Jon Petter Rui / Ulrich Sieber (eds.)

Non-Conviction-Based Confiscation in Europe

D1629284

Schriftenreihe des Max-Planck-Instituts für
ausländisches und internationales Strafrecht

Strafrechtliche Forschungsberichte

Herausgegeben von Ulrich Sieber

Band S 146

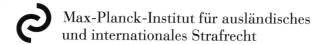

Max-Planck-Institut für ausländisches
und internationales Strafrecht

Non-Conviction-Based Confiscation in Europe

Possibilities and Limitations on Rules Enabling
Confiscation without a Criminal Conviction

Jon Petter Rui • Ulrich Sieber (eds.)

Duncker & Humblot • Berlin

Bibliografische Information der Deutschen Nationalbibliothek

Die Deutsche Nationalbibliothek verzeichnet diese Publikation in
der Deutschen Nationalbibliografie; detaillierte bibliografische
Daten sind im Internet über <http://dnb.ddb.de> abrufbar.

Umschlagbild: © iStock. by Getty Images
Druck: Stückle Druck und Verlag, Stückle-Straße 1, 77955 Ettenheim
Printed in Germany

ISSN 1860-0093
(Max-Planck-Institut)
ISBN 978-3-428- 14883-7 (Duncker & Humblot)
Gedruckt auf alterungsbeständigem (säurefreiem) Papier
entsprechend ISO 9706 ∞

In memory of our friend

Joachim Vogel

* 2 June 1963 † 17 August 2013

Preface

Traditional "repressive" criminal law is no longer sufficient to deal with the new threats posed by the global risk and information society. Terrorism, organized crime, economic crime, cybercrime, and other complex challenges demand new solutions that, above all, effectively prevent – rather than punish – crime. These new solutions are found primarily in new forms of "preventive" criminal law as well as in the combination of criminal law with other legal regimes in the areas of public and civil law and with self-regulating norms of private law. Examples for this paradigm shift in criminal policy include the increasing use of intelligence law against organized crime, the laws of war against terrorism, and self-regulatory compliance regimes against corporate crime.

Such solutions can indeed be quite innovative and effective in preventing crime. However, they pose serious threats to the protection of civil liberties if they disregard traditional human rights, particularly the traditional guarantees of criminal law which citizens have fought for since the Enlightenment. The newly developing security law must therefore seek to balance and combine the effectiveness of new innovative solutions with adequate human rights protection. This development towards a balanced combination of criminal law with other normative regimes shows that in criminal policy – as in other areas – innovation occurs primarily not at the center of traditional disciplines but in interdisciplinary and comparative research at the borders and overlaps of these disciplines, such as in the above-mentioned fields of law. For that reason, during the last decade, these questions have been the focus of the research program of the Max Planck Institute for Foreign and International Criminal Law.

Within this program, a most interesting interdisciplinary approach to crime represents "non-conviction-based confiscation" which is used especially in common law but now also in some European legal orders. The origins of this development lie in the extensive guarantees of criminal law concerning the trial of suspects and the related confiscation of the proceeds of crime. The resulting problems for the efficiency of traditional criminal-law based confiscation has led to the question of whether it is in accordance with human rights to confiscate the proceeds of crime, detected merely e.g. in the form of suspects' unexplained wealth, under a concept of unjust enrichment and re-establishment of the situation before a crime, and to do so without a conviction and by applying a set of less strict "civil"-law evidentiary rules. In cases in which such suspicion arises, the suspect must demonstrate the sources of his wealth. If he fails to do so and if a court is convinced of the assets' criminal origin, they can be confiscated – in some common law countries even when there is merely a preponderance of evidence that the property is tainted by crime. This means: no conviction of a person, no ethical blame, just a pragmatic "crime must not pay" approach under a civil law doctrine of unjust enrichment based on the preponderance of evidence and directed against property (*in rem* and not *in personam*). This kind of procedure gives rise to the question of whether its central concept of a "non-conviction-based confiscation" (NCBC) is just a false (civil law) label that facilitates the circumvention of the traditional guarantees of criminal law. The present book tries to answers this question and develop a new approach in order to create an effective new instrument for confiscation that does not contravene human rights guarantees.

*

The origins of this book go back to *Jon Petter Rui's* three-year stay at the Max Planck Institute for Foreign and International Criminal Law in Freiburg in 2010-2013. The pairing of his research on money laundering with the Max Planck Institute's research program on new answers to the challenges of the global risk society, developed in 2004 by *Ulrich Sieber*, proved a perfect match. Joint discussions on alternative concepts against new threats of crime led to a seminar on non-conviction-based confiscation in *Sommarøy*, Norway, in June 2012. The idea behind the seminar was for each of the carefully-selected participants to contribute a presentation on the topic of NCBC and for the organizers subsequently to prepare a comprehensive analysis of results. It is with great pleasure that we recall the inspiring contributions of the ten participants from five countries, the stimulating discussion, but also the extraordinary nature and the endless daylight that the beginning of June brings to the Norwegian north on the peninsula of *Sommarøy*. We thank all participants for their excellent contributions. Special thanks also go to the collaborators of the Max Planck Institute for Foreign and International Criminal Law, Ms. *Irene Kortel* for editing and Ms. *Indira Tie, M.A.,* for proofreading the contributions to the seminar published here. Our sincere thanks are also due to the Norwegian Finance Market Fund for its contribution financing the seminar.

*

Our memories of this seminar are particularly special since, for most of us, it was the last time we had the privilege of working with our colleague *Joachim Vogel* of the University of Munich. We remember not only his outstanding discussions and his brilliant analyses, but also his merry laugh, his relaxed manner, and the friendship we all shared. One of the most prominent scholars of criminal law in Europe, he lost his life one year later, just finishing his manuscript for the present book, at the age of 50 in a tragic boat accident in Venice. His contribution printed in this book is his last academic paper. We dedicate this book to him and to the memory of his outstanding work.

Bergen / Freiburg, August 2015 *Jon Petter Rui* and *Ulrich Sieber*

Contents

Chapter 1

Introduction

Jon Petter Rui

I. Background

For a long time, the ethos in most European criminal justice systems might have been described by the Latin phrase *pecunia non olet*, money does not stink. In essence, crime was fought by securing the criminal convictions and imprisonment of offenders. With the exception of rules making it possible to confiscate the instruments *(instrumentum sceleris)* or the object of crime *(objectum sceleris)*, most European legal systems did not provide for the confiscation of proceeds from crime *(producta/fructa sceleris)*.[1]

However, as organized crime increasingly became an international problem, first and foremost through drug crime, which exploded in the 1980s,[2] it became evident that the existing legal tools were insufficient to counter it. Firstly, because the few organized criminals who were put behind bars could enjoy the fruits of their criminal activity upon release. In addition, securing the conviction of one or a few other members of the criminal organization did not prove effective in disrupting the organization as such. Secondly, and perhaps more importantly, it seemed almost impossible to secure criminal convictions. Organized criminals used their power and intelligence to keep themselves removed from the crimes they were masterminding, and they were able to mask the criminal origin of their assets.

The global society's answer to the development of organized crime was the revitalization of rules making it possible to confiscate the proceeds of crime. Because of the difficulty of proving a link between organized criminals and crime, confiscation rules were "paired" with the establishment of a new criminal offense, namely money laundering.[3] Instead of having to prove a link between organized criminals and predicate offenses, e.g., drug trafficking, the subject matter of money laundering cases is whether the organized criminals can be linked to the money stemming from such crimes.

---

[1] *Stessens*, Money Laundering, p. 4.

[2] *Pieth/Aiolfi*, A Comparative Guide, p. 4; *Thony*, Money Laundering, p. 1.

[3] United Nations Convention Against Illicit Traffic in Narcotic Drugs and Psychotropic Substances, United States 1988.

The two first international instruments introducing these measures into national legal systems were the United Nations Convention Against Illicit Traffic in Narcotic Drugs and Psychotropic Substances and the Council of Europe Convention on Laundering, Search, Seizure and Confiscation of the Proceeds from Crime.[4] Since the introduction of those two conventions, numerous international instruments have been introduced by different international bodies over the last two decades. A clear trend has emerged that the various instruments overbid each other in placing requirements on national legislators to widen the scope of the rules aimed at fighting organized crime: The duties and incentives to criminalize money laundering and the obligations to implement rules on confiscation of the proceeds of crime have successively been strengthened. The same development is traceable as regards procedural mechanisms, such as the search, seizure, and freezing of assets as well as special investigative techniques and preventive measures to counter money laundering (regulatory and supervisory rules, i.e., anti-money laundering legislation).

However, looking back on two decades of fighting organized crime by means of this approach, the general picture is discouraging. The common experience in most European legal systems is that the criminalization of money laundering has not been an effective measure against organized crime; criminal convictions are almost non-existent.[5] As regards confiscation, the European Commission held in 2012 that "confiscation of criminal assets remains underdeveloped and underutilized"[6] and that "there is a significant underutilisation of asset confiscation laws throughout the EU."[7]

II. Confiscation without a previous criminal conviction at national levels

The evident main reason why confiscation is not effective is that, for several reasons, it is too difficult to achieve criminal convictions. To remedy the situation, several new strategies have been explored. One of the most radical but at the same

---

[4] CETS No. 141, Strasbourg 8 November 1990.

[5] Eurostat, Money laundering in Europe: Report on work carried out by Eurostat and DG Home Affairs, European Union 2010, pp. 54–67; Moneyval, Horizontal Review of Moneyval's Third Round of Mutual Evaluation Reports, Council of Europe 2010, pp. 8, 10.

[6] Proposal for a directive of the European Parliament and the Council on the freezing and confiscation of proceeds of crime in the European Union, COM (2012) 85 final, Brussels 12 March 2012, p. 2.

[7] Commission staff working paper. Accompanying document to the proposal for a directive of the European Parliament and the Council on the freezing and confiscation of proceeds of crime in the European Union, Impact assessment, SWD (2012) 31 final, Brussels 12 March 2012, p. 19.

time efficient legal tools developed to overcome the criminal conviction problem is the introduction of rules enabling confiscation without a former criminal conviction. Many terms are in use to describe this type of legislation: civil asset forfeiture, civil forfeiture, non-criminal confiscation and non-conviction-based confiscation. The latter will be applied in this book as an umbrella term, referred to as NCBC. The common denominator for NCBC legislation is that confiscation is possible without a criminal conviction of an offender.

The first jurisdiction to introduce NCBC legislation was the United States. In the late 1700s already, NCBC legislation was introduced in order to tackle problems with pirate ships and slave traders who operated out of lawless regions of the Caribbean.[8] The procedure of confiscating without the need for a criminal conviction of an offender was gradually developed and is today a cornerstone in the U.S. policy on confiscation.[9]

In Europe, Italy was the first country to develop NCBC legislation in 1965. The legislation has undergone several substantial changes since then.[10] In the following, I refer to the Italian legislation on NCBC as the *Italian approach*.

In 1996, comprehensive legislation on NCBC was developed in Ireland.[11] Seven years later, similar legislation came into force in the United Kingdom, through the Proceeds of Crime Act 2002 (POCA). It has been said that the non-conviction-based part of POCA was the most innovative but at the same time the most controversial.[12] A significant feature of NCBC schemes in common law jurisdictions is that the proceedings are directed at property and not at a person. I use the collective term *common law approach* when referring to Irish and UK NCBC legislation.

Legislation in other European countries also allows confiscation without there being a criminal conviction of an offender. In Germany, section 76a § 1 of the Criminal Code states that "(i)f for reasons of fact no person can be prosecuted or convicted of the offense, confiscation or deprivation of the object for the monetary value or destruction must or may be independently ordered if the conditions under which the measure is prescribed or available otherwise is met." The Code of Criminal Procedure section 441 § 3 stipulates that a court has to decide on confiscation in a ruling or judgment.[13]

In Norway, the Code of Criminal Procedure section 255 allows for confiscation without the criminal conviction of an offender:

---

[8] Pp. 19–20.
[9] Pp. 20–21.
[10] Pp. 119–122.
[11] Pp. 215–216.
[12] Pp. 31–32, 213, 215, 219–220.
[13] Pp. 75–77.

"If the prosecuting authority finds that a case should be decided by the imposition of a fine or confiscation, or both, the said authority may issue a writ giving an option to this effect (an optional penalty writ) instead of preferring an indictment."

Thus, in principle, the prosecutor has the option of issuing a writ on confiscation. If the writ is accepted by the defendant, the property is confiscated by the prosecuting authority without a court deciding on the matter. If it is not accepted by the defendant, the case has to be transferred to a court that decides whether confiscation should be executed or not. The court deciding on the matter is a criminal court. However, a criminal conviction of the defendant is not a prerequisite for a ruling on confiscation. The court may carry out a preliminary evaluation of the defendant's guilt if that is a condition for confiscation. There are no authoritative legal sources clarifying which evidence threshold the courts should apply when making the preliminary evaluation of criminal guilt. The practice seems to be that the criminal law threshold is applied, even though confiscation is not classified as a penal measure in Norwegian criminal law.

As the described procedure makes it possible to confiscate without a criminal conviction, Norwegian law, in principle, has NCBC legislation. It should be noted, however, that the NCBC procedure is almost never applied by the prosecuting authorities. When applied, it is in straightforward cases concerning petty offenses and the confiscation of relatively small amounts or property. The reasons for applying the NCBC procedure are mostly practical and jurisdictional obstacles to securing a criminal conviction. An example is contravention of fishery regulations by alien vessels. The NCBC procedure has never been applied in complex cases concerning, i.a., money laundering and organized crime. Two reasons are probably that the evidence threshold for confiscation is the same as that in a criminal trial and that the writ procedure in section 255 is not designed to be applied in complex cases.

As revealed above, German law also allows for NCBC in cases where no person can be prosecuted or convicted of an offense. According to the Norwegian Criminal Code, the point of departure is that a claim for confiscation has to be directed against the owner. However, section 37c allows for exceptions:

"When an object that has been seized is required to be confiscated, and when the owner is unknown or has no known place of sojourn in the realm, confiscation may be effected in proceedings against the offender or the person who was in possession at the time of seizure if this is considered reasonable according to the nature of the case and other circumstances […]. The owner shall as far as possible be notified of the proceedings.

If neither the offender nor the possessor is known or has a known place of sojourn in the realm, the District Court may order confiscation under circumstances similar to those mentioned in the first paragraph, without any person being made a defendant."

Even though the conditions differ, Norwegian law contains the same option as German law to launch confiscation proceedings without any person being made a defendant, even though the conditions differ. If an NCBC proceeding is launched against the property because there is no person who could be made defendant, it has to be stopped if such a person should appear during the proceedings. There are no authoritative legal sources or literature clarifying the evidence threshold in proceedings without a defendant. As confiscation is not classified as a penal measure in Norwegian law and the proceedings are not directed against a person, it is to be assumed that the general threshold in non-criminal cases applies (preponderance of evidence/balance of probabilities). To my knowledge, NCBC proceedings without a defendant are extremely rare.

In Denmark, the Code of Criminal Procedure section 832 features the same possibility as in Norwegian law for an offender to accept a claim for confiscation stated in a writ made out by the public prosecutor. A regulation defines the types of property for which confiscation can be accepted by the defendant without a trial.[14] It appears that the NCBC procedure in Danish law is also reserved for rather petty offenses, which do not raise particular questions of fact or law. The Danish Criminal Code does not afford the possibility to launch confiscation proceedings without any person being made a defendant.

In Swedish law, it is a general principle that confiscation requires a criminal conviction.[15] However, in limited circumstances, confiscation may be decided upon without there being a criminal conviction, i.a., when the person against which the proceedings are directed is someone other than the offender[16] and when the offender is unknown.[17] Confiscation without making a person subject to the proceedings is strictly limited.[18]

The common denominators of the German and Scandinavian countries' approach to NCBC are, firstly, that the procedure is prescribed for in criminal law and criminal procedure. Secondly, at least in German[19] and Norwegian law, the evidence threshold is higher than that in conventional civil cases, i.e., higher than preponderance of evidence. Thirdly, as a main rule, the case has to be directed against a person. Only under limited circumstances can an NCBC procedure be launched in cases where no person can be made part of the proceedings. I refer to NCBC legislation having these common denominators as the *German-Scandinavian approach*. In addition to the countries mentioned here, such an approach towards NCBC is found in Switzerland.[20]

---

[14] *Smith et al.*, Straffeprocessen, pp. 684–685.

[15] *Almkvist*, Förverkande, pp. 171, 179.

[16] *Op. cit.*, p. 179.

[17] *Op. cit.*, p. 177.

[18] *Op. cit.*, p. 168.

[19] P. 76.

[20] *Greenberg et al.*, Stolen Asset Recovery, pp. 111–113.

To make the picture complete, several jurisdictions in Europe have developed NCBC rules, e.g., Bulgaria,[21] Liechtenstein,[22] and Slovenia.[23] Due to the resources available for this study, these systems will not be dealt with in further detail.

III. Confiscation without a previous criminal conviction: International incentives

In the global arena, there are several legal instruments having provisions encouraging legal systems to implement rules making confiscation possible without criminal convictions. Firstly, the United Nations Convention Against Corruption (UNCAC) Art. 54 (1) (c) entails a provision which requests State Parties to consider taking measures to permit confiscation "without a criminal conviction, in cases in which the offender cannot be prosecuted by reason of death, flight or in other appropriate cases." This statement reflects the growing number of jurisdictions in which forfeiture can be ordered in the absence of a criminal conviction. With this endorsement, the UNCAC, for the first time in the text of a global criminal law convention, acknowledges the importance of non-conviction-based forfeiture for the recovery of criminal proceeds.[24] In UNCAC Art. 54 (1) (a), which addresses international cooperation for purposes of forfeiture, State Parties are obliged to enable domestic authorities to recognize and act on "an order of confiscation issued by a court of another State Party." Art. 54 (1) (b) sets out an obligation "to permit its competent authorities, where they have jurisdiction, to order the confiscation of such property of foreign origin." These provisions are broadly worded and will most likely encompass civil asset forfeiture measures.[25] In addition, UNCAC Art. 43 requires State Parties to consider assisting each other in investigations of and proceedings in civil and administrative matters related to corruption. This includes civil asset forfeiture proceedings and addresses the problem encountered in the past that states could provide legal assistance and cooperation in criminal matters but not in civil cases.[26]

---

[21] Transparency International: Forfeiture of Illegal Assets: Challenges and Perspectives on the Bulgarian Approach. National Report for Bulgaria, Sofia 2014, http://www.transparency.bg/media/cms_page_media/141/NationalReport_TI-BG_en_Forfeiture_of_Illegal_Assets_in_Bulgaria.pdf [last revised 12.7.2014].

[22] *Stephenson et al.*, Barriers to Asset Recovery, pp. 154–155.

[23] *Greenberg et al.*, Stolen Asset Recovery, p. 23.

[24] *Claman*, The promise and limitations of asset recovery, in: Pieth (ed.), Recovering Stolen Assets, p. 347.

[25] In the same vein, *Greenberg et al.*, Stolen Assets Recovery, p. 9.

[26] *Op. cit.*

Secondly, the fourth of the Financial Action Task Force's (FATF) Forty Recommendations states that countries "should consider adopting measures that allow such proceeds or instrumentalities to be confiscated without requiring a criminal conviction (non-conviction-based confiscation) [...] to the extent that such a requirement is consistent with the principles of their domestic law."[27] FATF is perhaps the most influential international organization in the field of combating money laundering and terrorist financing. The UN Security Council in Resolution 1617 "(s)trongly urges all Member States to implement the comprehensive, international standards embodied in the Financial Action Task Force's (FATF) Forty Recommendations on Money Laundering and the FATF Nine Special Recommendations on Terrorist Financing."[28] The EU is a member of FATF.

Thirdly, the G8 Countries' Best Practice Principles on Tracing, Freezing and Confiscation of Assets (para. 26) gives the following advice:

"Where they have not already done so, States are encouraged to examine the possibility to extend, to the extent consistent with the fundamental principles of their domestic law, confiscation by: permitting the forfeiture of property in the absence of a criminal conviction; requiring that the lawful origin of alleged proceeds of crime or other property be demonstrated by the claimant."

IV. Rules on confiscation without a previous criminal conviction at the EU level

On 24 February 2014, the European Parliament adopted the Directive of the European Parliament and of the Council on the freezing and confiscation of instrumentalities and proceeds of crime in the European Union.[29] Art. 4 is entitled "confiscation" and has the following wording:

"1. Member States shall take the necessary measures to enable the confiscation, either in whole or in part, of instrumentalities and proceeds or property the value of which corresponds to such instrumentalities or proceeds, subject to a final conviction for a criminal offense, which may also result from proceedings in absentia.

2. Where confiscation on the basis of paragraph 1 is not possible, at least where such impossibility is the result of illness or absconding of the suspected or accused person, Member States shall take the necessary measures to enable the confiscation of instrumentalities and proceeds in cases where criminal proceedings have been initiated regarding a criminal offense which is liable to give rise, directly or indirectly, to economic

---

[27] FATF, International Standards on Combating Money Laundering and the Financing of Terrorism & Proliferation. The FATF Recommendations, February 2012.

[28] Resolution 1617 (2005) adopted by the Security Council at its 5244th meeting on 29 July 2005 para. 7.

[29] Directive 2014/42/EU of the European Parliament and of the Council on the freezing and confiscation of instrumentalities and proceeds of crime in the European Union, published in the Official Journal of the European Union L 127, vol. 57, 29 April 2014.

benefit, and such proceedings could have led to a criminal conviction if the suspected or accused person had been able to stand trial."

No. 2 of the article requires Member States to introduce legislation making it possible to confiscate proceeds of crime without a criminal conviction. The NCBC approach referred to here will be referred to as the *EU approach*. Interpretation of the provision raises several questions, which will be dealt with in chapter 10.

Details on the drafting process of the directive is shrouded in darkness. However, the official documents reveal that the NCBC clause has been intensely debated in the Council and in Parliament. The most controversial topics seem to be whether and to what extent the EU has competence to legislate on NCBC and whether such legislation would be in compliance with European Human Rights.

The last word on NCBC at the EU level has not been spoken. In conjunction with a provisional agreement between the Council and the Parliament of 27 November 2013 on the text of the directive, the following declaration was provisionally agreed upon:

"The European Parliament and the Council *call on* the Commission to analyze, at *the earliest possible opportunity* and taking into account the differences between the legal traditions and the systems of the Member States, the feasibility and possible benefits of introducing further common rules on the confiscation of property deriving from activities of a criminal nature, also in the absence of a conviction of a specific person or persons for these activities."

The clear message to the Commission to analyse the possibility of EU legislation giving the opportunity to confiscate property deriving from activities of a criminal nature "also in the absence of a conviction of a specific person or persons for these activities," points towards a desire for more far-reaching NCBC legislation at the EU level. In this context, it should be noted that the Special Committee on Organized Crime, Corruption and Money Laundering of the European Parliament in its comprehensive report of 10 June 2013:[30]

"calls on the Member States, on the basis of the most advanced national legislations, to introduce models of civil law asset forfeiture, in those cases where, on the balance of probabilities and subject to the permission of a court, it can be established that the assets in question result from criminal activities or are used to carry out criminal activities."[31]

Furthermore the Committee:

"considers that, in compliance with constitutional national guarantees and without prejudice to the right of property and the right of defense, provision could be made for preventive models of confiscation, which should be applicable only following a court decision."[32]

---

[30] European Parliament, Special Committee on Organized Crime, Corruption and Money Laundering: Draft report on organized crime, corruption and money laundering: recommendations on action initiatives to be taken 2009–2014, 2013/2107 (INI), 10 June 2013.

[31] Para. 12.

[32] Para. 13.

There is no doubt that the Committee, in the first citation, is referring to the common law approach to NCBC. As we will see in chapter 5, the second citation is a reference to the Italian approach.

The current position at the EU level regarding NCBC might be summed up in three points: Firstly, the Member States are obliged to legislate on the minimum requirement set out in Directive Art. 4 No. 2. Secondly, the EU will "at the earliest possible opportunity" explore the possibilities on expanding the NCBC provision. Thirdly, the Special Committee on Organized Crime, Corruption and Money Laundering of the European Parliament strongly encourages Member States to consider introducing either the common law approach to NCBC or the Italian approach.

V. Creating effective systems of confiscation without criminal conviction in Europe: Possibilities and limitations

The main objectives of this book are: firstly, to analyse the concept of NCBC, more precisely which different approaches are available and what the advantages and disadvantages of the different models are. Secondly, the focus is directed towards Art. 4 No. 2 of the directive. Which type of NCBC legislation does the Article provide for? How could the requirements be implemented in the Member States? Thirdly, it is to be discussed whether and to what extent further NCBC legislation could and should be initiated at the EU level. Fourthly, it will be investigated whether and how NCBC systems might be introduced into national legislation in European countries, irrespective of whether and how further legislating action is being launched at the EU level.

In chapter 2, Assistant U.S. Attorney (Chief, Asset Forfeiture and Money Laundering Section District of Maryland) *Stefan D. Cassella* presents the American experience on non-conviction-based confiscation. American law is of special significance because the USA is the jurisdiction with the longest experience of having a system allowing confiscation without requiring a criminal conviction. Together with chapter 3, in which Barrister *Ian Smith* presents the NCBC system in the United Kingdom, the reader will acquire solid knowledge of the common law model of NCBC. The two chapters provide, e.g., analyses of human rights issues, which have been actualized by the NCBC rules. In addition, statistics on confiscation are presented, which give valuable information on how effective the legislation is in practice.

In chapter 4, Professor Dr. *Robert Esser* presents the German perspective on NCBC. One finding is that the common law approach to NCBC is incompatible with the German constitution. Professor *Esser* also presents the article in the German Code of Criminal Procedure that allows confiscation without a criminal conviction. In addition, he offers a thorough analysis of whether the common law approach is compatible with the ECHR and the provisions of the Charter of Fundamental Rights of the European Union.

In chapter 5, Associate Professors Dr. *Michele Panzavolta* and Dr. *Roberto Flor* give a presentation and analysis of the Italian approach to NCBC, which they call a "non-criminal system" of NCBC. *Panzavolta* and *Flor* analyse various human rights issues that have been raised in connection with the Italian approach.

In chapters 6 and 7, some important human rights issues are discussed: Postdoc. Dr. *Johan Boucht* carries out an in-depth analysis of non-conviction-based confiscation and the presumption of innocence, particularly in the light of the European Convention on Human Rights Art. 6 No. 2. Dr. *Els De Busser* (Head of Section European Criminal Law at the Max Planck Institute for Foreign and International Criminal Law) explores how data protection rules could be observed and implemented when creating NCBC systems in Europe.

Chapter 8 has the title "Civil Asset Forfeiture in Practice." Here, Senior Counsel *Alan Bacarese* and Pupil Barrister *Gavin Sellar* give an overview over some of the most important practical matters that have to be observed when establishing NCBC legislation.

The contribution by Professor Dr. *Joachim Vogel* (†) in chapter 9 reflects on the rationality and legitimacy of "civil" forfeiture. A theoretical framework is developed. Different types of confiscation are tested and deliberated upon in the light of this theoretical framework. *Vogel*'s contribution provides for a new and interesting perspective on the topic.

In chapter 10, the findings are brought together. The four questions outlined above are analysed, aiming to contribute to the debate on NCBC, both at the EU level and at the national level in European countries.

Bibliography

Almkvist, Gustaf, Förverkande av egendom. Stockholm 2014.

Claman, Daniel, The promise and limitations of asset recovery under the UNCAC. In: Mark Pieth (ed.), Recovering Stolen Assets. Bern 2008.

Greenberg, Theodore S./Samuel, Linda M./Grant, Wingate/Grey, Larissa, Stolen Asset Recovery. A Good Practices Guide for Non-Conviction Based Asset Forfeiture. Washington 2009.

Pieth, Mark/Aiolfi, Gemma, A Comparative Guide to Anti-Money Laundering. A Critical Analysis of Systems in Singapore, the UK and the USA. Cheltenham/Northampton 2004.

Smith, Eva/Jochimsen, Jørgen/Kistrup, Michael/Lund Poulsen, Jakob, Straffeprocessen. 2nd ed. Copenhagen 2008.

Stephenson, Kevin M./Grey, Larissa/Power, Ric/Brun, Jean Pierre/Dunker, Gabriele/Panjer, Melissa, Barriers to Asset Recovery. An Analysis of the Key Barriers and Recommendations for Action. Washington 2011.

Stessens, Guy, Money Laundering: A New International Law Enforcement Model. 3rd ed. Cambridge 2002.

Thony, Jean François, Money Laundering and Terrorist Financing: An Overview. Current Developments in Monetary and Financial Law, vol. 3/2005, 1–20.

List of Abbreviations

CETS	Council of Europe Treaty Series
COM	Working Document of the Commission
ECHR	European Convention on Human Rights
FATF	Financial Action Task Force
NCBC	Non-Conviction-Based-Confiscation
POCA	Proceeds of Crime Act
SWD	Commission Staff Working Document
UNCAC	United Nations Convention Against Corruption

Chapter 2

Civil Asset Recovery

The American Experience

*Stefan D. Cassella**

I. Introduction

In the United States, federal prosecutors routinely employ asset recovery as a tool of law enforcement. The approach takes two forms. In criminal cases, the prosecutor may seek to recover or "forfeit" property as part of the defendant's sentence, if the defendant is convicted. Alternatively, the prosecutor may commence a civil proceeding, naming the property as the defendant and seeking to forfeit the property independent of any criminal proceeding.

This chapter discusses the American experience with civil, or non-conviction-based, asset recovery. It discusses the prosecutor's motivations for seeking to forfeit assets, the types of property that may be forfeited, the procedures that govern civil asset forfeiture, the advantages of civil or non-conviction-based asset forfeiture over criminal forfeiture, and the ways in which the United States, through judicial decisions and legislation, has reconciled the non-conviction-based approach with the requirements of basic human rights and civil liberties.

– Terminology

In the United States, the term "civil forfeiture" refers to non-conviction-based forfeiture proceedings. It contrasts with "criminal forfeiture," which requires a criminal conviction and is imposed as part of a criminal sentence. Experience shows, however, that the term "civil forfeiture" can be confusing when employed in the international context.

---

* The views expressed in this chapter are solely those of the author and do not necessarily reflect the views of the United States Department of Justice or any of its agencies. This chapter is an updated version of an article entitled "Civil Asset Recovery: The American Experience" that appeared in eucrim: The European Criminal Law Associations' Forum 3/2013, pp. 98–103, and is an expanded version of a presentation given by the author at the seminar entitled "Civil Asset Forfeiture: Exploring the Possibilities for an EU Model," sponsored by the Max Planck Institute for Foreign and International Criminal Law, Freiburg, Germany and the University of Tromsø, Sammaroy, Norway, June 1–2, 2012.

The term "civil" means different things in different contexts. It evokes the distinction between civil and common law jurisdictions; it implies that the action is brought in a civil court as opposed to a criminal court; it suggests that the action is between private parties instead of between a private party and the government, or that the government is merely seeking compensation for a loss, instead of imposing a sanction for wrongdoing; and it implies that the process does not provide protections for human rights.

None of those connotations applies to the American civil forfeiture process. In the United States, civil forfeiture is a tool of law enforcement; it is an action commenced by the government in the same court in which a criminal action would be filed – often in parallel with an actual criminal action – both as a sanction and as a remedial device. Though the procedure may be civil in nature, with some important exceptions the same constitutional protections apply in civil cases as in criminal cases. Civil forfeiture is simply a procedural device that the criminal prosecutor uses to recover property in a situation in which all of the interests of the potential property owners may be adjudicated at one time, without the necessity of obtaining a criminal conviction of the property owner or of anyone else.

To avoid the confusion and unnecessary distraction created by the use of the term "civil forfeiture" when discussing asset recovery in the international context, I will use the term "non-conviction-based" forfeiture from this point forward.

II. Why Do Forfeiture?

The prosecutor may have multiple reasons for seeking to recover the assets involved in the commission of a criminal offense. Indeed, it would be the rare case if only one of the following motives were to apply. Frequently, they are overlapping and mutually reinforcing.

As the US Supreme Court recently recognized, forfeiture serves a multitude of punitive and remedial purposes.[1] First, forfeiture serves the non-punitive purpose of taking the profit out of crime.[2] Whatever benefit the wrongdoer obtained or retained as a consequence of his offense is simply forfeited to the government.

Second, forfeiture is seen as a form of punishment. Incarceration is a form of punishment but so is forcing the wrongdoer to disgorge the accouterments of the

---

[1] See *Kaley v. United States*, ___ U.S. ___, 134 S. Ct. 1090 (2014) (forfeiture serves to punish the wrongdoer, deter future illegality, lessen the economic power of criminal enterprises, compensate victims, improve conditions in crime-damaged communities, and support law enforcement activities such as police training).

[2] See *United States v. Ursery*, 518 U.S. 267, 291 (1996) ("[Forfeiture] serves the additional nonpunitive goal of ensuring that persons do not profit from their illegal acts.").

lavish lifestyle he acquired through his criminal acts. Indeed, many prosecutors relate that it was the loss of the luxury items acquired through a life of crime, not the period of time to be spent behind bars, that most distresses defendants.

Third, forfeiture serves as a deterrent. If one fraudster, child pornographer, corrupt politician, or drug dealer is not permitted to retain the fruits of his crime, perhaps the next person will be less likely to travel the same road.

Fourth, forfeiture is used as a form of prevention; it allows the government to deprive wrongdoers of the tools of their trade and the economic resources they would employ to commit similar or more serious crimes in the future.[3] In drug trafficking cases, for example, the prosecutor does not want the drug dealer to keep the airplane that might be used again to smuggle drugs or the land where he could produce another load of marijuana. The benefit of using the forfeiture laws to intercept the flow of guns to Mexico or the export of a flight simulator to a government that sponsors terrorism is obvious.

Fifth, another form of prevention is the disruption of criminal organizations.[4] Money is the glue that holds organized criminal enterprises together; they have to recycle the money in order to keep the scheme going to lull more victims into the fraud scheme, to buy more drugs, to finance acts of terrorism, or to pay bribes to corrupt officials. Moreover, it is often noted that it is harder for a drug organization to replace the money seized by law enforcement after the drugs have been distributed than it is to replace the drugs if they are seized beforehand. Thus, taking the money does more to interrupt the cycle of drug distribution than any number of buy/bust arrests of street dealers or seizures of drugs as they are being imported.

Sixth, forfeiture is used in the United States as a means of recovering property that has been taken from victims and of restoring it through processes known as "restitution" and "restoration." The United States has a robust set of restitution laws, but for procedural reasons, forfeiture is a more effective way of recovering money for victims than ordering the defendant to pay restitution.[5] Restitution orders may only be imposed after a defendant has been convicted, whereas forfeiture

---

[3] See *von Hofe v. United States*, 492 F.3d 175, 184 (2d Cir. 2007) ("Like imprisonment, which incapacitates convicted criminals, forfeiture may be said to incapacitate contraband.").

[4] See *Caplin & Drysdale v. United States*, 491 U.S. 617, 630 (1989) ("[A] major purpose motivating congressional adoption and continued refinement of the racketeer influenced and corrupt organizations (RICO) and [continuing criminal enterprise] forfeiture provisions has been the desire to lessen the economic power of organized crime and drug enterprises.").

[5] See *United States v. Blackman*, 746 F.3d 137, 143 (4th Cir. 2014) ("The Government's ability to collect on a [forfeiture] judgment often far surpasses that of an untutored or impecunious victim of crime [...]. Realistically, a victim's hope of getting paid may rest on the Government's superior ability to collect and liquidate a defendant's assets under the forfeiture laws.").

laws allow the government to seize and hold the property at the outset of the case, thus ensuring that it remains available to the victims as the case progresses.

Seventh, forfeiture is used to protect the community and to demonstrate to the community that law enforcement is working in its interest. If the police are able to use the forfeiture laws to shut down a *crackhouse* and turn it into a shelter for battered women, they have at once removed a hazard to public health and safety, provided a much-needed resource to a community, and created a visible demonstration of the effectiveness of the local law enforcement agency's efforts.

Finally, forfeiture is used as a way of encouraging cooperation between state and federal law enforcement agencies and of focusing their resources on the economic aspects of crime. Through a program called "equitable sharing," state and local law enforcement agencies, which assist federal law enforcement in investigating and prosecuting federal offenses leading to the forfeiture of assets, are allowed to use a portion of those assets to supplement their budgets, and thereby are given an incentive to dedicate resources to matters that have the highest federal priority. They are not, however, allowed to pay the salaries of the agents or officers who handle the cases.

III. Non-Conviction-Based Forfeiture

All of these motives apply equally to criminal and non-conviction-based forfeiture. The difference between the two approaches is procedural.

In a criminal case, forfeiture is part of the defendant's sentence.[6] After the defendant is found guilty beyond a reasonable doubt, the court determines on a balance of probabilities whether the property the government is seeking to forfeit was derived from, used to commit, or was otherwise connected to the crime in a way that would allow it to be forfeited to the government.[7] If the property is unavailable, the government may obtain a personal money judgment against the defendant and may satisfy this judgment out of any assets of equal value that the defendant may own – property known as "substitute assets."[8] Finally, the government must

---

[6] See *Libretti v. United States*, 516 U.S. 29, 39 (1995) ("[C]riminal forfeiture is an aspect of punishment imposed following conviction of a substantive criminal offense.").

[7] See Fed. R. Crim. P. 32.2(b); see, e.g., *United States v. Bader*, 678 F.3d 858, 893 (10th Cir. 2012) ("A forfeiture judgment must be supported by a preponderance of the evidence.") (citing *Cassella*, Asset Forfeiture Law in the United States § 15-3(d), New York, Juris 2007).

[8] See, e.g., *United States v. Vampire Nation*, 451 F.3d 189, 201–203 (3d Cir. 2006) (rejecting the argument that a forfeiture order must order the forfeiture of specific property; as an *in personam* order, it may take the form of a judgment for a sum of money equal to the

give notice of the forfeiture order to any third parties with an interest in the forfeited property and afford them an opportunity to contest the forfeiture on the ground that it belongs to the third party and not to the defendant.[9]

In a non-conviction-based forfeiture proceeding, there is no requirement of a criminal conviction or even of a criminal investigation.[10] The government brings the action against the property as the defendant *in rem*, and any person seeking to oppose the forfeiture action must intervene in order to do so.[11] This is why, in the United States at least, non-conviction-based forfeiture cases have such unusual names, such as *United States v. $65,000 in U.S. Currency* or *United States v. 2005 Mercedes Benz E500*.

The forfeiture process is straightforward and is described in detail in statutes and rules.[12] Basically, the government seizes the property and must provide notice to the owner and any other interested party of the forfeiture action and the right to intervene. If the property owner, universally referred to at this stage as the "claimant," chooses to intervene by filing a proper claim, the case proceeds through various stages in which the parties can conduct discovery to obtain evidence, the claimant may move to suppress evidence or to dismiss the government's case, and the government may move to strike the claim for lack of standing (i.e., the lack of a sufficient interest in the property). Finally, if the case goes to trial, the government has the burden of establishing on a balance of probabilities that a crime occurred and that the property was derived from, used to commit, or was otherwise involved in the offense in terms of the particular statute authorizing forfeiture. If the government meets that burden, the claimant then has the burden of establishing that he or she was an "innocent owner" or that the forfeiture of the property would be "grossly disproportionate to the gravity of the offense" on which the forfeiture is based.[13]

---

proceeds the defendant obtained from the offense, even if he no longer has those proceeds, or any other assets, at the time he is sentenced).

[9] See 21 U.S.C. § 853(n).

[10] See *United States v. One Assortment of 89 Firearms*, 465 U.S. 354, 361–362 (1984) (holding that acquittal on gun violation under 18 U.S.C. § 922 does not bar civil forfeiture under 18 U.S.C. § 924(d)); *One Lot Emerald Cut Stones & One Ring v. United States*, 409 U.S. 232, 234–235 (1972) *(per curiam)* (determining that acquittal on a criminal smuggling charge does not bar later civil forfeiture).

[11] See *United States v. $196,969.00 in U.S. Currency*, 719 F.3d 644, 646 (7th Cir. 2013) (in a civil forfeiture case, the defendant is "the thing;" the claimant is like a plaintiff in a "suit nested within the forfeiture suit"); *United States v. $8,440,190.00 in U.S. Currency*, 719 F.3d 49, 57 (1st Cir. 2013) (in a civil forfeiture case, the defendant is the property, and persons raising defenses to the forfeiture must establish standing to intervene).

[12] See 18 U.S.C. § 983 (2009); Fed. R. Civ. P. Rule G (Supplemental Rules for Admiralty or Maritime Claims and Asset Forfeiture Actions). The process is also described in detail in Chapters 3–14 of *Cassella*, Asset Forfeiture Law in the United States (hereinafter Asset Forfeiture Law).

[13] 18 U.S.C. § 983(d) & (g).

In older cases, the rationale for non-conviction-based forfeiture was that the property itself had done something wrong, but that is not the view taken today. The property is not being punished because it did something wrong; it is being confiscated because it represents the proceeds of a crime or property that was used to commit a crime and should, for those reasons, be taken out of the stream of commerce and out of the hands of those who committed the wrong or would use it to commit a wrong in the future. The government could, of course, try to recover the property in a criminal case in which the underlying criminal act is established but, as we will see, that is not always possible or desirable. Alternatively, it could bring a separate *in personam* civil action against each party with an interest in the property, but that would be cumbersome: the government would have to locate and serve all of them and conduct separate trials as to each person's interest before it could obtain clear title to the property.

Thus, as Supreme Court Justice Anthony Kennedy has explained, non-conviction-based forfeiture – as an *in rem* action against the property – is simply a procedural device that allows the government to litigate the interests of all persons with an interest in the property at the same time and to obtain clear title when the proceeding is complete.[14]

A. What Can Be Forfeited

Forfeiture actions in the United States may be brought against contraband, the proceeds of crime, and any property that is used to commit or facilitate the commission of a criminal offense. There are, however, statutes that sweep more broadly. In money laundering cases, for example, the government may forfeit all property involved in a money laundering offense, including untainted property that is commingled with the criminal proceeds at the time the money laundering offense takes place.[15] In racketeering cases brought under the Racketeer Influenced and Corrupt Organizations Act (RICO statute), the government may forfeit all property affording the defendant a "source of influence" over the racketeering enterprise, whether the property is tainted by the offense or not.[16] And in terrorism cases, the

---

[14] *Ursery*, 518 U.S. at 295–296 (Kennedy, J. concurring) (discussing how proceedings *in rem* are simply structures that allow the government to quiet title to criminally tainted property in a single proceeding in which all interested persons are required to file claims contesting the forfeiture at one time).

[15] See 18 § U.S.C. 981(a)(1)(A) (2011); 18 U.S.C. § 982(a)(1) (2012); see also Asset Forfeiture Law, *supra* note 12, at Chapt. 27.

[16] 18 U.S.C. § 1963(a)(2)(D) (2009); see also *United States v. Anderson*, 782 F.2d 908, 918 (11th Cir. 1986) ("A defendant's conviction under the RICO statute subjects *all* his interests in the enterprise to forfeiture regardless of whether those assets were themselves tainted by use in connection with the racketeering activity.") (emphasis added) (internal quotation marks omitted).

government is entitled to the forfeiture of every item of property that the terrorist owns.[17]

Though there are nuances and exceptions, the scope of the forfeiture statutes is generally the same whether the forfeiture is brought as part of a criminal case or as a non-conviction-based forfeiture action. Moreover, within each procedural construct – criminal or non-conviction-based – the procedures for forfeiting property are the same, regardless of the government's theory of forfeiture and regardless of the motive the government may have had for bringing the forfeiture action. So, if a defendant is convicted of a criminal offense, the procedure for forfeiting the property derived from or used to commit the offense is the same, regardless of the nature of the crime, the connection between the property and the crime, or the motive for seeking the forfeiture. Similarly, in a non-conviction-based forfeiture action, the government would have the same burden of proof and would follow the same procedural steps, whether it was seeking to forfeit property as criminal proceeds, facilitating property, or property involved in a money laundering offense and regardless of whether it viewed the forfeiture as punitive or remedial.

The reasons are largely pragmatic. Suppose, for example, a drug dealer uses a false name to purchase an automobile with drug proceeds and then uses the automobile to commit a further drug offense. From the property owner's point of view, it does not matter whether the government's forfeiture action is based on the theory that the automobile constitutes the proceeds of a crime, is property used to facilitate a crime, or is property involved in a money laundering offense. It also does not matter that the government brought the action to punish the property owner for committing the offense and to prevent him from using the same automobile to commit similar crimes in the future.

Moreover, if the procedures governing forfeiture were different depending on the government's theory or motive there would be endless litigation over exactly what theory or motive applied in a given case, with the prosecutor arguing that he was proceeding under the theory that invoked the less burdensome procedures and the claimant arguing the reverse. Given the overlapping and mutually reinforcing motives and theories that apply in forfeiture cases, determining which procedures apply in a given case based on the government's motive or theory would be a prescription for chaos in the courtroom.

B. History of Forfeiture in the United States

Forfeiture laws in the United States have been evolving for a long time. In the late 1700s, the United States had a serious problem with pirate ships and slave

---

[17] See 18 U.S.C. § 981(a)(1)(G).

traders who operated out of lawless regions of the Caribbean. There were times when the ship, the crew, and the cargo could be seized, but rarely was there an opportunity to bring the ship owner to justice. Accordingly the First Congress of the United States passed laws allowing the government to bring a forfeiture action against the ship itself – or its cargo – thereby forcing the owner to come forward to defend his property if he would do so. This is why the forfeiture cases decided throughout the 1800s arose for the most part in admiralty practice and have names like *United States v. The Brig Ann*.[18] Indeed, the modern rules of procedure for non-conviction-based asset forfeiture actions are still found in the Supplemental Rules for Admiralty and Maritime Cases and Asset Forfeiture Actions of the Federal Rules of Civil Procedure.[19]

Later, in the late 19th and early 20th centuries, the United States used its forfeiture laws to collect taxes due on the production of alcoholic beverages and then to enforce the prohibition on the consumption of alcohol altogether. This gave rise to another series of cases involving distilleries and vehicles used to transport bootleg whiskey or other illegal spirits.[20]

What brought non-conviction-based forfeiture into common use in the 1980s were drug trafficking cases. Just as it was often hard to find the owner of a slave ship in the 1790s and bring him to justice, it is often hard to find or lay hands on the mastermind behind an international drug organization; yet law enforcement still wants to confiscate his proceeds, his airplanes, his money laundering operation, or whatever else he might use to perpetuate his scheme and gain entry into the legitimate economy.

Beginning in 1978 and continuing through the following decade, Congress enacted a series of laws expanding the use of civil forfeiture with regard to drugs. As discussed below, this led to a great deal of litigation regarding the procedures necessary to ensure that basic civil liberties were protected, as it became apparent that the laws and procedures that were designed originally to deal with pirate ships and slave traders were ill-suited to dealing with the seizure and forfeiture of houses, cars, businesses, and bank accounts.

As these issues were resolved, the forfeiture laws were expanded, so that they now apply to most federal crimes. One of the problems with the piecemeal development of the law over two hundred years, however, is that instead of there being one broadly applicable statute, there are separate forfeiture statutes dealing with a wide variety of federal crimes spread throughout the U.S. Code. Inevitably, the

---

[18] 13 U.S. 289 (1815).

[19] The history of the development of asset forfeiture law in the United States is summarized in Chapter 2 of Asset Forfeiture Law, *supra* note 12.

[20] See, e.g., *Van Oster v. Kansas*, 272 U.S. 465 (1926); *J.W. Goldsmith, Jr.-Grant Co. v. United States*, 254 U.S. 505 (1921); *Dobbins's Distillery v. United States*, 96 U.S. 395 (1877).

scope of the legislation is inconsistent: some statutes authorize the forfeiture of the proceeds of the offense and nothing more; others authorize the forfeiture of facilitating property; still others authorize both; and some contain exemptions from the procedural changes that were enacted at the turn of the 21st century.[21] This is why U.S. forfeiture law is often confusing to the novice practitioner, but for the purposes of the discussion of non-conviction-based forfeiture in this chapter, the basic concepts are the same.

C. Statistics

To get a sense of the current scope of forfeiture in the United States, a few statistics may be useful. The figures given below are only from the forfeiture program administered by the U.S. Department of Justice. It is by far the largest forfeiture program in the United States, but it is not the only one. Each of the 50 states has a forfeiture program and so do several other federal agencies, such as the Internal Revenue Service and the Department of Homeland Security, which are not part of the Justice Department.

The Justice Department's analysis is divided into three categories of forfeiture: criminal, civil (i.e., non-conviction-based) and administrative. The administrative forfeitures are really non-conviction-based forfeitures that are uncontested. In these cases, the property is seized, notice is given, no one files a claim, and the property is forfeited by default. In the United States, the vast majority of forfeitures (in terms of the raw number of cases) are resolved that way.

Forfeiture Type	JUSTICE FUND					
	Number of Cases		Number of Assets		Forfeiture Amount ($)	
	2007	2011	2007	2011	2007	2011
Administrative	9,787	12,757	185,417	39,451	392,030,233	631,894,315
Civil/ Judicial	1,351	1,372	2,500	2,518	189,046,090	876,296,324
Criminal	2,030	3,007	5,574	8,618	791,974,573	617,231,644
Total	13,168	17,136	193,491	50,587	1,373,050,896	2,125,422,283

---

[21] For example, there is no "innocent owner defense" in cases brought under the Customs laws. See, e.g., *United States v. Davis*, 648 F.3d 84, 93–95 (2d Cir. 2011) (holding that there is no innocent owner defense to the forfeiture of property unlawfully imported into the United States in violation of 19 U.S.C. § 1595a).

The data illustrate a number of things. First, the forfeiture program in the U.S. is large – exceeding $2.1 billion in asset recoveries in 2011 – and it is mature, but it is still growing. Second, non-conviction-based forfeitures (judicial and administrative) are an enormous part of the success of the program; of the 17,000 cases in 2011, 14,000 were non-conviction-based, and they accounted for the forfeiture of $1.5 billion of the $2.1 billion forfeited, which is roughly 70 percent. Third, non-conviction-based forfeiture – with its administrative forfeiture component – is an enormously efficient use of time and resources; fully 80 percent of the cases remain uncontested, and they account for 30 percent of the money forfeited.

Law enforcement agencies in the United States do not measure the success of the asset forfeiture program solely in terms of dollars or assets: the real issue is how many crimes were deterred, wrongdoers punished, and victims compensated. The metrics set forth in these charts do not necessarily tell that story, but they do suggest some measure of success in those hard-to-quantify areas.

D. Advantages of Non-Conviction-Based Forfeiture[22]

We now turn to some examples in which asset recovery would not be possible were it not for the availability of non-conviction-based forfeiture proceedings or in which non-conviction-based forfeiture is at least the superior option.

1. When the Forfeiture Is Uncontested

If the government files a forfeiture action directly against the property, and no one files a disputing claim, the property may be forfeited to the government directly without any judicial forfeiture proceeding. In the United States, 80 percent of forfeiture cases – involving as much as $600 million in a recent year – are resolved in this fashion.

2. When the Defendant Has Died

The government can only obtain a forfeiture order as part of the sentence in a criminal case if the defendant lives long enough to be tried, convicted, and sentenced. If the defendant dies before his conviction is final, as in the case of *Kenneth Lay*, head of the *Enron Corporation*, non-conviction-based forfeiture becomes the principal means of recovering property traceable to the underlying crime.

---

[22] The advantages and disadvantages of criminal and non-conviction-based forfeitures under U.S. federal law are discussed in more detail in Chapter 1 of Asset Forfeiture Law, *supra* note 12. See also. *Cassella*, The case for civil forfeiture, 11 Journal of Money Laundering Control 8 (2008).

3. When the Wrongdoer Is Unknown

In the United States, law enforcement agents commonly find criminal proceeds in the hands of a courier – a person who was not himself involved in the commission of the crime. It is often clear from the circumstances that the money at issue is criminal proceeds, but neither the government nor (in most cases) the courier knows who the money belongs to or who committed the underlying criminal offense. In such cases, there is no chance of bringing a criminal prosecution, yet it is still desirable for the government to recover the money. Thus, it is not unusual in the United States to file a forfeiture case against a very large sum of currency that was seized from a courier. Many of these are drug trafficking cases, but the scenario appears in other contexts as well (the financing of terrorism being one prominent example).

4. When the Property Belongs to a Third Party

It is quite common for a person to commit an offense using property that belongs to a third party. For example, a robber may carry out a robbery using someone else's gun.

In a criminal case, the government cannot forfeit property that belongs to a third party if the third party has been excluded from the proceeding, as this would violate the third party's right to due process. In fact, criminal forfeiture laws have a procedure specifically designed to *exclude* the property of third parties from a criminal forfeiture order, even if the third party knew about or was complicit in the commission of the crime. Yet if the third party was aware that his property was being used for a criminal purpose – or was willfully blind to that fact – he should be made to forfeit the property. The procedural device for forfeiting property held by a non-innocent third party is non-conviction-based forfeiture.

5. When the Interests of Justice Do Not Require
a Criminal Conviction

There are many cases in which the interests of justice do not require a criminal conviction on the offense giving rise to the forfeiture. Some of them involve relatively minor crimes, while others involve property owned by a person who played a minor role in the offense and is not going to be prosecuted. In such cases, the forfeiture of the property in a separate non-conviction-based forfeiture action – and not criminal prosecution – is probably the best way to recover the property.

Finally, there are very serious cases in which the criminal defendant will admit to committing a particular offense but will not admit to other conduct that gave rise to the lion's share of his criminal proceeds. In such a case, non-conviction-based forfeiture is needed to recover the much larger body of assets involved in the scheme.

In all of these instances, the point is the same: because criminal forfeiture is imposed as part of the defendant's sentence, there can be no forfeiture if no one is convicted or if the property belongs to a person who was not convicted. So, where the interests of justice do not require a conviction, non-conviction-based forfeiture provides a means of imposing a punishment that fits the crime.

6. When the Wrongdoer Is a Fugitive

Criminal forfeiture is available only when there is a conviction, but there can be no conviction as long as the accused is a fugitive from justice. Non-conviction-based forfeiture, however, allows the government to file an action against the assets left behind by the fugitive or placed in a jurisdiction from which they may be recovered. For example, if a person steals money from a US aid program in Afghanistan and cannot be extradited to the US, but has placed the proceeds of the fraud in a country that recognizes and enforces external forfeiture judgments, the US may use non-conviction-based forfeiture to obtain a judgment against the money.[23] The fugitive retains the right to contest the forfeiture, but only if he is willing to surrender to face the criminal charges; he cannot ignore the process of the court in the criminal case and ask the court to protect his property interests in the civil one.[24]

7. When the Criminal Case Is Prosecuted by Another Sovereign

Finally, federal prosecutors use non-conviction-based forfeiture when the defendant has already been prosecuted elsewhere (in one of the 50 states or in a foreign country) and thus will not be prosecuted federally, but there are assets related to the crime that may be recovered under federal law. For example, if someone commits an offense in Norway or Nigeria and conceals the proceeds of the crime in the United States, a federal prosecutor can use the non-conviction-based forfeiture laws to recover that property, even though the defendant has already been convicted of the criminal offense in a Norwegian or Nigerian court. This can often be a more efficient way of recovering the property than trying to register and enforce a foreign confiscation order.

E. Civil Liberties and Due Process Concerns

In most instances, the protection afforded to property owners' civil liberties in non-conviction-based forfeiture cases is the same as it is in criminal cases. In both

---

[23] See *United States v. Sum of $70,990,605*, ___ F. Supp.2d ___, 2014 WL 824048, *8–9 (D.D.C. Mar. 4, 2014) (forfeiture action against funds fraudulently derived from aid for Afghanistan Reconstruction).

[24] See 28 U.S.C. § 2466 (codifying the "fugitive disentitlement doctrine").

proceedings, for example, the property owner can seek to suppress evidence obtained in violation of the Fourth Amendment protection against unreasonable searches and seizures; is entitled to fair notice and an opportunity to be heard as guaranteed by the Fifth Amendment Due Process Clause; is entitled to cross-examine witnesses and insist on the application of the Rules of Evidence; and is protected from the imposition of a forfeiture that is grossly disproportionate to the gravity of the offense under the Excessive Fines Clause of the Eighth Amendment. There is also a right to a trial by jury, which is actually more robust under the Seventh Amendment in the non-conviction-based context then it is in the criminal context.[25] In neither case is either the defendant or the property owner entitled to use property subject to forfeiture to finance his defense.[26]

For other purposes, however, the non-conviction-based proceeding does not contain the same constitutional protections for basic human rights that are available in a criminal proceeding. In non-conviction-based proceedings, the government's burden is to establish the forfeitability of the property by a balance of probabilities (not beyond a reasonable doubt); there is no right to remain silent and there is no right to the provision of counsel at government expense if the claimant is unable to afford counsel of his or her own choosing. As the Supreme Court has held, non-conviction-based forfeiture proceedings are not criminal proceedings for purposes of invoking the provisions of the Bill of Rights reserved for the protection of criminal defendants whose liberty is placed in jeopardy by the filing of criminal charges.[27]

The process of determining which constitutional protections would or would not apply in non-conviction-based forfeiture proceedings has evolved piecemeal over many years. The procedures governing civil forfeiture practice were borrowed from 18th century admiralty practice and needed to be modified to fit modern usage and the concept of due process. Many of the constitutional issues were addressed by the Supreme Court in the decade from 1992-2002; others were addressed legislatively in the Civil Asset Forfeiture Reform Act of 2000 (CAFRA).

The following is a brief discussion of how some of the most prominent issues were resolved.[28]

---

[25] Compare Fed. R. Civ. P. Rule G(9) *with* Fed. R. Crim. P. 3.22(b)(5).

[26] See *Caplin & Drysdale*, 491 U.S. at 630.

[27] *Ursery*, 518 U.S. at 291-292 (setting forth the test for determining whether a forfeiture proceeding constitutes punishment for purposes of applying the Double Jeopardy Clause of the Fifth Amendment).

[28] For a complete discussion of the development of asset forfeiture law in the United States, including the application of constitutional protections embodied in the Bill of Rights to non-conviction-based proceedings, see Chapter 2 of Asset Forfeiture Law, *supra* note 12.

1. Presumption of Innocence and the Burden of Proof

The practice in admiralty included a reverse burden of proof: once the government showed that it had a reasonable basis to believe the property was subject to forfeiture – which the courts in the United States call "probable cause" – the burden was on the property owner to prove that it was not.[29] The Supreme Court repeatedly held that this was constitutional: the presumption of innocence embodied in the Bill of Rights applies only in criminal cases.[30] But the presumption of innocence is so ingrained in American practice and culture, and in the expectations of the jurors who decide civil cases if they go to trial, that it made sense to modernize the procedure by placing the burden on the government to establish the connection between the property and a criminal offense in the first instance. This was accomplished with CAFRA.[31]

In practice, placing the burden of proof on the government has made very little difference in the outcome of cases. Generally, the government's evidence is fairly strong, and the number of cases in which the evidence was evenly divided, such that the allocation of the burden of proof mattered, were few. Indeed, the amount of property forfeited has more than tripled since CAFRA was enacted.

2. The Innocent Owner Defense *(Bennis)*

Finding a way to deal with innocent third parties who have an interest in the property subject to forfeiture has been more controversial. In *Bennis v. Michigan*,[32] the Supreme Court affirmed two centuries of precedent and held that imposing strict liability on third parties does not violate their due process rights. But in CAFRA, the Justice Department proposed, and Congress enacted, a uniform innocent owner defense. By statute, the defense gives third parties the opportunity to protect their property from forfeiture, even if it was derived from or used to commit a crime, if (1) they did not know of, or took all reasonable steps to prevent, the illegal use of the property, or (2) they acquired the property interest as a bona fide purchaser for value without reason to know that it was subject to forfeiture.[33]

---

[29] See 19 U.S.C. § 1615.

[30] See, e.g., *United States v. One "Piper" Aztec "F" Deluxe Model 250 PA 23 Aircraft Bearing Serial No. 27-7654057*, 321 F.3d 355, 360-361 (3d Cir. 2003) (explaining that there was no constitutional infirmity in the pre-CAFRA allocation of the burden of proof on the claimant).

[31] See 18 U.S.C. § 983(c).

[32] 516 U.S. 442, 446 (1996).

[33] See *United States v. One 1990 Beechcraft*, 619 F.3d 1275, 1278 (11th Cir. 2010) (explaining that § 983(d) was enacted in response to the Supreme Court's decision in *Bennis*, holding that an innocent owner defense is not constitutionally required, and to bring uniformity to federal forfeiture law, which contained a variety of inconsistent innocent owner provisions prior to CAFRA). The uniform innocent owner defense, codified at 18 U.S.C.

3. Due Process and Notice *(Dusenbery)*

There was also a great deal of litigation over the steps the government must take to provide notice of the forfeiture action to interested parties. In an *in rem* action, it is not always immediately apparent that the property owner is aware that a forfeiture action has been initiated. The rule that emerged, and was eventually codified, is that the government must send written notice to any person who appears to have an interest in the property within 60 days of its seizure and must also publish notice on the Internet on an official government website.[34]

4. The Eighth Amendment and the Excessive Fines Clause *(Bajakajian)*

Another controversial issue – and the subject of three separate Supreme Court cases in the 1990s – involved the proportionality of the forfeiture to the seriousness of the crime. A forfeiture may potentially be large enough to implicate the Excessive Fines Clause of the Eighth Amendment, making the forfeiture unconstitutional. Thus, in *United States v. Bajakajian*,[35] when a traveler leaving the Los Angeles airport with $347,000 concealed in his luggage committed the relatively minor offense of not reporting the currency on his Customs form, the Supreme Court held that the forfeiture of the entire $347,000 was unconstitutional because it was "grossly disproportional to the gravity of the offense." However, the Court did not say how much could be forfeited without being unconstitutional; lower courts have been wrestling with this question ever since.

Generally, the forfeiture of the actual proceeds of a crime is never problematic – it is difficult to envision how the forfeiture of a crime's proceeds could be disproportional, let alone grossly disproportional, to the gravity of the offense. But the situation may be different when valuable property, such as a person's home, is used to facilitate the commission of an offense. At what point, for example, does the forfeiture of the home become disproportional to the offense of collecting or producing child pornography, or subjecting children to sexual abuse?[36]

5. Self-incrimination, the Right to a Stay, and Adverse Inferences

Another set of issues arises when there is a non-conviction-based forfeiture action and a parallel criminal investigation or trial.

---

§ 983(d), is discussed in detail in: *Cassella*, The Uniform Innocent Owner Defense to Civil Asset Forfeiture, 89 Ky. L.J. 653 (2001).

[34] See *United States v. Dusenbery*, 534 U.S. 161, 167, 172–173 (2002).

[35] *United States v. Bajakajian*, 524 U.S. 321, 322–323 (1998).

[36] The case law on the application of the Excessive Fines Clause to civil and criminal forfeiture is discussed in detail in Chapter 28 of Asset Forfeiture Law, *supra* note 12.

Under the Fifth Amendment to the Bill of Rights, a criminal defendant has the right to remain silent and put the government to proof. When the government files a parallel civil forfeiture action, however, the defendant is presented with a Hobson's choice: does he invoke his right to remain silent so that what he says cannot be used against him in his criminal case but in doing so foregoes his opportunity to defend his property, or does he give evidence in the forfeiture case? There are various ways to deal with this problem, but the choice made in CAFRA was to allow the defendant subject to criminal liability in a related case to ask that a related non-criminal case be stayed until the criminal case is over, thus making it unnecessary for him to make the choice between his property and his right to remain silent.[37]

6. The Sixth Amendment Right to Counsel

A criminal defendant has the right to court-appointed counsel in a criminal case under the Sixth Amendment but, as mentioned earlier, this right does not extend to civil cases. In CAFRA, however, Congress created a limited right to court-appointed counsel if the property subject to forfeiture is the claimant's primary residence. The view was that no one should be at risk of losing his home without having counsel to defend him.

The right to counsel also arises when the defendant in a criminal case claims that he needs property that the government has seized or restrained under the forfeiture laws to pay for counsel of his choice in the criminal case. The Supreme Court has held that there is no constitutional right to exempt criminally derived property from forfeiture so that a defendant may use it to hire counsel;[38] but criminal defendants who demonstrate at the outset that they lack other funds with which to retain counsel do have a right to a pre-trial hearing at which the government must establish probable cause that the property is likely to be forfeited.[39]

7. Double Jeopardy *(Ursery)*

Finally, there is one other issue that threatened to derail the non-conviction-based forfeiture program for a time in the 1990s. In 1994, an appellate court in California held that because civil forfeiture is a form of punishment, forfeiting a person's property would necessarily prevent the government from bringing criminal

---

[37] See 18 U.S.C. § 981(g).

[38] See *United States v. Monsanto*, 491 U.S. 600 (1989).

[39] See *United States v. Farmer*, 274 F.3d 800, 804–805 (4th Cir. 2001) (defendant entitled to a probable cause hearing if property he needs to hire counsel in criminal case has been seized or restrained in related civil forfeiture case). Cf. *Kaley v. United States*, ___ U.S. ___, 134 S. Ct. 1090 (2014) (Roberts, C.J., dissenting) ("To even be entitled to the hearing, defendants must first show a genuine need to use the assets to retain counsel of choice.").

charges against that same person in a later criminal action.[40] Doing so, the court said, would constitute double jeopardy.[41] Almost overnight, forfeitures dropped by 40 percent in the United States as prosecutors feared that a forfeiture order in a civil forfeiture case would constitute a Get out of Jail Free card for a criminal defendant.

Two years later, however, the Supreme Court held in *Ursery*, that forfeiture is not punishment for committing a crime but is either a remedial measure (as it is when the government is recovering proceeds) or punishment for *allowing one's property to be used* to commit a crime and so does not constitute punishment for purposes of the Double Jeopardy Clause of the Fifth Amendment.[42]

IV. Conclusion

The American experience with civil, or non-conviction-based, asset forfeiture spans more than two centuries. In that time, it has become an essential tool of law enforcement, resulting annually in the recovery of over $2 billion in assets derived from or used to commit federal crimes. As the use of non-conviction-based forfeiture has expanded, enormous attention has been given to the protection of individual rights and civil liberties by the courts and the national legislature, with the result that litigants now have a high level of confidence that their rights will be protected regardless of what form the government's forfeiture action may take.

The process of refining the forfeiture laws and procedures is not yet complete. Matters of significance are litigated daily, and new cases are pouring in from the trial and appellate courts. But the major issues having been resolved, it is certain that non-conviction-based forfeiture will continue to play a significant role in efforts to deprive criminals of the fruits of their crimes, and it will take the instruments of crime out of the hands of those who would use them to violate the law. Indeed, with the globalization of the financial system and the resulting ease with which criminals of all persuasions are able to move criminal proceeds across international borders, it is highly likely that non-conviction-based forfeiture will assume an even greater role in recovering the proceeds of crime that are generated in one nation and transferred to another, particularly where the government has little likelihood of bringing the wrongdoer to justice through a traditional criminal trial.

---

[40] See *United States v. $405,089.23 in U.S. Currency*, 33 F.3d 1210 (9th Cir. 1994).

[41] 33 F.3d at 1222.

[42] *Ursery*, 518 U.S. at 291–292.

Bibliography

Cassella, Stefan D., Civil Asset Recovery: The American Experience. eucrim 3 (2013), 98–103.

– Asset Forfeiture Law in the United States. 2nd ed. New York 2013.

– The Case for Civil Forfeiture: Why in rem proceedings are an essential tool for recovering proceeds of crime. Journal of Money Laundering Control 8 (2008), pp. 8–14.

– The Uniform Innocent Owner Defense to Civil Asset Forfeiture. 89 Kentucky Law Journal (2001), pp. 653–654.

List of Abbreviations

CAFRA	Civil Asset Forfeiture Reform Act
Chapt.	Chapter
Cir.	Circuit
D.D.C.	District of D.C. (District of Columbia)
F.2d	Federal Reporter, Second Series
F.3d	Federal Reporter, Third Series
Fed. R. Civ. P.	Federal Rules of Civil Procedure
Fed. R. Crim. P.	Federal Rules of Criminal Procedure
F. Supp. 2d	Federal Supplement, Second Series
Ky. L.J.	Kentucky Law Journal
S. Ct.	Supreme Court Reporter
U.S.	United States Supreme Court
U.S.C.	United States Code
WL	Westlaw

Chapter 3

Civil Asset Recovery

The English Experience

*Ian Smith**

I. Outline of the civil recovery scheme[1]

Civil recovery[2] was introduced in 2003 by the Proceeds of Crime Act 2002 (POCA), with retrospective effect. It is the first scheme of its kind in the United Kingdom, following decades of operation of regimes for criminal forfeiture of the instrumentalities of crime and post-conviction confiscation of the proceeds of crime.

Civil recovery is designed to enable the state to remove from circulation the proceeds of crime where criminal prosecution is not possible or has failed rather than to determine or to punish for any particular offence.[3]

State agencies are able to sue for the recovery of "recoverable property," being property which has been obtained through unlawful conduct (including unlawful conduct abroad) or property which represents such property. These civil recovery powers were initially restricted to one agency, the Assets Recovery Agency, but were subsequently widened to a number of agencies, the most prominent users now being the National Crime Agency (which in October 2013 took over the functions of the now defunct Serious Organised Crime Agency) and the Serious Fraud Office. Civil recovery was intended to be a form of "proprietary remedy"[4] focusing on the criminal origin of property rather than the attributes of a current holder of that

---

* Although much of what I will say also applies to Scotland and Northern Ireland, for ease of understanding, I have restricted my presentation to the law of England and Wales.

[1] I have dealt with the main civil recovery scheme contained in the Proceeds of Crime Act 2002 and have not, in this chapter, dealt with other areas of "asset recovery" law, namely:

- the cash forfeiture provisions of POCA,

- forfeiture of the "instrumentalities" of crime,

- non-conviction-based confiscation under POCA in relation to a defendant who has absconded.

[2] Of the kind described in this chapter.

[3] *Gale v. Serious Organised Crime Agency* [2011] UKSC 49, [123].

[4] *Smith, Owen & Bodnar*, Asset Recovery: Criminal Confiscation and Civil Recovery, [1.1.45], citing the Attorney-General at the time of passage of POCA into law.

property. Proceedings are brought before the High Court (a civil court) against the person who is thought to hold the property in question.[5]

This new form of state-instigated civil law suit fits with a UK statute-law trend towards the erosion of the distinction between civil and criminal laws.[6]

The fact that a respondent could be charged with a criminal offence or has previously been acquitted of a criminal offence is not generally a bar to civil recovery proceedings in relation to the same subject matter.[7] Subject to further discussion below, the law in relation to this is more or less settled in the UK but is due to be subject to further argument before the European Court of Human Rights.[8] Conversely, the existence or conclusion of civil recovery proceedings does not bar criminal proceedings in relation to the same subject matter.[9]

Government guidance provides that, although the reduction of crime is best secured by criminal investigations and prosecutions, civil recovery is to be used where (a) it is not feasible to secure a conviction, (b) a conviction is obtained but a confiscation order is not made, or (c) a relevant authority is of the view that the public interest is better served by pursuing civil recovery than criminal prosecution.[10]

Civil recovery is backed by an array of powerful investigative powers and preservation measures, which may be used both before and during proceedings.[11] The following are available to state agencies: property freezing orders;[12] management receiving orders;[13] interim receiving orders;[14] production orders;[15] search and seizure warrants;[16] disclosure orders;[17] customer information orders;[18] and account monitoring orders.[19]

---

[5] POCA, s 243(1).

[6] *Smith, Owen & Bodnar,* [I.1.18–20]. By contrast with parliament, the courts declined to reduce the significance of the distinction between criminal and civil law, even when the result was leaving assets in the hands of offenders: *Smith, Owen & Bodnar,* [III.2.08].

[7] *Gale v. Serious Organised Crime Agency* [2011] UKSC 49, [133].

[8] *Gale* is appealing to the ECtHR.

[9] *R v. Levey* [2006] EWCA Crim 1902, [57]–[62].

[10] Joint Guidance of the Home Secretary and the Attorney-General given on 5 November 2009.

[11] Beyond the scope of this chapter.

[12] POCA, s 245A.

[13] POCA, s 245E.

[14] POCA, s 246.

[15] POCA, s 345.

[16] POCA, s 352.

[17] POCA, s 357.

[18] POCA, s 363.

[19] POCA, s 370.

Property which is made the subject of a "civil recovery" order becomes the property of the state rather than of any victim (although there are safeguards for victims who may intervene to protect their property interests). As yet, there are no asset-sharing agreements between the UK and other states to make mandatory the sharing of property recovered with other countries whose governments or citizens may have an interest in the property recovered.

There is no publicly available consolidated data as to the performance of all relevant state agencies. The most readily accessible information as to recent levels of civil recovery is that published by the Serious Organised Crime Agency in its recent annual reports. The reports show that in 2010/11 assets worth some £9.5 million were made the subject of civil recovery orders (the majority through consent orders, agreed to by respondents), in 2011/12 the figure was £14.1 million (the majority of recoveries were by orders of the court), and in 2012/13 the figure was £4.6 million (which included both orders of the court and consent orders). The Serious Fraud Office continues to achieve substantial civil recoveries, which it publishes in its press releases.

Lawyers for respondents have argued that "civil" recovery proceedings are in fact criminal in nature, giving rise to greater procedural safeguards that would include, amongst other things, the enhanced criminal standard of proof and the right against double-jeopardy.

These attempts to characterize the scheme as criminal in nature have failed in England, with the Supreme Court,[20] in *Gale v. Serious Organised Crime Agency* [2011], now ruling that the scheme is civil in nature.[21] The Supreme Court in Gale considered the three-factor ECHR definition of criminal proceedings in *Engel v. The Netherlands (No 1)* (1976),[22] namely (a) the national designation of the proceedings, (b) the essential nature of the proceedings, and (c) the nature and severity of the consequences to which the respondent is exposed, as well as a number of ECHR decisions in this area. The case of *Gale* is now the subject of an application to the ECHR.

The burden of proof remains with the state which must satisfy the court of its case on the balance of probabilities.[23]

The civil standard of proof is really the hallmark of civil recovery in the United Kingdom. If the civil standard of proof were to be replaced with the criminal one (beyond reasonable doubt), then the whole civil recovery regime would almost certainly be fatally damaged:

---

[20] Exceptionally composed of seven judges rather than the usual number of five.

[21] *Gale v. Serious Organised Crime Agency* [2011] UKSC 49, [54], [57], [113].

[22] *Engel v. The Netherlands (No 1)* (1976) EHRR 647.

[23] POCA, s 241(3).

- Firstly, civil recovery allegations would be as difficult to prove as criminal charges, therefore reducing the number of viable civil recovery actions.
- Secondly, it would not be possible for the state to make allegations of wrongdoing in civil recovery proceedings that have already been made and decided in favor of defendants in criminal proceedings on the same standard of proof (see below in relation to the presumption of innocence).
- Thirdly, the use of the criminal standard of proof may well render the proceedings criminal in nature under the *Engel* criteria (see above).

II. The presumption of innocence

Perhaps surprisingly, it has not been the due process of civil recovery proceedings themselves which has vexed the English court most. Instead, it is the impact of earlier criminal proceedings on civil recovery proceedings that has led to much argument before and a 7-justice judgment from the Supreme Court in the case of *Gale*, with reference to case law of the ECtHR.

Before turning to the Gale case and its analysis of the ECHR jurisprudence, I shall consider the following:

- A number of relevant ECHR cases themselves, some of which were considered by the Supreme Court in *Gale*.
- The Scottish case of *Scottish Ministers v. Doig, Doig & Cameron* concerning civil recovery proceedings, which came before the Inner House of the Court of Session.[24]

Sekanina v. Austria[25]

Mr. Sekanina was charged with murder. He had allegedly used a bucket to knock his wife out of a fifth-floor window, causing her to fall to her death. Mr. Sekanina was acquitted by jury verdict. He spent a year on remand pending trial and his acquittal, and he claimed compensation for that time. His claim for compensation was refused by the Court of First Instance, and this refusal was upheld on appeal in Austria. Under Austrian law, the courts could only order Mr. Sekanina to receive compensation if the suspicion that Mr. Sekanina had committed the murder had been 'dispelled.' The Austrian courts found that it had not been dispelled. Indeed

---

[24] *Scottish Ministers v. Doig, Doig & Cameron* [2009] CSIH 34 P260/04. The Inner House of the Court of Session is the Scottish equivalent of the English Court of Appeal.

[25] Application No 13126/87 *Sekanina v. Austria* (1994) 17 EHRR 221.

the courts made a number of comments affirming the view that a suspicion that he had committed the murder still existed.[26]

Mr. Sekanina took his case to the ECtHR. Prior to reaching the court itself, the Commission of the ECtHR found in his favor (by 18 votes to 1[27]) that the Austrian courts' continued remarks and findings that suspicions about the guilt of Mr. Sekanina persisted after his acquittal violated his right to be presumed innocent under Article 6(2) of the ECHR.[28] In the opinion of the Commission:

"... the criminal courts' judicial authority would be severely undermined if, after an acquittal, a suspicion could be maintained that the accused had committed the offences dealt with at trial. The role of the courts, as conceived in Article 6 in general and which also finds its expression in the principle of the presumption of innocence laid down in Article 6(2) excludes such a suspicion in the case of a person whose record has been cleared on final acquittal."[29]

The Commission in *Sekanina* relied on the earlier opinion of the Commission in *X v. Austria,*[30] which had stated:

"No authority may treat a person as guilty of a criminal offence unless he has been convicted by the competent court and in the case of an acquittal the authorities may not continue to rely on the charges which have been raised before that court but which have proved to be unfounded. This rule also applies to courts which have to deal with the non-criminal consequences of behaviour which has been subject to criminal proceedings. They must be bound by the criminal court's finding according to which there is no criminal responsibility for the acts in question although this naturally does not prevent them to establish, e.g. a civil responsibility arising out of the same facts."[31]

In respect of the applicability of Article 6(2), although the court would not express a general view on whether Article 6(2) applied to all authorities, it found that it did apply to the Austrian courts which had refused Mr. Sekanina compensation even though the refusal to award compensation had come several months after his acquittal. It declared that Article 6(2) was applicable because:[32]

- "Austrian legislation and practice nevertheless link the two questions – the criminal responsibility of the accused and the right to compensation – to such a degree that the decision on the latter issue can be regarded as a consequence and, to some extent, the concomitant of the decision on the former."
- The same court, albeit composed differently, had jurisdiction to try both the criminal charge against Mr. Sekanina and, following his acquittal, his claim for compensation;

---

[26] *Sekanina v. Austria*, [12] & [13].

[27] The English Commissioner, Sir Basil Hall, was the dissenter.

[28] *Sekanina v. Austria*, Commission's Opinion, [47]–[50].

[29] *Sekanina v. Austria*, Commission's Opinion, [48].

[30] Application No 9295/81 *X v. Austria*, Dec. 6.10.82, D.R. 30, p 227.

[31] *X v. Austria*, p 228.

[32] *Sekanina v. Austria*, [20].

- The Austrian courts relied heavily on the evidence from the criminal court's case file in order to justify their decision rejecting Mr. Sekanina's claims, which demonstrated that there was a link between the two sets of proceedings.

Proceedings came before the judges of the ECtHR. In reaching its decision as to whether Article 6(2) had been violated, the court stressed that Article 6(2) does not guarantee a person acquitted of a criminal offence compensation for his time detained on remand.[33] It also recognized that the ECtHR had not found Article 6(2) violations in previous cases brought against Germany, where suspicions had been voiced in cases which had been discontinued before final judgment, but Sekanina was different: the case had ended with Mr. Sekanina's acquittal.[34]

The ECtHR went on to find that there had been a violation of Article 6(2) for the following reasons. The findings of the Austrian courts which denied Mr. Sekanina compensation

"left open a doubt as to the applicant's innocence and as to the correctness of the [criminal] court's verdict ... [and the Austrian court's] undertook an assessment of the applicant's guilt on the basis of the [criminal] court's file. The voicing of suspicions regarding an accused's innocence is conceivable as long as the conclusion of criminal proceedings has not resulted in a decision on the merits of the accusation. However, it is no longer admissible to rely on such suspicions once an acquittal has become final."

Rushiti v. Austria[35]

Mr. Rushiti was charged with attempted murder and remanded in custody awaiting his trial. He was acquitted by a jury and claimed compensation in respect of his time spent on remand. The Austrian first-instance court dismissed Mr. Rushiti's compensation claim because, relying on the statement of the victim who gave evidence against Mr. Rushiti at the criminal trial, it found there had been a reasonable suspicion, which had not been dissipated, that Mr. Rushiti had committed the attempted murder. The Austrian appeal court held that the court deciding on whether or not to grant compensation was not entitled to examine the evidence that had been deployed in the criminal court but must limit itself to the reasoning of the jury for its findings. In Mr. Rushiti's case, the jury had been split 7 to 1 in favor of acquittal (meaning that one person thought him guilty) and had given its reasons for acquittal as "the evidential basis was insufficient." On this basis, the Austrian appeal court concluded that the suspicion that Mr. Rushiti had committed the murder had not been dissipated.

---

[33] *Sekanina v. Austria*, [25].

[34] *Sekanina v. Austria*, [27] & [28].

[35] Application No 28389/95 *Rushiti v. Austria* (2001) 33 EHRR 56.

The ECtHR followed its earlier decision of and reasoning – set out at paragraph 19(a) above – in *Sekanina* in respect of the applicability of Article 6(2).[36] In respect of the merits of Mr. Rushiti's case, the ECtHR found that there had been a violation of Article 6(2) for the following reasons:

- It was not satisfied that the Austrian court had confined itself to the jury's record of deliberation and no other considerations;[37]

- In any case, the fact that suspicions may have already been expressed in the course of a person's acquittal did not justify the voicing of those suspicions after that acquittal.[38]

Explaining the aim and effect of Article 6(2), the ECtHR had the following to say:[39]

"... the general aim of the presumption of innocence ... is to protect the accused against any judicial decision or other statements by State officials amounting to an assessment of the applicant's guilt without him having previously been proved guilty according to law ... The Court, thus, considers that once an acquittal has become final – be it an acquittal giving the accused the benefit of the doubt in accordance with Article 6(2) – the voicing of any suspicions of guilt, including those expressed in the reasons for acquittal, is incompatible with the presumption of innocence."

Hammern v. Norway[40]

Mr. Hammern was charged with the sexual abuse of a number of children under his care in a nursery. After spending periods of time remanded in custody, he was acquitted by jury verdict at this particular trial. About a year later, Mr. Hammern was awarded some compensation by professional judges who had presided alongside the jury in his criminal trial but, significantly, those judges refused Mr. Hammern compensation payable under Article 444 of the Norwegian Code of Criminal Procedure. This Article provided that compensation could be claimed by an acquitted person for damage suffered from the prosecution "if it is shown to be probable that he did not carry out the act that formed the basis for the charge." As a general rule, Norwegian case law provided that it was for the acquitted compensation-claimant to show, on the balance of probabilities, that it was more than 50% probable that he did not carry out the act on which the charge was based. Having considered both the evidence presented at Mr. Hammern's criminal trial together with further evidence on the compensation hearing itself, the Court of First Instance

---

[36] *Rushiti*, [27].

[37] *Rushiti*, [30].

[38] *Rushiti*, [31].

[39] *Rushiti*, [31].

[40] Application No 30287/96 *Hammern v. Norway* (final judgment rendered on 11 May 2003).

refused Mr. Hammern's compensation application. In doing so, it cited a number of features of the evidence before it, including evidence from medical experts as to a very high degree of probability that the children in question had been exposed to sexual abuse and the evidence pointing to Mr. Hammern as a perpetrator of that abuse. Mr. Hammern's appeal to the Norwegian Supreme Court was rejected. He brought his case to the ECtHR.

As it did in *O*, *Y* and *Ringvold* (see below), the ECtHR in *Hammern* recorded that the compensation proceedings in question were civil rather than criminal proceedings but that:[41]

• The compensation issue overlapped to a very large extent with that decided in Mr. Hammern's criminal trial;

• It was determined on the basis of evidence from the criminal trial by the same court, sitting largely in the same formation.

"Thus, the compensation claim not only followed the criminal proceedings in time, but was also tied to those proceedings in legislation and practice, with regard to both jurisdiction and subject matter. ..." and "the conditions for obtaining compensation were linked to the issue of criminal responsibility in such a manner as to bring the proceedings within the scope of Article 6(2), which is accordingly applicable."

The ECtHR found that the reasoning of the Norwegian Court of First Instance, which had reiterated the evidence of sexual abuse of the children by Mr. Hammern, clearly amounted to the voicing of suspicion against the applicant with respect to the charges of sexual abuse for which he had been acquitted. It furthermore found that even the more cautious findings of the Norwegian Supreme Court were capable of calling into doubt the correctness of Mr. Hammern's acquittal in a manner incompatible with the presumption of innocence in Article 6(2).[42]

O v. Norway[43]

O was charged with sexual offences in relation to his daughter L. He was acquitted by a Norwegian court following a jury verdict in his favor. Within three months of his acquittal, O filed an application to the same Norwegian court for compensation, requesting compensation under the Norwegian Criminal Code for compensation for the damage caused to him by the criminal proceedings. Approximately five months later, the court rejected O's compensation application. The court noted that, under the relevant law, it was a condition for obtaining compensation that the former accused person must prove on the balance of probabilities that he did not carry

---

[41] *Hammern*, [45]–[46].

[42] *Hammern*, [48].

[43] Application No 29327/95 *O v. Norway*.

out the acts in respect of which he had been charged and acquitted.[44] Dealing with the factual evidence before it, the court found:[45]

- That it was probable that L had been subjected to sexual abuse;
- That it had not been shown on the balance of probabilities that O did not engage in sexual intercourse with his daughter L.

O appealed to the Norwegian Supreme Court. The Supreme Court upheld the lower court's rejection of his claim for compensation, finding "no reason to depart from the [lower court's] assessment of the evidence."[46]

The ECtHR considered that the compensation proceedings in O's case were civil in character and went on to state that "[t]he issue is whether the compensation proceedings were nevertheless linked to the criminal trial in such a way as to fall within the scope of Article 6 § 2."

Considering this question, the ECtHR made the following observations:

- Noted that a compensation claim of the kind brought by O had to be brought within three months of the close of criminal proceedings, before the same court and, as far as possible, before the same judges who had presided at the criminal trial;[47]
- Considered it a "weighty consideration" that compensation proceedings engaged the responsibility of the state to pay any compensation awarded;[48]
- Noted that an acquittal in criminal proceedings was a prerequisite for a compensation claim;[49]
- Found that, notwithstanding the differing burdens of proof in the criminal proceedings and a subsequent compensation application, the issues in these proceedings "overlapped to a very large extent";[50]
- Noted that the compensation application was determined on the basis of evidence which had been adduced at O's criminal trial;[51]
- Noted that the compensation application was determined by the same court and judges that had presided in the criminal proceedings.[52]

The ECtHR found that Article 6 § 2 was "applicable" for the following reasons:[53]

---

[44] *O*, [13].
[45] *O*, [13].
[46] *O*, [14].
[47] *O*, [35].
[48] *O*, [36] & [37].
[49] *O*, [37].
[50] *O*, [37].
[51] *O*, [37].
[52] *O*, [37].

"... [T]he compensation claim not only followed the criminal proceedings in time, but was also tied to those proceedings in legislation and practice, with regard to both jurisdiction and subject matter. Its object was, put simply, to establish whether the State had a financial obligation to compensate the burden it had created for the acquitted person by the proceedings it had instituted against him. Although the applicant was not 'charged with a criminal offence', the Court considers that, in the circumstances, the conditions for obtaining compensation were linked to the issue of criminal responsibility in such a manner as to bring the proceedings within the scope of Article 6 § 2."

Citing *Rushiti*, the ECtHR stated "the Court reiterates that this provision [Article 6(2)] embodies a general rule that, following a final acquittal, even the voicing of suspicions regarding an accused's innocence is no longer admissible."[54]

The court did not find any grounds for distinguishing O's case from *Rushiti* and *Sekanina* and found that there had been a violation of Article 6(2)[55] on the basis that the Norwegian court's reasoning behind its refusal to grant compensation to O "clearly amounted to the voicing of suspicion against the applicant regarding the charges of sexual abuse on which he had been acquitted."[56]

Y v. Norway[57]

Y was charged with violent assault, sexual assault, and homicide of his cousin Ms. T. He was convicted of these charges by a criminal court composed of professional and lay judges, sentenced to a term of imprisonment, and ordered to pay compensation to T's family. Norwegian law provided that compensation should be payable, whether or not an accused has been convicted or acquitted, on the basis of that person's "intent or gross negligence."[58]

Y was subsequently acquitted by a jury in the appeal court. The day after that acquittal, professional judges in the appeal court who had presided over the appeal before the jury (receiving submissions on behalf of Y and Ms. T's family but hearing no further evidence) upheld the first instance court's decision to award compensation to Ms. T's family. It did so on the basis that it was "clearly probable that [Y] has committed the offences against [the victim]," which met the Norwegian legal requirement that, in cases where a person has been acquitted, it would only be permissible to order him to pay compensation if "it is clear on the balance of prob-

---

[53] *O*, [38].

[54] *O*, [39].

[55] *O*, [41].

[56] *O*, [39].

[57] Application No 56568/00 *Y v. Norway* (2005) 41 EHRR 7 (final judgment rendered on 11 May 2003).

[58] *Y*, [24] & [25].

abilities" that the accused has committed the "infringements specified in the indictment."[59]

Y's appeal to the Norwegian Supreme Court failed. Although the Norwegian Court used more careful language, it did not quash the lower court's decision. Y took his case to the ECtHR.

The ECtHR rejected Y's argument that the compensation claim in respect of Ms. T had amounted to a "criminal charge" against him.[60] The ECtHR went on to address Y's complaints under Article 6(2). It prefaced its findings with the following propositions:

• "If the national decision on compensation contains a statement imputing the criminal liability of the respondent party, this could raise an issue falling within the ambit of [Article 6(2)]."[61]

• "The Court will therefore examine the question whether the domestic courts acted in such a way or used such language in their reasoning as to create a clear link between the criminal case and the ensuing compensation proceedings as to justify extending the scope of the application of [Article 6(2)] to the latter."[62]

Finding that Article 6(2) was both applicable and violated, the ECtHR stated as follows:[63]

"... in seeking to protect the legitimate interests of the purported victim, the Court considers that the language employed by the High Court, upheld by the Supreme Court, overstepped the bounds of the civil forum, thereby casting doubt on the correctness of that acquittal. Accordingly, there was sufficient link to the earlier criminal proceedings which was incompatible with the presumption of innocence."

Ringvold v. Norway[64]

Mr. Ringvold was charged with the sexual assault of a child, G. The same court of first instance acquitted Mr. Ringvold and rejected G's compensation claim at a joined hearing of these two issues. G appealed the lack of compensation award to the Norwegian Supreme Court. In these appeal proceedings, the Supreme Court allowed evidence to be adduced which had been produced in the context of the earlier criminal proceedings. At the conclusion of G's appeal, the Supreme Court

---

[59] *Y*, [13].

[60] *Y*, [40] & [41].

[61] *Y*, [42].

[62] *Y*, [43].

[63] *Y*, [46].

[64] Application No 34964/97 *Ringvold v. Norway* (final judgment rendered on 11 May 2003).

found it clearly probable that Mr. Ringvold had sexually abused G and ordered him to pay compensation to G. Mr. Ringvold took his case to Strasbourg.

The ECtHR rejected Mr. Ringvold's argument that the compensation claim in respect of Ms. T had amounted to a "criminal charge" against him,[65] in doing so stating the following:

> "... while exoneration from criminal liability ought to stand in the compensation proceedings, it should not preclude the establishment of civil liability to pay compensation arising out of the same facts on the basis of a less strict burden of proof ..."[66]

As it did in *Y*, the ECtHR stated that, if the national decision on compensation were to contain a statement imputing criminal liability to the respondent party, this would raise an issue falling within the ambit of Article 6(2).[67] It also stated that "the question remains whether there were such links between the criminal proceedings and the ensuing compensation proceedings as to justify extending the scope of Article 6(2) to the latter."[68] Finding no violation of Article 6(2), the court stated as follows:[69]

> "The Court reiterates that the outcome of the criminal proceedings was not decisive for the issue of compensation. In this particular case, the situation was reversed: despite the applicant's acquittal it was legally feasible to award compensation. Regardless of the conclusion reached in the criminal proceedings against the applicant, the compensation case was thus not a direct sequel to the former. In this respect, the present case is clearly distinguishable from those referred to above, [including Sekanina and Rushiti] where the Court found that the proceedings concerned were a consequence and concomitant of the criminal proceedings ..."

Baars v. The Netherlands[70]

Mr. Baars was arrested in February 1993 on suspicion of bribery and forgery. In June 1995, he was informed that the preliminary judicial investigation against him had been closed but summoned before a criminal court on charges of forgery in August 1995. The criminal court, in October 1995, declared the case against Mr. Baars to be inadmissible on the basis that the judicial authorities had failed to deal with Mr. Baars' case with the required due diligence and had therefore violated his Article 6(1) right to a trial within a reasonable time. The prosecutor appealed this ruling but then, in August 1996, withdrew the appeal.

---

[65] *Ringvold*, [37]–[40].

[66] *Ringvold*, [38].

[67] *Ringvold*, [38].

[68] *Ringvold*, [41].

[69] *Ringvold*, [41].

[70] Application No 44320/98 *Baars v. The Netherlands* (final judgment given on 28 January 2004).

In January 1997, in the course of continued criminal proceedings against another individual, Mr. Baars was heard as a witness. The court dealing with that case convicted the other individual of forgery, having established wrongdoing by that individual in cooperation with Mr. Baars.

In November 1996, Mr. Baars had lodged a request for compensation under the Code of Criminal Procedure for reimbursement of his costs and expenses in relation to the criminal case as well as claiming damages in respect of his pre-trial detention. In April 1997, the criminal court rejected much of Mr. Baars' claim for costs and expenses and rejected the whole of his claim for damages in respect of his pre-trial detention. The Court of Appeal then upheld those decisions on the basis that Mr. Baars had forged a relevant document and that, had he been prosecuted, he would "in all likelihood ... have been convicted."[71]

The ECtHR found this reasoning to be a violation of Mr. Baars' Article 6(2) rights.[72] Critically, the ECtHR considered that the Dutch Court of Appeal had not merely indicated that there were strong suspicions against Mr. Baars[73] but also that its reasoning amounted to "a determination of [Mr. Baars'] guilt without [Mr. Bok] having been 'found guilty according to law'" and went on to add "It was based on findings in proceedings against another person, Mr. B. [Mr. Bok] participated in these other proceedings only as a witness, without the protection that Article 6 affords the defence."[74]

A.L. v. Germany[75]

A.L. was accused of insurance fraud in 1994 and indicted for the same in 1997. In 2000, the criminal proceedings were discontinued by the criminal court on the basis that A.L. had agreed to and did pay a sum of money to the Association to Aid Criminal Offenders. The court which discontinued the proceedings refused to grant compensation to A.L. in respect of his time spent on remand. A.L. appealed this refusal. This was shortly followed by a letter from the presiding judge of the criminal court addressed to counsel for A.L. It stated that, had criminal proceedings been pursued, A.L. would have been convicted with "predominant probability." In 2000, the Frankfurt/Main Court of Appeal and later the Federal Constitutional Court rejected A.L.'s appeal against the refusal to grant him compensation on the grounds that the courts were entitled to take into account "a remaining suspicion" when

---

[71] *Baars*, [17].

[72] *Baars*, [32].

[73] *Baars*, [30].

[74] *Baars*, [31].

[75] Application No 72758/01 *A.L. v. Germany* (final judgment rendered on 28 July 2005).

determining whether to grant compensation to a former accused person, as this did not involve the establishment or allocation of guilt but only constituted an admissible and necessary evaluation of the state of suspicion which had led to the prosecution.[76] A.L. brought his case to the ECtHR.

The ECtHR repeated its often quoted position that Article 6(2) gives no former accused person the right to compensation for his previous lawful detention and that a refusal to grant such compensation does not offend the Article 6(2) presumption of innocence.[77]

The ECtHR went on to note that a decision refusing to grant compensation to a former accused person may nonetheless amount to a violation of Article 6(2) "if supporting reasoning which cannot be dissociated from the operative provisions amounts in substance to a determination of the accused's guilt without his having previously been proved guilty according to the law and, in particular, without his having had an opportunity to exercise the rights of the defence."[78]

Citing an earlier decision, the ECtHR went on to note the distinction between decisions which describe a "state of suspicion" (compatible with Article 6(2)) and decisions which contain a "finding of guilt" (incompatible with Article 6(2)).[79]

Turning to A.L.'s case, the ECtHR found no violation of Article 6(2). It based its decision on the fact that it accepted the German government's argument that the presiding judge's letter to A.L. (which the ECtHR described as "ambiguous and unsatisfactory"[80]) did not constitute a formal part of the decision[81] on the compensation claim and had only "limited external effects."[82] It clearly agreed with the German appellate courts' decisions that the lower court had been entitled to take into account a remaining suspicion regarding the former accused person.

Orr v. Norway[83]

Mr. Orr was a pilot. He was accused of raping a fellow crew member, Ms. C. He was initially convicted but on re-hearing before a jury in the Norwegian High Court acquitted of the allegation. Ms. C maintained her civil claim for compensation be-

---

[76] *A.L.*, [14]–[18].

[77] *A.L.*, [32].

[78] *A.L.*, [33].

[79] *A.L.*, [34].

[80] *A.L.*, [38].

[81] *A.L.*, [37].

[82] *A.L.*, [38].

[83] Application No 31283/04 *Orr v. Norway* (final judgment rendered on 1 December 2011).

fore the High Court. The professional judges of the High Court gave a two-part judgment, firstly acquitting Mr. Orr and secondly finding Mr. Orr liable to compensate Ms. C. In order to reach this conclusion, the court found – as it had to do under Norwegian law – that it was "clearly probable" that Mr. Orr had had non-consensual sex with Ms. C.[84]

The Norwegian Supreme Court rejected Mr. Orr's appeal. In doing so, it described and upheld the Norwegian system in forthright terms:[85]

- It found that Article 6(2) does not constitute an obstacle to ordering that compensation be payable by an acquitted person;
- It noted that, according to the (Norwegian) Code of Criminal Procedure, a victim's civil claim may be heard alongside a criminal case provided that the civil claim was derived from the same act as in the criminal case;
- Parallel proceedings is procedurally economic and saves the victim from the financial and emotional burden of undergoing two trials;
- The evidentiary requirements of a civil claim are less stringent than those in a criminal case and an unavoidable consequence of this is that findings of civil liability may follow acquittals of criminal charges;
- In order to enable this resolution without creating doubts in respect of acquittals, strict requirements should apply to the reasoning contained in the judgment awarding compensation;
- It is not possible to avoid coming close to a criminal-law assessment, but what must be avoided is casting doubt over the correctness of the acquittal at the higher criminal evidentiary standard.

The (Norwegian) Supreme Court went on to find that the High Court had gone no further than was necessary in order to establish that the conditions for compensation were given and that it had used appropriate language in its findings, thus marking the necessary distance between the criminal acquittal and the finding of civil liability.[86]

The ECtHR prefaced its consideration of Mr. Orr's case by stating that it would examine his complaint in the light of the principles enunciated in its case law *Ringvold v. Norway* and *Y v. Norway*, namely by examining whether the compensation proceedings gave rise to a "criminal charge" and, in the event that this was not the case, whether the compensation case nevertheless was linked to the criminal

---

[84] *Orr*, [9].
[85] *Orr*, [13].
[86] *Orr*, [13].

trial in such a way as to fall within the scope of Article 6(2).[87] The ECtHR found that the compensation proceedings did not give rise to a "criminal charge."[88]

Finding, by a majority of 4 votes to 3, that there had been a violation of Mr. Orr's Article 6(2) right,[89] the ECtHR's judgment stated:

- The fact that the (Norwegian) High Court had dealt with the compensation issue in the same judgment as the criminal charges was a natural consequence of the fact that the two matters had been pursued in the course of the same proceedings and could not in itself bring the compensation issue within the ambit of Article 6(2);[90]
- The Norwegian Court had covered practically all those constitutive elements, objective as well as subjective, that would normally amount to the offence of rape under the Norwegian Penal Code;[91]
- (Citing *Y*), the language of the (Norwegian) High Court "did confer criminal law features on its reasoning overstepping the bonds [sic] of the civil forum;"[92]
- (Citing *Ringvold* and *Y*), that it was mindful of the (Norwegian) High Court's two-part judgment distinguishing the acquittal from its civil liability findings on a lower standard of proof,[93] but it was "not convinced that, even if presented together with such cautionary statements, the impugned reasoning did not 'set aside' [Mr. Orr's] acquittal or 'cast doubt on the correctness of the acquittal',"[94] and these shortcomings were not rectified on appeal to the Supreme Court.[95]

Cogent dissenting judgments were delivered by three judges of the ECtHR, in whose opinion there had been no violation of Article 6(2), which included the following reasoning:

- The fact that an acquittal of a criminal charge does not bar civil liability to pay compensation on findings relating to the same case facts is necessary in order to safeguard the interests of the victim and right of access to a court under Article 6;[96]
- There was insufficient linkage between the criminal and civil cases to justify the extension of Article 6(2) to the latter case, given that the outcome of the criminal cases was not decisive for the compensation issue (the opposite was the case).

---

[87] *Orr*, [47].
[88] *Orr*, [47]–[49].
[89] *Orr*, [55].
[90] *Orr*, [50].
[91] *Orr*, [51].
[92] *Orr*, [51].
[93] *Orr*, [52].
[94] *Orr*, [53].
[95] *Orr*, [54].
[96] *Orr*, Dissenting Opinion of Judge Jebens.

Therefore "the compensation case was not a direct sequel to the former or a consequence and concomitant of it ...";[97]

- The purpose of establishing civil liability to pay compensation (of a non-penal amount) is quite different from that of establishing criminal liability;[98]

- The ECHR jurisprudence accepts that the difference in standards of proof constitutes a sufficient distinction between a criminal charge on which there has been an acquittal and a civil claim arising out of the same events. So, the question now is not what view one takes of the system as such but whether the High Court was at fault in the language it used;[99]

- In fact, all the Norwegian cases finally turned on what the ECtHR thought of the way that the national courts had expressed themselves in their decisions, the court repeatedly saying that a decision containing a "statement imputing criminal liability" would raise an issue under Article 6(2);[100]

- The (Norwegian) Supreme Court had meticulously pointed out that the different result – as that between the acquittal and the finding of civil liability in respect of Mr. Orr's case – was differentiated only by the necessary standard of proof in each set of proceedings;[101]

- At no point did the (Norwegian) High Court's description of the facts or its reasoning go beyond what was necessary in order to present sufficient grounds for establishing civil liability. In fact, several times in its judgment, the High Court had even highlighted that civil liability was different from criminal liability[102] and, in doing so, had marked the necessary distinguishment between these findings.[103]

Bok v. The Netherlands[104]

Mr. Bok had been investigated, prosecuted, convicted, and sentenced to a term of imprisonment in respect of organized criminal activities but was cleared on appeal and granted some compensation by the appellate court under the Dutch Code of Criminal Procedure. Mr. Bok then went on to issue a civil claim for compensation against the Netherlands state, alleging that the case against him had wrongly pro-

---

[97] *Orr*, Dissenting Opinion of Judge Jebens.

[98] *Orr*, Dissenting Opinion of Judge Jebens.

[99] *Orr*, Dissenting Opinion of Judge Nicolaou joined by Judge Vajić.

[100] *Orr*, Dissenting Opinion of Judge Nicolaou joined by Judge Vajić.

[101] *Orr*, Dissenting Opinion of Judge Nicolaou joined by Judge Vajić.

[102] *Orr*, Dissenting Opinion of Judge Jebens.

[103] *Orr*, Dissenting Opinion of Judge Nicolaou joined by Judge Vajić.

[104] Application No 45482/06 *Bok v. The Netherlands* (final judgment rendered on 18 April 2011).

ceeded on a suspicion that had been unfounded from the outset. The Dutch Court of First Instance rejected Mr. Bok's claim on the basis that the investigating judges in the criminal proceedings had found that there was a reasonable suspicion against Mr. Bok and furthermore that the Court of Appeal had found that the investigative methods used against Mr. Bok were lawful. The Court of Appeal then upheld this decision. In rejecting his appeal, the Court of Appeal stated:

> "The Court of Appeal agrees with the Regional Court that the criminal investigation – the final judgment or otherwise – does not show that [Mr. Bok] was innocent ... of the crimes charged. The Court of Appeal notes that such a conclusion can only be drawn if the suspect's innocence is reasonably obvious ... This is not the case here given – on the one hand – the items of evidence ... and – on the other – the absence from the case file, in so far as made available ... of convincing disculpatory material ..."[105]

Mr. Bok complained to the ECtHR that the Dutch Court of Appeal had violated his Article 6(2) right when finding – despite his acquittal – that the original suspicion against him had not been dispelled as a ground for denying him compensation.

The ECtHR held, by 6 votes to 1, that there had been no violation of Article 6(2), basing this decision on the following reasoning:

- Mr. Bok had chosen to bring the civil claim, despite having already been awarded some costs and expenses of the criminal proceedings;[106]
- Mr. Bok bore the burden of proving his allegations, a decisive distinction between this case and other similar cases before the ECtHR;[107]
- The claimant had based his civil claim on the allegation that any suspicion against him had been groundless from the outset;[108]
- It was reasonable to expect the claimant to have to prove this allegation; his acquittal in the criminal proceedings was based on insufficiency of evidence to find him guilty beyond reasonable doubt, and his acquittal did not mean that Mr. Bok was dispensed from having to prove his claim for damages in civil proceedings;[109]
- Although the Dutch Court of Appeal's language in referring to Mr. Bok's lack of innocence and the lack of disculpatory material had been "unfortunate," the Court of Appeal had nonetheless been entitled to uphold the decision that it had been for Mr. Bok to prove his case that there were no grounds for suspicion against him.[110]

In his dissenting opinion, Judge Casadevall reasoned as follows:

---

[105] *Bok*, [18].
[106] *Bok*, [42].
[107] *Bok*, [43].
[108] *Bok*, [44].
[109] *Bok*, [45].
[110] *Bok*, [46]–[48].

- He found the distinction cited by the court – that Mr. Bok had initiated subsequent civil proceedings, despite having already been granted a sum of money towards his costs and expenses – to be "artificial," given that the prior award had nothing to do with the subsequent claim.[111]
- He effectively stated his opinion that the Dutch Court of Appeal had violated Mr. Bok's Article 6(2) right in the language used to reject his appeal.[112]

The Scottish Ministers v. Doig, Doig and Cameron[113]

Mr. Cameron was stopped in his Land Rover in October 2002. 2 kg of amphetamine were found in the car. He denied knowing anything about the drugs, claiming that they must have been put there by somebody whilst the car was parked in a garage or left unlocked by him. Mr. Cameron also possessed cash totalling £1442. His explanation was that this came from his dealing in cars, furniture, and jewelry. He was registered as unemployed and receiving state benefits.[114] Mr. Cameron was charged with being a drug supplier.

At the commencement of his criminal trial, surveillance evidence advanced by the prosecutor was ruled inadmissible by the criminal court on the ground that the surveillance had not been properly authorized. Following the court's decision as to this evidence, the prosecutor withdrew the case against Mr. Cameron who was then formally acquitted by the criminal court. This was in October 2003.

The Scottish Ministers subsequently[115] brought civil recovery proceedings in the Outer House of the Court of Session against Mr. Cameron and others, with reference to Mr. Cameron's alleged drug dealing, seeking to remove from their possession land, cash in accounts at financial institutions, insurance policies, and cars.[116] Amongst other things, the Inner House rejected Mr. Cameron's argument that some of the allegations made against him were incompatible with his Article 6(2) rights in respect of his acquittal before the criminal court. It found that there was "no suf-

---

[111] *Bok*, Opinion of Judge Casadevall, [9].

[112] *Bok*, Opinion of Judge Casadevall, [8] & [10].

[113] The decision of the Inner House of the Court of Session, *The Scottish Ministers v. Doig, Doig & Cameron* [2009] CSIH 34 P260/04. This case followed the proceedings before the Outer House of the Court of Session, reported as *The Scottish Ministers v. Doig* [2007] SLT 313, [2006] CSOH 176. I shall refer to the judgments of each court by reference to the Inner House or the Outer House judgments.

[114] Inner House judgment, [4].

[115] Neither the judgment of the Court of First Instance, the Outer House of the Court of Session, nor the appeal before the Inner House of the Court of Session state when the proceedings were commenced. Judgment was passed down by the Outer House on 23 November 2006 ([2006] CSOH 176, 2007 SLT 313) and by the Inner House on 1 May 2009.

[116] Inner House judgment, [8].

ficient linkage" between the civil recovery proceedings and the earlier criminal case to contravene Article 6(2).[117] The judge of the Outer House expressed the reasoning behind his decision as follows:

- The parties to the criminal litigation and civil recovery litigation were not the same and although the state was involved in both cases, it was so involved through different agencies carrying out different functions.[118]

- The subject matter of the two cases was different. The civil recovery case was proprietary in nature, the purpose being to recover wrongfully obtained property. By contrast, the earlier criminal proceedings had not been concerned with that property, their purpose instead being to establish whether or not Mr. Cameron was guilty of the alleged criminal conduct.[119]

- In the civil recovery case, it was not necessary for the Scottish Ministers to prove that Mr. Cameron was guilty of any criminal charge; it was sufficient that they prove that the property in question had been obtained by criminal conduct, albeit in this case that of Mr. Cameron[120] (although this need not have been the case).[121] The question of whether Mr. Cameron had committed any criminal offence was only of "evidential significance" and was not the "critical issue" in the case.[122]

- The aim of the civil recovery proceedings was not to call into question Mr. Cameron's acquittal, and the court was not entitled to make any findings as to his guilt regarding any particular criminal offence.[123]

- No conviction or punishment is sought in civil recovery proceedings.[124]

- Civil recovery proceedings are conducted in a civil court using civil procedures.[125]

Mr. Cameron appealed against these findings to the Inner House of the Court of Session.

The Inner House, finding insufficient linkage between the civil and criminal proceedings to make Article 6(2) applicable, endorsed the reasoning[126] given in the Outer House decision in the case.[127] The Inner House also:[128]

---

[117] Outer House judgment, [31] & [34].
[118] Outer House judgment, [31].
[119] Outer House judgment, [32].
[120] Outer House judgment, [32].
[121] Outer House Judgment, [33].
[122] Outer House judgment, [33].
[123] Outer House judgment, [33].
[124] Outer House judgment, [32].
[125] Outer House judgment, [32].
[126] Set out in paragraph 51 above.
[127] Inner House judgment, [29].

- Emphasized, as another reason for the lack of sufficient linkage between the civil recovery proceedings and the earlier criminal case, that proceedings for civil recovery may be brought regardless of whether there have been any criminal proceedings.
- Reiterated its agreement with the lower court that the functions of the state agencies responsible for civil recovery and criminal proceedings were distinct.

The Inner House considered the ECtHR case of Y and whether it gave rise to an additional ground for the application of Article 6(2), notwithstanding a lack of linkage between the two sets of proceedings. On this issue, the Inner House decided, "it is, we consider, perhaps not unreasonable to suppose that implicit in the decision [in Y] was an acceptance that the compensation proceedings were indeed sufficiently linked by law and practice to be regarded as, in effect, a consequence, and concomitant, of the criminal proceedings," noting that, "The decision on criminal liability and on liability to pay compensation was reached by the same court, at the same time and on the basis of the same evidence" and, moreover, that the decision in the case of Y was made by the same judges as in the case of O on the same day.[129]

The Inner House then went on to state that, even if this analysis of Y was incorrect, in the case of Mr. Cameron, there had been no assertions of criminal guilt on his part so as to justify a violation of Article 6(2) similar to that found by the ECtHR in the case of Y. The Inner House, noting that it was not necessary in a civil recovery case to allege the perpetration of a specific criminal offence or offences, went on to conclude:

"Although references are earlier made to [Mr. Cameron] having been concerned in [drug] supply, it is not obvious that the language is used in any specific technical sense or as necessarily imputing guilt of the particular offence provided for by [the section of the criminal statute]. More generally, and perhaps more importantly, the averments do not invite a finding of guilt of a particular offence, but rather a finding that conduct was 'unlawful'. It is true that section 241 [of POCA] provides that unlawful conduct occurring in any part of the United Kingdom is unlawful conduct if it is unlawful under the criminal law of that part, and it may be a fine distinction, but the effect of the provision may be said to provide that certain conduct has both civil and criminal consequences; the latter being that it is 'unlawful' for the purposes of civil recovery pro property. Just as, as it is accepted, a civil court, even after an acquittal in criminal proceedings, may in certain cases make a finding of liability to pay compensation on proof of the same facts as would constitute a criminal offence (e.g. assault or rape) without offending article 6(2), provided, no doubt, it is plain that the finding is of the delict of assault or rape, so too, it appears to us, a finding of 'unlawful conduct', albeit on the basis of the same facts as would constitute a criminal offence, could not be said to offend article 6(2). ... In such circumstances, the court could not be said to 'overstep the bounds of the civil forum', to adopt the expression used in Y v. Norway."

---

[128] Inner House judgment, [29].

[129] Inner House judgment, [31].

To use the court's wording, there is at best a fine distinction between an allegation that a person has committed a crime and an allegation that property was obtained by a person as a result of his criminal conduct. It is true that the former concerns liability and punishment of an individual, whereas the latter concerns the recovery of property. At their core, however, both approaches scrutinize the conduct of an individual and the key issue to be determined is whether or not that individual committed a criminal offence.

Gale v. Serious Organised Crime Agency[130]

This case concerns Mr. and Mrs. Gale, who, according to the judgment of Griffith Williams J in the High Court, engaged in criminal conduct in a number of jurisdictions, including Spain and Portugal. In the case of Mr. Gale, this was drug trafficking, money laundering, and tax evasion and in the case of Mrs. Gale, this was money laundering.[131]

Some £2 million in property held by the couple was made the subject of a civil recovery order. This was notwithstanding the fact that Mr. Gale had been prosecuted for but acquitted of drug trafficking in Portugal and had, in Spain, been the subject of a drug trafficking prosecution that had been discontinued because of a statute of limitations.[132]

In trying the civil recovery case, the High Court judge examined the evidence that had led to the Portuguese prosecution and the commencement of the Spanish prosecution as well as fresh evidence, including that of Mr. and Mrs. Gale in the civil recovery proceedings.[133]

The High Court judge dealt with the Portuguese acquittal and Spanish proceedings in the following way:[134]

"It is not contended that the doctrine of issue estoppels applies and clearly the criminal law principle of autrefois acquit has no application in civil proceedings. On behalf of DG, it was submitted that the Portuguese charges cannot be re-litigated without hearing from all the relevant witnesses or considering a full transcript which is not available. However, I do not accept this contention. To consider the evidence adduced in the Portuguese proceedings is not to re-litigate because what is in issue in these proceedings is not the commission of the specific offences alleged against DG in Portugal but whether on the evidence before this court of the material considered by the Portuguese Court, together with the evidence available to the Spanish Courts and other material not considered by the courts in either jurisdiction, the claimant has proved on the balance of prob-

---

[130] *Gale v. Serious Organised Crime Agency* [2011] UKSC 49.
[131] *Gale*, [11] & [12].
[132] *Gale*, [3], [12], & [141].
[133] *Gale*, [12].
[134] *Gale*, [11], citing paragraph 18 of Griffith Williams J's judgment.

abilities that DG's wealth was obtained through unlawful conduct of a particular kind or of one of a number of kinds, each of which would have been unlawful conduct: see section 242(2)(b) of POCA – that is to say drug trafficking, money laundering and tax evasion."

Turning to the conduct of Mr. and Mrs. Gale, the High Court judge said this:[135]

"I am in no doubt that DG and TG engaged in unlawful conduct – in DG's case, money laundering and drug trafficking, in TG's case money laundering. There is also evidence of tax evasion in four jurisdictions. They have acquired capital and various assets as a direct consequence of the money laundering and/or drug trafficking, but it is not possible to quantify the extent of the tax evasion or to estimate the extent, if at all, that it contributed to their capital wealth. For reasons given during the course of the judgment and below, I am satisfied the Receiver has correctly identified recoverable property. I found DG a witness whose evidence, on the central issues, was wholly unreliable. He was so often demonstrably lying. I am not prepared to believe the evidence of TG insofar as she purported to confirm his account or to explain her involvement; she too was shown to be a liar about matters of real moment. While I am prepared to accept that DG was the moving force behind all criminal conduct, she was hardly ignorant of what he was doing and played her full part in the money laundering."

The rationale of Mr. Gale's arguments before the Supreme Court was that Article 6(2) of the ECHR applied and once Mr. Gale had been acquitted of drug trafficking by the Portuguese Court, no adverse finding could be made that implicated him in the conduct of which he had been acquitted.[136]

The Supreme Court analyzed the ECHR cases referred to above. Lord Phillips (with whom three other Judges agreed[137]) had this to say in relation to the *Sekanina* and *Rushiti* decisions:[138]

"Taken at face value these decisions seem to convert a presumption of innocence prior to conviction which is rebuttable into an irrebuttable presumption of innocence after acquittal. Two matters demonstrate that this is not the case. The first is the relief granted, or more significantly denied, to the applicants. Each of the applicants sought damages by way of compensation for his detention on remand – ie the relief he had sought in the domestic proceedings, to which he was entitled under domestic law if suspicion of his guilt had been dispelled. This was denied on the ground that there was no connection between the violation of article 6(2) and the damage in question. If, however, the acquittals had been conclusive of the applicant's innocence his right to compensation would logically have followed. The other matter is the reasoning of the ECtHR in a number of subsequent applications against Norway, which were heard together."

Let us pause for a moment to consider the first point made by Lord Phillips, namely that acquittals not being conclusive of a right to compensation for time spent on remand, demonstrates that the presumption of innocence is not irrebuttable. With the greatest respect for the learned judge, this is not a watertight argument. Every country is free to choose whether or not to compensate acquitted de-

---

135 *Gale*, [12], citing paragraph 140 of Griffith Williams J's judgment.

136 *Gale*, [14].

137 Lord Mance, Lord Judge, and Lord Reed.

138 *Gale*, [25].

fendants. The decisions of *Sekanina* and *Rushiti* do not affect this position. What they do affect is the ability of the authorities and courts to question the earlier acquittals of persons during the process of determining whether compensation should be paid to those acquitted persons.

Lord Phillips went on to consider the three ECtHR cases involving Norway. He was critical of the ECtHR's attempts to distinguish between claims for compensation by acquitted defendants and claims for compensation by third parties against acquitted defendants:

> "With respect, I find unconvincing the attempts of the Strasbourg Court to distinguish between claims for compensation by an acquitted defendant and claims for compensation by a third party against an acquitted defendant. As the cases to which I have just referred show, the link between the criminal proceedings and the subsequent proceedings can be close in either case. The evidence may be common to both proceedings, as may the judges who have to consider it. In each case the compensation proceedings can put in issue the facts that were alleged as the foundation of the criminal charges. In each case facts were held proved according to the civil standard of proof which had not been established according to the criminal standard in the earlier proceedings. How can it credibly be said that the claim for compensation by the defendant is 'consequential and concomitant' to the criminal proceedings but not the claim by a third party? May it not be that the Strasbourg Court took a wrong turn in Sekanina and Rushiti? It might be thought that the judges who sat on the criminal proceedings will be well placed to determine the outcome of issues that depend upon the application of a lesser standard of proof to the same factual evidence; the Norwegian procedure, illustrated in Y, proceeded on that basis. Yet this is something that the Strasbourg jurisprudence appears to discourage. This confusing area of Strasbourg law would benefit from consideration by the Grand Chamber."

Concluding his analysis, Lord Phillips considered but rejected the possibility that the Convention cases render unviable the possibility that an acquitted person seeking compensation can be required to show on the balance of probabilities that he did not carry out the act which formed the basis of the charge.[139] It was rejected by Lord Phillips on the basis that "... if this were correct the effect of article 6(2) was to prejudice the rights of the defendant that it was designed to protect." With the greatest respect for Lord Phillips, there is no such apparent prejudice to a defendant from such an interpretation of Article 6(2).

Lord Phillips preferred an alternative, much narrower interpretation of Article 6(2):[140]

> "An alternative view is that all that the cases establish is that article 6(2) prohibits a public authority from suggesting that an acquitted defendant should have been convicted on the application of the criminal standard of proof and that to infringe article 6(2) in this way entitles an applicant to compensation for damage to reputation or injury to feelings. I am inclined to this view, albeit that it involves a remarkable extension of a provision that on its face is concerned with the fairness of the criminal trial – see my comment on Taliadorou and Stylianou v. Cyprus (Application Nos 39627/05 and 39631/05 (unre-

---

[139] *Gale*, [33].

[140] *Gale*, [34].

ported) 16 October 2008) in R (Adams) v. Secretary of State for Justice [2011] UKSC 18, [2011] 2 WLR 1180."

More specifically in relation to Mr. Gale, Lord Phillips concluded:

"On no view does this jurisprudence support [Mr. Gale's advocate's] submission that the appellant's acquittal in Portugal precludes the English court in proceedings under POCA from considering the evidence that formed the basis of the charges in Portugal. The link between the Portuguese criminal proceedings and the English civil proceedings, which Strasbourg would appear to consider so critical, is not there. Nor does this jurisprudence lend any support to the proposition that the criminal standard must be applied to proof of criminal conduct in proceedings under POCA. That proposition requires further consideration of Strasbourg authority."[141]

All seven judges of the Supreme Court determined in *Gale* that there was not a sufficient link between the civil recovery proceedings under POCA and the previous criminal proceedings (in which one of the defendants was acquitted) to justify the application of Article 6(2) of the ECHR.[142]

All seven judges of the Supreme Court were also in agreement that the High Court judge had not imputed criminal liability to Mr. and Mrs. Gale[143] on the basis that "... none of the judge's findings specifically calls into question the correctness of Mr. Gale's acquittal in Portugal." With the greatest respect, this appears to be a careful but ultimately erroneous denial of the obvious: that the High Court judge did take into consideration the Portuguese evidence when finding that Mr. Gale had committed drug trafficking crimes.

In conclusion, the UK's Supreme Court has found that civil recovery proceedings are in themselves not so closely connected to criminal prosecutions as to render Article 6(2) applicable. What they have left open is that Article 6(2) may become applicable if the making of a civil recovery order entails imputations of criminal liability; courts must be astute in order to avoid use of language creating such an impression.[144]

III. Discussion regarding the ECHR jurisprudence

The decisions in *Sekanina, Rushiti, Hammern, O, Ringvold* and *Orr* all appear to be based on the same premise that, in order for Article 6(2) even to be applicable, there must be a sufficient link, in law and practice, between the original criminal proceedings and the subsequent civil proceedings. By contrast, there was no explicit recitation or application of such a pre-condition in the cases of *Y, Baars* or *A.L.*

---

[141] *Gale*, [35].

[142] *Gale v. Serious Organised Crime Agency* [2011] UKSC 49, [35], [56], [111], [133].

[143] *Gale*, [58], [141] & [142].

[144] *Gale v. Serious Organised Crime Agency* [2011] UKSC 49, [115], [138].

If it *is* a necessary pre-condition for the applicability of Article 6(2) that there be a link between the criminal proceedings and subsequent civil proceedings, does this mean that extra-judicial statements by officials of an acquitted person's criminal guilt are not barred by Article 6(2)? Surely not. And if such a linkage is a necessary pre-condition, what will the ECtHR make of English civil recovery proceedings and whether or not there are sufficient links between such proceedings and earlier criminal cases to render applicable Article 6(2)? I return to this below.

Leaving aside the "linkage" question, the most consistent basis on which all cases before the ECtHR have turned is not whether or not there is a sufficient link between the relevant criminal and civil proceedings but whether, in fact, the language used by the civil courts has undermined an individual's acquittal. If this is the real test to be applied in each case, then what kind of language offends Article 6(2)? Should Article 6(2) bar even the voicing of suspicion of the guilt of the former accused, amounting to a violation of Article 6(2), or should it only prohibit findings that a person has committed the offence for which he has been convicted? One can find justification for each of these possibilities in the ECtHR's decisions.

What is not in doubt is that the ECHR jurisprudence provides some level of continued protection to persons acquitted of crimes. The fundamental question is what level of protection these persons should be given. The *Gale* case presents an opportunity for the ECtHR to reconsider the entirety of its jurisprudence to date, including its inconsistent rulings, and to enunciate in clear and unambiguous terms the true nature of Article 6(2) as it applies after the end of a set of criminal proceedings. Will the ECtHR use the *Gale* case as an opportunity to recast its jurisprudence on Article 6(2)?

In the context of English civil recovery proceedings, what appears to be particularly significant when considering Article 6(2) and civil recovery proceedings, are the following points:

- An individual needs greater protection from allegations of criminal conduct by the state than from similar allegations by private individuals (for example, victims). This is because allegations by public officials and agencies carry much more weight, as credible allegations, with the press and the public than those raised by private individuals.

- It is reasonable to expect that the activities of investigators and government-employed lawyers should observe the human rights of individuals under their purview. It is also reasonable to expect them to have higher standards than members of the public.

- Whilst it may be the case that civil recovery proceedings occur in a court that is designated as civil in nature, such a distinction is a fine one if one at all to the layperson. The public is largely ignorant of the structure of the English court system and misunderstands the distinction between the criminal and civil courts. This misunderstanding is most pronounced in relation to the Court of Appeal whose judgments are rarely reported by the press by reference to the distinction between the criminal and civil divisions of that court. Moreover, at the level of the Supreme Court, there is no distinction between civil and criminal matters: the same court deals with both. A pronouncement by a court, particularly a senior one with senior judges like the High Court, which deals with civil recovery cases, has a powerful effect in the media.

- The very fact that civil recovery proceedings focus on the property derived from crime does not mean that allegations are not made in respect of (if not against) particular identifiable individuals, and the evidence before the civil court will usually be identical in many respects to that which was presented before the criminal court.

- Individuals may not even be present at the hearing in question, where allegations are made about their criminal conduct, giving them no opportunity to defend themselves in this situation.

- In private law cases based on facts that could also found a criminal complaint, the alleged torts may require proof of similar or even identical facts but typically require proof of a different set of ingredients than those in criminal cases. There is, however, often an overlap in the relevant ingredients. By contrast, when compared with criminal cases, only the standard of proof is different in civil recovery cases.

- In many civil recovery cases, the allegations of wrongdoing have no equivalent in the civil private law system of torts and equitable wrongs. The best illustration of this are civil recovery cases concerning drug trafficking, where there is no equivalent tort. A finding of unlawful conduct of this kind can only be detrimental to an individual's reputation.

- In civil recovery cases, the objective of the claim by the relevant state agency is the forfeiture of certain property to the state rather than to compensate any identifiable individual victim of crime. Therefore, there is no interplay between the presumption of innocence afforded to an acquitted defendant and the Article 6 right of a victim to have access to justice in the courts.

The above points may be used in arguments that civil recovery, in a case such as that of Mr. Gale, does indeed violate his Article 6(2) rights. However, even proponents of the view that the English civil recovery regime can violate Article 6(2) must ask themselves these questions:

- Would it be right to treat acquitted defendants differently from those who have never been prosecuted?

- Is it not right that society can and should seek to remove from circulation property obtained through criminal conduct, in order to deny offenders benefit from crime and to prevent further use of said property by those with a propensity to commit crime?

- Is it not sufficient that a civil court can emphasize that its finding have no bearing on the acquittal of the defendant, the validity of which is not an issue the civil court can or should attempt to determine?
- Is it not sufficient protection that an informed observer of civil recovery proceedings or an informed reader of any civil recovery judgment will understand that any allegations or findings made are made on the basis of the lower standard of evidential proof in the civil court?

IV. Recovery of property obtained through unlawful conduct

A court must, subject to certain safeguards, make a civil recovery order, "vesting" the property in question in the hands of a government-appointed trustee for civil recovery ("trustee"), if it is satisfied that the property is "recoverable."[145]

"Recoverable property" is "property obtained through unlawful conduct."[146] This can be any property in the United Kingdom as well as any property outside the United Kingdom if the case being brought for civil recovery can be shown to have a sufficient connection with the part of the UK in which the case is being brought.[147] "Unlawful conduct" is:

- Any conduct occurring in the United Kingdom and which is "unlawful" under the criminal law of the part of the United Kingdom in which it occurs";[148]
- Any conduct in a country or territory outside the United Kingdom that is unlawful under the criminal law of that country or territory and that, had it occurred in a part of the United Kingdom, would also be unlawful in that part.[149]

It is not necessary for the law enforcement claimant to show that the unlawful conduct was of a particular kind if it is shown that the property was obtained through conduct of one of a number of kinds, each of which would have been un-

---

[145] POCA, s 266(1).

[146] POCA, s 304(1).

[147] SOCA ss 242 and 282A and Schedule 7A. These expressly extra-territorial provisions were inserted by the Crime and Courts Act 2013 as a direct response to the Supreme Court case of *Perry and others (Appellants) v. Serious Organised Crime Agency (Respondent), Perry and others No. 2 (Appellants) v. Serious Organised Crime Agency (Respondent)* [2012] UKSC 35 in which the majority of the Supreme Court Justices have ruled that POCA civil recovery proceedings, under the then POCA provisions, could not be extra-territorial in effect: [12(viii)], [53], [56], [63], [69]–[73], [79] and [136]. Dissenting judgments were given by two lords, Lords Judge and Clarke.

[148] POCA, s 241(1).

[149] POCA, s 241(2).

lawful conduct.[150] Although it is not sufficient for the claimant law enforcement agency simply to show that a respondent had no identifiable lawful income to warrant his holding of the property in question,[151] an untruthful explanation or a failure to offer an explanation may add strength to the case for civil recovery.[152]

In *Director of Assets Recovery Agency v. Green*,[153] Sullivan J gave guidance as to the level of specificity required in a civil recovery allegation (which was subsequently endorsed by the Court of Appeal[154]):

"For the purposes of Section 240 and 241(1)(2) a description of the conduct in relatively general terms should suffice, 'importing and supplying controlled drugs,' 'trafficking women for the purpose of prostitution,' 'brothel keeping,' 'money laundering' are all examples of conduct which if it occurs in the United Kingdom is unlawful under criminal law. It is possible that more detail might be required if conduct outside the United Kingdom was being relied upon ..."[155]

In the words of King J, in *Director of Assets Recovery Agency v. Jackson*[156] courts should take:

"... a global approach to the issue of proof that the property in issue is recoverable in the meaning of the Act ...I do not consider it essential that the court considers each property transaction on an item by item basis in the sense that the claimant has an obligation to show some particular unlawful actions by the defendant at some particular time which enabled the particular transaction."[157]

The "global" approach was followed in *SOCA v. Agidi*,[158] by Sweeney J, whose approach was that "It is obviously important to stand back from the detail and look at the broad picture provided by the factors as I have found them to be."[159]

The court may draw inferences from the primary facts of the case, so that a case may be determined on the basis of an "irresistible inference" that the property in question could only have been derived from crime[160] or, to put it another way, no other inference can be drawn fairly from the primary facts.[161] In doing so, courts

---

[150] POCA, s 242(2)(b).

[151] *Director of Assets Recovery Agency v. Szepietowski* [2007] EWCA Civ 766, [2008] Lloyd's Rep FC 10, Times, August 21, 2007, at [26]; *Director of Assets Recovery Agency v. Olupitan* [2008] EWCA Civ 104, at [16].

[152] *Director of Assets Recovery Agency v. Szepietowski* [2007] EWCA Civ 766, at [28]; *Director of Assets Recovery Agency v. Olupitan* [2008] EWCA Civ 104, at [16].

[153] *Director of Assets Recovery Agency v. Green* [2005] EWHC 3168 (Admin).

[154] *Director of Assets Recovery Agency v. Olupitan* [2008] EWCA Civ 104, at [22]–[24].

[155] *Director of Assets Recovery Agency v. Green* [2005] EWHC 3168 (Admin), [17].

[156] *Director of Assets Recovery Agency v. Jackson* [2007] EWHC 2553 (QB).

[157] *Jackson*, [116].

[158] *SOCA v. Agidi* [2011] EWHC 175 (QB).

[159] *Agidi*, [160].

[160] *Serious Organised Crime Agency v. Coghlan* [2012] EWHC 429 (QB), [14(6)].

[161] *Sweeney v. Coote* [1907] 1 AC 221, at 222.

are entitled to take a common sense approach to what inferences may be drawn[162] but must not arrive at inferences by light conjecture.[163]

In addition, courts will often be navigating documentary evidence and may not have received relevant evidence from respondents and others and have therefore not been able to see the evidence tested by cross-examination.[164]

The following are examples of the approach taken by the courts in admitting evidence in support of civil recovery:

- *Coghlan*:[165] C had been arrested on suspicion of murder, and a relatively large amount of money was found. He was charged with murder and drug supply, but the prosecution against him was stayed. The relevant agency[166] brought an action for the recovery of a real property. Despite C's denials of being involved in drug supply, his defense being that he had made a living through loan-sharking and lacked any previous conviction for a drug offence, the court was satisfied from the evidence that C had engaged in unlawful conduct as a drug dealer and derived his income from such source. To reach this conclusion, the court took account of a number of factors,[167] including (i) C's lack of a legitimate or any other source of income during the relevant period; (ii) C's association with convicted and well known drug dealers; (iii) C's lifestyle and expenditure (which included spending on luxury cars, one of which was an armor-plated BMW); (iv) the cash found following C's arrest; (v) a file containing information about money-laundering legislation in C's possession; (vi) payments from unidentified sources for the development and refurbishment of the property that was the subject of the civil recovery proceedings.

- *Robb*:[168] This case exemplifies how the court will take into account a range of previous misconduct by a respondent, including previous convictions, in order to determine a respondent's propensity to act dishonestly and commit fraud (it was alleged that the property held by R was derived from fraud) as well as how the respondent's credibility and reliability as a witness are assessed.

- *Jackson*:[169] The court, making civil recovery orders based upon findings that the property held by K represented his proceeds of drug dealing and mortgage fraud, took into account (i) K's previous convictions for drug supply; (ii) periods of time K was unable to engage in legitimate business trading for reason of his in-

---

[162] *Coghlan*, [14(5)].

[163] *Sweeney*, 222.

[164] *Coghlan*, [16].

[165] *Serious Organised Crime Agency v. Coghlan* [2012] EWHC 429 (QB).

[166] The Assets Recovery Agency, whose functions were taken over by the Serious Organised Crime Agency.

[167] Summarised at [99].

[168] *Serious Organised Crime Agency v. Gary John Robb* [2012] EWHC 803 (QB).

[169] *Director of Assets Recovery Agency v. Jackson* [2007] EWHC 2553 (QB).

carceration in prison; (iii) cash, jewelry, and watches found at K's home and in a safety deposit box he held; (iv) the fact that the cash seized from R's home was stored in a washbag and plastic supermarket bags; (v) much higher than normal levels of drug-particle contamination of the cash seized; (vi) K's own explanations that he registered vehicles under a false name to avoid speeding fines and did not pay tax on his earnings.

Property is obtained "through unlawful conduct" if it is obtained "by or in return for" that conduct.[170] In order for this to be the case (a) there must be a direct link between the unlawful conduct and the obtaining of the property[171] and (b) the unlawful conduct must have made a "material contribution" to the acquisition of the property in question.[172]

Recoverable property remains recoverable, subject to certain defenses, even if it has been disposed of: it may be "followed" to the hands of subsequent persons.[173]

Recoverable property may also be "traced" in that property which "represents" the original recoverable property may also be recovered,[174] e.g., if a stolen car is sold, the proceeds of sale will also be recoverable, but a civil recovery order cannot be made in relation to both the original recoverable property and the property which fully represents it.[175]

If it has been mixed with other property,[176] then the portion of the mixed property which is attributable to the recoverable property represents the property obtained through unlawful conduct.[177]

The fact that property which is the subject of a civil recovery order is "vested" in the trustee for civil recovery settles the question of ownership between the state and the individual – the state owns any property which has been vested.[178]

---

[170] POCA, s 242(1).

[171] *Director of Assets Recovery Agency v. Lord* [2007] EWHC 360 (QB), per Tugendhat J, [63ff].

[172] *R (Chief Constable of Greater Manchester) v. Salford Magistrates' Court* [2008] EWHC 1651 (Admin).

[173] POCA, s 304.

[174] POCA, s 305.

[175] POCA, s 279(2); in relation to property which only partially represents the original recoverable property, see POCA, s 279(3).

[176] POCA, s 306 gives examples, including recoverable property paid into a bank account already holding other funds and recoverable property used as partial payment for an asset.

[177] POCA, s 306.

[178] For example, a trustee will obtain legal and equitable title to real property vested in him: *Olden v. Serious Organised Crime Agency* [2010] EWCA Civ 143, [2010] Lloyd's Rep FC 432, cited in *Perry v. Serious Organised Crime Agency* [2011] EWCA Civ 578, [168].

Where recoverable property is "associated" with other property, that other property is regarded as "associated property,"[179] e.g., property held as tenant in common with recoverable property may be so associated. Where recoverable property is owned by "joint tenants," a tenant who obtained the property under circumstances in which it would not be recoverable against him is an "excepted joint owner." If the court considers it "just and equitable" to do so,[180] associated property or an excepted joint owner's property may be made the subject of a civil recovery order.[181] In doing so, the court may order the trustee who receives the associated property to make a compensating payment to the owner of the associated property or create interests or liabilities in relation to it in order to compensate the other owner,[182] with regard to the rights of any person holding associated property or who is an excepted joint owner as well as the state's interest in receiving the proceeds of the recoverable property.[183]

V. Protection for victims' and other third parties' interests in property

Property will not be recoverable under certain circumstances if it in fact belongs to a victim of crime or has come into the hands of another person under circumstances in which it would be unfair to recover it, as set out below.

A person who has been deprived of property belonging to him by means of unlawful conduct, e.g., through fraud or theft, may apply to the court for a declaration of that fact and the property which is the subject of the declaration will no longer be recoverable property.[184] It is considered that property protected in this way will include property which "represents" the original property as long as the victim retains an equitable interest in that representative property.[185] The court may make a declaration that property is, in principle, recoverable, pending applications by vic-

---

[179] POCA, s 245 sets out the definition of "associated property," which includes interests in the recoverable property and tenancies in common in the associated property.

[180] POCA, s 272(1)(b).

[181] POCA, s 272(2).

[182] POCA, s 272(3).

[183] POCA, s 272(4); for discussion of the rights of individuals holding associated property or who are excepted joint owners, see *Smith, Owen & Bodnar*, [III.2.39–41].

[184] POCA, s 281; however, this provision only applies to victims who owned property before it became recoverable property, *i.e.*, it will not entitle a person who has himself obtained the property through unlawful conduct to seek such a declaration on the basis that he was deprived of the property by means of unlawful conduct.

[185] There is no case law on this point, but it is the logical extension of equitable proprietary rights.

tims for declarations as to their interests in relevant property, and it will only go on to make any recovery order after determining victims' applications[186] (this makes sense where findings necessary for civil recovery would also support victims' applications). There may, however, be cases in which it would be more efficient for the court to determine victims' applications before considering whether it should try the civil recovery case as the subject of the civil recovery proceedings between the state and the respondent who appears to hold the property.

Property will cease to be recoverable if it is disposed of and the person who obtains the property does so in good faith, for value, and without noticing that it was recoverable property,[187] e.g., recipients of gifts are not protected from recovery of property they hold.[188]

Property which has been paid to or obtained from a defendant by a person pursuant to a judgment against that defendant, based on the defendant's unlawful conduct, ceases to be recoverable.[189]

Property will also cease to be recoverable if held by a person under the following circumstances:

- A person obtained the property in good faith;
- He took steps after obtaining the property which he would not have taken if he had not obtained it or he took steps before obtaining the property which he would not have taken if he had not believed that he was going to obtain it;
- If he took the steps he had without noticing that the property was recoverable;
- If a recovery order made in respect of the property would be detrimental to that person;
- If it would not be just and equitable to make a recovery order in respect of the property.[190]

For example, it is very unlikely that a recovery order would be made if an innocent person inherits recoverable property and, as a result, gives away other property he holds believing that he no longer needs that other property.

It is notable that the protection offered to innocent owners of otherwise recoverable property is dependent upon their ownership of the asset in question. There is

---

[186] *Serious Crime Agency v. Gary John Robb* [2012] EWHC 803 (QB).

[187] POCA, s 308(3); for a detailed analysis of these principles, see *Ulph*, Good Faith and Due Diligence, in: Palmer/McKendrick (eds.), Interests in Goods, pp. 403–427.

[188] It may be possible for the recipient of a gift, for example, to argue under Article 1 of Protocol 1 of the European Convention on this basis, as POCA explicitly provides that a recovery order may not be made if it is incompatible with convention rights: POCA, s 266(3)(b).

[189] POCA, s 308(3).

[190] POCA, s 266(3)(a) & (4).

no right for victims who have *in personam* claims or judgments against the person holding the property recovered to recover any part of the property made the subject of a recovery order. Instead, such persons are prohibited from law enforcement against any goods belonging to the debtor that are the subject of a property freezing order pending civil recovery,[191] and the court has the power to stay any enforcement proceedings in relation to frozen property.[192]

In a fraud case, the state may recover the proceeds of fraud from the perpetrator and keep those proceeds without even having to notify victims of the fraud of its claim and recovery and without reference to any need to compensate those victims. Is this just?

Would it be fairer for victims of fraud and other crimes who may have an interest in bringing a private civil claim against a wrongdoer to be warned of the effect that any civil recovery order would have? Should the state put in place a scheme for using recovered property to compensate the victims of the crimes on which the recoveries are based? Should it go even further and use recovered property to compensate other victims who come forward and complain about other kinds of criminal behavior on the part of the person from whom property has been recovered? These are political questions concerned with the fairness of civil recovery proceedings.

VI. International enforcement of foreign civil recovery orders in England and Wales

Foreign enforcement authorities and other persons seeking the enforcement of civil recovery orders or provisional and protective measures in civil recovery proceedings may use provisions in the Proceeds of Crime Act 2002 (External Requests and Orders) Order 2005[193] ("POCA Order 2005") for the recovery of property derived from criminal conduct. The property recovered in such proceedings goes to the state (the United Kingdom).

The relevant law enforcement authority in the United Kingdom is empowered to bring proceedings to enforce any order, which it thinks constitutes an "external order," by an overseas court when a request has been forwarded to it by the Secretary of State.[194] An "external order" is defined as an order made by an overseas court

---

[191] POCA, s 245D(1)(b).

[192] POCA, s 245D(1)(a).

[193] The Proceeds of Crime Act 2002 (External Requests and Orders) Order 2005, SI 2005/3181; in particular ch 5 of the Order.

[194] POCA Order, Article 143.

when property is found or believed to have been obtained as a result of criminal conduct and the order is for the recovery of specified property or a specified sum of money.[195]

"Criminal conduct" is defined as conduct constituting an offence in any part of the United Kingdom or which would be constituting an offence in any part of the United Kingdom if it occurred there.[196]

The POCA Order 2005 provides certain safeguards for victims and other third parties holding interests in property that is the subject of an "external order" of the kind afforded in domestic civil recovery proceedings.[197]

Outside the regime in the POCA Order 2005, the English courts will not directly or indirectly enforce any foreign judgment resulting in the enforcement of foreign penal, revenue, or public law[198] (although, in this last category, the Court of Appeal has held that there is no rule that all foreign public laws are unenforceable).[199]

The English courts' lack of jurisdiction stems from the general principles that (a) no state has the right to enforce its law outside its own jurisdiction, meaning that the English courts will not exercise their jurisdiction in support of such an attempt by a foreign state[200] and (b) that a claim for such enforcement is not justiciable in England.[201]

---

[195] POCA, s 447(2); POCA Order, Article 2.

[196] POCA, s 447(8). This provision mirrors the definitions of "criminal conduct" for the purposes of confiscation proceedings in England and Wales (POCA, s 76(1)), Scotland (POCA, s 143(1)), and Northern Ireland (POCA, s 224 (1)).

[197] POCA Order 2005, arts 177(5), 205(1) and 205(2).

[198] For the English and common law prohibition on enforcement of penal and revenue laws, see *Dicey, Morris & Collins*, The Conflict of Laws, [5-027]–[5-031]. Some doubt existed as to whether the prohibition included public laws but that is no longer the case. See the Privy Council decision in *The President of the State of Equatorial Guinea and Another v. The Royal Bank of Scotland International and Others* [2006] UKPC 7, [2006] 3 LRC 676, and *Mbasogo and another v. Logo Ltd and others* [2006] EWCA Civ 1370, [2007] 2 WLR 1062.

[199] *Government of the Islamic Republic of Iran v. The Barakat Galleries Ltd* [2007] EWCA Civ 1374, [2009] QB 22, at [125].

[200] This was suggested by the editors of the (1987) 11th edition of *Dicey & Morris* (as it was then called), substantially adopted by the House of Lords in *In re State of Norway's Application (Nos 1 and 2)* [1990] 1 AC 723, at 808.

[201] This term is used throughout the judgment of the Court of Appeal in *Government of the Islamic Republic of Iran v. The Barakat Galleries Ltd* [2007] EWCA Civ 1374, [2009] QB 22.

VII. International enforcement of English civil recovery orders in other countries and territories

The following is an outline of the difficulties of enforcing civil recovery in foreign courts.

The Judgments Regulation[202] and the Lugano Convention[203] apply only to "civil and commercial" judgments and both stipulate that they do not extend to "revenue, customs or administrative matters." The ECJ has held that cases involving judgments pursuant to the exercise of public functions by a public authority are outside their *ratione materiae*.[204] A claim will be founded on the exercise of public functions if it is founded on legal provisions which may be used by a state agency but which are not available to all persons in general.[205]

It is expected that declarations in favor of victims made under POCA[206] would, however, be recognized and enforced (where necessary, e.g, if the property were to be moved abroad after judgment), being remedies available to all persons and analogous to awards of compensation made within criminal proceedings enforceable under the Judgments Regulation and the Lugano Convention.[207]

Interestingly, the English Court of Appeal has recently decided that the Council of Europe Convention on Laundering, Search, Seizure and Confiscation of the Proceeds of Crime agreed in Strasbourg on 9 November 1990 and which came into force in 1993, applies to civil proceedings which lead to "confiscation" of property, contrary to the arguments of the Serious Organised Crime Agency in this case.[208]

---

[202] Council Regulation (EC) No 44/2001 of 22nd December 2000 on jurisdiction and the recognition and enforcement of judgments in civil and commercial matters, as amended from time to time and as applied by the agreement made on 19th October 2005 between the European Community and the Kingdom of Denmark on jurisdiction and the recognition and enforcement judgments in civil and commercial matters (OJ No. L 299 16.11.2005 at p 62). These regulations are frequently referred to by commentators as the "Brussels I Regulation." I have followed the terminology used in the Civil Procedure Rules 1998, rule 6.31(d).

[203] Convention on jurisdiction and the recognition and enforcement of judgments in civil and commercial matters between the European Community and the Republic of Iceland, the Kingdom of Norway, the Swiss Confederation, and the Kingdom of Denmark signed on behalf of the European Community on 30th October 2007 (OJ No. L 147 10.06.2009 at p 5).

[204] Case 814/79 *Netherlands State v. Rüffer* [1980] ECR 3807; Case 271/00 *Gemeente Steenbergen v. Luc Baten* [2002] ECR I-10527.

[205] Case 271/00 *Gemeente Steenbergen v. Luc Baten* [2002] ECR I-10527, [37].

[206] POCA, s 281.

[207] *Sonntag v. Waidmann* (Case C-172/91) [1993] ECR I-1963.

[208] *Perry v. Serious Organised Crime Agency* [2011] EWCA Civ 578, [69]–[88], overruled in other respects on appeal to the Supreme Court.

VIII. Further questions

This chapter has focused on being a description of the United Kingdom's civil recovery regime as it currently exists and has been interpreted by the courts. Obviously, there are a number of fundamental issues which observers of the United Kingdom's regime – particularly those planning a civil recovery regime – may wish to ask themselves:

- Are civil recovery cases – of the English kind – really criminal cases?
- Whether they are criminal or civil, are they penal in nature for the purposes of Article 7?
- Should civil recovery be restricted to assets shown to have been obtained by means of crime (as is the case in English civil recovery) or should it also extend to legitimate assets in cases in which a person has spent the monies he made from crime but still retains other assets (this kind of recovery is commonplace in the English criminal confiscation regime)?
- What standard of proof should be required for success in a civil recovery claim?
- What disclosure rights should be given to the parties and, in particular, to those whose assets are the subject of claims?
- Should a person holding assets which are the subject of a claim be allowed to use those assets to pay for his defence to the claim?
- Should information or documents obtained from a person in the course of civil recovery proceedings be available to investigators and prosecutors for use in a criminal prosecution?
- How can the presumption of innocence be properly observed?
- How should the rights of innocent owners and other third parties be protected?
- Should property recovered in civil proceedings automatically be used to give compensation to victims of crime?
- Should there be EU-wide mutual enforcement of civil recovery orders?
- Is civil recovery of the English kind really necessary and proportionate for a democratic state?
  - Is this the start of a shift towards a police state?
  - In cases involving non-state victims, would it be as effective or more effective for the state to provide more assistance and funding for private-sector civil actions instead?
  - Would money be better spent on other crime prevention or other criminal prosecution?

Ian Smith

Bibliography

Dicey, Morris & Collins, The Conflict of Laws. 14th ed. London 2014.

Smith, Owen & Bodnar, Asset Recovery: Criminal Confiscation and Civil Recovery, Looseleaf. Oxford 2014.

Ulph, J.S., Good Faith and Due Diligence. In: Norman E. Palmer/E. McKendrick (eds.), Interests in Goods. 2nd ed. London 1998, pp. 403–427.

List of Abbreviations

ECHR	European Convention on Human Rights
ECJ	European Court of Justice
ECtHR	European Court of Human Rights
POCA	Proceeds of Crime Act

Chapter 4

A Civil Asset Recovery Model

The German Perspective and European Human Rights

Robert Esser

I. Introduction

The confiscation of assets related to criminal offences and the levy of economic advantages resulting from criminal offences is a well-known and well-proven means of combating crime in many EU Member States. On the one hand, in most continental jurisdictions, it is only possible to confiscate assets in the wake of a criminal sentence imposed by a court. In Great Britain and in the United States, on the other, there is an action at hand that is directed against the asset itself.

In its communication to the European Parliament and the European Council of 20 November 2008 entitled *"Proceeds of organized crime – Ensuring that crime does not pay"*, the European Commission proposed the introduction of such legal actions in continental jurisdictions as well.[1] Non-governmental organizations, such as the Financial Action Task Force (FATF), also lobbied for the introduction of civil actions directed against the asset itself in order to confiscate it without there being a criminal conviction beforehand.[2] Legal scholars argued for the introduction of said actions in continental jurisdictions as well.[3] Other experts were well aware of the differences in existing legal traditions.

They therefore created the generalizing term *non-conviction-based forfeiture*; this term refers equally to civil, criminal, and administrative proceedings; the aim of this action – the confiscation or seizure of the asset – can be achieved by introducing an action against the asset itself *(actio in rem)* or a person closely related to it *(actio in personam)*, e.g., the owner.[4]

Notwithstanding the fact that an action of the state against an asset itself, as in the UK and in the US, is unknown to continental jurisdictions, this kind of action

---

[1] COM(2008)766 final.

[2] See no. 4 § 3 of the FATF Recommendations on International Standards on combating Money Laundering and the Financing of Terrorism and Proliferation of February 2012, available at http://www.fatf-gafi.org.

[3] Cf. *Stephenson et al.*, Barriers to asset recovery, pp. 66 ff.

[4] *Stephenson et al.*, Barriers to asset recovery, p. 67.

has implications on the fundamental rights and human rights of the person concerned.

Finally, non-conviction-based confiscation was taken out of the scope of Directive 2014/42/EU on the freezing and confiscation of the proceeds of crime in the EU adopted on 3 April 2014.[5] The agreement has been welcomed by many, but some parties have also demurred (for instance the European Criminal Bar Association – ECBA) that the new legislation could have an impact on the protection of fundamental rights and the proportionality principle. The new directive, however, has the merit of establishing a clearer legal framework that is able to invigorate the judicial cooperation between the Member States of the European Union. It has to be underlined, however, that the initial scope of the draft directive, as submitted by the Commission, was significantly reduced during the negotiations between European Parliament and Council.[6] The final text adopted does not permit or tolerate the initial proposal to also establish a full regime for "non-conviction-based confiscation." Even in the absence of a criminal conviction, this regime enables money or any assets to be confiscated if a civil court is satisfied or convinced that the money or assets derive from activities of a criminal nature (*in extenso* see below). This instrument is regarded by many as necessary in order to impede cross-border money laundering.

Nevertheless, the EU legislator did not enact this regime and adhered to a conviction-based confiscation requiring a final criminal conviction. The stated system in the new European directive thus presents itself differently from "civil asset forfeiture." The confiscation is taken against a person (so it is not an *actio in rem*) who would have had to face a criminal conviction if that person had been able to stand in a trial.

Art. 2 of the directive enlarges the "proceeds"[7] in respect to the past framework decision 2006/783/JHA and provides a new definition of "instrumentalities" and "property."[8]

---

[5] Only Poland voted against; UK and Denmark did not take part in the vote. The text was agreed upon with the European Parliament, which adopted its position on 25 February 2014.

[6] In comparison the Report on the proposal for a directive of the European Parliament and of the Council on the freezing and confiscation of proceeds of crime in the European Union COM(2012)0085 – C7-0075/2012 – 2012/0036 COD, 20 May 2013 and the final text as adopted.

[7] "Proceeds" are intended simply as "any economic advantage deriving directly or indirectly from a criminal offence; it may consist of any form of property and includes any subsequent reinvestment or transformation of direct proceeds and any valuable benefits," see Art. 2 No. 1.

[8] "Property" is intended as "property of any description, whether corporeal or incorporeal, movable or immovable, and legal documents or instruments evidencing title or interest in such property," see Art. 2 No. 2.

Art. 4 of the directive obligates the Member States to administer the necessary measures to enable confiscation "subject to a final conviction for a criminal offence" by clarifying that the power of confiscation subsists even in the case of proceedings *in absentia*. Only in case of illness or absconding and when criminal proceedings have been initiated regarding a criminal offence, shall the Member States take the confiscation of instrumentalities and proceeds without a final conviction (Art. 4 § 2). In conclusion, the attempts to widen the legal scope of non-conviction-based confiscation have been highly controversial. Not only because it is an almost unknown concept in many EU Member States that follow a so-called civil law system, but also because it is deemed to be a possible source of violation of human rights.[9]

However, Directive 2014/42/EU may turn out to be a starting point for a broader strategy of the Union for the confiscation of assets related to criminal offences in a few years. This conclusion can primarily be based on the recitals of the directive. Recital 1 of the directive declares that "the effective prevention of and fight against organised crime should be achieved by neutralising the proceeds of crime and should be extended, in certain cases, to any property deriving from activities of a criminal nature." Thus, the *actio in rem* can also be deduced as a possible confiscation instrument. In recitals 12 and 13, the directive gives leeway to the Member States to use their own measures to realize confiscation and forfeiture. The "broad definition of property" (Art. 2 No. 1) suggests that an *actio in rem* should also be taken into consideration. In recital 33, the directive focusses on the area of conflict between the rights of persons, not only of suspected or accused persons but also of third parties who are not being prosecuted: "It is therefore necessary to provide for specific safeguards and judicial remedies in order to guarantee the preservation of their fundamental rights in the implementation of this directive. This includes the right to be heard for third parties who claim that they are the owner of the property concerned, or who claim that they have other property rights ("real rights", *ius in re*), such as the right of usufruct. The freezing order should be communicated to the affected person as soon as possible after its execution."

If a third person has to be heard, the concept of an innocent owner has to be taken into account (*in extenso* see below).

The European Parliament indeed desisted from introducing a civil asset forfeiture model. Nonetheless, the directive cleared the way towards integrating such a non-conviction-based confiscation. Therefore, it is still questionable whether a rule similar to a *civil asset recovery model*[10] would be in harmony with the current German model of criminal procedure and the fundamental rights as guaranteed by the German constitution (Basic Law or *Grundgesetz*).

---

[9] Notably, Germany was explicitly opposed to the non-conviction based confiscation in case of death.

[10] *Kenney,* in: Klose (ed.), Asset Tracing and Recovery, p. 111.

II. Recovery of Civil Assets According to German Criminal Law

The conditions of confiscation of assets in criminal proceedings *(Verfall)* are laid down in Section 73 *et seq.* German Criminal Code *(Strafgesetzbuch* – StGB). The German system concentrates on the personal conviction of the perpetrator. The idea that the property itself may be the offender is totally alien to the concept of culpability in German criminal proceedings.

A. Confiscation of Assets *(Verfall)*

The basic provision concerning the confiscation of assets, **Section 73 § 1 StGB**, regulates as follows:

> If an unlawful act has been committed and the offender has obtained anything in order to commit it or obtained anything from it, the court shall in its judgment order the confiscation of what was obtained.

It results from this legislation that there are two conditions for the court to order the confiscation of assets: *First*, it has been established in court that the concerned person has committed an unlawful, punishable act[11] and the court observed all principles of a criminal law trial to actually reach the conviction that it is beyond reasonable doubt that the act has actually been committed. *Second*, it has further been established that the assets concerned were *obtained (erlangt)*. Subject to confiscation is "anything" *(etwas)* that is *directly* acquired either by the crime committed or for the purpose of the commission of the crime.[12]

Insofar as a confiscation of the directly obtained gains is no longer possible, "anything" includes benefits from said asset and objects which replace it, e.g., because the asset has been destroyed or sold in the meantime (Section 73 § 2 StGB). The confiscation of an object shall also be ordered if it is owned or subject to a right by a third party, who furnished it to support the act or with knowledge of the circumstances of the act (Section 73 § 4 StGB).[13]

---

[11] Not necessarily with guilt; according to the German criminal law, a perpetrator of an unlawful act acts without guilt if he cannot be held responsible for his young age or his mental state or if he cannot be expected to abide by the law for wanting to rescue himself or people close to him from imminent danger.

[12] See *Kempf/Schilling*, Vermögensabschöpfung, marginal no. 53 ff.; nonetheless it has to be an asset *from* the crime, not *for* (doing) the crime, BGH wistra 2013, 347 ff.; BGHSt 58, 152–158; BGH NStZ 2012, 383; Money from a loan that was distributed in the run-up to the offence and that has only been paid back with money obtained from the criminal offence cannot be confiscated from a third party acting in good faith, see OLG Rostock NStZ-RR 2013, 275.

[13] Compare BGH wistra 2014, 219–224: also, a third person can be the object of an action if he obtained assets from the criminal offence.

To order a confiscation pursuant to Section 73 StGB, the crime from which the economic gains result has to be the subject of the criminal conviction. A confiscation order can not only be based on premeditated crimes but also on criminal negligence.[14]

Section 111b et seq. of the German Code of Criminal Procedure (StPO) provides interim measures at the pre-trial stage of criminal proceedings. These measures consist of freezing and confiscating the assets concerned and are meant to ensure the possibility to ultimately confiscate them.

The confiscation order in many ways resembles private law regulating restitution after unjust enrichment (Section 812 et seq. of the German Civil Code – BGB) and has a strong connection to criminal law (see "unlawful act" above). According to criminal jurisprudence and a majority of legal scholars, the confiscation order nonetheless is neither a punishment nor a sanction resembling punishment. The prevailing opinion sees it as a measure sui generis aiming at taking away unlawfully obtained assets. Unlike the conventional fine, asset confiscation does not result from personal guilt and its amount is not connected to the personal income of the perpetrator.

"Anything" (as defined by Section 73 StGB) the perpetrator has obtained from the unlawful act is calculated without deducing costs and expenses borne by the perpetrator for committing the crime;[15] thus, gross economic gains that might have been obtained at any stage of the commission of the crime are to be confiscated as a whole.[16] This so-called Bruttoprinzip has applied to confiscation proceedings since 1992, meaning that every asset acquired by the perpetrator by means of committing the crime is subject to confiscation, not only the true profits (Gewinn) gained by him.[17] A number of legal scholars thus qualify the confiscation of assets as a punishment as such.[18] The German Federal Court of Justice and the German

---

[14] BGH NStZ 2012, 265, marginal no. 9.

[15] An exception to this rule can be found in Section 73c StGB. The court may refrain from confiscating if the confiscation would constitute an undue hardship for the convicted person. This can occur especially when the obtained assets never become real gains of the property of the accused; see BGH NStZ-RR 2014, 44 f.; BGH wistra 2012, 264–265 = NJW 2012, 2051. Nevertheless, the defendant cannot refer to undue hardship if he has distributed the gained assets to third persons, BGH NStZ 2014, 32 with a note by Engländer, NStZ 2014, 33.

[16] BGHSt 47, 369, 370; BGH NStZ 2012, 265, 266, marginal no. 11; nonetheless, the court has to describe the source of the "anything" as clearly as possible. "Money from drug dealing," e.g., is not accurate enough to fulfill the requirements of Section 73 StGB, see BGH NStZ-RR 2012, 313 f.

[17] Concerning the offence of tax evasion, the assets can be seen in the light of expenses saved the legal taxpayer, OLG Hamm ZWH 2013, 329–330.

[18] See Eser, in: Schönke/Schröder (eds.), Strafgesetzbuch, Kommentar, Introduction to Section 73, marginal no. 19; Kühl, in: Lackner/Kühl (eds.), Strafgesetzbuch, Kommentar, Section 73, marginal no. 4b; Dannecker, NStZ 2006, 683 f.

Federal Constitutional Court (BVerfG) have not joined the views of said legal scholars and insist on the preventive character of the confiscation of assets. They say the measure is neither a punishment as such nor does it resemble a punishment; it thus does not fall into the scope of the principle of culpability.

B. Extended Confiscation *(Erweiterter Verfall)*

While a confiscation of assets according to Section 73 StGB is only possible if the court can prove that the source of the confiscated assets lies in the unlawful act, the far-reaching so-called "Extended Confiscation" *(Erweiterter Verfall)* regulated in Section 73d StGB also allows for the confiscation of assets probably resulting from an unlawful act:[19]

> **Section 73d StGB** (Extended confiscation): **If an unlawful act has been committed** pursuant to **a law which refers to this provision**, the court shall also order the confiscation of objects of the principal or secondary participant **if the circumstances justify the assumption** that these objects were acquired as a result of unlawful acts, or for the purpose of committing them. The 1st phrase shall also apply if the principal or secondary participant does not own or have a right to the object merely because he acquired the object as a result of an unlawful act or for the purpose of committing it. [...].

At first glance, this provision does not fit into the constitutional framework of the German Constitution (Basic Law or *Grundgesetz*) because it seems to infringe the presumption of innocence and to invalidate the right to property to a decisive extent (Art. 14 GG).[20] *Extended confiscation* works on the *probability* (one might also call it a presumption) that the assets at stake result from an unlawful act. It should be stressed, however, that Section 73d StGB must be interpreted according to the German Constitution in such a way that an extended confiscation can only be ordered when the sitting judge is completely convinced[21] – after having considered the evidence – that the assets subject to the confiscation order emanate from unlawful deeds or that they were used to commit those deeds; the judge does not have to identify the suspected crimes in detail. A confiscation order pursuant to Section 73d StGB thus requires the determination that the assets in question are somehow related to unlawful deeds.[22] An *extended confiscation* is therefore always connected to the conviction of a person or at least to the declaration of an unlawful (personal)

---

[19] BGH NStZ-RR 2013, 207: extended confiscation, Section 73d StGB, is subsidiary to the confiscation in Section 73 StGB; see also BGH, 15.10.2013, 3 StR 224/13, marginal no. 17.

[20] See critical remarks by: *Julius*, ZStW 109 (1997), 58, 94 ff. (property) and *Hoyer*, GA 1993, 406, 413 (presumption of innocence).

[21] BGH NStZ-RR 2013, 207: The judge may not leave the question open if Section 73, 73a, or 73d StGB is concerned; he has to decide accurately which Section is at stake in the relevant case. The judge also has to justify his decision in a comprehensible manner, BGH wistra 2014, 192–193.

[22] OLG Hamm NStZ-RR 2012, 272.

act that has been committed. It is still not the property itself that is the focus of the proceedings.

In 2004, the German Federal Constitutional Court declared Section 73d StGB to be in conformity with the German Basic Law. The court did not see a violation of the principle of culpability *(Schuldgrundsatz)*, the right to property (Art. 14 GG), the right to silence, and the freedom from self-incrimination, the rule of certainty of criminal provisions, and the prohibition of retroactivity (Art. 103 GG) as well as the right of equality (Art. 3 GG).[23]

C. Confiscation by Independent Orders
(Selbstständiger Verfall)

Section 76a StGB and Section 440 *et seq.* of the German Code of Criminal Procedure (StPO) allow the execution of an independent confiscation order (Section 73, 73d StGB) – without regard to a personal conviction *(selbstständiges Einziehungs- und Verfallsverfahren)*.

Section 76a § 1 StGB (Independent orders): If **for reasons of fact** no person can be prosecuted or convicted of the offence, confiscation or deprivation of the object or the monetary value or destruction must or may be independently ordered if the conditions under which the measure is prescribed or available otherwise are met.

Section 76a StGB requires for a crime to actually have been committed[24] (an "unlawful act" is sufficient for confiscation); it further requires that criminal proceedings, e.g., the prosecution and conviction of a suspect, are not possible for *factual* reasons. This can be the case when the identity of the perpetrator cannot be determined or when the offender is untraceable or on the run.[25] On the contrary, an autonomous confiscation order will not be ordered, if *legal* reasons prevent the prosecution of an offence: lapse of time *(Verjährung)*,[26] no demand for a penalty, continuous inability to stand trial *(Verhandlungsunfähigkeit)*,[27] *ne bis in idem*.

Whether the death of the accused is a factual or legal obstruction in the sense of Section 76a StGB is disputed among legal scholars. A majority of them takes the view that the offender's death is no *factual* reason enabling the continuation of the criminal proceedings according to Section 76a StGB.[28] The main argument is that

---

[23] German Federal Constitutional Court (BVerfG), decision of 14.1.2004, BVerfGE 110, 1 = NJW 2004, 2073.

[24] *Schmidt*, Gewinnabschöpfung im Straf- und Bußgeldverfahren, marginal no. 492.

[25] *Temming*, in: Graf (ed.), StPO Kommentar, Section 440, marginal no. 3 f.

[26] OLG Hamm NJW 1976, 2222, 2223.

[27] OLG Celle NStZ-RR 1996, 209.

[28] See *Fischer*, Strafgesetzbuch, Section 76a, marginal no. 6; *Schmidt*, in: Leipziger Kommentar zum StGB, Section 76a, marginal no. 9; *Rönnau,* Vermögensabschöpfung in der Praxis, marginal nos. 159, 160; *Kempf/Schilling*, Vermögensabschöpfung, marginal

only such obstacles are relevant that do not hinder material punishability but restrict the procedural sanctioning; when the offender is dead, there is no longer any material culpability. Additionally, requirements for confiscation, as regulated in Section 73e StGB (property of the concerned), have not been fulfilled. A confiscation order can only be addressed to the person who has directly obtained the economic gain in question. A confiscation order is consequently no longer possible when the said person no longer exists. The offender's successors have only obtained the economic gain indirectly by means of succession.[29]

An autonomous confiscation order can be made notwithstanding the abatement of the proceedings (*Verfahrenseinstellung*, Sections 153, 153a StPO). The procedure, however, still remains a criminal one and implies a different understanding of the burden of proof than a civil law procedure *(in dubio pro reo)*.

At the request of the prosecution (or of a private claimant, or of a taxation authority as provided by Section 401 AO), an independent confiscation procedure can be executed based on Section 440 *et seq.* StPO. The application and its extent are subject to the judgment of the prosecution.[30] While Sections 440 *et seq.* StPO are concerned with the *form* of procedure, the admissibility of such an independent confiscation depends on Section 76a StGB (German Criminal Code): Furthermore, the order has to be "expectable according to the result of the investigations" laid down in the wording of Section 440 § 1 StPO, meaning that there has to be strong probability for that outcome. Since the procedure laid down in Section 440 StPO is not aimed at a specific accused person, the question of crime and guilt does not get examined. This will be done, however, where it is a condition for the order of a legal consequence.[31] The court gives its decision in a ruling (*Beschluss*, Section 441 § 2 StPO) or judgment (*Urteil*, Section 441 § 3 StPO) about the application. In case the court allows the application, it can also order a less severe measure than the one submitted (Section 74b § 2, 3 StGB). The items to be collected have to be named exactly by the court in a way that makes it clear which items the court is referring to.[32]

---

no. 207; different opinion expressed by OLG Stuttgart NJW 2000, 2598 (concerning extended confiscation, Section 73d StGB).

[29] OLG Frankfurt NStZ-RR 2006, 39.

[30] *Temming*, in: Graf (ed.), StPO Kommentar, Section 440, marginal no. 6.

[31] *Schmidt*, in: Hannich (ed.), Karlsruher Kommentar zur Strafprozessordnung, Section 440, marginal no. 1.

[32] *Schmidt*, in: Hannich (ed.), Karlsruher Kommentar zur Strafprozessordnung, Section 440, marginal no. 13 f.

III. Compliance of a Civil Asset Recovery Model with the German Constitution

A. General Remarks

The advantage of a mere civil procedure is that its result does not have a damaging effect concerning the reputation of the person. It is not completely unthinkable to integrate a forfeiture procedure, which follows civil procedural principles, into the German system of criminal procedure. Although the German criminal procedure system is bound to the principles of public prosecution and an *ex officio* investigation, it is not entirely free of partiality. This is shown, for example, by the following special types of procedure:

- Proceedings to force criminal prosecution (*Klageerzwingungsverfahren*, Section 172 *et seq.* StPO), by which the victim can force the prosecution service to bring a case before the court, if he has legitimate reasons for it;

- Proceedings for private prosecution (*Privatklage*, Section 374 *et seq.* StPO), by which the (alleged) victim can demand the prosecution of the crime directed against him by private action;[33]

- Adhesive procedure (*Adhäsionsverfahren*, Section 403 *et seq.* StPO), by which the victim or his heirs can bring a civil claim that results from the commission of a crime before the criminal court that has established the accused's guilt.

It still remains questionable, however, whether *civil asset forfeiture* complies with the standards of German basic rights, the European Convention on Human Rights (ECHR), and the European Charter of Fundamental Rights (EUC).

B. The Principle of Culpability und Presumption of Innocence in the Jurisdiction of the German Federal Constitutional Court (BVerfG)

The principle of culpability and the observation of the presumption of innocence would be at the focus of the constitutional review of a civil asset forfeiture procedure.

1. Meaning and scope of the principle of culpability

The principle "no punishment without guilt" *(nulla poena sine culpa)* is laid down in the guarantee of dignity and the right to free development of a person's personality (Art. 1 § 1 and Art. 2 § 1 GG):

---

[33] See *Klose*, in: Klose (ed.), Asset Tracing and Recovery, p. 608.

Article 1 GG [Human dignity ...]

(1) Human dignity shall be inviolable. To respect and protect it shall be the duty of all state authority.

Article 2 GG [Personal freedoms]

(1) Every person shall have the right to free development of his personality insofar as he does not violate the rights of others or offend against the constitutional order or the moral law.

According to this principle, penalties or similar sanctions have to be proportional to the gravity of the act and the default of the offender. The elements of a committed crime and the legal consequences thereof have to be adjusted appropriately. Therefore, the principle *nulla poena sine culpa* prohibits the punishment of a *criminal act* without addressing the liability of the offender.[34] A *penalty* is the imposition of a legal disadvantage because of an unlawful and illicit act. It is – notwithstanding its function to discourage the commission of future crimes and to resocialize the offender – an appropriate reaction to an action prohibited by criminal law. The hardship *(Übel)* comprised in every punishment is designed to compensate the culpable violation of a legal norm; it is an expression of retributive justice.[35]

A measure is not to be considered *similar to a penalty* just because there is a connection to a loss of freedom or assets and therefore an actual effect of an ill. Concerning the evaluation of the penal character of a legal consequence, further judgmental criteria should be used, especially the legal ground for the order and the intention the legislator pursues with it.[36] The German Federal Constitutional Court emphasizes that the absorption of illegally obtained profits is not necessarily a retributive sanction. The legislator can instead decide freely if and how, *i.e.*, under what conditions, he wants to withdraw illegally obtained economic assets.[37]

The absorption of illegally obtained profits can be ordered by the legislator autonomously notwithstanding the admission of a penalty that has to be appropriate, considering the level of guilt of the offender; in cases in which a penalty as such cannot be administered, an order to absorb the said profits can be ordered independently in objective proceedings. The legislator could also provide for a punitive

---

[34] BVerfGE 110, 1; see also: BVerfGE 20, 323, 331 = NJW 1967, 195; BVerfGE 45, 187, 228 = NJW 1977, 1525; BVerfGE 50, 125, 133 = NJW 1979, 1037; BVerfGE 50, 205, 214 f. = NJW 1979, 1039; BVerfGE 81, 228, 237 = NJW 1990, 1900; BVerfGE 86, 288, 313 = NJW 1992, 2947; BVerfG NJW 2004, 739.

[35] Cf. BVerfGE 9, 167, 171 = NJW 1959, 619; BVerfGE 22, 49, 79 f. = NJW 1967, 1219; BVerfGE 95, 96, 140 = NJW 1997, 929; BVerfGE 96, 10, 25 = NVwZ 1997, 1109; BVerfGE 110, 1.

[36] BVerfGE 110, 1; cf. BVerfGE 9, 137, 144 ff. = NJW 1959, 931; BVerfGE 21, 378, 383 ff. = NJW 1967, 1651; BVerfGE 21, 391, 403 ff. = NJW 1967, 1654; BVerfGE 22, 125, 131 = NJW 1967, 1748; BVerfGE 23, 113, 126 = NJW 1968, 1083; BVerfGE 27, 36, 40 ff. = NJW 1969, 1623; BVerfGE 80, 109, 120 ff. = NJW 1989, 2679; see also BVerfG NJW 2004, 739 [C III 2]; cf. *Volk*, ZStW 83 (1971), 405.

[37] BVerfGE 110, 1.

sanction that would at the same time absorb any obtained profits. In summary, it is up to the legislator to decide whether a measure to absorb profits obtained through the commission of a crime has a punitive character or not.[38]

The German legislator never intended to introduce a new form of punishment with Section 73d StGB. He instead views the extended confiscation as a mere extension – as the section's title already suggests – of the simple confiscation regulated in Section 73 StGB. The legislator views the absorption of profits not as an administration of hardship but as the removal of benefits that could lead to the commission of future crimes, were they not removed.[39]

The German Federal Constitutional Court sees no conflict between "extended confiscation" (Section 73d StGB) and the principle of culpability, because the extended confiscation has no punitive character. An interpretation of Section 73d StGB according to its wording, its systematic position in the criminal code, and its *travaux préparatoires* results in the finding that the absorption of profits does not intend to reproach the concerned with the criminal offence and to retaliate the offence by administering a hardship. Section 73d StGB instead aims to regulate the allocation of patrimony and stabilize the legal order. The procedure laid down in Section 76a StGB, according to which the extended confiscation can only be ordered independently of a criminal conviction, can only be properly understood when the non-punitive nature of extended confiscation is considered. The (criminal) absorption of profits is designed to correct an unlawful allocation of property.[40] This function, e.g., to regulate the allocation of property, does not make extended confiscation an instrument similar to punishment. The removal of a wrongful allocation of property does indeed require the establishment of facts deriving from the past and is retrospective in this respect. The correction of wrongful allocation of property, however, is in itself not a repressive act.

In summary, the absorption of profits laid down in Section 73d StGB is not a penal reaction to an unlawful act committed by the person concerned. It instead aims to correct a wrongful allocation of property by strengthening the legal order. The extended confiscation does not pursue repressive and retaliating goals but rather preventive goals; it does not fall into the scope of the principle of culpability.

---

[38] BVerfGE 81, 228 [238] = NJW 1990, 1900.

[39] BGH NJW 2014, 1399, 1402; the court has to take into consideration that the confiscation or the forfeiture could cause hardship for the convicted person. Therefore it has to take into account if the consequences of the confiscation lead to an undue hardship, see BGH NStZ-RR 2014, 44 f.

[40] See BT-Drucksache 11/6623, pp. 7 and 8.

2. Meaning and scope of the presumption of innocence

The German Federal Constitutional Court considers the presumption of innocence to be a special characteristic of the rule of law (Art. 20 § 3 GG), giving it the
priority of a constitutional principle. The presumption that someone is not guilty
has to be rebutted in an orderly trial, before provisions based on the indictment are
made that would require the establishment of guilt of the accused. The presumption
protects the accused from effects that amount to the establishment of the accused's
guilt or to punishment if there was no orderly trial to properly establish the accused's guilt and sentence him accordingly.[41]

On the one hand, the presumption of innocence does not allow one "to impose
any measures on the accused in the concrete proceeding, without a lawful and procedural – not necessarily legally binding – proof of guilt, which are in their effect
similar to a penalty, and to treat him as guilty in the proceedings; on the other, it
demands a legally binding proof of guilt before the convicted can be reproached
with it in legal relations."[42] Furthermore, the presumption does not offer protection
from those legal consequences not having a punitive character but only protecting
public order.[43]

Because of the fact that a punishable act is not a necessary condition for a forfeiture of assets, such a measure can be seen as an instrument of skimming excess
profit without a penal character.[44] With regard to the independent recovery procedure laid down in Sections 440, 441 StPO in connection with Section 76a StGB, it
is acknowledged that it does not have a penal character either, since a previous
conviction is not necessary. However, the criminal evaluation is a decisive condition for the order of a forfeiture of assets.[45]

According to the requirements of the German Federal Constitutional Court, the
confiscation and forfeiture of profits does not have a penal character as long as it
only aims at a correction of illegally developed assets. In fact, it rather compensates
for what civil law is not able to accomplish, as it can at most prohibit the validity of
an illegal transaction.

The German Federal Constitutional Court has tightened the scope of the presumption of innocence and has formally limited it to the *prohibition of punishment
or treatment similar to punishment* of a person before his guilt is established by a

---

[41] Cf. BVerfGE 19, 342, 347f. = NJW 1966, 243; BVerfGE 35, 311, 320 = NJW 1974,
26; BVerfGE 74, 358, 369 ff. = NJW 1987, 2427; BVerfGE 82, 106, 114 f., 118 ff. = NJW
1990, 2741.

[42] BVerfG NJW 1987, 2427.

[43] BVerwG Judgment of 20.3.2012 – 5 C 1.11, DVBl 2012, 843, marginal no. 45 (Refusal of naturalisation in Germany).

[44] BVerfGE 110, 1.

[45] Brandenburg Constitutional Court, decision of 17.10.1996 = NJW 1997, 451.

court. Thus, every measure relating to a criminal offence that inhibits the suspect's rights does not fall within the scope of the presumption of innocence if it does not reach a certain level of similarity to punishment.

3. Comparison according to the conventional "civil asset forfeiture model"

According to the Federal Constitutional Court, the German model of confiscation – without the establishment of the accused's guilt – does not violate the German constitution. A civil asset forfeiture would thus very likely be declared compatible with the presumption of innocence and the principle of culpability *if* the result of the proceedings would not amount to a punishment as such or a treatment resembling a punishment.

The conventional *civil asset forfeiture model*, similar to the rules of criminal law, requires a *substantial connection between the property and the offence.*[46] The difference, however, is that the procedure is not directed at the person – but at the item as such. The claimant as a *third person* carries the burden of proof of arguing that, with a strong probability, the item lacks any ground to get confiscated. By choosing the civil procedure, this reversal of the burden of proof could be seen as a sort of prejudgment.

Considering that *civil asset forfeiture* can be carried out independently of criminal proceedings, the guilt of the third party is assumed to some extent in the civil proceedings. This can be shown by the fact that 18 USC § 983 provides for the possibility of the so-called *innocent owner*.[47] Thus, the proof of innocence has to be brought forward by the third party's defence. This reversal of the burden of proof in order to obtain a maximum skimming of excess profit can therefore be seen as an avoidance of the presumption of innocence. Civil legal actions are taken so the government does not have to prove the guilt of the other party. Access to property and assets, however, has an effect similar to a conviction. One may see this as a clear violation of the presumption of innocence, which demands an open decision-making process from beginning to end.[48]

Nevertheless, assuming the German Federal Constitutional Court maintains its rigid interpretation of the scope of the presumption of innocence regarding the classification of measures inhibiting the accused's rights, which it adopted in 2004, all arguments before the court would be in vain: Neither the civil action brought against the asset itself, nor the objections of the concerned, or even the final confis-

---

[46] Cf. 18 USC § 983(c)(3) Burden of Proof (I).

[47] Cf. 18 USC § 983(d)(1) Innocent Owner Defence (I).

[48] Cf. *Esser*, in: Erb *et al.* (eds.), Löwe-Rosenberg, Die Strafprozessordnung und das Gerichtsverfassungsgesetz: StPO, vol. 11: EMRK/IPBPR, Art. 6 EMRK, marginal no. 445 f.

cation of the asset are related to an establishment of guilt, or the administration of punishment, or a treatment amounting thereto.

C. *Nemo tenetur* Principle

As seen above, a civil asset forfeiture is aimed at the assets as such and the owner of the assets only has the possibility to defend them by actively joining the procedure. It should therefore be explored whether such a forced intervention may, in addition to the issue of presumption of innocence, be in conflict with the *nemo tenetur* principle.

Under German constitutional law, this principle derives from the basic personal rights of the accused (commonly accepted interpretation of the application of the most essential basic rights laid down in Art. 2 § 1 GG, read together with Art. 1 § 1 GG) and from the rule-of-law principle, Art. 20 § 3 GG).[49] Through its codification in Art. 14 § 3 *lit.* g ICCPR[50] and deriving from the interpretation as an element of a fair trial (Art. 6 § 1 ECHR), it further has the rank of ordinary federal law *(einfaches Bundesrecht)*.

The constitutional guidelines, however, do not allow an unlimited guarantee of the *nemo tenetur* principle. As early as 1963, the German Federal Constitutional Court, in connection with a constitutional complaint on Section 142 StGB (illegally leaving the scene of a traffic accident), stated that self-incrimination caused by an order to stay at the accident location is not prohibited by human dignity or the rule-of-law principle. In this matter, the court stated in the relevant judgment:

> "The citizen is not debased, when the legal order demands him to be responsible for the consequences of his human failure and to at least not complicate or even prevent the clarification of the causes of the accident by escaping."[51]

As regards the regulation of extended confiscation (Section 73d § 1 StGB), the German Federal Constitutional Court, in its ruling in 2004, did not see a violation of the accused's right against self-incrimination because

> "the concerned did not have to comment on the criminal offence for which he was indicted nor to any other criminal offences that he might have committed to prevent a confiscation-order."[52]

At this point, we can find a crucial difference in a civil asset forfeiture procedure. As seen above, a defence plea is the only way to prevent the state's access to

---

[49] BVerfGE 56, 37, 43.

[50] Art. 14 § 3 ICCPR: "In the determination of any criminal charge against him, everyone shall be entitled to the following minimum guarantees, in full equality: […] (g) Not to be compelled to testify against himself or to confess guilt."

[51] BVerfGE 16, 19, 194.

[52] BVerfGE 110, 1, 31 = NJW 2004, 2073, 2079.

a person's private assets within the framework of a civil asset forfeiture procedure. The owner of the assets is therefore factually forced to do so. In this respect, it is problematic how this defence plea should be evaluated in later or parallel criminal proceedings. As, according to the Code of Criminal Procedure and well-established case law, infringing or circumventing the *nemo tenetur* principle results in a prohibition to exploit the evidence,[53] the introduction of a *civil asset forfeiture* in Germany would at least have to lead to an adequate statutory rule in the Code of Criminal Procedure concerning the exclusion of statements made during a civil asset forfeiture from the evidence (which would, of course, have to pass the constitutional test itself).[54]

D. The Right to Property

Civil asset forfeiture further raises concerns in relation to the right to property laid down in Art. 14 § 1 GG.

1. Scope of protection

Art. 14 § 1 GG protects the right to "own" and to "use" a specific item.[55]

Article 14 GG [Property – Inheritance – Expropriation]

(1) Property and the right of inheritance shall be guaranteed. Their content and limits shall be defined by the laws.

(2) Property entails obligations. Its use shall also serve the public good.

(3) Expropriation shall only be permissible for the public good. It may only be ordered by or pursuant to a law that determines the nature and extent of compensation. Such compensation shall be determined by establishing an equitable balance between the public interest and the interests of those affected. In case of dispute concerning the amount of compensation, recourse may be had to the ordinary courts.

"Property" in the sense of Art. 14 GG traditionally does not cover *assets as such* but *valuable legal positions*. The protection of assets as such *(Vermögen)* is granted only by the general freedom of action (Art. 2 § 1 GG).[56] With regard to *civil asset forfeiture*, seizure of all assets is possible. In case the legal protection of Art. 14 § 1 GG does not apply here, at least Art. 2 § 1 GG will; the latter provision actually offers the freedom from unlawful and unconstitutional impositions of payment ob-

---

[53] BGHSt 38, 214; *Diemer*, in: Hannich (ed.), Karlsruher Kommentar zur Strafprozessordnung, Section 136, marginal no. 10.

[54] See: OVG Lüneburg decision of 4.4.2012 – 8 ME 49/12, DVBl 2012, 705 (duty to report and disclose information of sea pilots in case of accident).

[55] *Papier*, in: Herzog *et al.* (eds.), Maunz/Dürig, Grundgesetz – Kommentar, Art. 14 GG, marginal no. 8.

[56] *Papier*, in: Herzog *et al.* (eds.), Maunz/Dürig, Grundgesetz – Kommentar, Art. 14 GG, marginal no. 160 f.

ligations deriving from public law and from other undue orders, which would amount to special sacrifices imposed in connection with the assets.[57]

According to a more recent opinion brought forward by legal scholars, however, even Art. 14 § 1 GG applies, as it is meant to protect asset rights and money (though not the value of the money as such), which are indeed equated with the ownership.[58] Following this view, most measures against assets in the context of a *civil asset forfeiture* would fall within the scope of protection granted by Art. 14 GG.

It should be noted that the application of private law may lead to the conclusion that a person who seems to be the owner actually is not, due to violations of criminal law during the transfer of ownership, often but not necessarily committed by that person (see especially Sections 134 and 935 BGB). If and to the extent that the assets concerned are therefore not attributable to a specific person, Art. 14 GG does not, of course, apply; any related confiscation regulation therefore is not an infringement of this basic right. In practice, this concerns mostly the confiscation of gains obtained from illegal drug selling.[59]

2. Protection of the right to property in civil proceedings

In a civil asset forfeiture model, the seizure of concrete items, which are covered by the protection of property, is decided within the framework of civil proceedings. The purpose of such proceedings is usually to settle matters raised within private legal relations. The protection of basic rights does not extend to these proceedings as the state is not a party to these private relations. The protection of basic rights, however, cannot be circumvented by a state intervention disguised as civil proceedings. There are no adversarial proceedings but rather a hierarchy, which is a typical situation in which basic rights are to be applied. Therefore, the scope of protection of basic rights would cover civil asset forfeiture proceedings.

3. Expropriation or determination of the content and limits of the right to property?

Once Art. 14 § 1 GG applies, the question needs to be explored of whether measures in connection with a *civil asset forfeiture* account for an expropriation *(Enteignung)* or (only) for a determination of the content and limits of property *(Inhalts- und Schrankenbestimmung)* as stated in Art. 14 § 2 GG.

---

[57] *Papier*, in: Herzog *et al.* (eds.), Maunz/Dürig, Grundgesetz – Kommentar, Art. 14 GG, marginal no. 161.

[58] *Michael/Morlok*, Grundrechte, Art. 14, marginal no. 386; BVerfGE 97, 350, 370 f.

[59] BVerfGE 110, 1; see BVerfGE 83, 201, 209 = NJW 1991, 1807; BVerfGE 95, 267, 300 = NJW 1997, 1975.

If civil asset forfeiture was to be regarded as an expropriation, which therefore would have to be "concrete instead of abstract, individual instead of general" and would leave no part of the assets to the individual, the state would be obliged, as a consequence thereof, to pay monetary compensation as provided by Art. 14 § 2 GG. This would obviously totally contravene the purpose of a maximum skimming of excess profit as intended by a civil asset forfeiture model.

The regulations for a confiscation and forfeiture of civil assets laid down in current German criminal law (Sections 73, 73d StGB) differ from an expropriation in the sense of Art. 14 § 1 GG in two crucial points: *first*, there is no connection to any special purpose of use which is, however, elementary for any formal expropriation, and, *second*, criminal law has a personal connotation, *i.e.*, confiscation and forfeiture are decided upon in criminal proceedings directed against a natural person. In other terms, unlike customary expropriation, the confiscation and forfeiture of assets under Sections 73, 73d StGB are not meant to serve a specific public interest but only aim at the extrusion of the present owner from his position, and forfeiture is not related to items but to persons.[60]

When assessing the constitutionality of Section 73d StGB, the German Federal Constitutional Court emphasized that the legislator had thus defined general and abstract rights and obligations, which regulate the content and limits of property in civil and public law; according to the BVerfG, the character of a measure as a regulation of the content and limits of the right to property (in contrast to an expropriation) is preserved even under the circumstances of a legal regulation (such as Section 73d StGB) completely or partly removing concrete assets from the owner or when providing the legal grounds for doing so in the individual case.[61]

Legal scholars agree that, even though Art. 14 GG does not explicitly provide for the forfeiture of assets to be a subsequent effect of a criminal conviction, the German constitution "obviously" accepts it. The principle of proportionality and compliance with procedural guarantees have to be seriously taken into account, which is, however, done sufficiently by providing proceedings for criminal and administrative offences following the rule of law.[62]

Taking this jurisdiction of the German Federal Constitutional Court as a legal basis, conventional *civil asset forfeiture* can be qualified as a regulation of the content and limits of property *(Inhalts- und Schrankenbestimmung)* as stated in Art. 14 § 2 GG.

---

[60] *Papier*, in: Herzog *et al.* (eds.), Maunz/Dürig, Grundgesetz – Kommentar, Art. 14 GG, marginal no. 656.

[61] BVerfGE 110, 1; see also *Sachs*, JuS 2004, 1092.

[62] *Papier*, in: Herzog *et al.* (eds.), Maunz/Dürig, Grundgesetz – Kommentar, Art. 14 GG, marginal no. 657.

4. Standards of the German Federal Constitutional Court (BVerfG) concerning a justified interference with property and comparison to a civil asset forfeiture

According to the well-established jurisdiction of the German Federal Constitutional Court, the forfeiture of illegally obtained property *as a consequence of a criminal conviction* is part of a restriction of the right to property.[63] However, *civil asset forfeiture* is not related to a *criminal* conviction but decided upon in civil proceedings totally separate from any criminal proceedings. It needs to be explored whether this approach complies with the high standards the German Federal Constitutional Court has set concerning the proportionality of any measure affecting basic rights, especially the right to property.

With regard to the preventive order of an arrest *in rem* of the assets of an accused during preliminary criminal proceedings (Section 111d StPO), the German Federal Constitutional Court expressed strict requirements relating to this (merely) interim measure:

"Because the loss of property as a consequence of a criminal conviction is traditionally seen as an acceptable restriction of the rights of property (see BVerfGE 22, 387, 422; see also 2nd Chamber, Decision from 14 January 2004 – 2 BvR 564/95 = BVerfGE 110, 1 = NJW 2004, 2073 = WM 2004, 1001), corresponding interim measures consisting of freezing the related assets are not excluded by the constitution in general. However, concerning its reasonableness and the procedure of its order, particular requirements have to be fulfilled. In this context it is to note that the assets which were possibly acquired by means of criminal offences are secured at a time where there is mere suspicion and no decision on the criminal liability has been made. In these cases the basic right to property requires an assessment by weighing the state's interest in securing the assets against the legal position of the person affected by the measure related to his property. The more intensively the state intervenes (by making interim measures and thus securing the assets concerned) in the individual's right of property the stricter the requirements to justify this intervention. If the assets of a person get entirely or nearly entirely confiscated by interim measures, the principle of proportionality does not only call for a presumption that these assets were obtained illegally but instead for an especially thorough assessment and a detailed explanation of the relevant actual and legal considerations in the interim measure so that the person concerned can effectively appeal against it."

In this context, it is important to stress that the rules on forfeiture set out in the StGB and the StPO always call for a connection to an unlawful criminal act; this is explicitly stated, for example, in Section 73d StGB (extended forfeiture) and in Section 73 StGB (ordinary forfeiture).

Upon a thorough analysis of the German Federal Constitutional Court's decision of 2004 related to the extended confiscation, it is worth noting that the court apparently regards the confiscation of assets as a proportionate (and therefore constitutional) regulation of the content and limits of the right to property only if the owner

---

[63] BVerfGE 110, 1; 22, 387.

(*i.e.*, the person concerned by the confiscation order) has committed at least *one* specific "unlawful act." Only if said specific unlawful act is proven, does the German Federal Constitutional Court consider the confiscation of other assets, which were *supposedly* obtained illegally, to be proportionate and reasonable; this analysis is underlined by the following two extracts from the German Federal Constitutional Court's decision:

> [...] By provision of Section 73d § 1 1st phrase StGB the perpetrator's assets which he obtained illegally can be confiscated even if they do not derive from the criminal offence which is object of the current criminal sentence but if they derive from other unlawful acts for which criminal prosecution may not be possible any longer.

> The confiscation of illegally obtained assets by means of extended confiscation is not unreasonable. [...] On the grounds of the Federal Court of Justice's interpretation of Section 73d § 1 1st phrase StGB there will be no infringement on legally obtained assets given that this interpretation requires the courts to be convinced that the assets concerned were obtained illegally.

The legislator also had in mind that the extended confiscation, which can be ordered relatively easily, is to be seen in connection with a criminal verdict:

> The relaxed conditions of proof as provided by Section 73d § 1 1st phrase could compensate difficulties arising from circumstances where perpetrators are in possession of assets, the criminal origin of which is to be presumed yet it cannot be established from which unlawful acts they actually derive, if they even derive from unlawful acts which are object of the current criminal proceedings.[64]

> The regulation aims at making asset confiscation (literally: confiscation of property) possible where the court's possibilities to elucidate the affair prove unable to state the origin of an item but where the perpetrator's income and estate as well as his previous acts make seem the unlawfulness of obtaining said item so highly likely that an objective observer would consider anything else as beyond imagination.[65]

The German Federal Constitutional Court emphasizes that an assumption of unlawful origin of an item as stated in Section 73d StGB (extended confiscation) is only justified when the judge is convinced of it [= the illegal origin] upon exhausting all the available evidence. A court therefore cannot order an extended confiscation in a situation of only a very high likelihood (instead of absolute certainty) of the unlawful origin of assets as long as further investigations, which might prove (or disprove) this unlawful origin, can still be carried out. This jurisprudence (case law) ensures that the legal ownership of an item changes only if this is necessary in order to correct a situation that is actually the result of illegal actions.[66]

The German Federal Constitutional Court further underlined that legal rights of third parties who suffered prejudices need to be protected; it called upon the legislator to examine whether these rights are appropriately respected in cases of ex-

---

[64] BT-Drucksache 11/6623, p. 5.

[65] BT-Drucksache 11/6623, p. 5.

[66] BVerfGE 110, 1; *Herzog/Achsnich*, Geldwäschebekämpfung und Gewinnabschöpfung, Section 11, marginal no. 7.

tended confiscation after the legislative changes which widened its scope were implemented.

If these strict constitutional guidelines are transferred to a *civil asset forfeiture model,* it becomes clear that this new procedure would constitute a breach of Art. 14 GG or at least of Art. 2 § 1 GG. A conventional *civil asset forfeiture model* does not comply with the demands of the German constitutional framework, especially not with the principle of proportionality.

In the national understanding, the skimming of excess profits fulfils the purpose of disabling the offender in order to withhold the illegally obtained items so that he cannot commit further crimes by using them. The fight against organized crime is indeed a *legitimate aim* of limitations of the right to property by the state. *Civil asset forfeiture* can also lead to a maximum of determent and therefore contribute to combating organized forms of crime *(suitability)*.

Deep concerns arise, however, with regard to the *necessity* of the measure, as it does not seem to be the mildest means of countering organized crime. It is obviously not the purpose of civil asset forfeiture proceedings to *re-establish* a lawful situation because, in such a case, the need would arise to identify the existence of an illegal situation in the first place, a mere high likelihood being insufficient. The most important premise of a *civil asset forfeiture* procedure is the fight against organized crime in a fast and effective manner. But the effectiveness of a means also has to be considered in the context of its intensity. Concerning the fight against organized crime, the maximum skimming of excess profit does not play a central role but rather the eradication of its roots. Isolated civil proceedings aiming at the weakening of financial assets to be used for organized crime are not able to obliterate these roots. In this respect, national proceedings for the forfeiture of assets, combined with the possibility of objective, independent, and interim proceedings, seem to be more effective but less intensive.

With regard to *appropriateness,* consideration of the conflicting interests has to take place. Though *civil asset forfeiture* considers the interests of third parties by means of hardship clauses and provides for the possibility of a release of the confiscated item in certain cases,[67] this does not change the prevailing rules of evidence in civil proceedings.

In Germany, civil and criminal proceedings particularly differ with regard to the level of proof needed for a judge to reach the state of personal conviction. In civil proceedings, the *belief of the court* referred to in Section 286 ZPO allows certain facts to be regarded as being set, whereas criminal proceedings require extensive proof of the facts and the accused's guilt, because the presumption of innocence applies. Within the scope of free judicial evaluation of evidence laid down in Sec-

---

[67] Cf. 18 USC § 983(f).

tion 261 StPO, it depends on the judge being convinced of the facts which constitute the accused's guilt "beyond any doubt."[68]

Concerning the order of forfeiture, the German Federal Court of Justice has found a general statement of a district court, according to which *mobile phones are typically used by drug addicts to contact their dealers or to be accessible for them at all times,* as unduly because of its generality.[69]

The mere *preponderance of evidence* would therefore be insufficient to justify the final confiscation of property in Germany. The fact that civil asset forfeiture proceedings are not aimed at the person but at the item itself does not change this impression. Due to the reversal of proof, it is the owner who is forced to initiate the proceedings if he wishes to defend his property.

Even though the decision is not aimed at the person, this can be seen as a preconception of the claimant's guilt, drawn from the presumed unlawfulness of his property. A mere strong likelihood concerning the unlawfulness of the property to be confiscated is not sufficient to justify the final deprivation of such property.

The German Federal Constitutional Court made this clear when stating the unconstitutionality of the so-called confiscatory expropriation penalty (*Vermögensstrafe*; Section 43a StGB, repealed by a decision of the German Federal Constitutional Court),[70] which provided the possibility to impose a monetary sanction on the convicted person based not on the offender's income but on his assets. Mere suspicion of an unlawful origin of assets cannot justify the confiscation of (the whole of) the offender's assets:

> Confiscating the whole of one's assets as provided by Section 43a StGB is an unconstitutional removal of property because this does not aim at proven producta sceleris and therefore cannot be reconciled with traditional confiscation as being in conformity with Art. 14 GG. Instead the whole assets are removed for mere suspicion of unlawful origin. This non fact-based confiscatory expropriation order is a disproportionate interference, the impact of which equates an expropriation and which is in contradiction not only with Art. 14 § 3 GG but also with general requirements imposed by the rule of law; these requirements make it indeed necessary to establish that there is certainty that the assets were obtained by means of the criminal offence which was the legal ground for the conviction.

Even if an *interim measure* to secure *the final confiscation of assets* (Section 111d StPO) is only justified if it is sufficiently secured that it is directed at illegally obtained assets,[71] such a standard has to be applied all the more for a (final) *civil asset forfeiture.* According to this approach, civil proceedings only require a sufficient explanation of the connection between the item of forfeiture and the commis-

---

[68] BGHSt 10, 208, 209 = NJW 1957, 1039.

[69] BGH, decision of 20.2.2002 – 3 StR 14/02.

[70] BVerfGE 105, 135.

[71] Cf. BVerfGE 110, 1.

sion of a crime. A predominant probability is sufficient. But as far as *civil asset forfeiture* is concerned, it accounts for a severe interference with Art. 14 GG due to its finality. Therefore, the assessment of the proportionality of such measure is subject to extremely strict requirements.

While a conventional *civil asset forfeiture model* acknowledges the principle of proportionality to be applied in the proceedings,[72] the proof of disproportionality still falls to the third party.

In German law, however, compliance with the principle of proportionality is a requirement for every regulation concerning the content and limits of the right to property. It is neither the task nor within the competence of private persons to ensure that constitutional principles are applied correctly. These needs are addressed by the Federal Court of Justice's interpretation of Section 73d § 1 1st phrase StGB.

> On the one hand, asset confiscation is made easier as it is not necessary to establish the exact unlawful act where the assets concerned are derived from; the court which is to decide on the confiscation may rely on indirect proofs. On the other hand, the competent court is required to be convinced that there is actually an unlawful origin of the assets concerned, hereby avoiding unconstitutional interferences within the right of property of the person concerned. Only this restrictive interpretation ensures, according to the Federal Court of Justice, that the right of property is appropriately protected.

Conventional *civil asset forfeiture* therefore does not comply with the principle of proportionality as a specification of the rule of law, Art. 20 § 3 GG.

5. Rights of third parties / Right to be heard

In connection with the review of the constitutionality of a so-called extended forfeiture (Section 73d StGB), the German Federal Constitutional Court already stated its concerns as to the valuable legal positions of damaged third parties, as the claims for damages of third parties do not have priority over the skimming of excess profits in criminal law – unlike in the application of the (ordinary) forfeiture laid down in Section 73 § 1 2nd phrase StGB. In this respect, an interference with the property interests of third parties comes into consideration.[73]

By all means, *civil asset forfeiture* considers possible rights of third parties by granting a right of appeal and a compensation to everyone having a legitimate interest in the matter.[74]

To be more specific, there is clearly no breach of the right to be heard as provided by Art. 103 § 1 GG,[75] as all affected parties have an extensive possibility to ap-

---

[72] Cf. 18 USC § 983(g)(1–4)(I).

[73] BVerfGE 110, 1, 30 f. = NJW 2004, 2073, 2078 f.: no decision by the BVerfG; see: *Sachs*, JuS 2004, 1092.

[74] Cf. broad interpretation of the term "owner," 18 USC § 983(d)(6)(A).

peal. By filing an appeal against the forfeiture, the aggrieved parties have the possibility to express objections against the forfeiture. The court has to take into account these objections and to address them appropriately in its judgment.

6. Conclusion

All in all, a *civil asset forfeiture model* contains valuable approaches as to the factual effectiveness of the fight against organized crime, but the key legal problem is – according to German constitutional law – the application of the burden of proof in civil law. *Civil asset forfeiture* is incompatible with the right to property as the procedure does not comply with the requirements of the principle of proportionality – the core element of Art. 14 GG. Because of this, the conclusion concerning the compatibility of *civil asset forfeiture* with the national standard of basic rights can only be: *Crime must not pay off, but not at any price!*

IV. European Human Rights: Exploring the Possibilities for a European Civil Asset Recovery Model

A. European Convention on Human Rights (ECHR)

Every Member State of the European Union has signed and ratified the European Convention on Human Rights (ECHR). The European Union itself will soon join the state parties in signing the Convention.[76] It will then be bound by the case law of the European Court of Human Rights (ECtHR) in Strasbourg, like every other contracting party (cf. Art. 6 § 1 TEU). Even today, whilst not yet party to the Convention, the EU recognizes the rights enumerated in the ECHR as common principles of European Union Law (cf. Art. 6 § 3 TEU). Therefore, any proposal by the European Union for the implementation of a *civil asset forfeiture model* into the national law of the EU Member States has to be in conformity with the standards set by the ECHR and the jurisprudence of the ECtHR on any human right that might be affected. The following analyses attempt to give an overview of the presumption of innocence, Art. 6 § 2 ECHR, and the right to property, Art. 1 of Protocol No. 1 to the ECHR. Since the presumption of innocence is extensively dealt

---

[75] Cf. *Schmid-Aßmann*, in: Herzog *et al.* (eds.), Maunz/Dürig, Grundgesetz – Kommentar, Art. 103 GG, marginal no. 66 ff.

[76] The draft accession agreement of the European Union to the European Convention on Human Rights has been finalized in the meantime. At present, there are only some doctrinal controversies concerning accession to the Convention to be solved. The EU has already submitted a road map to smooth the way for the joining process, see: European Commission proposes negotiation directives for Union's accession to the European Convention on Human Rights (ECHR), MEMO/10/84, 17 March 2010.

with by *Johan Boucht* (see chapter 6, pp. 151–189), the right to property stands in the foreground of the following analysis.

1. Presumption of Innocence, Art. 6 § 2 ECHR

In the first place, the court reiterates that the presumption of innocence enshrined in paragraph 2 of Art. 6 ECHR is one of the elements of a fair trial that is required by Art. 6 § 1 ECHR:[77]

Everyone charged with a criminal offence shall be presumed innocent until proved guilty according to law.

The presumption of innocence is violated if a judicial decision or a statement by a public official concerning a person charged with a criminal offence reflects an opinion that he is guilty before he has been proven guilty according to law.[78] Once an accused has been properly proven guilty of a particular criminal offence, Art. 6 § 2 ECHR can have no application in relation to allegations about an accused's personality as part of the sentencing process, unless they are of such a nature and degree as to amount to the bringing of a new charge within the autonomous meaning of the Convention.[79]

However, according to the ECtHR, under certain conditions it is not incompatible with the requirements of a fair trial in criminal proceedings against an accused to shift the burden of proof to the defence.[80] Nor is the fairness of a trial vitiated on account of the prosecution's reliance on presumptions of fact or law that operate to the detriment of the accused, provided such presumptions are confined within reasonable limits, which take into account the importance of what is at stake and maintain the rights of the defence.[81]

a) Application to a criminal "charge"

While a proposed *non-conviction-based forfeiture* is itself a civil action, it can still interfere with the presumption of innocence (Art. 6 § 2 ECHR) of the owner of the forfeited asset. In the U.S. and the UK, (civil) asset forfeiture proceedings are directed against the asset itself, not against its owner. The proceedings being civil and not criminal, the burden of proof rests on the third party, the owner of the asset,

---

[77] ECtHR *Deweer v. Belgium*, 27 February 1980, no. 6903/75, Series A no. 35, § 56; *Minelli v. Switzerland*, 25 March 1983, no. 8660/79, Series A no. 62, § 27.

[78] ECtHR *Natsvlishvili and Togonidze v. Georgia*, 29 April 2014, no. 9043/05, § 103.

[79] ECtHR *Phillips v. The United Kingdom*, 5 July 2001, no. 41087/98, § 35.

[80] See, as regards inferences drawn from an accused's silence: ECtHR *Condron v. The United Kingdom,* 2 May 2000, no. 35718/97, § 56, ECHR 2000-V.

[81] See ECtHR *Salabiaku v. France*, 7 October 1988, no. 10519/83, Series A, no. 141-A, § 28; *Pham Hoang v. France*, 25 September 1992, no. 13191/87, Series A no. 243, § 33.

to intervene in the proceedings and to prove that the asset was not involved in the crime.

Art. 6 § 2 ECHR protects every person accused of a crime, that is, every person accused in a criminal trial. The ECtHR takes the view that the presumption of innocence, guaranteed by Art. 6 § 2 ECHR, is violated if a judicial decision or a statement by a public official concerning a person charged with a criminal offence reflects an opinion that he is guilty before he has been proven guilty according to law.[82] However, whilst it is clear that Art. 6 § 2 ECHR governs criminal proceedings in their entirety, and not solely the examination of the merits of the charge, the right to be presumed innocent arises only in connection with the *particular offence* a person has been "charged" with.[83]

The preliminary issue to be decided is whether recovery proceedings against a person or specific items involve the determination of a criminal charge in such a way as to bring into play the presumption of innocence (Art. 6 § 2 ECHR) and the special rights for *charged* persons (Art. 6 § 3 ECHR).

The ECtHR takes three guiding criteria into account when deciding whether a criminal charge has been determined: the *classification of the matter in domestic law*, the *nature of the offence,* and the degree of severity of the penalty that the person concerned risks incurring.[84]

If, according to *domestic law,* recovery proceedings are regarded as *civil* instead of criminal, the proceedings remain "civil;" they are actually separate and distinct in timing, procedure, and content from the criminal proceedings, even though they may follow an acquittal for specific criminal offences.[85]

As to the second criterion, the *nature of the charge*, the ECtHR takes into account whether the *purpose* of the proceedings is punitive or deterring.

In *Phillips* and *Van Offeren,* the ECtHR took the view that the confiscation order impugned in those cases *followed* from the applicant's prosecution, trial, and ultimate conviction on charges of importing an illegal drug. It did not give rise to the determination of a separate or *new charge* against the applicant. The confiscation order was found by the court to be analogous to a sentencing procedure, to the extent bordering on the *criminal* sphere of Art. 6 ECHR.[86]

---

[82] ECtHR *Deweer v. Belgium* (n. 77) § 56; *Minelli v. Switzerland,* (n. 77) § 37; *Geerings v. The Netherlands*, 1 March 2007, no. 30810/03, § 41.

[83] ECtHR *Geerings v. The Netherlands* (n. 82), § 43.

[84] ECtHR *Ezeh and Connors v. The United Kingdom* [GC], 9 October 2003, nos. 39665/98 and 40086/98, § 82, ECHR 2003-X; *Engel and Others v. The Netherlands*, 8 June 1976, no. 5100/71, Series A no. 22, pp. 34–35, §§ 82–83.

[85] ECtHR *Phillips v. The United Kingdom* (n. 79), §§ 32, 39, ECHR 2001-VII; *Walsh v. The United Kingdom*, decision of 21 November 2006, no. 43384/05.

[86] ECtHR *Phillips v. The United Kingdom* (n. 79), §§ 34, 39; *Van Offeren v. The Netherlands*, decision of 5 July 2005, no. 19581/04.

In *Walsh v. UK,* the ECtHR regarded the recovery of assets that did not lawfully belong to the applicant as *non-punitive* because, before the national court, there was no finding of guilt of specific offences and the court, in making the order, had been very careful not to take into account conduct in respect of which the applicant had been acquitted of any criminal offence.[87] The special recovery order in *Walsh* was not regarded as being punitive in nature; while it involved a hefty sum, the ECtHR stressed that the amount of money involved is not itself determinative of the criminal nature of the proceedings.[88] For this reason, the proceedings *fell outside the criminal sphere* of Art. 6 § 1 ECHR.

In *Butler v. UK,* the court regarded a forfeiture order as a *preventive measure,* which cannot be compared to a criminal sanction, since it was designed to take out of circulation money that was presumed to be tied up with the international trade in illicit drugs.[89]

In *Saccoccia,* the ECtHR also held that the criminal sphere of Art. 6 § 1 ECHR did not apply to the proceedings relating to the enforcement of a forfeiture order of the Rhode Island District Court (here: *exequatur* proceedings). But the court also reached the conclusion that the final forfeiture order involved a *determination of the applicant's civil rights and obligations.*[90]

In *Geerings,* the ECtHR took a different approach:

"If it is not found beyond a reasonable doubt that the person affected has actually committed the crime, and *if it cannot be established as fact that any advantage, illegal or otherwise, was actually obtained,* such a measure can only be based on a presumption of guilt. This can hardly be considered compatible with Art. 6 § 2."[91]

The special aspect of the case, however, was that the impugned order related to the very crimes of which the applicant had in fact been acquitted.

In *Krasimir Aleksandrov Nedyalkov and Others,*[92] the ECtHR recapitulated its jurisdiction in *Dogmoch*[93] and *Dassa Foundation and Others:*[94] the provisional seizure of assets with a view to their forfeiture does not engage Art. 6 ECHR under

---

[87] ECtHR *Walsh v. UK* (n. 85).

[88] ECtHR *Walsh v. UK* (n. 85); with reference to ECtHR *Porter v. The United Kingdom,* decision of 8 July 2003, 15814/02, where the applicant was liable to pay some GBP 33 million in respect of financial losses to the local authority during her mandate as leader of a city council.

[89] ECtHR *Butler v. The United Kingdom* (dec.), 27 June 2002, no. 41661/98, ECHR 2002-VI.

[90] ECtHR *Saccoccia v. Austria,* 18 December 2008, no. 69917/01.

[91] See also ECtHR *Salabiaku v. France* (n. 81), § 28.

[92] ECtHR *Krasimir Aleksandrov Nedyalkov and Others v. Bulgaria* (dec.), 10 December 2013, no. 663/11.

[93] ECtHR *Dogmoch v. Germany* (dec.), no. 26315/03, ECHR 2006-XIII.

[94] ECtHR *Dassa Foundation and Others v. Liechtenstein* (dec.), 10 July 2007, no. 696/05.

its criminal or civil spheres.[95] Moreover, provisional coercive measures – such as pre-trial detention – imposed in connection with criminal proceedings are not in themselves incompatible with the presumption of innocence enshrined in Art. 6 § 2 ECHR.

b) Conclusion

The court has, in a number of cases, been prepared to treat confiscation proceedings following from a conviction *as part of the sentencing process* and therefore as *beyond* the scope of Art. 6 § 2 ECHR.[96] Once an accused has been properly proven guilty of an offence, Art. 6 § 2 ECHR can have no application in relation to allegations made about the accused's character and conduct as part of the sentencing process, unless such accusations are of such a nature and degree as to amount to the bringing of a *new* "charge".[97] The features that these cases had in common are: that the applicant was convicted of drug offences; that the applicant continued to be suspected of additional drug offences; that the applicant demonstrably held assets whose provenance could not be established; that these assets were reasonably presumed to have been obtained through illegal activity; and that the applicant had failed to provide a satisfactory alternative explanation. Nevertheless, if the (later) recovery of assets has a kind of link to the original charge and can therefore be seen as "part of the sentencing process," or as a preventive measure (separate from the criminal proceedings), or if it has been interpreted as a *new charge* against the person concerned, seems to depend on the specific circumstances of the case and the special features of national law. The ECtHR is obviously avoiding any clear general approach on this matter (for more details on this point, refer to the chapter of *Johan Boucht* on the presumption of innocence).

A *civil asset forfeiture* model of the classic style (without any former conviction of a person needed) seems to fall outside the criminal sphere of Art. 6 § 1 and § 2 ECHR, since the ECtHR clearly focusses on the *purpose* of the proceedings, which, under a civil asset forfeiture model, do not have a deterrent or punitive character.

2. Protection of Property (Art. 1 of Protocol No. 1)

a) Scope of protection

Art. 1 of Protocol No. 1 enshrines the right to the peaceful enjoyment of one's possessions; this right to property is guaranteed to every natural person and legal entity:

---

[95] ECtHR *Krasimir Aleksandrov Nedyalkov and Others v. Bulgaria* (n. 92), §§ 104, 107.

[96] ECtHR *Phillips v. UK* (n. 79), § 34; *Van Offeren v. The Netherlands* (n. 86).

[97] ECtHR *Phillips v. UK* (n. 79), § 35.

Article 1 ECHR: Protection of property

(1) Every natural or legal person is entitled to the peaceful enjoyment of his possessions. No one shall be deprived of his possessions except in the public interest and subject to the conditions provided for by law and by the general principles of international law.

(2) The preceding provisions shall not, however, in any way impair the right of a State to enforce such laws as it deems necessary to control the use of property in accordance with the general interest or to secure the payment of taxes or other contributions or penalties.

The use of one's property can be regulated by the state if the regulation serves the common interest (Art. 1 § 2 of Protocol No. 1). Furthermore, the state can expropriate, under certain circumstances laid down in Art. 1 § 1 phrase 2 of Protocol No. 1. However, the fundamental provision is to be seen in Art. 1 § 1 2nd phrase of Protocol No. 1: The state must respect the right to peaceful enjoyment of property. The ECtHR oftentimes only considers this fundamental provision when it sees itself unable to determine whether the measure in question is a regulation of the use of property or an expropriation.

The scope of Art. 1 of Protocol No. 1 is rather wide: It covers not only the possession of physical assets but also the possession of claims and other acquired rights; intellectual property is also covered by Art. 1 of Protocol No. 1.[98] The concept of "possessions" in the first paragraph of Art. 1 of Protocol No. 1 thus has an autonomous meaning not limited to the ownership of material goods and is independent from the formal classification in domestic law.[99] Even if a person is not the owner of assets concerned by a forfeiture order, the ECtHR may regard these assets as "possessions."[100] Art. 1 of Protocol No. 1 certainly does not guarantee the right to obtain profit.[101]

b) Interference: Expropriation or regulation of the use of property?

Encroachments into the right to property are possible through *expropriation* on the one hand and *regulation of the use of property* on the other hand. Moreover, each interference must strike a "fair balance" between the demands of the general interest of the community and the requirements of the protection of the individual's fundamental rights.[102]

In case of an expropriation Art. 1 of Protocol No. 1 does not require the state expressly to compensate the expropriated person; however, the ECtHR has ruled that

---

[98] See ECtHR (Grand Chamber), *Anheuser Busch Inc. v. Portugal*, 11 January 2007, no. 73079/01, ECHR 2007-I.

[99] ECtHR *Gáll v. Hungary*, 25 June 2013, no. 49570/11, § 32.

[100] ECtHR *Saccoccia v. Austria* (n. 90), § 85; ECtHR *Gáll v. Hungary* (n. 99), § 32.

[101] ECtHR *R & L, S.R.O. and others v. The Czech Republic*, 3 July 2014, nos. 37926/05, 25784/09, 36002/09, 44410/09 and 65546/09, § 103.

[102] ECtHR *Gáll v. Hungary* (n. 99), § 41.

compensation is required by the principle of proportionality.[103] Any expropriation without compensation will therefore be disproportional and a breach of the Convention.[104] When considering the proposals for Civil Asset Forfeiture it has to be acknowledged that Civil Asset Forfeiture would be totally ineffective to combat organized crime if there was any form of compensation. Therefore, any Civil Asset Forfeiture is only conceivable as a regulation of the use of property (Art. 1 § 2 of Protocol No. 1).

Although it involves a deprivation of possessions, confiscation of property does not necessarily fall within the scope of the second phrase of the first paragraph of Art. 1 of Protocol No. 1.[105] Accordingly, the ECtHR has viewed the seizure of property without compensation in the wake of a criminal conviction as a *regulation of the use of property* as defined by Art. 1 § 2 of Protocol No. 1.[106]

In *Saccoccia v. Austria,* the ECtHR considered the execution of a forfeiture order, though depriving the applicant permanently of the assets at issue, under the so-called *third rule*, relating to the state's right "to enforce such laws as it deems necessary to control the use of property in accordance with the general interest."[107]

c) Justification of a regulation of the use of property

Each regulation of the use of property (Art. 1 § 2 of Protocol No. 1), including the execution of a confiscation or forfeiture order, must have a *clear sufficient basis in national law*. The legal basis must have a certain quality, namely it must be compatible with the rule of law and must provide guarantees against arbitrariness.[108] Although the ECtHR's power to review compliance with domestic law is limited, the court is willing to control it if the national courts dealt in detail with the applicant's arguments, gave extensive reasons for their findings, and did not go beyond the reasonable limits of interpretation.[109] "Law" must be understood to in-

---

[103] See *Esser*, in: Erb *et al.* (eds.), Löwe-Rosenberg, Die Strafprozessordnung und das Gerichtsverfassungsgesetz: StPO, vol. 11: EMRK/IPBPR, Art. 1 ZP-EMRK, marginal no. 31; *Jacobs/White/Ovey*, The European Convention on Human Rights, pp. 493 f.

[104] See ECtHR *Holy Monasteries v. Greece*, 9 December 1994, nos. 13092/87 and 13984/88, Series A no. 301-A, § 71; ECtHR (Grand Chamber), *Former King of Greece v. Greece*, 23 November 2000, no. 25701/94, ECHR 2000-XII. Cf. *Leach*, Taking a case to the European Court of Human Rights, marginal no. 6.646.

[105] See ECtHR *Handyside v. The United Kingdom*, 7 December 1976, no. 5493/72, Series A no. 24, § 63; *AGOSI v. The United Kingdom*, 24 October 1986, no. 9118/80, Series A no. 108, § 51; *Raimondo v. Italy*, 24 February 1994, no. 12954/87, § 29.

[106] See ECtHR *Butler v. The United Kingdom* (n. 88); *AGOSI v. UK* (n. 104), § 51.

[107] ECtHR *Saccoccia v. Austria* (n. 90), § 86.

[108] ECtHR *Gáll v. Hungary* (n. 99), § 46.

[109] ECtHR *Saccoccia v. Austria* (n. 90), § 87; *Duboc v. Austria*, Decision of 5 June 2012, no. 8154/04, § 52.

clude both statutory law and judge-made law. In sum, the "law" is the provision in force as the competent courts have interpreted it.[110]

With particular reference to the control of the use of property and therefore interference with proprietary rights, the state has a *wide margin of discretion* as to what is *in accordance with the general interest* (see Art. 1 § 2 of Protocol No. 1). Property, including privately owned property, also has a social function which, given the appropriate circumstances, must be put into the equation in order to determine whether the "fair balance" has been struck between the demands of the general interest of the community and the individual's fundamental rights. Consideration must be given, in particular, to whether the applicant, on acquiring the property, knew or should have reasonably known about the restrictions on the property or about possible future restrictions.[111]

Striking for a fair balance between the interests at stake, it first has to be checked whether the execution of a forfeiture order *pursues a legitimate aim*. Enhancing international co-operation to ensure that assets derived from drug dealing are actually forfeited and promoting measures, which are designed to block movements of suspect capital, are seen by the ECtHR as an effective and necessary weapon in the fight against drug dealers. Thus, the execution of a confiscation order to combat drug trafficking or other forms of organized crime serves a *general interest* acknowledged by the court.[112]

The ECtHR, however, demands a fair balance to be struck between the demands of the general interest and a person's interest in the protection of his right to peaceful enjoyment of his possessions. In making this assessment, with regard to the wide margin of appreciation the contracting states enjoy in such matters,[113] the ECtHR in *Raimondo v. Italy* reduced that "fair balance" to a general remark on the fight against organized crime by the recovery of assets:

> The Court is fully aware of the difficulties encountered by the Italian State in the fight against the Mafia. As a result of its unlawful activities, in particular drug-trafficking, and its international connections, this "organisation" has an enormous turnover that is subsequently invested, inter alia, in the real property sector. Confiscation, which is designed to block these movements of suspect capital, is an effective and necessary weapon in the combat against this cancer. It therefore appears proportionate to the aim pursued, all the more so because it in fact entails no additional restriction in relation to seizure.[114]

---

[110] ECtHR *R & L, S.R.O. and others v. The Czech Republic* (n. 101), § 114.

[111] ECtHR *Potomska and Potomski v. Poland*, 29 March 2011, no. 33949/05, § 67.

[112] ECtHR *Raimondo v. Italy* (n. 105), § 30; *Saccoccia v. Austria* (n. 89), § 88.

[113] See above, ECtHR *AGOSI v. The United Kingdom* (n. 104), § 52; *Saccoccia v. Austria* (n. 90), § 88. Cf. *Jacobs/White/Ovey*, The European Convention on Human Rights, pp. 502 f.; ECtHR *Gáll v. Hungary* (n. 99), §§ 32, 59.

[114] ECtHR *Raimondo v. Italy* (n. 105), § 30.

Although not explicitly mentioned in Art. 1 of Protocol No. 1, the ECtHR stresses the *importance of procedural requirements*.[115] The proceedings at issue must afford the individual a reasonable opportunity of putting his or her case to the relevant authorities for the purpose of effectively challenging the measures interfering with the rights guaranteed by this provision.[116] In particular, there must be a *reasonable relationship* of proportionality between the means employed and the aim sought to be realised.[117]

In *Butler v. UK*, the court offered more insight on how a "reasonable relationship of proportionality between the means employed by the authorities in the instant case to secure the general interest of the community and the protection of the applicant's fundamental right to the peaceful enjoyment of his possessions" can be achieved:

- the powers of the Customs' authorities were confined by the terms of the 1994 Act
- the authorities did not have unfettered discretion to seize and forfeit the applicant's money
- the exercise of their powers was subject to judicial supervision
- the applicant was able to have a re-hearing of the case against him
- the authorities relied on forensic and circumstantial evidence
- the applicant, assisted by counsel, was able to dispute the reliability of this evidence at oral hearings
- the applicant was not faced with irrefutable presumptions of fact or law
- it was open to the applicant to adduce documentary and oral evidence in order to satisfy the domestic courts of the legitimacy of his assets
- the domestic courts weighed the evidence before them, assessed it carefully, and based the forfeiture order on that evidence
- the domestic courts refrained from any automatic reliance on presumptions [...] and did not apply them in a manner incompatible with the requirements of a fair hearing.

Nevertheless, the ECtHR stressed the fact that, in assessing whether a fair balance has been struck between these interests, due weight has to be given to *the*

---

[115] ECtHR *Gáll v. Hungary* (n. 99), § 63; ECtHR *Microintelect OOD v. Bulgaria*, 4 March 2014, no. 34129/03, § 44.

[116] ECtHR *Jokela v. Finland,* 21 May 2002, no. 28856/95, § 45; *AGOSI v. The United Kingdom* (n. 104), § 55. Cf. *Leach*, Taking a case to the European Court of Human Rights, marginal no. 6.653 f.; in *Lavrechov v. The Czech Republic*, 20 June 2013, no. 57404/08, § 55, the Court states that the forfeiture of a bail is then lawful if the accused was given the possibility to appear before the court to plead against the forfeiture.

[117] ECtHR *Microintelect OOD v. Bulgaria* (n. 115), § 41.

wide margin of appreciation that the respondent state enjoys in formulating and implementing policy measures in this area.

Against this background, one has to bear in mind that the cases decided by the ECtHR had always been preceded by *criminal proceedings* against the owner of the asset (*Saccoccia*: money laundering; *Raimondo*: preventive seizure of assets; suspicion of belonging to a mafia-type organisation; acquittal).

A question not yet decided by the ECtHR is whether a conventional *civil asset forfeiture* could be considered proportional, *i.e.*, without parallel or foregoing criminal proceedings or even a conviction of the owner of the asset.

In *Paulet*,[118] the applicant successfully applied for three jobs using a false French passport. He had used the false passport to support his assurance that he was authorized to work in the UK. All of his employers subsequently stated that they would not have employed him without this assertion. The applicant earned a total gross salary of about 73,000 pounds sterling from his employment. On 4 June 2007, the applicant pleaded guilty in the Crown Court at Luton to three counts of dishonestly obtaining a pecuniary advantage by deception. In addition to the custodial sentence and the recommendation for deportation, the prosecution sought a *confiscation order* under section 6 of the Proceeds of Crime Act 2002 in respect of the applicant's earnings. After deducting tax and national insurance payments, it was agreed that the applicant still had assets of GBP 21,949.60. On this basis, the trial judge imposed a confiscation order to the sum of GBP 21,949.60 upon the applicant, with a consecutive sentence of twelve months' imprisonment to be served in default of payment.

The applicant complained that the confiscation order had been a *disproportionate interference* with his right to peaceful enjoyment of his possessions within the meaning of Art. 1 of Protocol No. 1. In particular, he tried to argue that his case could be distinguished from cases that concerned serious criminal offences, such as drug trafficking and organised crime, and in which there was clearly a compelling need to deter such criminal behaviour. He argued that the "public interest" that persons who had applied to enter the United Kingdom from overseas would feel justifiably underprivileged if those who had "skipped the queue could retain the savings earned through illegal employment".[119] The applicant further assured that no harm had been caused either to his employers or the state: the sentencing judge even indicated that the state had gained more in taxes from the applicant's employment than he himself had saved. Thus, the applicant argued that there was a discrepancy between the offence that he was convicted of (deceiving his employers) and the alleged justification for the confiscation order.[120]

---

[118] ECtHR *Paulet v. The United Kingdom*, 13 May 2014, no. 6219/08.

[119] ECtHR *Paulet v. The United Kingdom* (n. 118), § 55.

[120] ECtHR *Paulet v. The United Kingdom* (n. 118), §§ 57, 58.

The ECtHR concluded in *Paulet* that, at the time the applicant brought the domestic proceedings, the scope of the review carried out by the domestic courts was too narrow to satisfy the requirement of seeking the "fair balance" inherent in the second paragraph of Art. 1 of Protocol No. 1.[121] An interference with Art. 1 of Protocol No. 1 is disproportionate if the property owner concerned has to bear "an individual and excessive burden," such that "the fair balance which should be struck between the protection of the right of property and the requirements of the general interest" is upset.[122] The confiscation order in the present case was "oppressive" and thus an "abuse of process."[123] Therefore, the ECtHR held that there had been a violation of Art. 1 of Protocol No. 1 to the Convention.

d) Conclusion

In summary, for a civil asset forfeiture to be introduced would have to comply with four basic requirements regarding the protection of property laid down in Art. 1 of the First Additional Protocol to the ECHR: The forfeiture would have to be based on a formal statute passed by the legislator, it would have to be reasonably foreseeable, and – most importantly – it would have to remain within the limits of the principle of proportionality. Lastly, a civil asset forfeiture would need to comply with basic procedural requirements regarding the rights of the affected person.

B. Charter of Fundamental Rights of the European Union

1. Scope of protection and binding force of the Charter

With the entry into force of the Treaty of Lisbon on 1 December 2009, the European Union has recognized the Charter of Fundamental Rights of the European Union (EUC) as binding law equivalent to the treaties TEU and TFEU (Art. 6 § 2 TEU). A specific right in the EUC, which is also guaranteed by the ECHR, is to be interpreted in a way that its standard of protection is at least as high as the standard of the corresponding right in the ECHR (Art. 52 § 3 1st phrase EUC). Additionally, both are to be interpreted in the light of the jurisprudence of the ECtHR. Both the presumption of innocence and the right to property are protected by the Charter and by the ECHR. Consequently, the standard of protection of these rights finds its minimum in the standard of the ECHR.

---

[121] ECtHR *Paulet v. The United Kingdom* (n. 118), § 68.
[122] ECtHR *Paulet v. The United Kingdom* (n. 118), § 65.
[123] ECtHR *Paulet v. The United Kingdom* (n. 118), § 67.

The Charter shall have the same legal value as the treaties, as it is stipulated in Art. 6 § 1 TEU. It is thus part of primary European Union law. As such, it is binding for all Member States. Its effect on the Member States is detailed in Art. 51 § 1 1st phrase EUC: The Charter is only ever applicable when Member States are "implementing Union law." This limitation of the scope of European Union fundamental rights was already known in the jurisprudence of the European Court of Justice (ECJ) prior to the entry into force of the Charter on 1 December 2009. By "implementing Union law," the Member States are bound by the Charter on all levels: Both legislative action, e.g., the transformation of an EU directive, and administrative action are bound by the Charter. The scope of the binding effect of the Charter is rather difficult to determine, especially when Member States transpose EU directives: Member States sometimes have a margin of appreciation when transposing a directive; however, they are bound by the Charter when making use of that margin because the margin itself is determined by European Union law.[124]

In *Fransson,* the ECJ enlarged the scope of application of the Charter and therefore its own competences at the same time:

"It is not possible to construct a case, in which the Union law is concerned without the concurrent implementation of the Charter. Thus the implementation of the Union law involves automatically the implementation of the Charter."[125]

In *Melloni,* the ECJ even consolidated its jurisdiction and raised the grade of the Charter to be ranked higher than the national legislation of constitutional character.[126] As a result, the Charter may overrule the national constitutional order of the Member States in cases in which the standard of protection is lower than the one guaranteed by the Charter.

Consequently, should the European Union issue a directive prescribing the implementation of a civil asset forfeiture model, Member States would be bound by the Charter when transposing it into national law, even if there were a margin of appreciation left for them.

2. Presumption of innocence, Art. 48 § 1 EUC

The Charter protects the presumption of innocence (Art. 48 § 1 EUC), as does the ECHR:

Presumption of innocence [...]

(1) Everyone who has been charged shall be presumed innocent until proved guilty according to law.

---

[124] Cf. ECJ, C-400/10 *(McB.)*, EuGRZ 2010, 741, para. 52; C-411/10 and C-493/10 *(N.S. v. Secretary of State for the Home Department)*, NVwZ 2012, 417, paras. 65 ff.; C-571/10 *(Servet Kamberaj v. IPES)*, NVwZ 2012, 950, para. 80.

[125] ECJ, C-617/10, NJW 2013, 1415, para. 19.

[126] ECJ, C-399/11, EuZW 2013, 305, 309.

In 2008, well before the Charter entered into force, the Court of First Instance of the European Union (simply called "General Court" since the entry into force of the Treaty of Lisbon) ruled: "As regards the principle of the presumption of innocence, the Court recalls that that principle, which constitutes a fundamental right set forth in Art. 6 § 2 ECHR and Art. 48 § 1 EUC, confers rights on individuals which are enforced by the Community Courts."[127]

Even before the Charter entered into force with the Treaty of Lisbon on 1 December 2009, the ECJ had acknowledged the existence of the presumption of innocence in antitrust lawsuits:

> "It must also be accepted that, given the nature of the infringements in question and the nature and degree of severity of the ensuing penalties, the principle of the presumption of innocence applies to the procedures relating to infringements of the competition rules applicable to undertakings that may result in the imposition of fines or periodic penalty payments."[128]

The presumption of innocence has become relevant mostly in antitrust suits before the European courts. Quite often, the courts had to decide whether public statements made by Commission officials violated the presumption of innocence of the accused in the antitrust proceedings:

> "In addition, as the applicant admits, the scope of the Commission's power to adopt and publish decisions [...] and the scope of the protection of professional secrecy must be interpreted in the light of general principles and fundamental rights, which are an integral part of the Community legal order, and, in particular, of the principle of presumption of innocence – as reaffirmed in Art. 48 of the Charter of Fundamental Rights of the European Union proclaimed in Nice on 7 December 2000 – which applies to the procedures relating to infringements of the competition rules applicable to undertakings that may result in the imposition of fines or periodic penalty payments."[129]

As the ECJ has to construe Art. 48 § 1 EUC in the light of the findings of the ECtHR, it is very difficult to discern whether the ECJ will adopt a more general approach than the ECtHR on the question under what circumstances the *criminal* sphere of proceedings applies to a *civil asset forfeiture model*. One could guess that the ECJ will also address the question on a case-by-case basis.

3. Right to property, Art. 17 EUC

The Charter protects the right to property in its Art. 17:

---

[127] Court of First Instance, T-48/05 *(Franchet and Byk v. Commission)*, Collection 2008, II-1585, para. 209.

[128] ECJ, C-199/92P *(Hüls v. Commission)*, Collection 1999, 4287, para. 150.

[129] Court of First Instance, T-474/04 *(Pergan Hilfsstoffe v. Commission)*, Collection 2007, II-4225, para. 75 = EuR 2008, 703 with Annotations by *Wegener*. See also Court of First Instance, T-48/05 *(Franchet and Byk v. Commission)*; *Niestedt/Boeckmann*, EuZW 2009, 71 f.

Right to property

(1) Everyone has the right to own, use, dispose of and bequeath his or her lawfully acquired possessions. No one may be deprived of his or her possessions, except in the public interest and in the cases and under the conditions provided for by law, subject to fair compensation being paid in good time for their loss. The use of property may be regulated by law in so far as is necessary for the general interest.

As the right to property is equally protected by Art. 1 of Protocol No. 1 to the ECHR, Art. 17 EUC must be interpreted in the light of that provision.[130] However, Art. 17 EUC and Art. 1 of Protocol No. 1 to the ECHR are different in their wording: While Art. 17 EUC refers to "lawfully acquired possessions," Art. 1 of the Protocol to the ECHR does not have any similar limitations. It remains to be seen whether Art. 17 EUC is applicable when the forfeited asset was the product of or the instrument in a criminal offence. Some legal scholars have come to the conclusion that this is not the case, considering the clear wording of Art. 17 EUC.[131] The minimum standard clause of Art. 53 EUC would not alter this result.[132] Others think that Art. 17 EUC is applicable when at least the acquisition of the asset itself was lawful.[133]

Concerning the justification of interferences, it is very likely that the ECJ will make use of the "four requirements" the ECtHR has already set out (see IV.A.2.c).

4. Principle of proportionality

The principle of proportionality is a general safeguard for all fundamental rights (Art. 52 § 1 phrase 2 EUC). Even before the Charter entered into force, the ECJ had recognized the principle of proportionality as a general principle of European Union law.[134]

---

[130] See ECJ, C-402/05 *(Kadi and Al-Barakaat)*, Collection 2008, I-6351, para. 356.

[131] Cf. *Calliess*, in: Calliess/Ruffert (eds.), EUV/AEUV, Kommentar, Art. 17 EUC, marginal no. 7; *Depenheuer*, in: Tettinger/Stern (eds.), Kölner Gemeinschafts-Kommentar, Europäische Grundrechte-Charta, Art. 17 EUC, marginal no. 23.

[132] Cf. *Callies*, in: Calliess/Ruffert (eds.), EUV/AEUV, Kommentar, Art. 17 EUC, marginal no. 6 with reference to European Commission for Human Rights, *Pezoldová v. Czech Republic*, Decision of 11 April 1996: "... the right to acquire property, which is not covered by Art. 1 of Protocol No. 1." See also *Jarass*, NVwZ 2006, 1091, 1092.

[133] Cf. *Jarass*, Charta der Grundrechte der Europäischen Union – Kommentar, Art. 17 EUC, marginal no. 7; *Jarass*, NVwZ 2006, 1089, 1090 f.; *Bernsdorff*, in: Meyer (ed.), Charta der Grundrechte der Europäischen Union, Art. 17 EUC, marginal no. 16; *Streinz*, in: Streinz (ed.), EUV/AEUV, Art. 17 EUC, marginal no. 14; *Frenz*, Handbuch Europarecht, vol. IV, Europäische Grundrechte, marginal no. 2880 ff.

[134] ECJ C-310/04 *(Spain v. European Council)*, Collection 2006, 7285, para. 97; ECJ, C-189/01 *(Jippes et al.)*, Collection 2001, 5689, para. 81; ECJ, C-133/93 *(Crispoltini et al.)*, Collection 1994, 4863, para. 41; ECJ, C-331/88 *(Fedesa et al.)*, Collection 1990, 4023, para. 13.

The relevant jurisprudence of the ECJ can be used even after the coming into force of the Charter.[135] The principle of proportionality is linked to "objectives of general interest recognized by the Union" and "the rights and freedoms of others." The objectives of general interest recognized by the European Union are not only those enumerated in Art. 3 TEU but also other interests protected by special regulations such as Art. 4 § 1 TEU, Art. 35 § 3 TFEU, and Arts. 36 and 346 TEU. The link to Art. 4 TEU permits the incorporation of objectives belonging to the field of public security into the term "objectives of general interest." The Commission refers to the common interest of combating crime laid down in Art. 67 TEU in its proposal for a directive. Considering the explanations to the Charter, the ECJ will certainly accept the reference to Art. 67 TEU by the Commission.

The ECJ considers the principle of proportionality in two steps: *First*, it considers whether a measure is in principle suitable in order to attain the aim proposed by it. *Second*, the ECJ mixes necessity and proportionality *stricto sensu* together:

> "It is for the national courts to ascertain whether such publicity is both necessary and proportionate to the aim of keeping salaries within reasonable limits.[136] The principle of proportionality, which is one of the general principles of European Union law, requires that measures implemented by acts of the European Union are appropriate for attaining the objective pursued and do not go beyond what is necessary to achieve it."[137]

This results in the contrasting interests of other parties already being considered while examining the necessity of a measure. This contrasts with the way the ECtHR and the German Constitutional Court (BVerfG) consider the principle of proportionality. The ECJ's way to consider the principle of proportionality leads to a rather cursory examination of the case when it comes to proportionality. That being said, the concept of proportionality *stricto sensu* is known to the European courts.

> [The principle of proportionality] requires that the measures concerned satisfy criteria of **aptitude, necessity** and **proportionality stricto sensu**.[138]

Some legal scholars venture the hope that the ECJ will be forced to develop a more sophisticated consideration of the principle of proportionality by the minimum standards clause (Art. 52 § 3 phrase 1 EUC) and the thus required consideration of the jurisprudence of the ECtHR in the future.

Finally, one has to conclude that the ECJ has not yet developed new aspects in its consideration of the principle of proportionality since the entry into force of the Charter.[139] A *civil asset forfeiture model* to be implemented in the Member States would be an adequate area for such an experiment.

---

[135] Cf. ECJ C-92/09 *(Schecke GbR v. Land Hessen)*, EuZW 2010, 939 (943), para. 74.

[136] ECJ C-465/00 *(Österreichischer Rundfunk et al.)*, Collection 2003, I-4989, para. 88.

[137] ECJ C-92/09 (see n. 135), para. 74.

[138] Opinion of Advocate General *Jääskinen* in case no. C-249/09 *(Novo Nordisk)*, para. 48.

[139] It should be said that, up until now, there has been only one case in which the ECJ considered Art. 52 § 3 EUC since the Charter entered into force.

V. Final Conclusion

The implementation of a civil asset forfeiture model in Germany would be in conformity with the principle of culpability and the presumption of innocence – as interpreted by the German Federal Constitutional Court. It will not be possible, however, to bring such a model in line with the right to property as guaranteed by Art. 14 GG.

On the ECHR level, a civil asset forfeiture model seems to be outside the criminal sphere of Art. 6 § 1 ECHR as long as the three *Engel* criteria are not fulfilled in their specific patterns. Consequently, the presumption of innocence, Art. 6 § 2 ECHR, does not apply. Some more or less procedural restrictions will follow from the ECtHR's jurisdiction on the right to property, Art. 1 of Protocol No. 1 to the ECHR. However, the "constitutional standards" of the ECHR seem to be lower than those of the German Basic Law.

The standards of the EUC seem to follow those of the ECHR unless the ECJ opts for a "self-confident" approach.

Bibliography

Calliess, Christian/Ruffert, Matthias (eds.), EUV/AEUV, Das Verfassungsrecht der Europäischen Union mit Europäischer Grundrechtecharta, Kommentar. 4th ed. Munich 2011.

Fischer, Thomas, Strafgesetzbuch. 61st ed. Munich 2014.

Frenz, Walter, Handbuch Europarecht, vol. IV, Europäische Grundrechte. Berlin/Heidelberg 2009.

Graf, Jürgen Peter (ed.), Strafprozessordnung: StPO. Mit Gerichtsverfassungsgesetz und Nebengesetzen. Kommentar. 2nd ed. Munich 2012.

Hannich, Rolf (ed.), Karlsruher Kommentar zur Strafprozessordnung mit GVG, EGGVG und EMRK. 7th ed. Munich 2013.

Herzog, Felix/Achsnich, Gernot, Geldwäschebekämpfung und Gewinnabschöpfung: Handbuch der straf- und wirtschaftsrechtlichen Regelungen. Munich 2006.

Hoyer, Andreas, Die Rechtsnatur des Verfalls angesichts des neuen Verfallsrechts. GA 1993, 406–422.

Jacobs, Francis/White, Robin C. A./Ovey, Clare, The European Convention on Human Rights. 5th ed. Oxford 2009.

Jarass, Hans D., Charta der Grundrechte der Europäischen Union – unter Einbeziehung der vom EuGH entwickelten Grundrechte und der Grundrechtsregelungen der Verträge, Kommentar. 2nd ed. Munich 2013.

– Der grundrechtliche Eigentumsschutz im EU-Recht. NVwZ 2006, 1089–1095.

Julius, Karl-Peter, Einziehung, Verfall und Art. 14 GG. ZStW 109 (1997), 58–102.

Kempf, Eberhard/Schilling, Hellen, Vermögensabschöpfung. Bonn 2007.

Klose, Bernd (ed.), Asset Tracing and Recovery. Berlin 2009.

Lackner, Karl/Kühl, Kristian (eds.), Strafgesetzbuch, Kommentar. 28th ed. Munich 2014.

Leach, Philip, Taking a case to the European Court of Human Rights. 3rd ed.Oxford 2011.

Leipziger Kommentar, Strafgesetzbuch (StGB), Großkommentar, Heinrich Wilhelm Laufhütte/Ruth Rissing-van Saan/Klaus Tiedemann. 12th ed. Berlin 2008-2014.

Löwe-Rosenberg, Die Strafprozessordnung und das Gerichtsverfassungsgesetz: StPO, Volker Erb/Robert Esser/Ulrich Franke/Kirsten Graalmann-Scheerer/Hans Hilger/Alexander Ignor (eds.), vol. 11: EMRK/IPBPR. 26th ed. Berlin 2012.

Maunz-Dürig, Grundgesetz – Kommentar, Roman Herzog/Rupert Scholz/Matthias Herdegen/Hans H. Klein (eds.). Munich 2013.

Meyer, Jürgen (ed.), Charta der Grundrechte der Europäischen Union. 4th ed. Baden-Baden 2014.

Michael, Lothar/Morlok, Martin, Grundrechte. 4th ed. Baden-Baden 2014.

Niestedt, Marian/Boeckmann, Hanna, Verteidigungsrechte bei internen Untersuchungen des OLAF – das Urteil Franchet und Byk des Gerichts erster Instanz und die Reform der Verordnung (EG) Nr. 1073/1999. EuZW 2009, 70–74.

Rönnau, Thomas, Vermögensabschöpfung in der Praxis. Munich 2003.

Sachs, Michael: Reichweite des Schuldgrundsatzes und der Unschuldsvermutung – Verhältnismäßige Eigentumsbeschränkung durch die Regelungen über den erweiterten Verfall. JuS 2004, 1092–1094.

Schmidt, Wilhelm, Gewinnabschöpfung im Straf- und Bußgeldverfahren. Munich 2006.

Schönke, Adolf/Schröder, Horst (eds.), Strafgesetzbuch – Kommentar. 29th ed. Munich 2014.

Stephenson, Kevin M./Gray, Larissa/Power, Ric/Brun, Jean-Pierre/Dunker, Gabriele/Panjer, Melissa, Barriers to asset recovery: An analysis of the key barriers and recommendations for action. The International Bank for Reconstruction and Development/The World Bank, Washington 2011.

Streinz, Rudolf (ed.), EUV/AEUV: Vertrag über die Europäische Union und Vertrag über die Arbeitsweise der Europäischen Union. 2nd ed. Munich 2012.

Tettinger, Peter J./Stern, Klaus (eds.), Kölner Gemeinschafts-Kommentar, Europäische Grundrechte-Charta. Munich 2006.

Volk, Klaus, Der Begriff der Strafe in der Rechtsprechung des Bundesverfassungsgerichts. ZStW 83 (1971), 405–434.

List of Abbreviations

AEUV   Vertrag über die Arbeitsweise der Europäischen Union

AO   Abgabenordnung

BGB	Bürgerliches Gesetzbuch
BGH	Bundesgerichtshof
BGHSt	Entscheidungen des Bundesgerichtshofs in Strafsachen
BT-Drucksache	Bundestagsdrucksache
BVerfG	Bundesverfassungsgericht
BVerfGE	Entscheidungen des Bundesverfassungsgerichts
COD	Ordentliches Gesetzgebungsverfahren, früher auch Kodezisionsverfahren
COM	Europäische Kommission (Commission)
dec.	decision
DVBl	Deutsches Verwaltungsblatt (Journal)
ECHR	European Convention on Human Rights
ECJ	European Court of Justice
ECtHR	European Court of Human Rights
EGGVG	Einführungsgesetz zum Gerichtsverfassungsgesetz
EMRK	Konvention zum Schutze der Menschenrechte und Grundfreiheiten
EUC	European Charter of Fundamental Rights
EuGRZ	Europäische Grundrechte-Zeitschrift (Journal)
EuR	Europarecht (Journal)
EUV	Vertrag über die Europäische Union
EuZW	Europäische Zeitschrift für Wirtschaftsrecht (Journal)
FATF	Financial Action Task Force
GA	Goltdammer's Archiv für Strafrecht (Journal)
GBP	Britisches Pfund
GbR	Gesellschaft bürgerlichen Rechts
GC	Grand Chamber
GG	Grundgesetz für die Bundesrepublik Deutschland (Federal Law – German Constitution)
GVG	Gerichtsverfassungsgesetz
ICCPR	International Covenant on Civil and Political Rights
Inc.	Incorporated
IPBPR	Internationaler Pakt über bürgerliche und politische Rechte
JHA	Rat für Justiz und Inneres der EU (Journal)
JuS	Juristische Schulung (Journal)
NJW	Neue juristische Wochenschrift (Journal)
NStZ	Neue Zeitschrift für Strafrecht (Journal)
NStZ-RR	Neue Zeitschrift für Strafrecht – Rechtsprechungsreport (Journal)

NVwZ	Neue Zeitschrift für Verwaltungsrecht (Journal)
OLG	Oberlandesgericht
OVG	Oberverwaltungsgericht
StGB	Strafgesetzbuch
StPO	Strafprozessordnung
TEU	Treaty on European Union
TFEU	Treaty on the Functioning of the European Union
UK	United Kingdom
U.S.	United States
USC	United States Code
wistra	Zeitschrift für Wirtschafts- und Steuerstrafsachen (Journal)
WM	Wertpapier-Mitteilungen, Zeitschrift für Wirtschafts- und Bankrecht (Journal)
ZP-EMRK	Zusatzprotokoll der Konvention zum Schutze der Menschenrechte und Grundfreiheiten
ZPO	Zivilprozessordnung
ZStW	Zeitschrift für die gesamte Strafrechtswissenschaft (Journal)

Chapter 5

A Necessary Evil?

The Italian "Non-Criminal System" of Asset Forfeiture

Michele Panzavolta and *Roberto Flor*[*]

I. Introduction

In the Italian legal system, confiscation (or, to use an equivalent term, asset forfeiture),[1] is of a hybrid, multi-faceted nature. There are different types of forfeiture and it is difficult to categorize each one into a clear and precise theoretical framework.

Traditionally, confiscation in Italy falls within the area of crime prevention, as being distinct from punishment. Formally, this remains true in that the major forms of confiscation are qualified by the law as preventative tools. Nevertheless, the picture is complicated and blurred by three factors: the multi-faceted shape of prevention in and outside the system of criminal justice, the thin dividing line between prevention and repression, and the recent introduction of a number of special confiscation provisions applicable to certain offences only, which is sometimes difficult to reconcile with the general framework.

Crime prevention has always been a legitimate aim of every civilized country, often considered more "noble" than mere repression.[2] Western democracies have

---

[*] *Michele Panzavolta* has drafted paras. I.–III. and V.–XIX. This contribution was written within the framework of a Marie Curie fellowship. *Roberto Flor* has drafted para. IV.

[1] In the present article, confiscation and asset forfeiture are used as synonyms to indicate the deprivation of a defendant of a title to property, which is hence transferred to the state. This is not the case in other countries: in the UK, for instance, forfeiture of assets is distinct from confiscation: while the former takes away the proprietary right of the individual to some property, the latter is an order for payment of a specified sum of money (see *Dickson*, Towards more effective asset recovery, 436).

[2] See, for instance, *Blackstone*, Commentaries, pp. 248 ff. Blackstone recognized as commendable that English laws provided for means of crime prevention, "since *preventive justice* is upon every principle, of reason, of humanity, and of sound policy, preferable in all respects to *punishing justice*; the execution of which, though necessary, and in its consequences a species of mercy to the commonwealth, is always attended with many harsh and disagreeable circumstances." When defining and enlisting the means of prevention, Blackstone writes: "This preventive justice consists in obliging those persons, whom there is probable ground to suspect of future misbehaviour, to stipulate with and to give full assurance to the public, that such offence as is apprehended shall not happen; by finding pledges or securities for keeping the peace, or for their good behaviour."

always made use of some amount of preventative tools. In theory, there is a clear dividing line between prevention of crime and repression of crime: prevention looks forward, repression looks backward; prevention is concerned with future crimes, repression with committed crimes. In practice, however, that is no more than a very fine line. Even if confined within a strict retributive boundary, punishment always entails prevention. When prevention takes the form of afflictive (or coercive) measures (i.e., measures that erode, limit, intrude fundamental rights) it closely resembles punishment. Albeit being formally aimed at prevention, confiscation could easily be qualified as an afflictive measure, in that it entails a deprivation of the right to property.

Prevention itself can have different facets. The label of prevention covers different approaches. For instance, it is one thing to prevent criminals from committing other crimes (incapacitation) and a different thing to deter all citizens from crime (general deterrence), removing the conditions that could stimulate the commission of further offences or proving to citizens that crime does not pay. Another distinction must be made between preventative measures imposed *ante* or *praeter delictum* (i.e., when a person has committed no crime or, to put it in other terms, regardless of the finding of a commission of a crime) and measures imposed *post delictum* (when the dangerousness of the offender has materialized in the commission of a crime). Furthermore, there are preventative measures imposed outside of the criminal law system and others issued within criminal proceedings (and, in the latter case, it also makes a difference when the measures are issued: before, after or regardless of a criminal conviction).

The shape of Italian confiscation calls into question all these distinctions. There are types of confiscation that can be imposed only within criminal proceedings (criminal confiscation). Some must follow a conviction; others do not require a finding of liability against the defendant. There is also a type of confiscation that is issued outside of criminal proceedings, in a distinct and autonomous set of proceedings.

Confiscation of criminal properties has, for a long time, been confined to a marginal role within the array of instruments for fighting crime. In the past decades, it has gained significant importance in line with the general trend (in Europe and worldwide), which favours profit-oriented policies as a means of crime prevention.[3] The new approach towards countering criminals is to "hit them where it hurts the most,"[4] i.e., hit their economic interests. The emphasis is placed on the need to remove the economic incentive of crime and to reduce the amount of resources at the criminals' disposal. Most countries have introduced new forms of forfeiture or

---

[3] For the criminal policy approach of "taking the profit out of crime" in the English-speaking world, see *Levi*, Taking the Profit Out of Crime, 228–239; *Kilchling*, Tracing, Seizing and Confiscating, 264–280.

[4] *Nelen*, Hit them, 517–534.

broadened the existing ones. The majority of countries have enacted forms of extended confiscation against convicted criminals in order to deprive them of their illicit gains, regardless of a direct connection with the offence for which the conviction was passed.[5] Other countries, particularly common law countries (England, United States), have developed types of confiscation of criminal assets that are detached from the machinery of criminal justice, by making use of civil forfeiture remedies. Within this scenario, Italy stands out for a peculiar form of "confiscation" called "preventive confiscation," which is imposed outside of the criminal justice system, albeit not having a strict civil nature. In other words, it is a type of confiscation that shares some similarities with the civil forfeiture of common law and yet retains features of its own, which makes it a unique instrument within the European legal landscape.

The aim of this paper is to offer an illustration of the Italian system of "preventive non-criminal confiscation" within the larger array of confiscation measures. The first part of this paper will offer a brief overview of the Italian system of criminal sentencing, and it will contextualize confiscation in the sentencing system, according to the general provisions of the criminal code (para. II.). Then, it will focus on the abovementioned type of preventative confiscation, which is issued outside of the field of criminal justice. The illustration will start by describing the historical roots of non-criminal confiscation (paras. V.–VI.), then it will concentrate on its present shape (paras. VII.–XII.), and finally it will evaluate its nature and compliance with fundamental rights (paras. XIII.–XIX.).

II. The general framework of criminal confiscation within the Italian criminal sentencing system

In the provisions of the Italian criminal code (drafted in 1930 and still in force today), the sentencing regime was built around the logic of a "double track system": penalties, on the one hand, "security measures" *(misure di sicurezza)*, on the other. Penalties are aimed at punishing the convicted offender, while security measures are aimed at preventing the offender from committing further harm.

---

[5] Extended confiscation refers the power of a court to forfeit assets of a convicted person other than those directly linked to the crime. It can take different shapes: it can consist in the power to confiscate property acquired through similar crimes to the one for which the person was convicted, or in the power to confiscate all property probably acquired through the same type of crime on other occasions, or even in the power to forfeit all assets disproportionate to the income of the person (in this respect, see Article 3 § 2 Framework Decision 2005/212/JHA of 24 February 2005 on Confiscation of Crime-Related Proceeds, Instrumentalities and Property, OJ L 68/49).

Criminal penalties are of two kinds: custodial penalties and financial penalties. They are imposed against individuals found criminally liable at the end of the criminal proceedings as a just desert for the crime they committed. Criminal penalties have to be proportionate to the gravity of the crime (although the judge may also take into account the personality of the culprit at the sentencing stage) and are determinate in length (save for the remaining cases of crimes punishable with life sentences).

Security measures normally follow a conviction of the individual but they need not always follow a conviction. They in fact follow a different logic: they are intended to prevent dangerous individuals from committing further crimes. Nonetheless, security measures require at least the finding that a person committed a crime: e.g., in the case of a person acquitted on the basis of an insanity defence. It is only in a few exceptional instances that a security measure can be imposed for facts that do not constitute an offence (see Article 202 of the criminal code).[6] Security measures can also be of two kinds: personal (i.e., restrictive of personal liberty) or financial. Due to their preventive finality, security measures are indeterminate in length and their termination depends upon an assessment of the (lack of) actual dangerousness on the part of the offender.

Criminal penalties and security measures share a major common feature. They both fully belong to the realm of criminal justice. Even in the limited amount of cases in which security measures do not require a previous conviction, they can only be imposed in a criminal trial, i.e., be applied with all due safeguards provided for by the criminal (substantive and procedural) law. Hence, they are characterized by the fact that their preventive rationale remains confined within the boundaries of the strong safeguards offered by criminal justice.

III. Criminal confiscation as a security measure (Article 240 Italian criminal code)

According to the criminal code, criminal confiscation is a financial security measure. Nonetheless it has specific features. It differs from other security measures in that it does not require an assessment of the dangerousness of the individual. In fact, according to the traditional approach, criminal confiscation is justified by the dangerousness of an object or of a certain piece of property.[7]

---

[6] This is the case, for instance, for an attempt to commit a crime that was inherently unable to succeed (Article 49 section 4 of the criminal code) or the case of instigation to commit an offence if not followed by the commission of the crime (Article 115 of the criminal code).

[7] *Mantovani*, Diritto penale, p. 895.

The general rules on confiscation are set out in Article 240 of the Italian criminal code in relation to the different objects that can be forfeited.[8] The article provides that, when a conviction is passed, the judge may impose the confiscation of: 1) the instrumentalities of the crime; 2) the product of the crime; 3) the profit gained from the crime.

There are also cases of mandatory confiscation. With regard to the "price" of the crime, i.e., the retribution received for committing the crime, Article 240 section 2 holds that the judge must "always" order the confiscation of such retribution. Legal scholars have debated whether the judge is under an obligation to impose the confiscation of the price, even if the defendant is acquitted or if the measure is available only when a conviction is passed.[9] The Italian Supreme Court recently concluded in the latter sense, but only if the acquittal is not based on a reasoning on the merits (e.g., the person is found liable, yet acquitted due to the application of the statute of limitations).[10] Another case of mandatory confiscation concerns items that are *per se* dangerous (contraband property, i.e., property that is *per se* in violation of the law) and, in this case, there is no doubt that the confiscation is always compulsory, even in case of acquittal.[11]

The rationale behind this multi-faceted regime depends on the different degree of dangerousness of the property. On the one hand, there are objects that are inherently dangerous (contraband), for which confiscation must always be imposed, regardless of the criminal liability of the defendant and even of the finding of the existence of a crime. On the other hand, there are objects that prove to be dangerous in light of their connection with a crime or with a culprit (the price, the product, and the profits of a crime); hence, they may be confiscated only when the courts establish the commission of an offence and/or the personal liability of the defendant. The price of the crime is seen as an incentive to commit the crime; hence, the law

---

[8] This marks the distance from the historical experience of the *confiscation générale*, when confiscation was a penalty that would deprive the culprit of all properties, see *Mantovani*, Diritto penale, p. 895.

[9] In historical perspective: *Vassalli*, La confisca. Later, see *Alessandri*, Confisca, p. 45 (according to whom the confiscation of assets is not connected to the dangerousness of the person, as it is proven by the fact that it can/must be imposed even when the execution of the sentence against the defendant has been suspended).

[10] Cass., sez. un., 10 July 2008, Di Maio. Nevertheless, there still is some controversy in the case law with regard to the need for a formal conviction to be passed. Some further decisions have taken a slightly broader approach. They have held that it is not necessary for the conviction to be formally passed, as long as the defendant's liability is asserted in the reasons for decision. This refers particularly to those cases in which the statute of limitation bars the possibility to convict the defendant, albeit the defendant's responsibility having been ascertained by the court. See, Cass., sez. II, 5 October 2011, Ciancimino, rv. 251195. The opposite position is taken by Cass., sez. VI, 9 February 2011, Ferone, rv. 249590.

[11] For a general overview of the cases of confiscation without a previous conviction, see *Panzarasa*, Confisca senza condanna, 1672 ff.

requires the judge to order confiscation. It is different in the case of the profits and product of the crime, where the judge is left free to decide. The judge's discretionary evaluation shall consider the effective dangerousness of the property if left in the defendant's possession.[12]

A terminological clarification seems necessary. The concept of proceeds of crime, as it is commonly understood in Europe ("any economic advantage from criminal offences", Article 1 Framework Decision 2005/212), encompasses two distinct notions of Italian criminal legislation: the "product of the crime" and the "profit of the crime." The former refers to the material goods that constitute the result of the crime (for instance, forged coin in cases of counterfeiting, abusive constructions in violation of the infringement of local building regulations or stolen property),[13] while the latter concerns the economic gain derived from the crime. Courts and scholars have debated whether the direct economic advantages are the only forfeitable gains or whether they also extend to indirect advantages. In 2008, the Supreme Court endorsed the first approach. By emphasizing the need to identify advantages in light of their direct derivation from the crime, the court refused the application of purely economic criteria (net or gross principles) in the determination of the amount of the profit.[14]

The distinction between some of the aforementioned concepts – price, product, and profits of crime – is not always sharp, although it bears significant legal consequences on the regime of the confiscation (depending on the object, confiscation is either mandatory or discretionary) and some scholars have proposed abolishing it altogether.[15]

Save for the case of inherently dangerous items, whose confiscation is always mandatory, the judge must establish the existence of a causal link between the crime and the property to be confiscated in all other cases.[16] The forfeited goods must be clearly connected to the crime.[17]

---

[12] *Guarneri*, Confisca, p. 42; *Trapani*, Confisca, p. 2.

[13] Cass., sez. un., 3 July 1996, Chabni, Cassazione penale, 1997, 974; Cass., sez. V, 18 May 2005, Marchionni, Ced cass., rv. 232289, according to which the property of a company sold by the administrator in consequence of a private bribery scheme constitutes the product of the crime. In Cass., sez. III, 4 December 2001, Carletto, Ced cass., rv. 220329, the estate where there had been an infringement of local building regulations was deemed to be the product of the crime.

[14] Cass., sez. un., 27 March 2008, Fisia Italimpianti Spa, rv. 239925.

[15] *Maugeri*, Le sanzioni patrimoniali.

[16] *Alessandri*, Confisca.

[17] Cass., sez. un., 27 March 2008, Fisia Italimpianti Spa, rv. 239925.

Although it is formally labelled a security measure, the scholars and the courts often observe that criminal confiscation more closely resembles a criminal penalty, due to its afflictive nature and its indifference to the dangerousness of individuals.[18]

IV. Special cases of criminal confiscation

For a long time, the provision of Article 240 of the criminal code represented the whole of the Italian confiscation system,[19] with only few special provisions related to specific offences being contained in separate statutes.[20] Overall, asset forfeiture was confined to a marginal role within the array of legal instruments to fight crime.

Eventually, the parliament started acknowledging the importance of criminal confiscation, particularly in fighting criminal networks. Profit-oriented strategies were first enacted during the 1970s and they have experienced increasing success since then. The change in policy has brought about the introduction of a number of new cases of confiscation, linked to the conviction for certain crimes (for instance, in the field of drug smuggling, contraband, violations of local building regulations, bribery, etc.) or to cases in which the offender is a legal entity. The new rules have been devised with regard to specific offences; hence, they prevail over the general provisions of Article 240. Most of them are in fact characterized by a stricter regime, according to which the confiscation of the price, the profit, and the product of the crime is always mandatory.[21] Furthermore, in some of these new cases, the parliament also introduced the possibility of imposing value confiscation (i.e., confiscation of property other than the one directly connected to the crime, for a value equivalent to the price, profit, or product of the crime).

A further development in the strategy of depriving criminals of their assets dates back to the years 1992–1994, when the Italian lawmaker enacted a form of extended confiscation (Art. 12-*sexies* decree law 8 June 1992, n.° 306),[22] which empowers the judge to order against convicts for certain offences (public briberies, mafia

---

[18] *Alessandri*, Confisca.

[19] Besides the general provision of Article 240, the criminal code originally contained only few specific rules, mostly related to gambling offences, which made it mandatory to forfeit gambling means and profits (Articles 718–722).

[20] For example, provisions on confiscation for offences related to the export/import of goods, fishing and hunting activities, agricultural products fraud.

[21] *Fiandaca/Musco*, Diritto penale, p. 845.

[22] Extended confiscation was introduced in 1994 after a ruling by the Constitutional Court that had quashed the provision of a 1992 statute introducing an offence of possession of assets incompatible with a person's income with subsequent confiscation (judgement n. 48 of 1994).

association, joint criminal enterprises to commit trafficking in human beings, etc.)[23] the confiscation of all the assets that are disproportionate with their income if the persons cannot justify their lawful acquisition.[24]

When looking at these special cases, legal scholars and the courts gained the impression that they blur the traditional preventative aim of confiscation even more. In some instances, particularly with regard to value confiscation and extended confiscation, it appears to many that the real rationale is a punitive one.[25] Regardless of their nature, all these new cases share the feature of being criminal justice measures, issued at the end or as a result of criminal proceedings.

The multiplication of cases of criminal confiscation has simultaneously been accompanied by an entirely different strategy, which has consisted in establishing a type of confiscation of criminal assets outside of the criminal justice system. Parliament in fact decided to introduce a form of preventive confiscation, issued within an autonomous set of judicial proceedings and regardless of the conviction of the person.

V. Moving outside of the criminal justice system: from "criminal confiscation" to "preventive confiscation"

A clearer understanding of the system of non-criminal confiscation requires a brief review of the historical developments of the Italian system regarding the so-called "preventative measures."

As is widely known, Italy is home to criminal connections, the "mafia" above all. In the mid-sixties of the last century, the Italian government decided to experiment with new legal tools to fight criminal networks. The criminal justice system had until then proven to be inefficient in repressing such criminal networks. In particular, prosecutors had experienced severe difficulties in bringing to a successful end trials with charges of organized crime. This was partly due to the high standard of proof for criminal cases (equivalent to the common law maxim "beyond reasonable doubt") and partly due to the difficulty of bringing solid and consistent evidence before the court (particularly testimonial evidence, given the general fear of people to testify against powerful violent criminals).[26]

---

[23] Recently also with reference to computer crime and cybercrime: see L. 12/2012.

[24] On the powers of extended confiscation, see *Fondaroli*, Le ipotesi speciali di confisca.

[25] See *Fondaroli*, Le ipotesi speciali di confisca; *Nicosia*, La confisca; *Menditto*, Le misure di prevenzione.

[26] *Fiandaca/Musco*, Diritto penale, p. 845; *Gallo*, Misure di prevenzione, p. 5.

With a view to tightening the fight against mafia mobs, the Italian parliament passed a bill that introduced the possibility to impose restrictive measures on individuals who were suspected of being part of a mafia association (Law 1965, n. 575) outside the criminal law system. Mafia suspects could be placed under surveillance, forced not to enter certain areas of the country or even to live in a confined part of the country, thus being restricted in their personal liberty and/or freedom of movement. These were "preventive" measures in that they were issued to prevent the commission of crimes (*praeter delictum* or *ante delictum*) and without having to go through criminal proceedings.

Preventive measures of such a kind were by no means new to the Italian system. In enacting the new anti-mafia tools, the parliament built upon an already existing piece of legislation dating back to 1956, which allowed the imposition of "preventive measures" to limit the personal liberty and/or the freedom of movement of individuals deemed dangerous in accordance with the parameters set forth by the law (Law 1423/1956).[27] According to the 1956 act, certain categories of dangerous individuals could be placed under special surveillance, be forced to live in a specific area of the country, or be banned from some parts of the national territory. The constitutionality of such measures had always been in question but, despite general criticism, the measures survived several challenges before the Constitutional Court.[28] The Constitutional Court, in particular, considered the 1956 Act legitimate because it required that the measures be imposed by a judge and that the categories of individuals potentially affected be sufficiently determined.

Until 1965, preventive measures had been devised mostly as a form of incapacitation against small street criminals. The 1965 act built on the 1956 act in that it extended the system of personal preventative measures with regard to mafia suspects. The novelty of the 1965 act was that, in the case of mafia suspects, there was no need to assess the present danger of the individual: anyone suspected of being part of a mafia association was automatically considered dangerous, hence liable to be subjected to a preventive measure. The legislator had introduced a presumption of dangerousness. According to the 1956 act, the dangerousness of the individual had to be assessed in light of the circumstances of the case, following the parameters offered by the law. In the 1965 act, mafia suspects were deemed to be inherently dangerous, without any need to carry out a factual assessment of their dangerousness.[29]

---

[27] The 1956 act had its predecessor in a 1931 act (T.U.L.P.S.), Consolidated Text of Laws on Public Security, which provided for administrative police measures to control dangerous individuals and activities. See *Manna*, Measures of Prevention, 248 ff.

[28] Corte costituzionale 27/1959, 73/1963, 23/1964, 45/1960.

[29] *Gallo*, Misure di prevenzione, p. 5.

It soon appeared that the 1965 reform contained two major flaws. The first was the absence of a legal definition of "mafia association,"[30] which made it very difficult to precisely identify the targets of the preventive action. The second was the limited incapacitation effect of such measures to successfully prevent large-scale organized crime. To put mafia suspects under surveillance or to force them to live in a certain area of the country was not sufficient to effectively tackle the strength of mafia associations. In fact, the new measures soon proved to be highly ineffective in preventing mafia associates from carrying on their regular criminal activities.

Furthermore, in that same period, the structure of mafia mobs was undergoing a major change. Around the seventies, mafia mobs began restructuring their criminal networks along business principles. They developed what was later called a "mafia enterprise" or "mafia company."[31] On the one hand, the criminal network was reorganized so as to assure greater efficiency and maximize profits. On the other hand, the "mafia" groups started getting involved in ordinary economic activities; they ran regular businesses, which had an inherent advantage over their competitors that was derived from the use of illegal means (violence, threats, systematic bribery, etc.) and from the laundering of large amounts of criminal money (collected through channels of more traditional criminal activities, ranging from all sorts of illegal trafficking to racketeering, etc.).

The "mafia-run enterprise" outperforms competitor companies. It distorts competition because of its capacity to resort to criminal activities (briberies, threats, etc.) and because it can count at all times on a large amount of liquidity at its disposal stemming from other criminal deeds. The "mafia company" is in fact largely funded by the monies that the organization needs to launder.[32] In light of this development, personal preventive measures were ineffective in reaching their aim. At first, the Italian institutions did not recognize this paradigm shift towards an economically oriented approach but, as we shall see, they eventually did. The 1965 act was in fact only the beginning of a new wave of anti-mafia legislation.

In 1975, the parliament passed a new bill to tighten the fight against crime (Law 152/1975, so-called "Legge Reale") along the lines of the 1965 act, i.e., through the imposition of preventive measures. The statute extended the list of possible targets (deemed inherently dangerous) so as to include suspects of political crime (terrorism and other serious crimes against the integrity of the state, Articles 18 and 19). What is more important, a new measure was introduced to counter mafia crimes

---

[30] *Manna*, Measures of Prevention, 249.

[31] *Paoli*, The paradoxes, 58; *Mattina*, The transformations, 230 ff. In the Italian literature, see *Arlacchi*, La mafia imprenditrice, pp. 95 ff.; *Fiandaca*, Criminalità organizzata, 8; *Turone*, Il delitto di associazione mafiosa, p. 25; *Balsamo*, Le misure di prevenzione patrimoniali, p. 38; *Centorrino*, Mafia ed economie locali, p. 251.

[32] *Guzzini*, The "Long Night of the First Republic", 41; *Maugeri*, I modelli di sanzione patrimoniale, pp. 7 ff.

more effectively. It consisted in the temporary deprivation of the individual right to administer one's properties, with the exclusion of property related to the professional or business activity of the target (Article 22). It was the first shy sign that the Italian parliament recognized the need to challenge criminals, particularly mafia criminals, on the same grounds of economic interests.

The effects of the 1965 and 1975 acts were still far from satisfactory and, in the eyes of many, they brought about only modest results.[33] A change in pace took place in 1982 when the Italian parliament revolutionized its previous strategy. A new bill was passed (Law 646/1982, so-called "Legge La Torre-Rognoni") which, on the one hand, provided for a new offence of mafia association (hence, establishing a legal definition of the concept) and, on the other, introduced an array of preventive measures of a financial nature, in particular the seizure and confiscation of criminal assets.[34]

The origin of the system of financial preventive measures, as we know it today, can be traced back to the 1982 act. The introduction of financial preventive measures responded to the idea of tackling mafia groups in the field of their economic interests and earnings. It was based on a simple assumption: an effective strategy to counter the mafia and other similar associations requires depriving criminal networks of their property and profits. The underlying logic was that mafia properties were to be considered just as dangerous as single individuals. However, the logic was not taken to its fullest extent. The legislator did not simply permit the forfeiting of the assets that were found to have been obtained through unlawful mafia-related activities. Instead of establishing two separate profiles of dangerousness – the dangerousness of the individual and the dangerousness of the property – the law kept the two profiles intertwined. Not only did the imposition of a financial measure require an assessment of the subjective condition of the person (as being a suspect of certain crimes) but, even more, financial measures could be imposed only in connection with a personal measure. The freezing and forfeiture of property could be imposed only on those individuals against whom a personal preventive measure (special surveillance or other measure) had already been imposed or requested by the authorities.

Another major innovation in the 1982 act, together with the introduction of financial preventive measures, was the possibility to carry out investigations with a view to tracing and discovering the illicit property of the suspected individuals. One of the most famous magistrates in the fight against organized crime, Giovanni Falcone, who was eventually brutally murdered by the mafia, had in fact observed that the "Achilles' heel" of criminal networks is the trail of cash flow and illicit profits that they generate and move.

---

[33] *Balsamo*, Le misure di prevenzione patrimoniali, p. 35.

[34] *Fiandaca*, Misure di prevenzione, p. 108.

VI. Recent developments – Towards the autonomy of financial measures from personal measures

In the late '80s and at the beginning of the '90s, the Italian parliament was very active in the field of preventive measures. Several statutes were enacted to amend the previous provisions, all in the direction of toughening the preventive system of financial measures (for instance, by increasing investigating powers for tracing assets, allowing the adoption of urgent forms of freezing of property, etc.). More recent reforms in 2008, 2009, and 2010 have brought about further changes. In particular, the 2008 reform introduced an innovative provision, according to which financial preventive measures became detached from personal ones. The law established that it was no longer necessary to impose a personal measure prior to issuing a seizure/confiscation order against an individual. On this point, however, the law left a major incoherence. While declaring that a financial measure could be imposed independently from a personal one, it did not separate the two proceedings. Hence, the request to seize/confiscate could be filed only on condition that proceedings for the imposition of a personal preventive measure were underway, save for the exceptions expressly provided for by the law.[35]

Finally, in 2011, the entire subject underwent a major legislative restructuring. Preventive measures had developed chaotically throughout the years, with each reform following a piecemeal approach. Consequently, legislation in the field was muddled, with overlapping statutes, incoherent provisions, and misleading or incorrect cross-references. The situation had gotten even worse with the 2008–2010 insertions. This resulted in a general confusion as to the applicable rules, a situation which could no longer be tolerated.

In 2011, a new item of legislation entered into force to replace all the previous statutory instruments (Legislative decree 159 of 2011). It was a sort of consolidation, since it aimed at collating all previous rules scattered throughout the many different statutes. It did not bring about major innovations. It mostly reorganized previous existing provisions, attempting to ensure the necessary consistency between them. Nonetheless, some novelties were introduced and, after all, a consolidation made through the adoption of a new law is inevitably a codification. It is no surprise that the new act goes by the name of "Anti-mafia code" (A.M.C.).[36]

The following paragraphs will be devoted to an illustration of the rules provided for by the A.M.C. Reference to the case law will be made where appropriate.

One further remark: It would be wrong to believe that the fight against the mafia and other serious criminal networks was conducted only through the adoption of

---

[35] *Maugeri*, La riforma delle sanzioni patrimoniali, pp. 135 ff.

[36] For an overview of the Antimafia code see, *Malagnino* (ed.), Il codice antimafia; *Menditto*, Le misure di prevenzione.

preventive measures. It is correct to say that the parliament made use of all available instruments, outside and inside the criminal justice system. On the one hand, it broadened the offences related to organized crime and it toughened the system of criminal confiscation. On the other hand, it resorted to preventive instruments, which were placed outside the criminal justice system, mostly to circumvent the difficulties encountered in the criminal proceedings. The criminal proceedings and preventive proceedings were concurrently used to counter organized crime. Preventive measures were not simply intended as a "safety valve" to ensure greater efficiency of crime prevention, while keeping unaltered the architecture of criminal law, and of its traditional principles. The parliament did not refrain from introducing changes within the ambit of criminal law, mostly along the lines of a mitigation – or betrayal – of the principle of the classical school of criminal law (legality, harm, proportionality of punishment, etc.), particularly with the introduction of new inchoate offences. The provision of the 1982 act, which enacted a new offence of mafia association, is just one example of this approach. The development of cases of criminal confiscation (and particularly the adoption of a form of extended confiscation[37]) in parallel with preventive confiscation is another example.

VII. Confiscation as a preventive measure

Criminal confiscation and preventive confiscation show differences and similarities. They are similar in that they both entail the forfeiture of individual proprietary rights and the material apprehension of the assets by state authorities. However, while confiscation requires – at least in the majority of cases – a conviction, the same is not true for preventive measures, which were conceived as an alternative to the criminal justice process. Preventive confiscation, just like all other preventative measures, is wholly independent from a criminal conviction, although in practice there is often a link between the preventive measures and criminal proceedings in that preventive measures are often imposed when criminal proceedings are underway. They are often based on elements collected during the investigations into a criminal offence – this can also be seen in the requirements for imposing a preventive measures.

Preventive measures formally remain outside of the criminal justice system. They belong to an area that is formally administrative law (administrative punitive law), where substantive and procedural rules are looser.[38] Nevertheless, preventive proceedings remain fully judicial proceedings. It is only a court that can impose preventive measure; hence, a minimum of safeguards for the defendant is assured.

---

[37] *Supra*, para. IV.

[38] See also *infra*, para. XIII.

The A.M.C. provides for different types of financial measures, all issued by an order of the competent tribunal: seizure (i.e., temporary freezing of property), confiscation (i.e., forfeiture of property or control of assets), bail (deposit of a sum), judicial administration of personal property (Art. 33), and judicial administration of economic activities (Art. 34).

Preventive (i.e., non-criminal) confiscation is the decision by which an individual is deprived of ownership rights to suspicious property and the property is transferred to the state.

Seizure is instead a temporary measure, which precedes the confiscation order. It consists in the freezing of property, and it has the effect of temporarily precluding the exercise of property rights but does not entail the transfer of property to the state. In order to impose a (preventive) confiscation of property, the court must always issue an order of (preventive) seizure first.

VIII. Substantive requirements

According to the A.M.C., substantive requirements for preventative measures are of two kinds. First, the measures can be imposed only against one of the possible targets identified by the law. Second, the tribunal can issue a confiscation order against the property of listed targets only when certain conditions are met.

A. Targets

The law lists the people against whom the measure can be issued. It is quite an extensive catalogue, which corresponds (save for one category of subjects) to the list of individuals against whom personal preventive measures can be imposed. Article 4 states that financial preventive measures can be imposed against the following categories of individuals:

a) Suspects belonging to a mafia association (as defined by Article 416-*bis* of the criminal code);

b) Suspects of very serious offences (as listed in Article 51-*bis* of the code of criminal procedure), such as criminal associations committing human trafficking, drug trafficking, counterfeiting, contraband, mafia-related crimes, etc.;

c) Individuals who are considered dangerous because, in the alternative,

   i. They are habitually involved in the commission of criminal activities (career criminals);

   ii. They are considered as habitually living, even in part, on the proceeds of crime;

iii. Their outward conduct gives good reason to believe that they have tendencies to commit crimes that harm or put in danger the physical or moral integrity of minors, the public health, the public security, or the public tranquillity;

d) Individuals who carry out, alone or jointly with others, preparatory acts intended to commit crimes in order to subvert the democratic regime of the state (e.g., crimes of national or international terrorism, politically motivated crimes of insurgency, devastation, mass murder and kidnapping, and other similar acts);

e) Individuals who were part of dissolved and banned political associations (under Law 20 June 1952, n. 645), particularly the National fascist party, and for whom there is reason to believe that they still carry on a similar activity;

f) Individuals who carry out preparatory group activities intended to recreate the National fascist party, particularly by promoting or exercising violence;

g) Individuals who have been convicted of a crime concerning weapons (under Law 2 October 1967, n. 895 and Law 14 October 1974, n. 497, Articles 8 ff.) when there is reason to infer from their subsequent behaviour that they are inclined to committing a similar sort of crime;

h) Individuals who act as instigators, aiders, or abettors to the crimes listed above (including those who provide economic support by having knowledge of the criminal use made of the funds);

i) Suspects of aiding/abetting groups who have taken part in violent riots on the occasion of sports events.

Furthermore, financial preventive measures can be imposed against individuals included in the freezing list of the UN Security Committee or another competent international institution (Article 16, section 1, letter b). The latter is the only category of subjects against whom a personal measure cannot be issued.

Targets are identified either for the likelihood that they may commit crimes in the future (for instance, letter c, iii or g), either with regard to a past conduct that gives rise to the suspicion of having committed a serious crime (letters a–b), or a series of criminal activities (letter c, i, ii), or of being in the process of committing a crime (letter d).

In practice, the most common targets are individuals involved in organized crime (particularly mafia crime) or in violent political activities (e.g., terrorism).

B. Conditions

The goods seized and eventually confiscated must be property whose provenance the target cannot justify, and it must be:

a) Either disproportionate with regard to the declared income or to the activity carried out;

b) Or of illicit origin (i.e., deriving from an offence) or the result of reinvestment of proceeds of crimes.

Such property can be confiscated if the target owns it or possesses it either directly or indirectly (e.g., through a fictitious person). Hence, it is possible to impose a seizure/confiscation of property formally owned by a person different from the dangerous individual (third party).

If the targeted individuals conceal or sell their assets, the tribunal can seize and confiscate other properties of the person for an equivalent value (Article 25).

It is worth mentioning that the law also provides for a case of forfeiture that does not require the connection with a suspected or dangerous owner. When there is a reasonable suspicion that an economic activity is exercised with a view to favouring the commission of the activities related to mafia associations or other serious crimes (listed in letters a and b of Article 4) or of aiding the activities of a target, the law empowers to judge to put the business under the administration of a person appointed by the judge for a period of up to twelve months. At the end of this period, the judge can order the forfeiture of the business and all the assets, which reasonably appear as the fruits of a crime or their reinvestment (Article 34).

As mentioned, the contextual request or application of a personal measure is no longer a requirement. The A.M.C. explicitly repeats the provision that was introduced by the 2008 reform, according to which financial and personal measures can be requested and imposed disjunctively. In addition, it clearly makes the two proceedings (for the application of a personal measure, on the one hand, and of a financial measure, on the other) independent of one another.[39] The application of financial measures is also possible irrespective of the dangerousness of the person at the time of the filing of the request (Article 18 section 1).

IX. Measures against an absent person?

It often happens that (mafia) criminals are at large. This is particularly true with regard to mafia suspects who have often been able to hide successfully for years from judicial authorities. One recent example is the case of the most famous *mafioso* Bernardo Provenzano, who was found by the police after years of intense research in the Sicilian countryside. What then if prevention proceedings are instituted against absent individuals?

Originally, it was not possible to seize or confiscate assets if the suspected person could not be found. Confiscation against the absent person was precluded.

---

[39] See *infra*, para. XI.

Eventually, the legislator changed the rule to allow confiscation in such situations, because it would otherwise have been too easy for criminals (especially for high-profile criminals) to escape forfeiture.

At present, the rule is to be found in Article 18 section 4. According to this provision, proceedings for the imposition of financial preventive measures can be initiated (instituted) or continued when the individual is absent or lives abroad but only with regard to the property for which there is reason to believe that it is the proceeds (fruits) of illicit activities or their reinvestment.[40]

X. Measures against a deceased person?

Over the years, a large debate took place over the possibility to issue a seizure/confiscation measure against a deceased person, when the death had occurred during the proceedings or even before their commencement. It was not just an academic debate. The number of cases in which a person had died after the start of proceedings was astonishingly high. In the field of criminal networks, the rate of mortality is much higher than in ordinary life. The average criminal cannot expect to live as long as an ordinary person. Furthermore, it is well the case that the risk of death increases when the authorities initiate preventive proceedings against the person. The high frequency of cases in which death occurred while preventive proceedings were already underway reflects the approach of criminal networks, which may be willing to sacrifice one of their members to save their assets.

Until recently, the statutes did not provide for a specific rule. The courts (including the Court of Cassation) first favoured a more restrictive approach based on the argument that the individual could no longer be considered dangerous once deceased. Furthermore, until 2008, confiscation had to be connected to a personal measure, and it was technically impossible to impose the latter against the deceased (defunct). This position was backed by two rulings of the Constitutional Court, which considered the restrictive interpretation to be legitimate.[41] Since the mid '90s, however, the Italian Court of Cassation changed its line of reasoning. The court's new reasoning moved from the rationale of the instrument. In the court's view, preventive confiscation is not just intended to prevent dangerous individuals from harming society but it also aims at removing from the economic cycle (circuit) assets derived from a crime. In light of such a rationale, the constitutional judges eventually upheld the new line of reasoning that permitted preventive proceedings to be continued against the person who had died after a request of seizure/confiscation against him had already been filed. As long as the assessment of

---

[40] See *Malagnino*, Le misure di prevenzione patrimoniali, p. 58.

[41] Corte costituzionale 721/88; 355/96.

the dangerousness of the individual had been made during the course of prevention proceedings, the proceedings for the imposition of a confiscation measure could legitimately lead to a forfeiture decision.[42]

The 2008 reform supported the latest jurisprudential developments by allowing the possibility to seize/confiscate the assets of a deceased person. The provisions went one step further to even permit the commencement of confiscation proceedings against the assets of a defunct. These latest changes have been confirmed by the present A.M.C. According to Article 18 section 2, once the request for seizure/confiscation has been filed, the prevention proceedings carry on, even in case of the death of the target. In such a case, the proceedings continue against the heirs and successors in title. Furthermore, it is possible to request and to impose a measure against a deceased person, i.e., against universal or particular heirs, but only within five years after the deceased person's death (Article 18 section 3). The reason for the five year time-limit is grounded in the need to assure some degree of certainty for economic operators, hence assuring some forms of protection to commerce and other economic activities.[43]

The Constitutional Court recently dismissed a constitutionality complaint concerning the breach of the right to defence of the parties when proceedings are commenced (or continued) against a deceased person. In the court's view, it goes without saying that a deceased person is not a party to prevention proceedings and hence he does not enjoy the right to defence. The proceedings in such a case are instituted against third parties (the heirs) who are given an adequate possibility to defend themselves.[44] One of the points at issue was that the third party may have little knowledge of the deceased's conduct or lifestyle; hence, they may not be able to produce enough evidence to justify the absence of the substantive requirements of the measure. In essence, the question concerned not just the mere existence of the heirs' right to defence but whether the right could ever be effective. The court dismissed this problem as an ordinary evidentiary problem which parties may ordinarily incur. Whether this is correct or not, it seems that the court overlooked one important element. It is in fact not without significance that, in the different case of the dangerous person being absent or abroad, the proceedings for seizure/confiscation may continue but only with regard to the property for which there is reason to believe that it constitutes the proceeds of illicit activities or their reinvestment.

---

[42] Cass., sez. V, 20 January 2010, De Carlo, rv. 246863.

[43] The proceedings are radically void if they are instituted after the five-year time-limit: Cass., sez. VI, 20 October 2011, Abbate, rv. 251648.

[44] Corte costituzionale, judgement 25 January 2012, n. 21.

XI. Preventive confiscation:
procedural requirements

In confirming the separation of financial preventive measures from personal ones, the A.M.C. remedies the major flaw of the previous statutes, which did not clearly separate the two set of proceedings. Now it is clear that proceedings for the application of a financial measure can be instituted independently from the request of a personal measure (Article 18 section 1). The procedure nonetheless remains very similar to the one provided for the personal measure, with a few adaptations.

As mentioned, the proceedings for the imposition of a financial measure are divided into two phases. The first phase revolves around the adoption of a preventive seizure (i.e., an order to temporarily freeze the property). The second phase involves the application of a confiscation order, with forfeiture of the proprietary rights.

The first phase is a mandatory precondition of the second, in that the confiscation order may be issued only against the property that is already under seizure. Both phases constitute judicial procedures: the seizure and the subsequent confiscation can only be imposed by order of the competent court.

Prevention proceedings can be commenced upon the initiative of different subjects: the chief of police of the province *(questore)*, the district public prosecutor (i.e., the chief of the prosecution office established by the tribunal in the cities where the courts of appeal sit), the director of the anti-mafia brigade *(Direzione Investigativa Antimafia*, DIA).

Before filing their request, the above-mentioned subjects can conduct financial investigations to trace all sources of income. They can investigate the lifestyle, the financial situation, and the properties and belongings of the target. They can also conduct investigations on the economic activities exercised by the targeted individual. In carrying out their investigations, they can avail themselves of police forces specialized in economic matters *(guardia di finanza)* or in criminal investigations *(polizia giudiziaria)*. Article 19 section 2 A.M.C. allows investigations into possession by the target of licenses or authorizations to run a commercial business or carry out entrepreneurial activities, membership in professional associations (e.g., members of the bar), enrolment in public registers (e.g., estate registers, car registers, etc.) and into whether the target received funds from the state, the European Union, or other public entities. Investigations can also be conducted against the target's partner and offspring and whoever cohabited with him in the previous five years. The investigations can extend to all connected individuals, legal entities, companies, and associations when it appears that the target has, in whole or in part, directly or indirectly, property of the said subjects at his/her disposal (Article 19 section 3). Furthermore, the law now provides that the investigating authorities may obtain any type of document from public administration offices and from private and public companies (Article 19, section 4). The tribunal also enjoys the said investigative powers once the proceedings have been commenced (Article 19, section 5).[45]

It is intensely debated whether the request for application of a financial measure is subject to a principle of legality or opportunity.[46] Some argue that the request is mandatory, in that the competent authorities are under an obligation to file it whenever there is sufficient evidence that the person falls within the list of targets and that he possesses, directly or indirectly, suspicious property.[47] Nonetheless, there is no express provision in the A.M.C. that allows one to reach a similar conclusion.[48] Furthermore, while it is normal in Italy to bind the public prosecutor to the legality principle (since the public prosecutor's office is an independent body under Italian law), it would appear awkward to apply the same principle to the initiatives of officers of the executive who naturally enjoy political discretion. It is in fact noticeable that the proceedings can be instituted not only upon the initiative of a judicial authority (the public prosecutor is part of the judiciary in Italy) but also upon that of executive officers. Despite the criticism of some scholars,[49] when enacting the A.M.C., the parliament decided to uphold the power of impulse of said police officers. After all, the judiciary does not have a monopoly on crime prevention and some tasks of crime prevention can legitimately be given to the offices of the executive power.

The request is directed to the tribunal located where the person resides (Article 5 section 4). A panel of three judges has to decide whether the suspicious property is to be seized. In urgent cases, however, when there is a real risk that the property may be disposed of, dispersed, or concealed by the target, the seizure may be ordered upon request of the competent authorities by the president of the tribunal alone within five days of the request. The order must then be validated by the court in a regular hearing within thirty days of the request (Article 22 section 1). Upon request of the competent authorities, the president of the tribunal may also impose

---

[45] According to Cass., sez. II, 23 January 2007, Giordano, rv. 236129, it is entirely legitimate for the tribunal to exercise the investigating powers *motu proprio*.

[46] Strong criticism against the opportunity principle has been expressed by *Filippi*, La confisca di prevenzione, 270, due to the fact that it is based an on uncontrolled discretion on the part of the prosecuting authorities.

[47] *Filippi/Cortesi*, Il codice delle misure di prevenzione, p. 120.

[48] Some scholars have argued their position in favour of a mandatory activation of preventive proceedings on the basis of a provision contained in a different statute (Article 23-*bis*, law 13 September 1982, n. 646), according to which all public prosecutors, when they start investigations for the offences of mafia association or drug trafficking association, are under a duty to make a communication to the competent colleague for the parallel commencement of prevention proceedings (see *Filippi/Cortesi*, Il codice delle misure di prevenzione, p. 120).

[49] *Filippi/Cortesi*, Il codice delle misure di prevenzione, p. 120.

an urgent seizure when preventive proceedings have already been instituted (Article 22 section 2).

The seizure is normally ordered by the tribunal at a hearing. The conditions of the seizure are in principle no different from those required for the confiscation. However, the case law has sometimes highlighted that, since the seizure is a temporary measure whereas the confiscation is a final one, the standard of proof for the former is naturally lower than what is required for the latter.[50]

The second phase opens up once the seizure (i.e., temporary freezing of property) has been imposed, leading to the decision on the confiscation. The decision is taken by the tribunal after a hearing. The hearing can be held in public if the person so requests (Article 7 section 1). The possibility of a public hearing was recently introduced in consequence of several decisions of the European Court of Human Rights (ECtHR) against the Italian state. The ECtHR judgements were eventually followed by a ruling of the Constitutional Court, which quashed the rule prescribing that the hearing be held behind closed doors without exceptions.

The target and all other interested parties receive a notice of the hearing ten days in advance at the latest (Article 7 section 2). At the hearing, the person against whom the measure has been requested is entitled to elicit a counsel of her own choice (Article 7 section 2). If the person does not have a counsel, a duty counsel will be appointed. The presence of the prosecutor and the counsel is mandatory (Article 7 section 4) and the hearing is void if one of the two is absent. The person has a right to be present and to be heard. The hearing is adjourned if the person cannot be present as long as she requests to be heard in person by the tribunal (Article 7 section 5).[51] If the person is detained, she can be heard by a judge before the hearing, unless there is a possibility of establishing a direct connection via videolink (Article 7, section 4, referring to Article 146-*bis* of the code of criminal procedure).

In principle, the person has a right, not a duty, to be present.[52] Nevertheless, if the prosecutor, the police, or the judge wants to hear the person, the president of the tribunal can order that the person be coercively brought before the court (Article 7, section 6).[53]

---

[50] *Maugeri*, La riforma delle sanzioni patrimoniali, pp. 155.

[51] There is no similar provision in case of an impediment of the counsel (see the criticism of *Filippi/Cortesi*, Il codice delle misure di prevenzione, p. 120). The consequence is that, if the attorney is absent, a duty counsel will be specifically appointed by the court for the hearing, so the hearing will not be adjourned (Cass., sez. un., 22 September 2006, Passamani, Diritto Penale e Processo, 2006, 1333).

[52] *Filippi/Cortesi*, Il codice delle misure di prevenzione, p. 146.

[53] The latter provision has been strongly criticized by some scholars in that it would constitute a breach of the right to remain silent: *Filippi/Cortesi*, Il codice delle misure di prevenzione, p. 147.

With regard to evidence, the A.M.C. only provides for the possibility to hear witnesses from a distance via video-link (Article 7, section 8). Nonetheless, Article 7 section 9 makes the rules of the criminal proceedings applicable to prevention proceedings insofar as they are compatible. In particular, it provides that, for all matters not expressly regulated by the A.M.C., the rules concerning the execution of judgements in criminal matters should apply (Article 7 section 9, referring to Article 666 of the code of criminal procedure). Hence, it is possible to introduce witnesses and other types of evidence. Yet the problem remains as to what rules are exactly applicable.

The case law has addressed some evidentiary issues. For instance, a recent decision has ruled that the use in preventive proceedings of elements collected in criminal proceedings is made conditional upon due respect of the rules with respect to citizens' fundamental rights. If the evidence was collected within criminal proceedings in violation of the fundamental rights of the individual, it may not be used in prevention hearings. The decision concerned the interception of communications but, in light of the court's argumentation, it is likely to apply to other kinds of criminal evidence.[54]

Although it is often the case that the evidence presented by the prosecutors comes from criminal trials, other evidence can also be produced, in particular evidence collected in the course of the financial investigations,[55] but also evidence from civil cases or from other administrative authorities. In practice, it is common for the plaintiff to introduce police reports (which are, on the contrary, banned from the criminal trial).

The confiscation order of the tribunal must be issued within a year and a half of the day of execution of the seizure. The term can, however, be prolonged for a period of six months no more than two times, if the proceedings entail complicated investigations or if the amount of property at stake is particularly consistent (Article 24 section 2).

The decision taken by the tribunal can be appealed both on procedural grounds and on the merits before the Court of Appeal. The Court of Appeal decision can be further appealed before the Supreme Court *(Corte di cassazione)* but only on grounds of correct interpretation of the law, not on issues of facts (Article 27).

---

[54] Sez. un., 25 March 2010, Cagnazzo.

[55] See *supra* in this paragraph.

XII. Third parties' rights

Third parties who enjoy property/real estate rights (hence with the exclusion of mere legal obligations related to the object, as is for instance the case of a promissory purchaser)[56] on the seized evidence are invited to participate in the hearing within thirty days of the seizure (Article 23 section 2). They also have a right to a counsel of their own choice and they can produce all the evidence that they deem necessary to their case (Article 23 section 3). If the tribunal decides not to issue a confiscation order, the property is restituted to said third parties.

Third parties are required to prove that they legitimately acquired the property without being aware of its illicit origin. The Supreme Court has clarified that this does not conflict with the Italian Constitution (Articles 3, 24, 47 Italian Constitution, concerning the right to property, the right of defence, and the principle of equal and uniform treatment), namely the imposition on third parties of the burden of proof that they acquired the property in a diligent and proper manner (that is, third parties fulfilled a duty to collect information and ascertained to the best of their knowledge that the property did not have an illicit origin) and hence they reasonably placed faith in the giver.[57]

XIII. An actio in rem?

What is the exact aim of preventive confiscation? Is it intended as a tool for the incapacitation of the dangerous individual or is it instead a means for blocking the dangerousness of certain property? To put it in other terms, is it an *actio in personam* or an *actio in rem*?

Browsing the case law of the Italian Supreme Court and the Italian literature, one can find several statements that prevention proceedings are devised for the removal of criminal assets from the economic circuit.[58]

Before the enactment of the A.M.C., the matter was at the core of much debate concerning confiscation of the assets of a deceased person, giving rise to several controversies. After the 2008 separation of personal and financial measures, all the more so with the entry into force of the A.M.C., several commentators now believe that the issue has been settled. They have welcomed the complete separation of financial preventive measures from personal ones and they have argued that the system of financial measures is now wholly focused on the dangerousness of the

---

[56] With regard to the position of the promissory purchaser, see Cass., sez. I, 3 May 2007, Giaraffa, rv. 236843.

[57] Cass., sez. I, 29 April 2011, MPS Gestione Crediti Banca Spa e Paleari, rv. 250910.

[58] See, for instance, Cass., sez. I, 15 June 2005, Libri, rv. 231755.

property.[59] In their view, it constitutes an *actio in rem* and no longer an *actio in personam*, because the property can be confiscated irrespective of the dangerousness of the individual. It is, however, difficult to completely subscribe to such opinion without making some further remarks. When looking at the substantive conditions provided for by the law, it does not appear entirely proper to categorize the Italian system of preventive confiscation as a pure *actio in rem*, simply directed against the property.

Even after the most recent reforms, the approach remains to a certain degree based on the link with an individual,[60]

– Although financial measures have been separated from personal ones (and so have the proceedings);
– Although dangerousness is presumed in most cases and suspicion of commission of certain offences is sufficient.

It is not just the link of the property with the crime that matters; there must be also a link of the property with a suspect or dangerous person. In other words, even if clear evidence were available that a crime had been committed and that certain property were derived from it, it would still be necessary to identify a suspect at least roughly. The only case in which there is no need to establish a link with a person is the one provided for in Article 34,[61] which appears to be a true case of *actio in rem*.

All in all, the system seems to be a hybrid that leans very much towards an *actio in rem*, albeit still requiring a connection with an individual. On the one hand, it is possible to forfeit assets even when a direct causal link with the commission of the crime has not been clearly established.[62] On the other hand, the property cannot be forfeited on the sole basis of a causal connection with a crime (save for the case of Article 34) but in connection with an individual. Whether or not one believes that the assets are confiscated in that they are deemed inherently dangerous, it is that the assets are identified and apprehended only in connection with a person deemed (or presumed) dangerous.

It would, however, also be wrong to categorize the system as one against dangerous individuals. In fact, it is no longer necessary that: a) the dangerousness of the person is a present one; b) a link exists between the assets and the dangerousness of the person.[63]

---

[59] *Balsamo*, Le misure di prevenzione patrimoniali, p. 38; *Fiorentin*, Serve il coordinamento, XXIV.

[60] *Maugeri*, La riforma delle sanzioni patrimoniali, pp. 154 ff.

[61] See *supra*, para. VIII.

[62] The case law on this point is rather firm: Cass., sez. VI, 27 May 2003, Lo Iacono e a., rv. 226655.

[63] Cass., sez. I, 11 February 2014, Mondini, rv. 260104 (the Court expressly held that "with regard to a thing *(res)*, particularly for things that are dangerous because of their connection with the individual owner, it is meaningless to require that dangerousness be

It seems, in other words, that the dangerousness of the individual who falls under the list of targets is no more than a way of identifying assets that are deemed to be dangerous. In sum, it is a system in which the dangerousness of an item is identified with regard to the link with the (past, present, presumed) dangerousness of the individual.

XIV. Interconnections with criminal proceedings

Does preventive confiscation require the commission of a crime? Not necessarily, it depends on the category of individuals who are the target of the preventative action. This is the case when the target belongs to one of the categories of suspects of a crime. In such cases, preventive proceedings can run parallel to criminal proceedings and the two sets of proceedings can intertwine.

This is hardly surprising. When looking at the list of targets, it is evident that the subjective conditions for a preventative measure are often equivalent to those for opening a criminal investigation. A person suspected of being a mafia associate can face both a criminal charge and a request for the application of preventive proceedings and this is what in fact often happens in practice.

Nonetheless, the two proceedings formally run independently and follow their own rules (Article 29 A.M.C.). Some interconnections are inevitable though. For instance, nothing prevents the introduction and use in preventive proceedings of evidence acquired in criminal proceedings (while the opposite would not normally be permitted, save for evidence which qualifies as documents).

An issue that has arisen in the case law concerns the consequences within preventive proceedings of an acquittal in a parallel criminal trial. The courts move from the premise that preventive proceedings are wholly independent from criminal trials and they subsequently hold that the acquittal of the target in a parallel criminal trial does not automatically exclude the possibility to issue a confiscation order.[64] Hence, a suspect can be acquitted in criminal trials for mafia associations (or other crimes) and then suffer preventive confiscation. And the courts do not find it necessary to evaluate whether this outcome is in compliance with the presumption of innocence in light of some of the ECtHR's rulings.[65]

---

present (immediate), because the staticity of goods does not allow to identify changes in terms of the possibility of danger, at least until the property is not seized or confiscated").

[64] See Cass., sez. V, 17 January 2006, Pangallo, rv. 233892; Cass., sez. V, 17 November 2011, Serafini e a., rv. 251719; Cass., sez. II, 9 May 2000, Coraglia, rv. 217801 makes clear that it is possible to use against the defendant the elements collected in a criminal trial ended with an acquittal of the same defendant.

[65] ECtHR, *Geerings v. The Netherlands*, 1 March 2007, appl. no. 30810/03, according to which a previous acquittal does not justify any subsequent orders of confiscation of assets.

Another possible overlap between preventive proceedings and criminal proceedings concerns seizure orders issued against the same property. It can happen that the property seized during a criminal investigation is later seized/confiscated in preventive proceedings or vice versa. The traditional rule gave preference to the order issued in the criminal proceedings. The A.M.C. has now enacted an opposite rule, according to which the order passed in preventive proceedings is to prevail (Article 30). The reason for this is that the law on preventive confiscation provides for a more efficient management of the forfeited assets (which are devolved to an administrative agency).[66]

XV. Standard of proof

To what extent must each of the conditions be proven by the prosecutor? And to what extent can the prosecutors rely on presumptions to meet the burden of proof? What degree of suspicion is necessary to impose a measure?

The major difference between preventive proceedings and criminal proceedings concerns the standard of proof. Even in those cases in which the preventive measure requires the finding of a crime, the assessment need not be as rigorous as it would be in a criminal trial. Financial preventive measures were introduced to circumvent the fact-finding difficulties encountered within the system of criminal justice due to the rules on evidence applicable in criminal trials.

It is clear that the standard of proof in preventive proceedings is lower than that employed in criminal trials. Nevertheless, the exact "shape" of the standard of proof remains partly obscure.

What does it mean that a person is a suspect of certain crimes? The courts have made clear as early as 1969 that a person can be considered a suspect for the application of a personal preventive measure only on the basis of evidence that offers a reasonable and objective basis to argue that the individual committed the crime.[67] In other words, a mere subjective suspicion, based on weak evidence, would not suffice.

It is hence clear that the assessment must be grounded on objective facts based on evidence. Beyond this statement, however, the case law is not of much help in understanding how high the standard of proof should be. The courts hardly use

---

[66] Agenzia Nazionale per l'amministrazione e la destinazione dei beni sequestrati e confiscati alla criminalità organizzata (website: http://www.benisequestraticonfiscati.it/Joomla /index.php).

[67] Cass., sez. I, 29 October 1969, Tempra, Cassazione penale, 1971, 1419. See *Scaglione*, Le misure di prevenzione patrimoniali.

clear and direct words. They often hide under nebulous expressions, such as the autonomy of prevention proceedings from criminal proceedings, and make it difficult for the reader to clearly understand the position taken. To say that the assessment made in prevention proceedings is different and autonomous from the one carried out in criminal proceedings does not give clear guidance as to the standard of proof to be employed. The only certain conclusion is that the finding of a crime, and the individual's involvement in it, need not be proven beyond reasonable doubt.

Often, the courts state that there must be enough evidence that the individual committed a crime or that the commission of a crime must be ascertained with some degree of probability, though certainty is not required and not even high probability.[68] They do not, however, go much further than this. They never talk of a balance of probabilities; hence, it remains unclear what is intended when they say that the commission of the crime must be probable. Furthermore, it is not clear whether the assessment of a likely probability must concern all the elements of the offence. In practice, the courts hardly go so far in their reasoning as to make a detailed assessment of each and every element of the crime and sometimes even the allegations are slightly nebulous.[69]

There is a contrast in the case law as to the rigorousness required in the evaluation of the evidence. Some courts hold that the circumstantial evidence available must be as strong, clear, and precise as it is needed for a conviction in a criminal trial by Article 192 of the code of criminal procedure.[70] The majoritarian approach however favours a looser approach,[71] but it is difficult to understand the exact degree of license allowed.

The courts repeat that there is not always a need to establish a direct link between the assets and the alleged crime,[72] since it is also possible to forfeit property

---

[68] Cass., sez. VI, 19 June 1997, Di Giovanni, rv. 208310; Cass., sez. I, 20 February 1992, Barbaro, rv. 189334. *Balsamo*, La sfera soggettiva, p. 65.

[69] Cass., sez. VI, 19 June 1997, Di Giovanni, rv. 208310 states that since the standard of proof consists in a degree of likely probability, the allegations need not be extremely detailed.

[70] Cass., sez. II, 9 February 2011, Battaglia e a., rv. 249364.

[71] Cass., sez. I, 21 October 1999, P.g. in c. Castelluccia, rv. 215117 (excluding, in particular, the need to apply Article 192 section 3 of the code of criminal procedure concerning corroboration of an accomplice's statements).

[72] See, for instance, Cass., sez. I, 20 November 1998, Iorio, rv. 212444 e; Cass., sez. VI, 22 March 1999, Riela, rv. 214507. According to both these rulings, it is irrelevant that the confiscation order does not give reasons for the link between the property and the crime of which the individual is suspected (in both cases, mafia association), as long as it is clear that the property derives from any illegal activities of the target. In other terms, the courts can forfeit assets of a mafia suspect, even if they are not in connection with mafia crimes but with other criminal activities instead. For another application, Cass., sez. VI, 27 May 2003, Lo Iacono e a., rv. 226655, which forfeited assets of the targets that were the fruits of tax evasion.

that is disproportionate with the individual's income and whose provenance the individual cannot justify.[73] Nonetheless, they disagree with regard to the scope of forfeitable property. The problem revolves around assets which are found to be disproportionate to the individual income and for which the person cannot offer evidence of a licit acquisition. Some courts believe that the property to be forfeited is only the property acquired in temporal connection with the involvement of the individual in the crime[74] and that assets acquired prior to engagement in the criminal network cannot be forfeited. The majoritarian approach allows instead the confiscation of all the disproportionate assets, even if they were acquired before involvement in the criminal association.[75]

XVI. Scholarly criticism – Burden of proof and presumptions

Scholars have raised strong criticism against preventive measures and proceedings. However, while there is unanimous disapproval of personal preventive measures, the positions differ when it comes to financial preventive measures.

The majority believe that financial measures are fully legitimate in that they encroach upon the right to property, which right is protected in the Constitution and the European Convention of Human Rights (ECHR) less strongly than personal liberty.[76] Other scholars hold instead that even financial preventive measures raise concerns of compatibility with human rights protection, both in their substantive requirements and procedural profiles.

With regard to substantive requirements, scholars criticize that several of the listed categories of individual targets are defined in too vague a manner.[77] Even greater concerns are directed toward the procedure, in that it breaches the right to the defendants and entails a reversal of the burden of proof.[78] The basic assumption for this opinion is that prevention proceedings are of a criminal nature; hence, they

---

[73] Cass., sez. II, 23 June 2004, Palumbo e a., rv. 229725.

[74] Cass., sez. V, 23 March 2007, Cangialosi e a., rv. 236920. In slightly milder terms, Cass., sez. I, 11 February 2014, Mondini, rv. 260104 (the Court held that, although the assets need not have been acquired in direct connection with the period of commission of the crime, their acquisition also cannot be completely detached from the involvement in the mafia group).

[75] Cass., sez. VI, 15 January 2010, Quartararo, rv. 246084; Cass., 20 October 2010, Stagno e a., rv. 249012; Cass., sez. V, 21 April 2011, Cuozzo, rv. 250917.

[76] See, for instance, *Fiandaca/Musco*, Diritto penale, p. 845; *Mantovani*, Diritto penale, p. 911.

[77] *Filippi*, La confisca di prevenzione, 270.

[78] *Filippi/Cortesi*, Il codice delle misure di prevenzione, *passim*.

should entail a system of rules and safeguards similar to those normally applicable in criminal proceedings.[79]

Who is to prove that the property was lawfully/unlawfully acquired? The issue is a very delicate one, which directly intertwines with the precise determination of the object of proof in preventive proceedings. Those who lament a reversal of the burden of proof argue that the law places upon the defendant the burden to prove that the property has been lawfully acquired.[80] The courts and other scholars have excluded that the law codifies a reversal of the burden of proof.[81] The burden for the defendant, so they argue, arises only when the prosecution has proven that the property is disproportionate to the individual's lifestyle or that it has an illicit origin. Hence, the burden of proof is placed on the shoulders of the prosecution/plaintiff, in line with the traditional principle of the presumption of innocence. It is only when the prosecution can successfully prove the aforementioned requirements that the targeted individual is required to offer evidence to the contrary.[82]

The latter position is formally correct. In fact, it is first for the prosecutor (or other competent authority) to prove: 1) that the person falls within the list of targets; 2) that the person directly or indirectly controls property that is suspicious, either because i) it is entirely discrepant with the person's lifestyle; ii) it is of illicit origin. Only when all these elements have been successfully proved against the defendant, can he then rebut by showing the lawfulness of the purchase or acquisition of the assets.

Nonetheless, this formal approach does not offer a conclusive answer to the problem. From a substantive point of view, in fact, the legal issue at hand could be rephrased in the following terms: how difficult is it for the plaintiff authority to successfully fulfil its burden of proof? Is it not the case that the burden of proof for the applicant authority is so light that the defendants are always forced to give evidence of a licit acquisition of the assets? To put it in other words: it might be true that the prosecutor (or the other competent authority) has first to formally prove that certain conditions have been met but, if those conditions are very general or based on presumptions, the prosecutor can easily meet his burden of proof, and the defendants are in essence always and inevitably required to offer evidence of the contrary. The focus should hence be placed on the effective evidentiary effort required of the plaintiff prosecutor, which is, however, difficult to measure in light of the nebulous statements concerning the applicable standard of proof. The impres-

---

[79] *Filippi/Cortesi*, Il codice delle misure di prevenzione, pp. 4, 12.

[80] *Filippi/Cortesi*, Il codice delle misure di prevenzione, p. 156.

[81] Cass., sez. I, 26 novembre 1998, Bommarito, rv. 212103; Cass., sez. V, 17 February 1998, Petruzzella G. e a., Cassazione penale, 1998, 1597 (rv. 210809). Cass., sez. V, 12 December 2007, Campione, rv. 238871.

[82] *Maugeri*, La riforma delle sanzioni patrimoniali, pp. 157. *Contraffatto*, L'oggetto della confisca, p. 90.

sion is that the burden of proof for the plaintiff is sufficiently high if he has to prove that the property is linked with the crime. The plaintiff's effort has instead been simplified by the law with regard to the presumption of illicit origin of all assets incompatible with the individual income and whose provenance the individual cannot justify. Such a conclusion could reinforce the doubts as to the compatibility of Italian preventive forfeiture with fundamental rights, but only if it can be safely said that preventive proceedings are of a criminal nature.

XVII. The nature of preventive confiscation

To properly address the issues of fundamental rights, it is hence necessary to establish whether financial preventive measures can be considered a criminal penalty.

Within the Italian system, as almost everywhere in Europe, criminal penalties are defined according to a purely formal parameter: whether they are categorized as such by the law. From this perspective, preventive measures, whether personal or financial, are clearly not criminal penalties. Can they nonetheless be considered criminal penalties from a substantive point of view, despite the label given by the legislator? In other words, what is the real nature of confiscation? The answer to these questions is not easy and is made more complicated by the fact that the same nature of criminal confiscation is unclear.

The Italian Supreme Court addressed the issue of the nature of preventive confiscation on several occasions. It affirmed that preventive confiscation does not constitute a preventive measure (in that it is not intended to prevent the commission of further crimes by dangerous individuals); neither is it a criminal penalty. It rather constitutes an administrative penalty, which is equivalent to criminal confiscation in terms of effects.[83]

There is always a fine line between administrative punitive law and criminal law. There is no doubt that, if confiscation orders are formally labelled as criminal measures, they fall under the legal notion of criminal punishment,[84] although they may not constitute a criminal charge separate from the trial in which the defendant was found liable.[85] The same is not true, however, when the national qualification

---

[83] Corte di cassazione, Sezioni unite, 3 July 1996, Simonelli and others, Cassazione penale, 1996, 3609. See also Cass., sez. V, 20 January 2010, De Carlo, rv. 246863; Cass., sez. I, 15 June 2005, Libri, rv. 231755.

[84] *Welch v. U.K.*, 9 February 1995, appl. no. 17440/90, § 27. For another application of Article 7 to a case of criminal confiscation, ECtHR, *Sud Fondi S.r.l. et autres c. Italie*, 20 January 2009, appl. no. 75909/01, §§ 111–118 (Italy was convicted for the lack of clarity and foreseeability of the law). See also ECtHR, *Varvara v. Italy*, 29 October 2013, appl. no. 17475/09.

[85] ECtHR, *Phillips v. U.K.*, 5 July 2001, appl. no. 41087/98, §§ 34–35.

is administrative. When looking at the ECtHR case law, the Strasbourg Court has held on several occasions that the formal qualification of a punishment as criminal or administrative is not binding and that the assessment of the criminal or administrative nature of a charge must also be made in light of the nature of the offence and the nature and degree of severity of the penalty.[86] These parameters are indeed slightly vague. Nonetheless, they can offer inspiration to solve our problem. First, there are cases where a person is deprived of personal liberty, which naturally fall under the notion of criminal punishment in light of the severity of the measure, regardless of any other considerations. With regard to measures restricting property rights, a distinction should instead be made based on whether the measure is applied in relation to conduct of the individual or not. If a financial measure is taken not on the basis of the conduct of an individual and with a view to punishing it, but only for removing from the economic circuit the illegal gains, irrespective of a person's liability, it seems appropriate to qualify it as an administrative measure. When seizure/confiscation/forfeiture is solely aimed at blocking illegal profits, it appears to have no punishing features and simply amounts to a measure aimed at protecting the legal economy.[87]

In sum, if the measure is intended to forfeit property derived from the crime without taking into account any conduct or behaviour on the part of the individual, it seems that the measure can truly be qualified as "preventive" and "administrative." In other words, it appears sensible to qualify confiscation as an administrative measure when the forfeiture order is solely based on the finding of a causal link between the property and the crime, as is the case of the civil forfeiture mechanisms of common law.[88]

The Italian law does not always require the finding of a causal link between the property and the crime. It is in fact possible to forfeit the assets of a suspect that are

---

[86] ECtHR, *Öztürk v. Germany*, 21 February 1984, appl. no. 8544/79, § 50; ECtHR, *Bendenoun v. France*, 24 February 1994, appl. no. 12547/86, § 47. With specific regard to the sphere of military service, ECtHR, *Engels and others v. The Netherlands*, § 82. *Trechsel*, Human Rights, pp. 16 ff.

[87] ECtHR, *Butler v. U.K.*, 27 June 2002, appl. no. 41661/98. Dealing with a case of English civil forfeiture, the court held that "the forfeiture order was a preventive measure and cannot be compared to a criminal sanction, since it was designed to take out of circulation money which was presumed to bound up with the international trade in illicit drugs." For a slightly different approach, see ECtHR, *Dassa Foundation and others v. Liechtenstein*, 23 December 2004, appl. no. 696/05, which equates the Liechtenstein civil forfeiture orders to an action against unjustified enrichment. However, such a comparison seems inappropriate because unjustified enrichment is a civil restitution measure, which is based on some loss of earnings of another private individual. It seems awkward to view civil forfeiture orders as a form of restitution of the unjust enrichment to the state, unless moving away from the premise that the state is the natural owner of all properties not lawfully belonging to any individuals.

[88] For an overview of cases of civil-asset forfeiture, see *Rui*, The Civil Asset Forfeiture Approach, 164.

incompatible with his individual income and whose provenance the individual cannot justify. The situation in which property can be forfeited without any direct connection with a crime but simply because it is in the possession of an individual who is a suspect (or, in other cases, is presumed to be dangerous) seems to lean more toward a form of punishment of the individual than a measure to prevent that illegal profits negatively impact on society and its economy. And since the conduct can, in most cases, also be punished as a criminal offence, and since the degree of severity of preventive confiscation is the same for criminal confiscation, it would seem inevitable to qualify this case of confiscation as a form of criminal punishment.

XVIII. The tolerant approach of the ECtHR

The approach of the ECtHR has been tolerant with regard to the Italian system of "non-criminal" confiscation. In assessing whether financial preventive measures are in compliance with fundamental rights, the Strasbourg Court has mostly answered in the affirmative.

The issue can be approached from a twofold perspective. First, whether financial preventive measures affect some fundamental rights protected by the Convention and, if the answer is positive, whether the safeguards provided for by the Convention and its protocols are respected. Second, the question is whether such measures are considered by the ECtHR to fall within the notion of "criminal matters" (criminal charge), with the consequent obligation to respect the stricter rules provided for by Article 6-2 and 6-3.

With regard to the first perspective, financial measures entail a restriction of the right to property granted by Article 1 Protocol 1 of the Convention. However, the safeguards provided for by the protocol are rather weak when compared to the right to personal liberty protected by Article 5 ECHR. In fact, the Convention permits to deprive people of their possessions when it is "in the public interest and subject to the conditions provided for by law and by the general principles of international law." Section 2 furthermore states that: "The preceding provisions shall not, however, in any way impair the right of a State to enforce such laws as it deems necessary to control the use of property in accordance with the general interest or to secure the payment of taxes or other contributions or penalties." Hence, the states can impose measures that restrict private property as long as they can justify them on grounds of public interest and do so by providing for a clear legal basis.[89]

---

[89] *Trechsel*, Human Rights, p. 561.

With regard to respect for the right to property, the ECtHR has so far dismissed all complaints that have lamented a breach of the right to the peaceful enjoyment of private property. The court has repeatedly held that the freezing/confiscation of property interferes with the right to private property, but it does so in a manner consistent with the safeguards of the Convention, since the measure is established by the law and pursues a general public interest.[90] Furthermore, the restriction is deemed to be proportionate in light of the crime-prevention policy pursued by the measures.

In *Raimondo*,[91] the ECtHR observed with regard to preventative seizure (under the regime of section 2 *ter* of the 1965 Act) that it "is clearly a provisional measure intended to ensure that property which appears to be the fruit of unlawful activities carried out to the detriment of the community can subsequently be confiscated if necessary. The measure as such was therefore justified by the general interest and, in view of the extremely dangerous economic power of an 'organisation' like the Mafia, it cannot be said that taking it at this stage of the proceedings was disproportionate to the aim pursued."[92] With regard to confiscation, the court stated that "the Court is fully aware of the difficulties encountered by the Italian State in the fight against the Mafia. As a result of its unlawful activities, in particular drug-trafficking, and its international connections, this 'organisation' has an enormous turnover that is subsequently invested, *inter alia*, in the real property sector. Confiscation, which is designed to block these movements of suspect capital, is an effective and necessary weapon in the combat against this cancer. It therefore appears proportionate to the aim pursued, all the more so because it in fact entails no additional restriction in relation to seizure."[93]

In *Arcuri*, the court expressly maintained that "even though the measure in question led to a deprivation of property, this amounted to control of the use of property within the meaning of the second paragraph of Article 1 of Protocol No. 1, which gives the State the right to adopt 'such laws as it deems necessary to control the use of property in accordance with the general interest'."[94] Several subsequent decisions have upheld this conclusion.[95]

---

[90] ECtHR, *Riela et autres c. Italie*, 4 Septembre 2001, appl. no. 52439/99.

[91] ECtHR, *Raimondo v. Italy*, 22 February 1994, appl. no. 12954/87.

[92] *Ibid.*, § 27.

[93] *Ibid.*, § 30.

[94] ECtHR, *Arcuri c. Italie*, 5 July 2001, appl. no. 52024/99 (inadmissibility decision)

[95] ECtHR, *Arcuri c. Italie*, 5 July 2001, appl. no. 52024/99 (inadmissibility decision). ECtHR, *Pozzi c. Italie*, 26 July 2011, appl. no. 55743/08, §§ 27–30; ECtHR, *Capitani et Campanella c. Italie*, 17 May 2011, appl. no. 24920/07, §§ 33–35; ECtHR, *Leone c. Italie*, 2 February 2010, appl. no. 30506/07, § 36–37; ECtHR, *Paleari c. Italie*, 26 July 2011, appl. no. 55772/08, § 37.

In a similar vein, the Italian Supreme Court has ruled out any contrasts of financial preventative measures with the provisions of the Convention.[96] It has also held
that the proprietary rights of third parties are not unduly restrained by preventive
confiscation in that *bona fide* third parties are allowed to intervene in the proceedings and given ample possibility to offer evidence to prove their blameless position
and their unawareness of the connection of the property with criminal activities or
individuals.

The compatibility of the system of preventive measures with fundamental rights
should then be tested from the different perspective of Articles 6 and 7 of the
ECHR. On several occasions, the Italian system of financial preventive measures
has been challenged before the ECtHR on the grounds of a violation of Article 6.
Save for what concerns the publicity of the hearing, the European Court did not
find the Italian system to be incompatible with the safeguards provided for by the
European Convention and its protocols.

In particular, the court has repeatedly held that Italian preventative sei-
zure/confiscation cannot be considered a criminal penalty. The issue was directly
addressed in *Arcuri*, in which the court had observed that preventive measures "do
not involve a finding of guilt, but are designed to prevent the commission of offences;" hence, they are "not comparable to a criminal sanction" and "the proceedings under these provisions did not involve the determination ... of a criminal
charge."[97]

The same conclusion was upheld in following decisions. In *Riela*, the court explicitly held that

> "les mesures de prévention prévues par les lois italiennes de 1956, 1965 et 1982
> n'impliquent pas un jugement de culpabilité, mais visent à empêcher l'accomplissement
> d'actes criminels. En outre, leur imposition n'est pas tributaire du prononcé préalable
> d'une condamnation pour une infraction pénale. Dès lors, elles ne sauraient se comparer
> à une peine."[98]

It is for these reasons that the Strasbourg Court has consistently concluded that
Article 6 cannot apply to preventive proceedings in the part concerning criminal
proceedings but only in the part related to all judicial (including civil and administrative) proceedings. And, in fact, when the applicants have expressly raised the
issue of compatibility with Article 6-2 concerning the presumption of innocence,
the court has not directly addressed the complaint, implicitly rejecting the approach
that the proceedings could be considered of criminal nature.[99]

---

[96] Cass., sez. V, 17 November 2011, Casucci e a., rv. 251717.

[97] ECtHR, *Arcuri c. Italie*, 5 July 2001.

[98] ECtHR, *Riela et autres c. Italie*. In the same words, ECtHR, *Capitani et Campanella
c. Italie*, § 37.

[99] ECtHR, *Pozzi c. Italie*, §§ 31–36; ECtHR, *Paleari c. Italie*, §§ 33–38.

In *Licata*,[100] the applicant brought a direct challenge against the procedure and the presumptions it entails. The court declared the complaint inadmissible. It observed that the Italian prevention proceedings involve an adversarial procedure before three different courts (Tribunal, Court of Appeal, and Supreme Court), where the individual has the right to intervene and the possibility to raise objections and produce evidence to refute the allegations against him. The judges cannot base the decision on a mere suspicion, but they have to take a decision on the basis of objective facts that are grounded on evidence.[101] Hence, the right of the interested party to defend herself are sufficiently safeguarded.

So far, the court has convicted the Italian state only for what concerns the violation of Art. 6-1 with regard to the safeguard of a public hearing.[102] Until very recently, the statutes in fact did not provide for the possibility to hold a public hearing, and therein the ECtHR found a violation of the safeguard provided for by Article 6-1. Publicity is a guarantee that should, in principle, apply to all judicial litigations. Only limited exceptions can be tolerated. Despite the fact that prevention proceedings deal with very technical issues, the court did not find it a sufficient justification to depart from the principle of publicity. It is noticeable, however, that the court did not consider prevention proceedings to fall within the legal notion of "criminal matters." It stressed that Art. 6-1 contains a set of safeguards concerning all judicial procedures.[103]

XIX. Concluding remarks

Originally confiscation in Italy occupied a marginal role within the array of legal instruments to fight crime, the emphasis being placed on the instruments which entailed a deprivation of the freedom of movement and personal liberty. When the Italian parliament recognized that crime and criminals needed to be tackled on the grounds of their economic interests, forfeiture assumed a more central role and the statutes started multiplying the cases of confiscation. New cases of criminal confiscation were introduced, including value confiscation and extended confiscation.

---

[100] ECtHR, *Licata v. Italy*, 27 May 2004, appl. no. 32221/02 (inadmissibility decision).

[101] *Ibid.* The Court expressly held that "les juridictions italiennes ne pouvaient pas se fonder sur de simples soupçons. Elles devaient établir et évaluer objectivement les faits exposés par le parties et rien dans le dossier ne permet de croire qu'elles aient apprécié de façon arbitraire les éléments qui leur ont été soumis." See also ECtHR, *Pozzi c. Italie*, § 35.

[102] See also *supra*, para. XI.

[103] ECtHR, *Bocellari et Rizza c. Italie*, 13 November 2007, appl. no. 399/02; ECtHR, *Perre et autres c. Italie*, 8 July 2008, appl. no. 1905/05; ECtHR, *Leone c. Italie*, 2 February 2010, appl. no. 30506/07; ECtHR, *Pozzi c. Italie*; ECtHR, *Capitani et Campanella c. Italie*, 17 May 2011, appl. no. 24920/07; ECtHR, *Paleari c. Italie*, 26 July 2011, appl. no. 55772/08.

With a view to making confiscation an even more powerful and effective instrument, particularly against mafia criminals, the parliament decided to create a form of asset forfeiture detached from the criminal justice system, hence doing away with some of the strong safeguards typical of criminal justice. In order to do so, the parliament emphasized the preventative aim at the origin of criminal confiscation. Since prevention is a function that does not belong exclusively to the machinery of criminal justice, a form of preventive confiscation could be created within the realm of administrative law.

Nevertheless, it remains unclear whether the preventative nature of non-criminal confiscation is aimed at removing the assets derived from crime or at incapacitating certain individuals. The difference is not irrelevant. It is easier to defend an administrative (non-criminal) system of confiscation if the focus is more on the apprehension of illicit gains than on the incapacitation of an individual; but the consequence should then be that the requirements for forfeiture ought to be construed only around the derivation of property from unlawful behaviour, regardless of any subjective link to a suspect. Hence, the non-criminal forfeiture system should simply revolve around the assessment of a causal link between the property and an offence. The Italian law has taken steps to move in the direction of creating an *actio in rem* but it has not quite gotten there yet. The law still identifies the property to be forfeited in its connection with a suspect or a dangerous individual (whether or not presently dangerous) and not for its connection with a wrongful action. The overall approach remains unclear and it inevitably raises doubts as to whether it is entirely compatible with fundamental rights. If the forfeiture of property is justified by the fact that it belongs to a certain individual, irrespective of a direct connection with an ascertained crime, Italian preventive confiscation could easily be qualified as a form of punishment with all the relevant consequences in terms of burden of proof and due process safeguards (Article 6 ECHR). The ECtHR has so far dismissed all human rights concerns and it has ruled out the criminal nature of preventive confiscation. Nevertheless, it seems that the ECtHR has done so mostly because it acknowledges the peculiarity of the Italian situation with regard to the pressing need to fight organized crime. It is indeed true that the Italian situation is almost unique within the European scenario. However, this does not *per se* justify a departure from the protection of fundamental rights.

Albeit having been recently reformed, Italian administrative preventive confiscation still requires some adjustments. If transformed into a pure form of *actio in rem*, purely aimed at forfeiting properties causally linked with serious forms of crime, preventive confiscation can remain a legitimate and powerful tool by which to tackle the mafia, without raising concerns about the protection of the fundamental rights of the individuals.

Bibliography

Alessandri, Alberto, Confisca. Digesto delle discipline penalistiche. Torino 1989, pp. 39 ff.

Arlacchi, Pino, La mafia imprenditrice. Dalla Calabria al centro dell'inferno. Milano 2007.

Balsamo, Antonio, Le misure di prevenzione patrimoniali come modello di "processo al patrimonio". Il rapporto con le misure di prevenzione personali. In: Antonio Balsamo (ed.), Le misure patrimoniali contro la criminalità organizzata. Milano 2010, pp. 33–57.

– La sfera soggettiva di applicazione delle misure patrimoniali. In: Antonio Balsamo (ed.), Le misure patrimoniali contro la criminalità organizzata. Milano 2010, pp. 59–85.

Blackstone, William, Commentaries on the laws of England, vol. IV. Oxford 1769.

Centorrino, Giovanni, Mafia ed economie locali: un approfondimento dei tradizionali modelli di analisi. In: Giovanni Fiandaca/Salvatore Costantino, La mafia, le mafie. Bari/Roma 1994, pp. 251 ff.

Contraffatto, Vania, L'oggetto della confisca di prevenzione e lo standard della prova. In: Antonio Balsamo (ed.), Le misure patrimoniali contro la criminalità organizzata. Milano 2010, pp. 87–139.

Dickson, David J., Towards more effective asset recovery in Member States – the UK example. ERA Forum 10 (2009), 435–451.

Fiandaca, Giovanni, Criminalità organizzata e controllo penale. Indice penale 1991, 1 ff.

– Misure di prevenzione (profili sostanziali). Digesto discipline penalistiche, VIII. Torino 1994, 108 ff.

Fiandaca, Giovanni/Musco, Enzo, Diritto penale. Parte generale. 6. ed. Bologna 2010.

Filippi, Leonardo, La confisca di prevenzione: un'anomalia tutta italiana. Diritto penale e processo 3 (2005), 270 ff.

Filippi, Leonardo/Cortesi, Maria Francesca, Il codice delle misure di prevenzione. Torino 2011.

Fiorentin, Fabio, Serve il coordinamento del procuratore distrettuale. Guida al diritto 42 (2011), XXIV.

Fondaroli, Désirée, Le ipotesi speciali di confisca nel sistema penale. Ablazione patrimoniale, criminalità economica, responsabilità delle persone fisiche e giuridiche. Bologna 2007.

Gallo, Ettore, Misure di prevenzione. Enciclopedia giuridica Treccani, XX, 1996, 1.

Guarneri, Giuseppe, Confisca (diritto penale), Novissimo Digesto Italiano, IV. Torino 1968, 40.

Guzzini, Stefano, The "Long Night of the First Republic": years of clientelistic implosion in Italy. Review of International Political Economy 2(1) (1995), 27–61.

Kilchling, Michael, Tracing, Seizing and Confiscating Proceeds from Corruption (and other Illegal Conduct) Within or Outside the Criminal Justice System. European Journal of Crime, Criminal Law and Criminal Justice (2001), 264–280.

Levi, Michael, Taking the Profit Out of Crime: The UK Experience. European Journal of Crime, Criminal Law and Criminal Justice (1997), 228–239.

Malagnino, Mario Erminio, Le misure di prevenzione patrimoniali. In: Mario Erminio Malagnino (ed.), Il codice antimafia. Torino 2011, 49–80.

– (ed.), Il codice antimafia. Torino 2011.

Manna, Adelmo, Measures of Prevention: Dogmatic-Exegetic Aspects and Prospects of Reform. European Journal of Crime, Criminal Law and Criminal Justice, Vol. 5/3 (1997), 248–255.

Mantovani, Ferrando, Diritto penale. Padova 2001.

Mattina, Cesare, The transformations of the contemporary mafia: a perspective review of the literature on mafia phenomena in the context of the internalization of the capitalist economy. International Social Science Journal 62 (2012), 230 ff.

Maugeri, Anna Maria, I modelli di sanzione patrimoniale nel diritto comparato. In: Anna Maria Maugeri (ed.), Le sanzioni patrimoniali come moderno strumento di lotta contro il crimine: reciproco riconoscimento e prospettive di armonizzazione. Milano 2008, 7 ff.

– La riforma delle sanzioni patrimoniali: verso un'actio in rem?. In: Oliviero Mazza/ Francesco Viganò (eds.), Misure urgenti in materia di sicurezza pubblica. Torino 2008, 135 ff.

– Le sanzioni patrimoniali come moderno strumento di lotta contro il crimine organizzato, http://www.lex.unict.it/eventi/s200107/maugeri.pdf.

– Le moderne sanzioni patrimoniali tra funzionalità e garantismo. Milano 2001.

Menditto, Francesco, Le misure di prevenzione personali e patrimoniali. Milano 2012.

Nelen, Hans, Hit them where it hurts the most. Crime, Law and Social Change 41 (2004), 517–534.

Nicosia, Emanuele, La confisca. Le confische. Torino 2012.

Panzarasa, Marco, Confisca senza condanna? Uno studio de lege lata e de iure condendo sui presupposti processuali dell'applicazione della confisca. Rivista italiana di diritto e procedura penale (2010), 1672 ff.

Paoli, Letizia, The paradoxes of organized crime. Crime, Law and Social Change (2002), 37, 51–97.

Rui, Jon Petter, The Civil Asset Forfeiture Approach to Organised Crime: Exploring the possibilities for an EU model. eucrim (2011), 164.

Scaglione, Antonio, Le misure di prevenzione patrimoniali: problemi attuali e prospettive di riforma. In: La magistratura (2007), 193 ff. (also available at http://www.associazione magistrati.it/media/54026/17%20-%20Scaglione.pdf).

Trapani, Mario, Confisca. Enciclopedia Giuridica Treccani, XXXX, 1988, 1.

Trechsel, Stephan, Human Rights in Criminal Proceedings. New York 2006.

Turone, Giuliano, Il delitto di associazione mafiosa. Milano 2008.

Vassalli, Giuliano, La confisca dei beni. Storia recente e profili dommatici. Padova 1951.

List of Abbreviations

A.M.C.	Anti-mafia code
appl.	application
Cass.	Corte di cassazione (Italian Court of Cassation)
DIA	Direzione Investigativa Antimafia
ECHR	European Convention of Human Rights
ECtHT	European Court of Human Rights
ICT	Information and Communication Technology
rv.	Numero di rivista (Official number of the legal principle of the judgement in the official database of the Italian Supreme Court of Cassation)
sez. un.	Sezioni unite (Italian court of cassation sitting in full plenary composition)
T.U.L.P.S.	Testo Unico delle Leggi Pubbliche di Sicurezza (Consolidated act of public safety laws)

Chapter 6

Civil Asset Forfeiture and the Presumption of Innocence under Art. 6(2) ECHR

*Johan Boucht**

Abstract. This article deals with so-called civil asset forfeiture (CAF), or non-conviction-based confiscation, and the presumption of innocence (POI). CAF measures are civil actions, directed against proceeds of crime, which facilitate the forfeiture of suspected criminal proceeds, even when it has not been possible to achieve a criminal conviction. CAF emphasises the unlawful provenance of the property, rather than the guilt of the property holder, and is generally considered to be preventive, rather than punitive, in nature. One of the central concerns raised in relation to CAF is that the respondent can be excluded from some of the basic safeguards normally conferred on a defendant in criminal proceedings, including the POI. This article analyses the relationship between CAF and the POI as expressed in Art. 6(2) of the European Convention on Human Rights (ECHR). Overall, it is concluded that Art. 6(2) will normally not be applicable to CAF proceedings. However, even if the POI were considered to apply, it is concluded that it would be unlikely that this would have a dramatic effect on the operation of forfeiture proceedings, as the ECHR is mainly concerned with issues of procedural fairness rather than substantial unreasonableness.

I. Introduction

A fundamental principle underpinning criminal justice policy is that the perpetrator must not profit from his crime. It follows that criminal confiscation following a

---

* The article was written within the framework of a post-doctoral project on extended asset recovery and mainly financed by the Norwegian Research Council (FRISAM) as well as in part by the Functionality of the Criminal Justice System project at the Faculty of Law, University of Bergen. The author wishes to thank *Andrew Ashworth, Iain Cameron, Michele Panzavolta, Julian V. Roberts*, and *Jon Petter Rui* for valuable comments on earlier drafts of this paper. This article has been previously published in: New Journal of European Criminal Law (2014), 221–253 and is re-published here with kind permission of the Intersentia.

conviction is an important mechanism to deprive a defendant of financial benefit derived from his criminal behaviour.[1]

However, criminal confiscation is not always possible due to the difficulties inherent with showing that the property derives from a particular criminal offence. This can be the case, for example, when individuals suspected of involvement in more serious criminality committed with the intent of achieving economic profit (e.g., trafficking in narcotics, smuggling, and money laundering) possess property to an extent that does not reasonably correspond to their lawful income. Although it may be clearly probable that the property or goods in question originate from criminal activity, a confiscation claim may be rejected if it cannot be shown that the property derives from a particular criminal offence. In order to address situations such as these, and to make it "easier" for the state to successfully claim confiscation, rules on so-called extended confiscation have been introduced.[2] In extended confiscation, the requirement to concretise the criminal offence from which the assets originate has been moderated, so that instead of targeting a particular preceding offence, extended confiscation often pursues proceeds from more vague preceding criminal activity. Traditional criminal procedural safeguards have usually also been watered down, for example by a reversed burden of proof or a lowered standard of proof (or both).

However, the opportunities provided by confiscation and extended confiscation are not considered sufficient in light of intensified transnational and international, economically motivated (and often organised) criminality.[3] Some European countries, for example the United Kingdom, Italy, Bulgaria, and Slovenia, have therefore introduced so-called Civil Asset Forfeiture (CAF), or non-conviction-based confiscation, schemes in order to increase efficiency in the field of asset recovery.[4] In the United States, CAF schemes have existed for a long time, both at federal and state levels.[5] The EU has also discussed the possibility of introducing a common non-conviction-based confiscation scheme amongst Member States.[6]

---

[1] Instrumentalities *(instrumentum sceleris)* and the produce of crime *(productum sceleris)* are also normally subjected to confiscation (or forfeiture).

[2] See *Boucht*, European Journal of Crime, Criminal Law and Criminal Procedure (2013), 127–162.

[3] See, e.g., Proposal for a directive of the European Parliament and of the Council on the freezing and confiscation of proceeds of crime in the European Union, COM(2012) 85 final, p. 2, in which the Commission concluded that "although regulated by EU and national laws, confiscation of criminal assets remains underdeveloped and underutilised."

[4] See, e.g., European Parliament Report on the proposal for a directive of the European Parliament and of the Council on the freezing and confiscation of proceeds of crime in the European Union (COM(2012)0085 – C7-0075/2012 – 2012/0036(COD)), A7-0178/2013, 34.

[5] See *Cassella*, Asset Forfeiture Law, pp. 1–27.

[6] See COM(2012) 85 final. The final Directive on the freezing and confiscation of instrumentalities and proceeds of crime in the European Union (2014/42/EU L127/39) does

Civil forfeiture measures that are directed against tainted property (*i.e.*, the proceeds of crime) are detached from possible criminal proceedings and pursued in order to forfeit suspected criminal proceeds, even when it has not been possible to secure a criminal conviction. CAF thus rests upon the principle that a holder of property cannot rightfully own property that has been obtained by unlawful conduct; and these measures therefore target the proceeds of unlawful activity that the respondent does not have any right to retain.[7] CAF is normally considered to be preventive in nature, and to emphasise the unlawful nature of the property, rather than being punitive and deterrent.[8]

Arguably, the trend towards more extensive forfeiture schemes as general law enforcement tools can be seen as part of a new stream in criminal justice policy, particularly in response to organised crime oriented towards the financial profits of crime, which "strives to curb crime by taking away the profits of crime, rather than by punishing the individuals who have allegedly committed the crimes."[9] However, from a criminal justice point of view, this trend also gives rise to questions as to how such measures comply with fundamental principles of criminal law and criminal procedural law. This is such because it is in the nature of CAF to be in the borderland between criminal and civil measures. One such basic principle, of particular interest for this inquiry, is the presumption of innocence (POI) as expressed in Art. 6(2) of the European Convention of Human Rights (ECHR).[10]

---

not, however, provide for the establishment of a non-conviction-based confiscation regime in the EU (see also 2012/0036(COD), 28.11.2013). Art. 4(2) states instead that where "regular" confiscation would not be possible, "at least where such impossibility is the result of illness or absconding of the suspected or accused person, Member States shall take the necessary measures to enable the confiscation of instrumentalities and proceeds in cases where criminal proceedings have been initiated regarding a criminal offence which is liable to give rise, directly or indirectly, to economic benefit, and such proceedings could have led to a criminal conviction if the suspected or accused person had been able to stand trial." For a critical discussion of the original proposal, see *Rui*, Non Conviction Based Confiscation in the EU, ERA Forum 13 (2012), 349–360.

[7] See *Smith/Owen/Bodnar,* Asset recovery, p. I-1023. See also *Cecil Walsh v. Director of the Assets Recovery Agency* [2005] NICA 6, p. 7, and Justice Stevens in *U.S. v. Ursery*, U.S. U20022 (1996).

[8] *Emmerson et al.*, Human Rights, p. 204.

[9] See *Stessens*, Money laundering, p. 12.

[10] See *Rui*, eucrim 4 (2011), 164. *Rui* also points at other potentially problematic issues: 1) the self-incrimination defence in Art. 6(1) ECHR, 2) the *ne bis in idem* principle in Prot. 4 of Art. 7 ECHR, and 3) the possible applicability of the prohibition of retroactivity in Art. 7 ECHR. See also *King*, Legal Studies (2013), 1–24.

II. Overview

In this article, I will discuss the relationship between CAF and the POI as formulated in Art. 6(2) ECHR and the jurisprudence of the European Court on Human Rights (ECtHR). Having briefly described the general characteristics of CAF proceedings in section 3 and having explored the content of Art. 6(2) ECHR in section 4, I will, in section 5, look at whether Art. 6(2) is applicable to CAF proceedings. To this end, I will explore the following questions: does a non-conviction-based forfeiture order constitute a criminal charge?, and, if not, could there nevertheless be a sufficient link to criminal proceedings in order to encompass CAF within Art. 6(2)? If Art. 6(2) were to apply, what would the consequences be? In this regard, I will look at four dimensions of the POI: 1) how does the civil standard of proof correspond to Art. 6(2)?; 2) is a reversed onus of proof in CAF proceedings legitimate in view of the requirements set up by Art. 6(2)?; 3) is the use of statutory presumptions compatible with Art. 6(2)?; and 4) what is the relationship between *in rem* proceedings and *mens rea*?

III. CAF as a Legal Concept

As differences exist between how CAF schemes are constructed in different countries, it is difficult to use any specific model as a point of departure. Thus, it seems more fruitful in this context to identify the main features common to the various CAF regimes and to use these as a reference later in the text.[11]

The first distinguishing characteristic relates to the nexus between the property subjected to forfeiture and the underlying offence in question. In criminal confiscation, a triggering criminal conviction is always necessary (with confiscation proceedings taking place either in connection with the criminal charge or in separate proceedings), whilst the causality requirement varies from being a particular offence to more vague preceding criminality. The purpose of CAF, however, is to forego the causality requirement between the property in question and the offence and to detach the proceedings from any criminal proceedings. CAF proceedings can therefore normally be initiated irrespective of the existence of a criminal conviction, *i.e.*, after an acquittal, after the discontinuation of criminal proceedings for other reasons, or where there are no criminal proceedings at all.

Secondly, criminal confiscation is directed against the defendant *(i.e., in personam)*, whilst CAF measures are against the property in question rather than a par-

---

[11] See also *Kennedy*, Journal of Financial Crime (2006), 132–163, for a number of issues that need to be addressed when a CAF scheme is designed.

ticular respondent *(i.e. in rem)*. Attention is therefore strictly on the unlawful derivation of the property, not on the conduct of the property holder.[12]

Third, as criminal confiscation is normally conducted through criminal proceedings, criminal procedure is normally applied, although the standard of proof required may vary.[13] CAF proceedings, however, are carried out on a civil basis, and the relevant rules are those of civil procedure, which include the civil standard of proof.[14]

Fourth, it is often argued that the purpose of CAF and criminal confiscation differ, although both share the same goal of removing the economic benefits of crime. Criminal confiscation is closely linked to criminal proceedings (initiation of confiscation proceedings requires conviction of a triggering offence) and, thus, is often seen as a part of the sentencing process. Although considered an alternative reaction to crime rather than a fine or additional punishment,[15] confiscation can nevertheless to some extent be interpreted as containing a penal and deterrent element.[16] CAF's main aim, however, being detached from the criminal proceedings, is normally considered to be preventative by facilitating the removal from circulation of criminally tainted property and thereby preventing further crime (e.g., corruption), the use and reinvestment of illegitimate property in the legal economy, and the dis-

---

[12] This is sometimes described as the "taint doctrine", *i.e.*, "property becomes 'tainted' at the moment it facilitates or is derived from criminal activity." See *Worrall*, Policing: An International Journal of Police Strategies & Management (2004), 234.

[13] In some countries, e.g., Finland, the criminal standard of proof is applied. In other criminal confiscation regimes, however, the standard of proof applied is lower, e.g., Norway (qualified balance of probabilities) and the UK (balance of probabilities).

[14] See, e.g., *Kennedy*, Journal of Financial Crime (2006), 139, according to whom it is necessary that the respondent is not able to argue that the central issue of whether the property originates from a criminal offence ought to be proven beyond any reasonable doubt. He further notes (p. 139) that this is the case in the models of the UK, Ireland, Australia, ACT, Northern Territories, New Zealand, Fiji, Ontario, Manitoba, Alberta, Saskatchewan, British Columbia, South Africa, Antigua and Barbuda, and Commonwealth.

[15] See, e.g., *Andenæs*, Alminnelig strafferett, p. 513; and *Jareborg/Zila*, Straffrättens påföljdslära, p. 55.

[16] See, e.g., *Welch v. the UK*, appl. 17440/90, 9.2.1995. See also *R v. Waya* [2013] 1 AC 294, para. 2, where Lord Steyn's much quoted statement in *R v. Rezvi* [2002] UKHL 1, para. 14 that "its purposes are to punish convicted offenders, to deter the commission of further offences and to reduce the profits available to fund further criminal enterprises," was qualified by Lord Walker in regard to the reference to punishment. The distinction between deterrent and preventative measures, as suggested by the ECtHR (although punitivity is seen by the Court as the main distinguishing feature of a criminal penalty, the deterrent character of the measure in question is also normally mentioned in the same breath), is somewhat confusing, at least from a conceptual perspective. Deterrence is, conceptually, one form of prevention (see *Ashworth/Zedner*, Preventive Justice, pp. 17–18). However, it becomes clearer if the former is understood as referring to the effect of the measure in deterring others or the respondent from future unlawful activity, whilst the latter concerns concrete prevention of the subject (either property or individuals) from being involved in future unlawful activity, *i.e.*, incapacitation.

ruption of the credibility and predictability of the financial system.[17] CAF is sometimes also considered "reparative," as it takes away from individuals, property that was never legally owned by them.[18]

CAF has both advocates and critics. The former argue that CAF represents an important means for removing from circulation in the financial system proceeds likely to originate in criminal activities. Moreover, civil forfeiture laws are considered necessary in order to allow the state to recover criminal proceeds in situations where it is not possible to obtain a confiscation order within criminal proceedings. According to *Cassella*, such situations can occur when the defendant has died, when the wrongdoer is unknown, when the property belongs to a third party, when the interests of justice do not require a criminal conviction, when the wrongdoer is a fugitive, and when the criminal is prosecuted in one country but the property is in another country.[19]

The critics, however, often claim that CAF circumvents the basic standards of criminal law and criminal procedural law. *Smith*, *Owen* and *Bodnar* argue as follows:

"there is no doubt that the consequence of both criminal confiscation and civil recovery is to circumvent [the] staple aspects of due process protection in criminal law. First, there is no need to allege a specific unlawful act. ... In civil recovery the state only has to allege that a person holds unlawfully obtained material. ... Second, the absolute prohibition on relying on upon evidence obtained by compelled testimony, save in a prosecution for perjury or as rebuttal evidence in a criminal trial, is now replaced by a power to compel the provision of information which can be used in either confiscation or civil recovery proceedings. ...Third, the need to adduce cogent and persuasive evidence in order to prove an allegation is diluted in so far as the rule against hearsay does not apply. Fourth, the need to prove the allegation to a respectably high standard, given the serious nature of the allegation, is again diluted in for as it will not be necessary to prove the matter beyond reasonable doubt. Fifth, there are no absolute jurisdictional bars to beginning civil recovery proceedings and then opting for criminal proceedings; or alter-

---

[17] See, e.g., Recovering the Proceeds of Crime, Performance and Innovation Unit, Cabinet Office, June 2000, section 5.2 and *Kennedy,* Journal of Financial Crime (2004), 16. Occasionally, as the government did in *Austin v. United States* 509 U.S. 602 (1993), it is argued that CAF is remedial. The general assumption is that forfeiture both removes the instruments of unlawful activity, and thereby protects the community from the threat of it, and compensates the government for the expense of law enforcement activity and for its expenditure on societal problems (urban blight, drug addiction, and other health concerns resulting from the drug trade). The US Supreme Court did, however, reject both arguments. It declared (quoting *One 1958 Plymouth Sedan v. Pennsylvania* 380 U.S. 693, 699 (1965)) that "there is nothing even remotely criminal in possessing an automobile" and that the "forfeiture of property ... [is] a penalty that ha[s] absolutely no correlation to any damages sustained by society or to the cost of enforcing the law." The position of the Supreme Court seems reasonable.

[18] See Recovering the Proceeds of Crime, Performance and Innovation Unit, Cabinet Office, June 2000, section 5.2. It can, however, be discussed whether it is accurate to classify CAF as reparative, as reparation normally involves returning the property to its owner, which does not occur here.

[19] See *Cassella*, Journal of Money Laundering Control 11 (2008), 8–13.

natively, starting civil recovery proceedings in the wake of an unsuccessful criminal prosecution."[20]

Hadaway reasons along similar lines and holds that "civil forfeiture is often used as a proxy for a criminal prosecution."[21] Criticism has also been directed at the lower standard of proof applied in CAF proceeding as well as at the so-called innocent owner problem, *i.e.*, when property is forfeited due to the actions of a third party.[22] *Hadaway* concludes the following:

> "in rem forfeiture may only be justified where the government has an established revenue interest in the property seized. If the forfeiture is not being brought to enforce a revenue interest in the property, such as a customs duty, then it should only be brought subsequent to a criminal conviction, whereby the forfeiture is justified by proof beyond a reasonable doubt that the owner committed the offense, and that the property forfeited was a proceed or instrumentality of the crime."[23]

IV. The Presumption of Innocence in Art. 6(2) ECHR

The general principle in regard to a fair trial is stated in Art. 6(1), under which a respondent who faces either allegations on civil rights and obligations or a criminal charge is entitled to a fair and public hearing within a reasonable time by an independent and impartial tribunal established by law.[24] In the case of a criminal charge, additional safeguards are provided in Art. 6(2) and Art. 6(3).

---

[20] *Smith/Owen/Bodnar*, Asset recovery, p. I-1022.

[21] *Hadaway*, University of Miami Law Review 109 (2000). However, in England, where there was also a fear that CAF would be used in place of criminal proceedings when POCA was introduced, it seems that this has not happened as a consequence of the legislative steer in Pt. 1 POCA that directs criminal proceedings wherever possible. See *Smith/ Owen/Bodnar*, Asset recovery, p. III-2005.

[22] In the US, questions have been raised as to the conformity of CAF with, *inter alia*, the double jeopardy clause (5th Amendment) and the excessive fines and punishment clauses (8th Amendment). See *Worrall*, Policing: An International Journal of Police Strategies & Management (2004), 225–226.

[23] *Hadaway*, University of Miami Law Review 121 (2000).

[24] The ECtHR has not given any general definition of a civil right or obligation but, according to *Cameron*, An introduction, pp. 97–98, it has provided some guidelines for this heading of Art. 6 to be applicable: 1) there must be a genuine and serious difference of opinion between the parties as to the nature and scope of a right or obligation; 2) the dispute must concern a right that already exists under domestic law; and 3) the outcome of the dispute must be decisive for a right of "civil" character, which is, in turn, determined by the Court on a case-by-case basis. Considering that the presumption of innocence also forms a part of the requirement of a fair trial according to Art. 6(1), the conditions of Art. 6(2–3) may still apply "the back way." In *Bochan v. Ukraine*, appl. 7577/02, 3.5.2007, para. 78, the ECtHR noted that the provisions of Article 6 §§ 2 and 3 have a certain relevance outside the strict confines of criminal law in that these principles are enshrined in the general notion of a fair trial as embodied in Article 6 § 1 of the Convention. See also the

The POI, the purpose of which is to safeguard a fair trial, is fundamental in criminal proceedings and is often seen as an important part of the so-called *Rechts-staatsprinzip*.[25] A wrongful conviction, against which the POI is an important protection, causes both injustice and substantial moral harm.[26] There are a number of readings of the POI, ranging from strictly formal to more substantive[27] but, in this context, I refer to the mainly procedural conception of the POI embodied in Art. 6(2) of the ECHR:

"Everyone charged with a criminal offence shall be presumed innocent until proved guilty according to law."[28]

Art. 6(2) has several fundamental implications for the criminal justice process, but the following appear to be of particular relevance in this context. First of all, the burden of proof (of *actus reus* and *mens rea*) is on the prosecution and any doubt should benefit the accused *(in dubio pro reo)*.[29] Thus, as a main rule, the presumption of innocence will be infringed where the burden of proof is shifted from

---

dissenting opinions by Judges Bratza and Vajic in *Phillips v. The United Kingdom*, appl. 41087/98, 5.7.2001.

[25] *Pellonpää*, Europeiska människorättskonventionen, p. 396. The elemental character is further shown by the fact that there can be no waiver of the right to be presumed innocent. See *Aall*, Nordic Journal of Human Rights (2011), 255.

[26] See *Dworkin*, in: Tapper (ed.), Crime, Proof and Punishment, p. 201.

[27] See, e.g., *Ashworth*, International Journal of Evidence & Proof (2004), 243. See also the Commission Green paper COM (2006) 174 final on The Presumption of Innocence, pp. 5–9, where the POI is considered to encompass pre-trial pronouncement of guilt, pre-trial detention, the burden of proof, privilege against self-incrimination, the right to silence, and the right not to produce evidence and in absentia proceedings. For a more substantial account, see, e.g., *Träskman*, in: Höglund *et al.* (eds.), Festskrift till Lars Welamson, p. 484, who argues that the POI also influences the shaping of material criminal law, and *Tomlin*, The Journal of Political Philosophy (2012), 1–23, according to whom the POI extends to the process of criminalisation, as the risk for punishing persons for non-punishment-worthy conduct should elicit the same level of concern as the risk of punishing persons for crimes they have not committed.

[28] The general aim of Art. 6(2), as explained in *Allen v. The United Kingdom*, appl. 25424/09, 12.7.2013, para. 94, is "to protect individuals who have been acquitted of a criminal charge, or in respect of whom criminal proceedings have been discontinued, from being treated by public officials and authorities as though they are in fact guilty of the offence charged. ... Without protection to ensure respect for the acquittal or the discontinuation decision in any other proceedings, the fair trial guarantees of Article 6 § 2 could risk becoming theoretical and illusory. What is also at stake once the criminal proceedings have concluded is the person's reputation and the way in which that person is perceived by the public." The POI is also regulated in Art. 48(1) of the Charter of Fundamental Rights of the European Union (2010/C 83/02): "Everyone who has been charged shall be presumed innocent until proved guilty according to law." The content of Art. 48 correlates to Art. 6(2–3) of the ECHR and is therefore not further analysed in this context. On the Charter, see *Mock/Demuro*, Human Rights in Europe, pp. 299–301.

[29] See, e.g., *Barberá, Messegué and Jabardo v. Spain*, appl. 10590/83, 6.12.1988, para. 77.

the prosecution to the defence.[30] Exceptions do, however, exist, for example by means of legal presumptions.[31]

Secondly, the accused is at no point in the process to be addressed as if he were guilty until the court has so decided, subsequent to a fair trial and according to law, where the defendant is provided with an opportunity to exercise a defence.[32] This requirement also extends outside the actual court proceedings to, for instance, pre-trial procedures[33] and concerns any representative of the state.[34] A closely connect-ed implication is the general aim of the POI to prevent a person acquitted of a crim-inal charge from being treated as guilty by public officials after the trial has been concluded.[35]

Whether Art. 6(2) also encompasses a certain standard of proof is, however, not entirely clear.[36] This is further discussed below.

---

[30] This was the case in *Telfner v. Austria*, appl. 33501/96, 20.3.2001, where the defend-ant refused to give testimony and was convicted of a traffic offence even though there was no direct evidence against him. The ECtHR concluded that in requiring "the applicant to provide an explanation although they had not been able to establish a convincing prima facie case against him, the courts shifted the burden of proof from the prosecution to the defence" (para. 18). Thus, there had been a violation of Art. 6(2) ECHR. See also *John Murray v. The United Kingdom*, appl. 18731/91, 8.2.1996, para. 54.

[31] See *Salabiaku v. France*, appl. 10519/83, 7.10.1988, para. 28.

[32] *Minelli v. Switzerland*, appl. 8660/79, 25.3.1983, para. 37, which concerned a court decision on paying court costs and compensation of expenses following termination of criminal charges due to statutory limitation. See also *Adolf v. Austria*, appl. 8269/78, 26.3.1982.

[33] See *Allenet de Ribemont v. France*, appl. 15175/89, 10.2.1995, in which some of the highest-ranking officers in the French police referred to the accused, without any qualifica-tion or reservation, as one of the instigators of a murder and, thus, as an accomplice in that murder. In establishing a breach of Art. 6(2), the Court found that this clearly amounted to a declaration of the applicant's guilt, which encouraged the public to believe him guilty and prejudged the assessment of the facts by the competent judicial authority. See also admissibility decisions in *Krause v. Switzerland*, appl. 7986/77, 3.10.1978 and *X v. Aus-tria*, appl. 9077/80, 6.10.1981.

[34] *X v. Austria*, appl. 9077/80, 6.10.1981.

[35] See *Sekanina v. Austria*, appl. 13126/87, 25.8.1993, para. 30; *Asan Rushiti v. Austria*, appl. 28389/95, 21.3.2000, para. 31, in which Sekanina was re-affirmed. The Court thus distinguished between cases where the criminal proceedings are discontinued by a final acquittal and cases where they have been discontinued for other reasons, for example that the conviction was quashed on appeal because the prosecution was time-barred when the case was brought to trial. See, however, *Allen v. The United Kingdom*, appl. 25424/09, 12.7.2013, in which a less rigid approach was applied.

[36] For example, *Ashworth*, International Journal of Evidence & Proof (2006), 243, un-derstands the POI as incorporating a requirement that proof must be established beyond reasonable doubt.

V. CAF and Article 6(2) ECHR

A. Introduction

Despite consensus in principle on the fundamental character of the POI in criminal proceedings, some commentators argue that it is under threat from various directions. *Ashworth* identifies four dangers: *confinement* "by defining offences so as to reduce the impact of the presumption," *erosion* "by recognizing more exceptions," and *side-stepping* "by imposing restrictions on the liberty of unconvicted persons that fall only slightly short of depriving them of their liberty." The fourth threat, *evasion*, that is, circumvention of the basic protections of the criminal procedure by introducing civil law procedures, is of particular interest in this context.[37] It seems, *prima facie*, that CAF proceedings under certain circumstances might exemplify this fourth threat.

Two questions are crucial: does CAF represent a "criminal charge" in the meaning of Art. 6(2) and, if answered in the negative, can there nevertheless be a sufficient link to criminal proceedings so as to bring it within the scope of Art. 6(2)? If answered in the positive, this raises issues as to the compatibility of CAF with the requirements of Art. 6(2).

I will, in the following section, endeavour an analysis of this by first setting out the general principles and then applying them to CAF. Thus far, the ECtHR has not had the opportunity to scrutinize the issue thoroughly and therefore everything said here is inevitably tentative. It should be stressed that the analysis does not depart from any particular CAF scheme. Considering that every system has its own characteristics, the value of such an exercise would probably be limited for my purposes here. Instead, I attempt an analysis based on the general characteristics of CAF identified in section 3.

B. Art. 6(2) and criminal confiscation

Before analysing the relationship between CAF and Art. 6(2), it may be useful to see how the ECtHR has interpreted Art. 6(2) in relation to criminal confiscation.

An important case is *Phillips v. the UK*, in which a criminal confiscation order was imposed on X after, but in conjunction with, him being sentenced to nine years imprisonment for drug offences.[38] In contrast to the usual burden of proof in crimi-

---

[37] See *Ashworth*, International Journal of Evidence & Proof (2006), 244, 270–274. See also *de la Cuesta Arzamendi*, Resolutions, p. 177, who points out that non-criminal sanctions should not be employed in order to circumvent the guarantees of substantive and procedural criminal law.

[38] *Phillips v. The United Kingdom*, appl. 41087/98, 5.7.2001.

nal proceedings, it was for the applicant to prove, on the balance of probabilities, that he acquired the property in question in other ways than through drug trafficking. In determining whether and to what extent the defendant had benefited from drug trafficking, the Crown Court applied a statutory presumption that any property appearing to have been held by the defendant at any time since his conviction, or during the six-year period prior to the date on which the criminal proceedings were commenced, had been received as a payment or reward in connection with drug trafficking, and that any expenditure incurred by him during the same period was paid for out of the proceeds of drug trafficking. The presumption could be set aside in relation to any particular property or expenditure if it was shown to be incorrect or if there would be a serious risk of injustice if it were applied. The applicant alleged that the legislation was in breach of his right under Art. 6(2).

The ECtHR first noted that, once an accused has properly been convicted of an offence, Art. 6(2) has no application in relation to allegations made about the accused's character and conduct as part of the sentencing process, unless the accusations are of such a nature and degree as to amount to the bringing of a new "charge." The confiscation proceedings were analysed in the light of the Engel criteria (see below section 5.3), and the court concluded that the purpose of the procedure was neither the conviction nor acquittal of the applicant for any other drug-related offence. Instead, it was to enable the national court to assess the amount at which the confiscation order should properly be fixed. It was therefore "analogous to the determination of the amount of a fine or the length of a period of imprisonment to be imposed on a properly convicted offender."[39] The ECtHR therefore held that Art. 6(2) was not applicable.[40]

---

[39] *Ibid.*, para. 34. See also the speech by Lord Bingham in Privy Council in *McIntosh v. Lord Advocate and Another* [2003] 1 A.C. 1078, para. 14 in which he concludes that a confiscation order is not a criminal charge on the following grounds: "(1) The application is not initiated by complaint or indictment and is not governed by the ordinary rules of criminal procedure. (2) The application may only be made if the accused is convicted, and cannot be pursued if he is acquitted. (3) The application forms part of the sentencing procedure. (4) The accused is at no time accused of committing any crime other than that which permits the application to be made. (5) When, as is standard procedure in anything other than the simplest case, the prosecutor lodges a statement under section 9, that statement (usually supported by detailed schedules) is an accounting record and not an accusation. (6) The sum ordered to be confiscated need not be the profit made from the drug trafficking offence of which the accused has been convicted, or any other drug trafficking offence. (7) If the accused fails to pay the sum he is ordered to pay under the order, the term of imprisonment which he will be ordered to serve in default is imposed not for the commission of any drug trafficking offence but on his failure to pay the sum ordered and to procure compliance. (8) The transactions of which account is taken in the confiscation proceedings may be the subject of a later prosecution, which would be repugnant to the rule against double jeopardy if the accused were charged with a criminal offence in the confiscation proceedings. (9) The proceedings do not culminate in a verdict, which would (in proceedings on indictment) be a matter for the jury if the accused were charged with a criminal offence." In *Cecil Walsh v. Director of the Assets Recovery Agency* [2005] NICA 6,

The question was also addressed in the admissibility decision *van Offeren v. the Netherlands*.[41] In this case, A was convicted by the Court of Appeal of having transported one or more quantities of cocaine, and of having held 640 g of cocaine and 535 g of a substance destined to dilute cocaine, but was acquitted of trafficking cocaine. In separate proceedings, a confiscation order was imposed, as the national court, in the light of the convictions as well as a criminal financial investigation, considered that there were "sufficient indications that [A] has committed the offence of cocaine-trafficking." The ECtHR, finding the application manifestly ill-founded, held that the confiscation order procedure did not amount to a "criminal charge" but was, applying *Phillips*, to be considered analogous to the determination by a court of the amount of punishment to be imposed on a person properly convicted of one or more drug offences.

In *Geerings v. the Netherlands* the outcome was different. X was convicted on certain theft charges but acquitted of others by a national court and was sentenced to 36 months imprisonment.[42] In separate proceedings, a confiscation order, which would be transformed into detention if not paid, relating to illegally obtained economic benefit was issued. The ECtHR confirmed the ruling in *Phillips* (and *van Offeren*) but distinguished the facts on five grounds: 1) the applicant was convicted of drug offences; 2) the applicant continued to be suspected of additional drugs offences; 3) the applicant demonstrably held assets whose provenance could not be established; 4) these assets were reasonably presumed to have been obtained through illegal activity; and 5) the applicant had failed to provide a satisfactory alternative explanation.[43]

---

p. 7 the Court of Appeal in Northern Ireland found that many of the characteristics identified in this passage are present in the case of CAF proceedings.

[40] The decision was not unanimous (5-2). Judge Bratza, joined by Judge Vajic, expressed the view that the majority position was too narrow on the role of Art. 6(2) in the context of proceedings relating to a criminal charge. They argued, *inter alia*, that a distinction had to be made between situations where, as in *Engel*, the facts are undisputed and where they are not. There is, further, a close relationship between cases in which presumptions are applied at the trial stage for the purpose of determining a defendant's guilt of the offence charged and cases, such as the present, in which presumptions are applied after conviction and as part of the sentencing process for the purpose of determining which of the defendant's assets are to be regarded as having been derived from the proceeds of drug trafficking and are thus liable to confiscation. Thus, 'the Court of Appeal in [R v] *Benjafield and Others* [[2001] 3 W.L.R. 75] was correct in holding that the confiscation procedure had to be considered on the basis that it was subject to the requirements of both paragraph 1 and paragraph 2 of Article 6 read together and in seeing the requirement of "fairness" in this context as substantially importing the requirements laid down by the Court in *Salabiaku* [v. France, appl. 10519/83, 7.10.1988] and *Pham Hoang* [v. France, appl. 13191/87, 25.9.1992].'

[41] *Van Offeren v. the Netherlands*, appl. 19581/04, 5.7.2005.

[42] *Geerings v. The Netherlands*, appl. 30810/03, 1.3.2007.

[43] *Geerings v. The Netherlands*, appl. 30810/03, 1.3.2007, para. 43. It can be noted that, in Geerings, the Court seems to depart from the position that the impugned order in van

Even though X had obtained unlawful benefit from the crimes in question, he was never shown to have been in possession of any assets for whose provenance he could not give an adequate explanation. The confiscation order related only to the crimes for which the applicant had been acquitted. The court thus concluded that criminal confiscation was an inappropriate measure in regard to assets that were not known to have been in the possession of the person affected, particularly if it related to a criminal act of which he had not actually been found guilty. The court continued (para. 47): "If it is not found beyond a reasonable doubt that the person affected has actually committed the crime, and if it cannot be established as fact that any advantage, illegal or otherwise, was actually obtained, such a measure can only be based on a presumption of guilt." Applying *Rushiti* (above), the court found that such voicing of suspicion regarding A's innocence was no longer admissible.[44]

What may be concluded from these cases? First of all, it seems clear that criminal confiscation proceedings following a conviction are treated as a part of the sentencing process. Thus, Art. 6(2) is not applicable once the accused has been proven guilty of that offence, unless the allegations constitute a new charge. A criminal confiscation order (even extended confiscation) issued in conjunction with a preceding criminal conviction does not therefore constitute a "criminal charge" *per se*.[45] However, *Phillips* does not necessarily rule out that a confiscation order with a penal and deterrent purpose might fall within the scope of Art. 6(2) in situations in which there has been no prior conviction.[46]

Secondly, a distinction should be made between cases where the defendant is convicted on some charges but acquitted of others, and where he is acquitted of all charges. If the defendant is partly acquitted and partly convicted, the outcome depends on the facts *in casu*. For example, under some rules on extended confiscation, the criteria for issuing a confiscation order can be fulfilled, even if the defendant is partly convicted and partly acquitted and the assets subject to confiscation are wholly connected to the offence for which he was acquitted. In this situation, the confiscation order might, in line with *Geerings*, amount to a new charge.[47]

Offeren did not relate to the crimes of which the applicant had been acquitted. However, it does in fact seem that he was acquitted of precisely those crimes. See *Mahmutaj*, Criminal Law Review (2009), 790.

[44] For some reason, Rushiti was not considered in van Offeren although the situation was similar.

[45] See *Cameron*, An Introduction, p. 101 (footnote 101).

[46] See *Strandbakken*, Uskyldspresumsjonen, p. 256. It seems that this distinction was not made by the Court of Appeal in Northern Ireland in *Cecil Walsh v. Director of the Assets Recovery Agency* [2005] NICA 6, 7–8.

[47] This was the situation in the Norwegian Supreme Court case Rt. 2004 s. 1126. The Court found Art. 6(2) to be applicable. See also *R. v. Briggs-Price* [2009] UKHL 19, where Lord Phillips concluded that "if the defendant is acquitted of offences with which he is charged, it is not legitimate to infer that he has benefited from those offences."

It should also be noted, with reference to *Phillips*, that even if Art. 6(2) would not be applicable to confiscation proceedings, the POI as implied in Art. 6(1) would still apply "throughout the entirety of proceedings for 'the determination of ... any criminal charge', including proceedings whereby a sentence is fixed" (which can be important in situations in which Art. 6(2) will not apply).[48] This includes confiscation proceedings and can be crucial when the proceedings in question are not covered by Art. 6(2). In view of this, the court's reasoning in *Geerings* can be read as having a further consequence if the forfeiture measure targets property that has not been shown to have been held by the defendant, and if he has not been charged with the offence from which it supposedly derives. In this case, arguably, as held by the House of Lords in *R v. Briggs-Price*, the prosecution must prove beyond reasonable doubt that the defendant has committed offences from which he is claimed to have achieved benefit if the assets are not known to have been in his possession.[49]

C. CAF and the requirement of a "criminal charge" under the Engel criteria

According to the jurisprudence of the ECtHR, Art. 6(2) will only apply if the individual is charged with a "criminal offence." In defining a "criminal charge," the ECtHR applies a principle of autonomous interpretation in order not to undermine the protections of the ECHR.[50] This means that the meaning of a concept under the Convention does not necessarily equal the meaning of a similar concept in national law.

The meaning of "criminal" was first analysed in the case *Engel and Others v. The Netherlands*, in which the court established three criteria of assessment: 1) the classification of the offence in national law; 2) the nature of the offence; and 3) the nature and severity of the punishment that is risked.[51] The criteria are to be as-

---

[48] Although Art. 6(2) did not apply in Phillips, the POI as part of Art. 6(1) did. It was, however, not infringed, as an application of the presumptions in question "was confined within reasonable limits given the importance of what was at stake and that the rights of the defence were fully respected" (para. 47).

[49] Lord Brown in *R v. Briggs-Price* [2009] 1 AC 1026, para. 94. It can be noted that Lord Brown dissented with the majority and found Art. 6(2) to be applicable but satisfied in the case. Geerings was therefore distinguished solely on the ground that, in Briggs-Price, the judge was satisfied beyond reasonable doubt that the defendant was guilty of trafficking in cannabis (although he was not charged for it).

[50] See, e.g., *Janosevic v. Sweden*, appl. 34619/97, 23.7.2002, para. 65, *Welch v. the United Kingdom*, appl. 17440/90, 9.2.1995, para. 27.

[51] *Engel and others v. The Netherlands*, appl. 5100/71; 5101/71; 5102/71; 5354/72; 5370/72, 8.6.1976. These criteria have been upheld in numerous later cases, see, e.g., *Ezeh and Connors v. The United Kingdom*, appl. 39665/98 and 40086/98, 9.10.2003, para. 82, and *Allen v. The United Kingdom*, appl. 25424/09, 12.7.2013, para. 95.

sessed separately, although they tend to blend into each other to a certain extent. The assessment has, in numerous later cases, been elaborated so as to include a number of relevant factors. The second and third criteria are alternative and not necessarily cumulative, although a cumulative approach is not precluded when a separate analysis of each criterion would not lead to a clear conclusion. As noted by *Harris et al.*, it is not easy to rationalize the case law as a whole, and the process of applying the second and third criteria to particular offences and sentences in specific legal systems "almost inevitably leads in some contexts to decisions based upon the particular facts."[52] Much has been written about the Engel criteria and I will not repeat that exercise. Instead, I will briefly illustrate how the criteria are applied in practice by using two cases from the court.[53]

In the first case, *Benham v. the UK*, the question was whether the proceedings relating to a liability order involved the determination of a "criminal charge" or not.[54] The facts were as follows: X failed to pay a community charge of £325 imposed on him, whereupon the magistrates' court issued a liability order to commence enforcement proceedings against him. However, the enforcement was unsuccessful, as there were no goods that could be seized and sold in order to pay the debt. Upon concluding that the failure to pay was due to the offender's culpable neglect, the court ordered X to go to prison for 30 days (a decision later found erroneous by the divisional court). The question arose as to whether or not this amounted to a criminal charge.

As to the first criterion, the court agreed with the government that, under national law, the proceedings in question were regarded as civil rather than criminal but noted that this factor is of relative weight and serves only as a starting point.[55]

---

[52] *Harris et al.*, Law of the European Convention, p. 206.

[53] In its assessment, the Court also seems to consider certain national particularities to some extent. See, e.g., *Raimondo v. Italy*, appl. 12954/87, 22.2.1994, para. 30: "the Court is fully aware of the difficulties encountered by the Italian State in the fight against the Mafia. As a result of its unlawful activities, in particular drug-trafficking, and its international connections, this 'organization' has an enormous turnover that is subsequently invested, inter alia, in the real property sector. Confiscation, which is designed to block these movements of suspect capital, is an effective and necessary weapon in the combat against this cancer. It therefore appears proportionate to the aim pursued, all the more so because it in fact entails no additional restriction in relation to seizure." The position was similar in *Arcuri and others v. Italy*, appl. 52024/99, 5.7.2001: "The Court … observes that in Italy the problem of organised crime has reached a very disturbing level. The enormous profits made by these organisations from their unlawful activities give them a level of power which places in jeopardy the rule of law within the State. The means adopted to combat this economic power, particularly the confiscation measure complained of, may appear essential for the successful prosecution of the battle against the organisations in question … The Court cannot therefore underestimate the specific circumstances which prompted the action taken by the Italian legislature."

[54] *Benham v. the UK*, appl. 19380/92, 10.6.1996.

[55] See also, e.g., *Öztürk v. Germany*, appl. 8544/79, 21.2.1984, para. 51. In *Deweer v. Belgium*, appl. 6903/75, 27.2.1980, para. 44, the Court noted that it also has to look "behind the appearances and investigate the realities of the procedure in question."

Regarding the second criterion, the nature of proceedings, the court particularly noted three elements of the proceedings in question: 1) the national law that regulated the case was of general application to all citizens; 2) they were brought by a public authority under statutory powers of enforcement; and 3) they comprised some punitive elements, for example, that the court could only exercise its power of committal to prison on a finding of wilful refusal to pay or of culpable neglect.[56] Finally recalling that the applicant faced a relatively severe maximum penalty of three months' imprisonment, and was in fact ordered to be detained for thirty days, the court concluded that there had been a breach of Art. 6(2).[57]

The other case, *Garyfallou AEBE v. Greece*, addressed the question of whether a fine of 500,000 drachmas (that the applicant company had been ordered to pay for having violated rules concerning the import and export trade), amounted to a criminal charge or not. As to the first criterion, the court noted that it was apparent that the fine imposed was not characterised under domestic law as a criminal sanction and then proceeded to analyse the second and third criteria. The court thus observed that the applicant company risked a maximum fine nearly three times the amount actually fined, as well as, in the event of non-payment, the seizure of the applicant company's assets and, more importantly, the detention of its directors for up to one year.[58] With regard to these circumstances, the court concluded that the sanction imposed on the company was sufficiently punitive to warrant the charge against them to be criminal under Art. 6(2).

How then would CAF be assessed under this jurisprudence? In regard to the first criterion, CAF is generally either statutorily defined or considered by the courts as being a civil action governed by the rules of civil procedure.[59] In fact, one of the main objectives of CAF is to be classified as not being part of the criminal proce-

---

[56] Other factors used by the Court include: how other European council Member States have classified the procedures (*Maaouia v. France*, appl. 39652/98, 5.10.2000); whether the relevant act is connected to the (national) criminal law context (*Öztürk v. Germany*, appl. 8544/79, 21.2.1984) as well as the terminology employed (*Gradinger v. Austria*, appl. 15963/90, 23.10.1995); whether or not the purpose of the sanction proscribed in the rule is punitive being a "customary distinguishing feature of a criminal penalty" (*Janosevic v. Sweden*, appl. 34619/97, 23.7.2002) as a compensatory or preventive purpose will not suffice (*Arcuri and others v. Italy*, appl. 52024/99, 5.7.2001); what kind of procedure is involved (*Ziliberberg v. Moldova*, appl. 61821/00, 1.5.2005); and whether or not different evidentiary standards are used (*Y v. Norway*, appl. 56568/00, 11.2.2003).

[57] See *Bendenoun v. France*, appl. 12547/86, 24.2.1994 and *Welch v. the United Kingdom*, appl. 17440/90, 9.2.1995.

[58] It is the potential maximum penalty that is ascribed relevance, not the punishment *in concreto*. See *Grabenwarter/Pabel*, Europäische Menschenrechtskonvention, p. 395 marginal no. 20. It should be noted that the amount of money involved is not in itself determinative. See *Porter v. the United Kingdom*, appl. 15814/02, 8.7.2003.

[59] See, for example, *Cassella*, Journal of Money Laundering Control 11 (2008), 9, *Kennedy*, Journal of Financial Crime (2006), 145, and *Serious Organised Crime Agency v. Gale and another* [2011] 1 WLR 2760.

dure. Thus, it seems fairly clear that CAF would normally not be considered criminal under the first criterion.

Several of the factors ascribed relevance by the ECtHR in assessing the second and third criteria (the nature of the offence/proceedings and the severity of the sanction) concern strictly procedural issues and would therefore probably be of minor relevance here, particularly when considering that CAF is normally classified as a civil procedure (applying the civil standard of proof) detached from the criminal law context.[60] Although the severity of the sanction may be relevant, and forfeiture orders may total considerable amounts, this factor is not decisive *per se*. As has been repeatedly pointed out by the court, many non-penal measures of a preventive character may have a substantial impact on the person concerned.[61] Whether imprisonment can follow upon failure to pay the forfeiture order may also be relevant but, as imprisonment is normally not an option for failure to pay a CAF order, this criterion probably has little relevance in the present context.[62]

An important factor seems to be to what extent forfeiture proceedings establish guilt on the part of the respondent (and whether the degree of culpability affects the magnitude of the forfeiture order). It is often argued that guilt is not an issue in CAF proceedings, as they focus on the illicit origin of property (*in rem*) rather than on the conduct of the individual who holds it.[63] This issue was touched upon in *Air*

---

[60] The proceedings do not involve the preferring of a charge against the appellant, and he does not acquire a criminal conviction if he is found liable to deliver up the assets. Nor will a forfeiture order give rise to a criminal record. Indeed, the same evidence may be used in subsequent forfeiture proceedings as in criminal proceedings that resulted in an acquittal, but this (at least as far that it relates to the objective facts) will hardly in itself be considered sufficient for bringing the claim within the realm of Art. 6(2).

[61] See, e.g., *Welch v. the UK*, appl. 17440/90, 9.2.1995, para. 32, and *Walsh v. the United Kingdom*, appl. 43384/05, 21.11.2006.

[62] In *McIntosh v. Lord Advocate and Another* [2003] 1 A.C. 1078, para. 14, Lord Bingham noted, in regard to criminal confiscation, that even though imprisonment could follow on failure to pay the sum he is ordered to pay according to the confiscation order, the term of imprisonment is imposed not for any new offence but for failure to pay the sum ordered and to procure compliance. Imprisonment would, in other words, follow for non-compliance with a court order. I do not, however, find the argument entirely convincing. Imprisonment is, due to its severity, normally considered a punishment and should therefore reasonably only follow on non-compliance with other forms of punishment, e.g. failure to pay fines. Confiscation, however, is not classified as punishment (although it can be said to retain a punitive element due to its connection with the criminal conviction). It therefore does not seem adequate to enforce non-compliance with a confiscation order with imprisonment; this should instead be done by way of civil enforcement. It can also be noted that in *Dassa Foundation and others v. Liechtenstein*, appl. 696/05 10.7.2007, the ECtHR found the fact that failure to pay a confiscation order would not entail imprisonment to be one reason for not finding a confiscation under Liechtenstein law to be a punishment. It can further be noted that similar legal arrangements can also be found in many other countries, e.g. Finland, Norway, and Sweden.

[63] It is clear that the distinction between *in personam* and *in rem* proceedings can be subjected to criticism and its adequacy contested (see e.g. *Naylor*, Crime, Law and Social

Canada v. the UK, where an aircraft operated by Air Canada, worth over £60 million, was seized upon discovery that 331 kg of cannabis resin with a street value of £800 000 had, unknown to the company, been transported on the aircraft into the UK on a regular scheduled flight (no criminal proceedings were initiated).[64] The aircraft was later (the same day) delivered back to the applicant company on payment of a penalty of £50,000. The ECtHR was persuaded by the reasoning of the Court of Appeal that, although the description of a relevant provision as being "civil" did not preclude it from being in effect "criminal" in nature, the provision in question concerned a process *in rem* against the property and therefore did not constitute a "criminal charge." Also in *Butler v. the UK*, the court referred to this reasoning in support of its conclusion that Art. 6 under its criminal heading did not apply to the relevant forfeiture proceedings.[65]

In view of this, it seems that the court approves of the *in rem/in personam* distinction, which again makes it more difficult to argue that CAF imputes criminal guilt to the respondent.[66]

Another important factor in this context is the purpose of CAF proceedings and, more specifically, whether or not they can be considered penal, which, according to the court, is the customary distinguishing feature of a criminal penalty. This issue has been discussed by the ECtHR in a number of cases and in regard to various kinds of confiscation proceedings. In *M v. Italy*, the property of the applicant, who was convicted *inter alia* of membership in a criminal organisation, was seized and subsequently confiscated.[67] The government argued that a confiscation order of this type, which did not intend to establish that a particular offence had been committed or to impose an appropriate penalty, was to be regarded as a preventative measure. The Commission agreed and held that such preventive measures must, in principle, be regarded as distinct from both criminal penalties as well as disciplinary, administrative, and other penalties, "since they are not designed to punish a specific offence," but rather to prevent the unlawful use of the property that is subject to the order. Thus, such measures do not include a finding of guilt.[68]

Change (1999), 41; *King*, Legal Studies (2013), 8–9. But this question will not be addressed here.

[64] *Air Canada v. the United Kingdom*, appl. 9/1994/456/537, 26.4.1995. See also *Agosi v. the United Kingdom*, appl. 9118/80, 24.10.1986.

[65] *Butler v. The United Kingdom*, appl. 41661/98, 27.6.2002.

[66] The original EU Commission's proposal for non-conviction-based forfeiture (see COM(2012) 85 final) seems to come closer to a criminal charge in this regard. The proceedings were *in personam*, not *in rem*, with the wording indicating that it had to be clear that the person would have been convicted had he been present at the trial. This clearly suggests something closer to a finding of guilt.

[67] *M v. Italy*, appl. 12386/86, 15.4.1991.

[68] The Commission also noted that the confiscation in question was conditional upon a prior declaration of dangerousness to society based on suspected membership of a mafia-

A similar issue was discussed in the admissibility decision *Arcuri v. Italy,* which referred to the compliance with Art. 6(1) of forfeiture procedures designed to prevent criminal offences by individuals linked to the mafia. Considerable property of the applicant had been seized and later confiscated following a suspicion that the applicant was a member of a criminal organisation involved in drug trafficking. In rejecting the complaint, the court again ruled that "the preventive measures ... which do not involve a finding of guilt, but are designed to prevent the commission of offences, are not comparable to a criminal 'sanction'" and therefore do not involve the determination of a criminal charge.[69]

The compliance with Art. 6(2) of cash forfeiture provisions under English law was discussed in the admissibility decision *Butler v. the UK.*[70] In this case, £240,000 that belonged to the applicant was seized by customs officers from a car at the border. The money was subsequently forfeited in civil recovery proceedings, applying a civil standard of proof, based on strong circumstantial evidence that it was to be used for drug trafficking. The court did not agree with the applicant that forfeiture of his money represented a criminal sanction. Finding the case inadmissible, and quoting *inter alia* the cases cited above, the court again concluded that a forfeiture order of this kind was a preventive measure that "cannot be compared to a criminal sanction, since it was designed to take out of circulation money which was presumed to be bound up with the international trade in illicit drugs." The reasoning in *Butler* was also relied upon in a similar admissibility decision, *Webb v. the UK.*[71]

Two conclusions can be drawn from these cases. First, that the ECtHR approves of preventive measures, distinct from criminal charges, *per se* and that preventative measures do not engage the safeguards normally required by "criminal charges" or "penalties."[72] Second, it seems to be an established position of the court to treat proceedings resembling CAF proceedings as preventative measures.[73]

---

type organisation and was subsidiary to the adoption of a preventive measure restrictive of personal liberty (residence order).

[69] *Arcuri and others v. Italy*, appl. 52024/99, 5.7.2001. See also *Ciulla v. Italy*, appl. 11152/84, 22.2.1989 (custodial order); *Raimondo v. Italy*, appl. 12954/87, 22.2.1994 (special supervision); and *Guzzardi v. Italy*, appl. 7367/76, 6.11.1980 (compulsory residence).

[70] *Butler v. The United Kingdom*, appl. 41661/98, 27.6.2002.

[71] *Webb v. The United Kingdom*, appl. 56054/00, 10.2.2004.

[72] It has been argued that this position does not sit easily with *Ezeh and Connors v. the UK*, appl. 39665/98 and 40086/98, 9.10.2003, where the Court found that disciplinary sanctions within a prison constituted a "criminal charge" (see *King*, Legal Studies (2013), 10). However, the relevance of this case to CAF proceedings can be discussed. First, the Court has repeatedly (both in Ezeh and in subsequent judgments) approved of distinctions *per se* between criminal, disciplinary, and preventative sanctions. Ezeh was also particular as to the facts: it concerned a prison environment where there was concurrent disciplinary and criminal liability, and where the sanctions in question were meted out to punish the applicants for offences they committed after a finding based on culpability. It may also be

However, it should be noted that preventative purposes have not always been approved by the ECtHR. In *Welch v. the UK*, which related to the application of Art. 7, a confiscation order following a criminal conviction for drug trafficking (essentially a confiscatory and preventive measure) was considered to be punitive when all elements of the order were considered together (para. 33): the sweeping statutory assumptions applied, that the confiscation order targeted all proceeds involved and was thus not limited to the defendant's actual enrichment, the discretion of the trial judge in fixing the amount of the order, to have regard to the degree of culpability of the accused, and the possibility of imprisonment in default of payment by the offender.[74] Although the crucial argument is not, as illustrated by *Welch*, whether the purpose is preventative or not (but rather whether the measure is punitive or not).[75] It seems that a preventative purpose is approved of as long as the justification for it is reasonable and the elements of the measure, considered together, do not give rise to the conclusion that the measure is substantially and significantly punitive. In other words, as long as CAF were to be classified as predominantly preventative, which it is likely to be, Art. 6(2) would probably not be applicable.[76]

This having been said, it is important to note that sanctions such as CAF can serve more than one purpose. This position was expressed by the US Supreme Court in *United States v. Halper* and seems relevant also in this context: "a civil sanction that cannot fairly be said solely to serve a remedial purpose, but rather can only be explained as also serving either retributive or deterrent purposes, is punishment."[77] It could also be argued that the ECtHR's approach to "preventative

---

noted that the judgment was not unanimous: six judges delivered convincing dissenting opinions.

[73] See also *Emmerson et al.*, Human Rights, p. 204. For a discussion about coercive preventive measures, see *Ashworth/Zedner*, Preventive Justice, pp. 20–25.

[74] *Welch v. the UK*, appl. 17440/90, 9.2.1995, para. 28. The fact that confiscation was not limited to actual enrichment is likely to be of considerable importance.

[75] See *Ashworth/Zedner*, Preventive Justice, p. 16.

[76] This has also been concluded in several challenges to the civil recovery regime by UK courts, see, e.g., *Walsh v. Director of the Assets Recovery Agency* [2005] NICA 6; *Scottish Ministers v. Doig* [2009] CSIH 34; and *Serious Organised Crime Agency v. Gale and others* [2011] 1 WLR 2760 (see also the judgment by the Court of Appeal, [2010] EWCA Civ 759).

[77] 490 U.S.435 (1989). The fact that forfeiture serves a penal purpose besides other purposes has also been concluded by the U.S. Supreme Court in several cases. 380 U.S. 693 (1965). See also the case of *Austin v. United States* and *Boyd v. United States*, 116 U.S. 616 (1886). One should perhaps question what the punishment is for. Probably it is, as a House of Representatives' committee submitted, that "civil forfeiture is being used to punish a property owner for alleged criminal activity." See House of Representatives, Report 106–192, 18.6.1999, p. 13. In *Plymouth Sedan v. Pennsylvania*, in which the claimant had transported in his car 31 cases of liquor not bearing Pennsylvania tax seals, the court found that "a forfeiture proceeding is quasi-criminal in character. Its object, like a criminal proceeding, is to penalize for the commission of an offense against the law." I feel inclined to

measures" is too deferential to national law and national policy. The court has itself emphasised that it is important not only to consider the prescribed purpose but also to look behind appearances to the actual consequences imposed on the individual. In light of this, it seems difficult to disregard the fact that civil recovery measures, depending on their construction, can potentially be both far-reaching and unfair, even if procedurally impeccable. This might have been in the court's mind in *Welch v. the UK*, when it held, in regard to the preventive purposes of a UK confiscation scheme, that:

> "[i]t cannot be excluded that legislation which confers such broad powers of confiscation on the courts also pursues the aim of punishing the offender. Indeed the aims of prevention and reparation are consistent with a punitive purpose and may be seen as constituent elements of the very notion of punishment."[78]

In other words, even if the main objective of CAF is preventative, this should not necessarily rule out that a particular CAF scheme could potentially also be seen as having a partly punitive (and deterrent) "secondary purpose." Thus, the question of what constitutes punitiveness under Art. 7 arises.

In *Welch v. the United Kingdom*, the court held that the starting point of the assessment under Art. 7 was whether the measure in question was imposed following conviction for a "criminal offence," but that there are also other relevant factors: the characterisation of the measure under domestic law, its nature and purpose, the procedures involved in its making and implementation, and its severity.[79] The court concluded, as noted above, that confiscation in this case was punitive in spite of its preventative purpose.

In the admissibility decision *Dassa v. Liechtenstein*, the court arrived at a different conclusion.[80] It concluded that the rules on seizure (and confiscation) under Liechtenstein law had a preventative aim in depriving the person concerned of the profits of his crime as well as in safeguarding the enforcement of civil law claims of third persons. Seizure and subsequent forfeiture of assets were a civil law consequence of the fact that a perpetrator or other beneficiaries had obtained assets originating from an unlawful act (*i.e.*, it aimed at guaranteeing that crime did not pay). The gravity of the orders alone was not considered decisive. *Dassa* was distinguished from *Welch* on all four of the "aggravating" elements: forfeiture was restricted to the actual enrichment of the beneficiary of an offence, there were no statutory assumptions of the same kind applied, the degree of culpability of the

---

agree with *Worrall* who argues that "it is naïve to assume that civil forfeiture does not punish" (*Worrall*, Policing: An International Journal of Police Strategies & Management (2004) 235).

[78] *Welch v. the United Kingdom*, appl. 17440/90, 9.2.1995, para. 30.

[79] *Welch v. the UK*, appl. 17440/90, 9.2.1995, para. 28.

[80] *Dassa Foundation and others v. Liechtenstein*, appl. 696/05 10.7.2007. The Convention utilizes a uniform concept of punishment that applies to both Art. 6 and Art. 7 ECHR (see, for instance, *Göktan v. France* appl. 33402/96, 2.7.2002, para. 48).

offender was irrelevant for fixing the amount of assets declared forfeited,[81] and forfeiture orders under Liechtenstein law could not be enforced by imprisonment in default of payment. Forfeiture was also limited to assets that originated in a punishable act. In conclusion, the court was inclined to find forfeiture under Liechtenstein law "more comparable to a restitution of unjustified enrichment under civil law than to a fine under criminal law" (despite the fact that the relevant national provisions were located in the criminal code and in the code of criminal procedure and dependant on the commission of a criminal offence). Forfeiture therefore did not amount to a penalty within the meaning of Art. 7(1).

What can then be said about this? Although *Dassa* does not necessarily, considering the particular nature of forfeiture under Liechtenstein law, exclude the possibility of CAF being considered partly penal, it is noteworthy that most of the factors used in distinguishing *Welch* from *Dassa* are also characteristic of CAF. Thus, it seems likely that, under Art. 7, CAF would not be considered to have even a partly penal purpose sufficient to bring it under Art. 6(2).

It is somewhat difficult, however, when looking beyond appearances towards the potential consequences of the individual concerned, to entirely depart from the impression that CAF schemes, in reality, seem to be designed to be *quasi* as deterrent as they can be without making them criminal.[82] CAF schemes allow the state to forfeit property by reference to its criminal origin by applying a lower standard of proof, even after an acquittal or without any criminal proceedings ever having been initiated. Besides the fact that the state is thus permitted "a second shot" at the respondent by taking away his property even if a conviction has not been secured, justified by criminal policy considerations,[83] a clear message is sent to potential offenders that committing criminal offences in order to gain profit is, simply put, "not worth it."

---

[81] This issue was also discussed in a similar way in *Austin v. United States*, 509 U.S. 602 (1993), sect. III C.

[82] See also *King*, Legal Studies (2013), 8. In *McIntosh v. Her Majesty's Advocate* [2001] JC 78, Lord Prosser, in finding that Art. 6(2) did apply, stated that: "… By asking the court to make a confiscation order, the prosecutor is asking it to reach the stage of saying that he has trafficked in drugs. If that is criminal, that seems to me to be closely analogous to an actual charge of an actual crime, in Scottish terms. There is of course no indictment or complaint, and no conviction. And the advocate depute pointed out a further difference, that a Scottish complaint or indictment would have to be specific, and would require evidence, whereas this particular allegation was inspecific and based upon no evidence. But the suggestion that there is less need for a presumption of innocence in the latter situation appears to me to be somewhat Kafkaesque and to portray a vice as a virtue. With no notice of what he is supposed to have done, or any basis which there might be for treating him as having done it, the accused's need for the presumption of innocence is in my opinion all the greater."

[83] *Kennedy*, Journal of Financial Crime (2004), 10, notes that while it would be more desirable if successful criminal proceedings could be instituted, "the operative theory is that 'half a loaf is better than no bread'."

If CAF would indeed prove to be partly penal, the question arises as to whether or not the penal element of forfeiture would suffice to bring CAF within the scope of Art. 6(2). This issue was addressed by the Northern Ireland Court of Appeal in *Walsh v. Director of the Assets Recovery Agency*, in which it was concluded that it would not:

> "even though the confiscation of the applicant's property was to be regarded as a penalty within the meaning of article 7 of the convention, since the purpose of the confiscation procedure was not to secure the conviction of the applicant, it did not constitute the preferring of a charge against him within the meaning of article 6."[84]

I agree that it can be argued, as the Court of Appeal did (with reference to *Phillips*), that the POI will not be applied, as the aim is not to secure any conviction of the respondent for a criminal charge. However, the reasoning still gives the impression of being tautologous: CAF is not a criminal charge because no criminal charge is involved.[85] Instead, there seems to be a good claim to in applying Art. 6(2) precisely in situations where the measure in question, besides being preventative, is also considered to have penal purposes.[86]

Summing up, what then is the general conclusion in this section? First of all, in light of existing jurisprudence and the main characteristics of CAF proceedings, it seems unlikely, particularly considering the CAF's *in rem* character and preventative purpose, that CAF would be considered a criminal charge *per se* under the Engel criteria (at least as long as the respondent's position is not held to be procedurally totally intolerable). Having said this, although unlikely, it is not necessarily ruled out that a particular CAF scheme could still, in light of the discussion above, be considered to have partly penal characteristics and thereby fall within the scope of Art. 6(2).

D. CAF as a sufficient link to prior criminal proceedings

1. Introduction

Even if not a "criminal charge" under the Engel criteria, Art. 6(2) might still be applied to subsequent judicial proceedings, provided that they are sufficiently linked to prior criminal proceedings. Over the years, the court has assessed the applicability of Art. 6(2) to judicial proceedings following the conclusion of criminal proceedings, either by way of discontinuation or acquittal, in a number of different settings, including the obligation to bear court costs, the imposition of civil liability

---

[84] *Walsh v. Director of the Assets Recovery Agency* [2005] NICA 6, para. 31.

[85] See also *Benham v. the UK*, appl. 19380/92, 10.6.1996.

[86] As noted by the Court in *Welch v. the UK*, appl. 17440/90, 9.2.1995, para. 30, "the aims of prevention and reparation are consistent with a punitive purpose and may be seen as constituent elements of the very notion of punishment."

to pay compensation to the victim, disciplinary issues, a former accused's request for defence costs, etc. There has been no single approach adopted by the court to ascertain the circumstances under which a sufficient link between proceedings, which follow the conclusion of criminal proceedings, and when Art. 6(2) is violated. This area of Strasbourg law has also been criticised for being confusing, inconsistent, and unclear.[87]

In assessing the applicability of Art. 6(2) in this area, a distinction should be made between whether or not Art. 6(2) is applicable, and, if it is applicable, what protections Art. 6(2) affords.[88]

2. A sufficient link to prior criminal proceedings

In relation to the establishment of a sufficient link, the court has considered a number of different factors. These include how close the link between criminal responsibility of the accused and the right to compensation is in national legislation and practice,[89] whether or not the claim has followed criminal proceedings in time, and how the proceedings have been connected in legislation and practice with regard to both jurisdiction and subject-matter.[90] Other factors that have been considered are jurisdictional issues, the composition of the court, the procedure followed, differences in evidentiary standards, and the extent to which the same evidence is used in subsequent proceedings.[91] In *Y v. Norway*, which concerned the imposition of civil liability to pay compensation to the victim, the court found that similar objective constitutive elements of a criminal offence, notwithstanding its gravity, could not *per se* bring the subsequent proceedings within the realm of Art. 6(2).[92]

---

[87] See, e.g., Lord Phillips in *Serious Organised Crime Agency v. Gale* [2011] 1 WLR 2760, para. 32, King 2013, 16–17.

[88] See, e.g., *Allen v. the UK*, appl. 25424/09, 12.7.2013.

[89] *Sekanina v. Austria*, appl. 13126/87, 25.8.1993 (compensation for detention on remand). The Court applied *X v. Austria*, appl. 9295/81, 6.10.1982, p. 228, where the Commission found that the POI also applies to courts having to deal with non-criminal consequences of behaviour that has been subject to criminal proceedings and that they "must be bound by the criminal court's finding according to which there is no criminal responsibility for the acts in question although this naturally does not prevent them to establish e.g. a civil responsibility arising out of the same facts."

[90] *Hammern v. Norway*, appl. 30287/96, 11.2.2003 (compensation for detention on remand).

[91] See, e.g., admissibility decisions *Moullet v. France*, appl. 27521/04, 13.9.2007 (disciplinary sanctions); *H.K. v. Finland*, appl. 36065/97, 27.9.2005 (maintenance of child care order); *Lundkvist v. Sweden*, appl. 48518/99, 13.11.2003 (refusal of civil claims lodged by the applicant against insurers).

[92] *Y v. Norway*, appl. 56568/00, 11.2.2003, para. 41. Compare *Orr v. Norway*, appl. 31283/04, 15.5.2008 (imposition of civil liability to pay compensation to the victim).

Whether or not the criminal proceedings are decisive for the issue of compensation has also been ascribed relevance.[93]

In the Grand Chamber judgment *Allen v. the UK* (unanimous), these principles were recently reviewed and, to a large extent, verified.[94] The facts of the case were as follows: In 2000, A was convicted by a jury of the manslaughter of her four-month old son and sentenced to three years' imprisonment. Subsequently, A was granted leave to appeal out of time. The Court of Appeal, hearing evidence from a number of medical experts, quashed the conviction as being unsafe. Following this, A initiated compensation proceedings for miscarriage of justice, which were re-fused. The High Court concluded that there had been powerful evidence against A, but that new evidence created the possibility that, when taken with the evidence given at the trial, a jury might properly acquit the claimant; this was not, however, consistent with the proposition that, at the conclusion of a new trial, a trial judge would have been obliged to direct the jury to acquit A.

Subsequent to a review of the older authorities, and with the aims of Art. 6(2) and existing case law in mind, the ECtHR reached three conclusions.[95] First, in order for Art. 6(2) to apply to judicial proceedings that follow concluded criminal proceedings, there must be a link between the criminal proceedings and subsequent proceedings. Second, the existence of that link must be demonstrated by the applicant. Third, this applies "[w]henever the question of the applicability of Article 6 § 2 arises in the context of subsequent proceedings," *i.e.*, to all kinds of cases.

A sufficient link is, according to the court, likely to be present, for example, "where the subsequent proceedings require examination of the outcome of the prior criminal proceedings and, in particular, where they oblige the court to analyse the criminal judgment; to engage in a review or evaluation of the evidence in the criminal file; to assess the applicant's participation in some or all of the events leading to the criminal charge; or to comment on the subsisting indications of the appli-

---

[93] *Ringvold v. Norway*, appl. 34964/97, 11.2.2003 (imposition of civil liability to pay compensation to the victim). This case was not unanimously decided (6:1) and Judge Costa gave a strong dissenting opinion in which he argued that Art. 6(2) ought to apply and that it had been breached. He pointed out: "What benefit, then, did the applicant derive from his acquittal (apart from the important fact that he was not subject to criminal penalties)? He was told that he had been acquitted of the offence with which he had been charged, but he was subsequently told (on the basis of the same facts) that it was clear that he had committed the offence, and ordered to pay compensation to the victim. Where is the legal certainty in all that?... It cannot simultaneously be maintained that a man has been lawfully declared innocent of an offence...and that he nonetheless probably did commit the offence (even if the probability is only 51%!) and should pay for it. Just as revenge is not justice, compassion is no ground for circumventing justice."

[94] *Allen v. the UK*, appl. 25424/09, 12.7.2013.

[95] The ruling in *Allen v. UK* was applied in *Müller v. Germany*, appl. 54963/08, 27.3.2014.

cant's possible guilt."[96] As the national court in *Allen* engaged in a scrutiny of the criminal judgment, the court concluded that A had established the existence of the necessary link.

At a general level, it seems very questionable to argue, in light of the criteria used by the ECtHR, that a sufficient link between CAF and prior criminal proceedings is likely to exist. CAF proceedings are normally not dependent on preceding criminal proceedings in order to be initiated, but are free-standing civil proceedings. In other words, there is normally no need to examine the outcome of prior criminal proceedings.[97] Nor is there normally a sufficient link in law and practice (as the procedure, and standard of proof, is civil) or any finding of guilt *in personam*. Temporally, CAF proceedings might indeed be close to criminal proceedings, and the finding might be based on similar evidence, but this can hardly in itself be sufficient to bring proceedings under Art. 6(2).[98]

If, however, the national court for some reason would engage in a review or evaluation of the evidence in the criminal file in order to decide on the CAF issue, this could, under *Allen*, potentially establish a sufficient link. However, as noted above, this does not yet mean that Art. 6(2) is infringed.

3. A sufficient link by way of incriminating language

Besides establishing a link based on circumstances mentioned in section 5.4.2, it seems to be the case under certain older authorities that a link can also be established if incriminating language has been used in the subsequent judicial decision.[99]

---

[96] *Allen v. the UK*, appl. 25424/09, 12.7.2013, para. 104. In this particular case, a sufficient link was considered to exist. This was due to the fact that a compensation issue could only be assessed by examining the preceding judgment in order to identify whether the reversal of the conviction, which resulted in an acquittal in the present applicant's case, was based on new evidence and whether it gave rise to a miscarriage of justice.

[97] However, one circumstance that seems to distinguish CAF proceedings from both compensation claims by the defendant himself and third parties previously dealt with by the ECtHR, is that it is the state that, for a second time, initiates proceedings, although not criminal, based on the same (or similar) facts against the acquitted person. It is, as noted by *Mahmutaj*, Criminal Law Review (2009), 792, "difficult to see how post-acquittal forfeiture proceedings would be instigated at all were it not for the unsuccessful outcome (for the prosecution) of the prior criminal proceedings."

[98] As Lord Dyson put it in *Serious Organised Crime Agency v. Gale and another* [2011] 1 WLR 2760, para. 133, civil forfeiture proceedings "are free-standing proceedings instituted whether or not there have been criminal proceedings against the respondent or indeed anyone at all," and consequently "[t]here is no link at all."

[99] For this interpretation, see also the speech by Lord Dyson in *Serious Organised Crime Agency v. Gale and others* [2011] 1 WLR 2760, paras. 134–139. In *Scottish Ministers v. Doig* [2009] CSIH 34 the Court also accepted the possibility that *Y* might be read as "supporting a wider potential approach to the question of linkage." A different matter is of course that it could be argued, *sententia ferenda*, that language should merely relate to the

In this scenario, the assessment of whether Art. 6(2) is applicable or not, and what protections it awards, merge into one.

Y v. Norway concerned the imposition of civil liability to pay compensation following an acquittal on charges of violent assault, sexual assault, and homicide. The court concluded that the statement by the national court that the evidence adduced in the case as a whole made it "clearly probable that [A] has committed the offences against Ms T. with which he was charged," was of such a nature so as to cast doubt on the acquittal and thereby create a necessary link to the criminal proceedings.[100] This also seems to have been at issue in the admissibility decision *Moullet v. France*. In this case, a city official in Marseilles was subjected to disciplinary sanctions (compulsory retirement) by the Mayor following the discharge (on formal grounds) of charges of bribery as well as aiding and abetting fraud against him.[101] The ECtHR found that the disciplinary sanction could not be considered a criminal charge under the Engel criteria. Nor did it find that the national court had used such language so "as to create a clear link between the criminal case and the ensuing administrative proceedings," as it confined itself to determining the facts without suggesting any criminal characterisation at all.

This approach to the constructing of the necessary link so as to engage Art. 6(2) does not seem to be ruled out by the court in *Allen*, even if it is not specifically mentioned by the court. First of all, the conclusions were made with due regard to earlier case law, and the list of situations likely to create a link was not exhaustive. Second, the linguistic link applied in *Y* was mentioned by the court (in para. 101) and not overruled later. Third, the court's example of commenting on the subsisting indications of the applicant's possible guilt could be read so as to include the linguistic link.

In view of the analysis thus far, perhaps the strongest ground for successfully claiming that Art. 6(2) is applicable to CAF proceedings, and that the POI has been infringed, would be to argue that incriminating language was used in a subsequent forfeiture decision.[102] However, incompatibility in this regard would only concern a particular decision, not a CAF scheme as such.

What then would be the kind of language that would be permitted under Art. 6(2)? In older case law, fairly strict criteria applied. In, for example, *Sekanina v. Austria*, the court concluded that "the voicing of suspicions" regarding an ac-

---

"material dimension" of Art. 6(2) and not be understood as also potentially facilitating a sufficient link so as to apply the POI.

[100] *Y v. Norway*, appl. 56568/00, 11.2.2003. See also *Orr v. Norway*, appl. 31283/04, 15.5.2008 and the admissibility decision *Lundkvist v. Sweden*.

[101] *Moullet v. France*, appl. 27521/04, 13.9.2007.

[102] In this scenario, it appears that the POI could be applicable when the preceding criminal proceedings were discontinued by an acquittal or on formal grounds.

cused's innocence is no longer admissible following a final acquittal.[103] This position was confirmed in *Rushiti v. Austria*.[104] In *Y v. Norway*, the court also established a breach by reference to doubt on the correctness of the acquittal cast by the national judgment in the compensation case.[105]

In *Allen v. the UK*, having reviewed the principles in the area, the court made three important conclusions. First of all, it emphasised that "the language used by the decision-maker will be of critical importance in assessing the compatibility of the decision and its reasoning" with Art. 6(2). Second, attention has to be paid "to the nature and context of the particular proceedings," and, consequently, that "even the use of some unfortunate language may not be decisive." Third, this norm is generally applicable to all kinds of cases ("in all cases and no matter what the approach applied").[106]

Thus, in *Allen*, the court noted that the relevant national provision required the domestic courts to refer to the judgment of the Court of Appeal quashing the conviction, in order to identify the reasons for the acquittal and the extent to which it could be said that a new fact had shown beyond reasonable doubt that there had been a miscarriage of justice. Thus, the language used, when considered in the context of the exercise the judges were required to undertake, did not undermine A's acquittal or treat her in a manner inconsistent with her innocence.[107]

By making clear that some "unfortunate language" does not necessarily suffice to establish a breach when the nature and context of the proceedings is taken into consideration, the rigid approach taken in some of the older cases now appears to have been modified. It now seems to mean that the national court must be permitted to use such language as required (*i.e.*, as necessary) in order to establish the claim in question, but that it may go no further than that.[108] Whether or not a statement can be considered to impute criminal liability has always, to a non-negligible degree, been a question of semantic interpretation, but *Allen* now articulates that the threshold should not be set too low. Nevertheless, the distinction between un-

---

[103] *Sekanina v. Austria*, appl. 13126/87, 25.8.1993, para. 22.

[104] *Asan Rushiti v. Austria*, appl. 28389/95, 21.3.2000, para. 31.

[105] For examples of where the language has not been considered to infringe Art. 6(2), see admissibility decision *Reeves v. Norway*, appl. 4248/02, 8.7.2004; *A.L. v. Germany*, appl. 72758/01, 28.4.2005; and *Daktaras v. Lithuania*, appl. 42095/98, 10.10.2000.

[106] These principles were confirmed in *Müller v. Germany*, appl. 54963/08, 27.3.2014, para. 46.

[107] In *Müller v. Germany*, appl. 54963/08, 27.3.2014, which concerned the language used by a national court in refusing to order the applicant's probationary release, the Court confirmed the position in *Allen*. The Court found that a close reading of the impugned sentence, given the nature and context of the proceedings, excluded an understanding that would touch upon the applicant's reputation and the way he is perceived by the public, and thus constituted an infringement of Art. 6(2).

[108] This line of reasoning can also be seen in older case law, e.g., *Moullet v. France*, appl. 27521/04, 13.9.2007.

fortunate language, which infringes the POI and unfortunate language which does not, is not necessarily easy to make.[109] Although the court has, to some extent, clarified the applicable principles, the national courts will probably still face difficulties in assessing what can and cannot be said in subsequent judicial proceedings.[110]

In light of all this, an infringement could potentially arise in CAF proceedings if the court, for example, imputes criminal liability through an allegation that the respondent has in fact committed the offence. Therefore, it seems important that the allegation, and any subsequent decision granting the civil forfeiture order, be strictly confined to a determination of the facts and the criminal origins of the property in question, without any suggestion of a criminal characterisation involving guilt in regard to the respondent.[111]

In CAF proceedings, the agent most likely to make a statement that could potentially create a link is the court making the decision. However, a related question is whether or not statements by the applicant (being a state agency) could also qualify, for example, if they invite a finding of guilt for a particular offence. Some commentators argue that they should,[112] although this is not necessarily an obvious conclusion to draw. An interesting case is *Daktaras v. Lithuania* (although this case concerned a statement before acquittal/conviction), in which a prosecutor's statement about the defendant's guilt in dismissing a request to discontinue the criminal proceedings was not considered to infringe Art. 6(2), because, *inter alia*, it had been made in the context of criminal proceedings.[113] This could, *e contrario*, sup-

---

[109] See also the partly dissenting opinion of Judge De Gaetano, joined by Judge Yudkivska, in *Müller v. Germany*, appl. 54963/08, 27.3.2014.

[110] The outcome in Allen could be viewed as an attempt at rationalising the application of principles already in use by the Court in assessing post-acquittal statements by national authorities. It is nevertheless not unlikely that the outcome of some older cases would have been different in light of Allen. See also, however, *Rui*, Tidsskrift for strafferett (2014), 119–143, who argues that the principles expressed in Allen in fact constitute a substantive shift that increases the leeway for national authorities.

[111] For example, the Scottish Court of Session, Inner House, in *Scottish Ministers v. Doig* [2009] CSIH 34, para. 32, rightly concludes that "[j]ust as, as is accepted, a civil court, even after an acquittal in criminal proceedings, may in certain cases make a finding of liability to pay compensation on proof of the same facts as would constitute a criminal offence (e.g. assault or rape) without offending article 6(2), provided, no doubt, it is plain that the finding is of the delict of assault or rape, so too, it appears to us, a finding of 'unlawful conduct', albeit on the basis of the same facts as would constitute a criminal offence, could not be said to offend article 6(2) … In such circumstances, the court could not be said to 'overstep the bounds of the civil forum'."

[112] See *Mahmutaj*, Criminal Law Review (2009), 792. It also seems to be indicated by the Scottish Inner House in *Scottish Ministers v. Doig* [2009] CSIH 34, para. 32, where it was found that "the averments do not invite a finding of guilt of a particular offence, but rather a finding that conduct was 'unlawful'."

[113] *Daktaras v. Lithuania*, appl. 42095/98, 10.10.2000. Compare *Lavents v. Latvia*, appl. 58442/00, 28.11.2002, where the judge of the criminal proceedings expressed her surprise in two daily newspapers that the applicant was persisting in denying the charges and called on him to prove his innocence. The Court found a breach of Art. 6(2). As noted by *Harris*

port the following assertion: A statement of guilt by a prosecutor in an ongoing criminal trial is accepted, but a similar statement inviting a finding of guilt for a particular offence in CAF proceedings, being civil proceedings, is another matter. Thus, there might be reason to argue that, if an allegation were made by the applicant in CAF proceedings, being a state agent, this might qualify as applying Art. 6(2) if it invites a finding of guilt on behalf of the defendant, rather than a finding that the property originated from conduct that was "unlawful."

VI. Consequences of Art. 6(2) Being Applicable to CAF

A. General remarks

If it were determined that a particular CAF scheme was a "criminal charge" the question arises as to what the consequences would be.[114] One possible consequence is illustrated in *Lord Steyn's* remark that "[a]t the very least, if article 6(2) is held to be directly applicable, it will tend to undermine the effectiveness of confiscation procedures generally."[115] It could also be argued, considering that CAF does not arguably belong to "the core" of criminal charges, *ergo* that the POI should be restricted to a "POI light," meaning that the safeguards set out in Art. 6(2) would not operate with full force.[116]

Perhaps, the most probable consequence would be that, even if Art. 6(2) did apply with full force, this would not necessarily have a significant impact on the functionality of CAF.

---

et al., Law of the European Convention, p. 305, it is probable that an infringement would have been established in Daktaras had it been the judge who made the statement.

[114] There seems to be an important difference here between Art. 6(2) incompatibility based on systemic considerations, on the one hand, and *in casu* incompatibility based on incriminatory language, in a particular decision, on the other.

[115] *R v. Rezvi* [2002] UKHL 1, para. 12.

[116] In fact, in *Jussila v. Finland*, appl. 73053/01, 23.11.2006, para. 43, the ECtHR opened up to this possibility: "Notwithstanding the consideration that a certain gravity attaches to criminal proceedings ... it is self-evident that there are criminal cases which do not carry any significant degree of stigma. ... What is more, the autonomous interpretation adopted by the Convention institutions of the notion of a 'criminal charge' by applying the Engel criteria have underpinned a gradual broadening of the criminal head to cases not strictly belonging to the traditional categories of the criminal law, for example administrative penalties ..., prison disciplinary proceedings ..., customs law ..., competition law ..., and penalties imposed by a court with jurisdiction in financial matters ... consequently, the criminal-head guarantees will not necessarily apply with their full stringency." See also *Rui*, The Civil Asset, 165.

In the following, I will address four potential areas of CAF that would be implicated by Art. 6(2): the standard of proof, the burden of proof, the use of legal presumptions, and the concept of *in rem* proceedings in light of *mens rea*.

B. Standard of proof

The basic requirement in criminal proceedings that guilt must be proven beyond reasonable doubt is often associated with the POI.[117] One of the more controversial aspects of CAF is that the civil standard of proof is applied to determine the nexus between the property and the criminal activity. If Art. 6(2) were to apply to CAF proceedings, a question arises as to whether the ECHR would have bearing on this. Two questions must be addressed: 1) does Art. 6(2) ECHR establish requirements as to the standard of proof and, if so, 2) does this have a bearing on the standard applied in CAF proceedings in regard to the origin of the property in question?

Whether or not Art. 6(2) sets out a minimum standard of proof is not quite clear. The wording of Art. 6(2) does not in itself do so. The locution "until proved guilty according to law" refers mainly to the standard of proof in national jurisdictions.[118] There also does not seem to be any clear statement in the case law of the ECtHR that Art. 6(2) requires a standard corresponding to "beyond reasonable doubt."[119] Considering that the court is not concerned with the assessment of evidence (as long as it is convinced that the national courts have assessed it sufficiently carefully and based their decision on that evidence) but rather with evaluating whether the proceedings considered as a whole have been fair, this may not necessarily be sur-

---

[117] See, e.g., *Ashworth*, International Journal of Evidence & Proof (2006), 243.

[118] In *Serious Organised Crime Agency v. Gale and another* [2011] 1 WLR 2760, the respondents argued that a rebuttal of the presumption of innocence required proof of guilt to the criminal standard as implicit in the locution "according to law." According to the Supreme Court, this was not case. See also *Cecil Walsh v. Director of the Assets Recovery Agency* [2005] NICA 6 where the same was asserted. The Court of Appeal ruled that it should not be the case.

[119] See *Harris et al.*, Law of the European Convention, p. 302, *Strandbakken*, Uskyldspresumsjonen, p. 342. This was also concluded by the UK Supreme Court in *Serious Organised Crime Agency v. Gale and another* [2011] 1 WLR 2760, para. 34. The ECtHR has nevertheless touched upon the standard of proof in national jurisdictions in some cases. See, e.g., *Austria v. Italy*, 6 Yearbook of the European Convention on Human Rights (1963), p. 782, 784; *Barberá, Messegué and Jabardo v. Spain*, appl. 10590/83, 6.12.1988, para. 77; and *Geerings v. The Netherlands*, appl. 30810/03, 1.3.2007. It seems that the Court can, to some extent, materially assess under Art. 6(2) whether the weight of the evidence presented suffices for conviction. See *Telfner v. Austria*, appl. 33501/96, 20.3.2001, paras. 17–18. There are, however, a vast number of cases that address the standard of proof that the Court itself applies when assessing evidence of complaints. In this evaluation, it is clear that the "beyond reasonable doubt standard" applies, even though such proof may also follow from the coexistence of sufficiently strong, clear, and concordant inferences or from similar unrebutted presumptions of fact. See *Ireland v. the United Kingdom*, appl. 5310/71, 18.1.1978, para. 161.

prising.[120] However, the position of the court in *Barberá,* that the presumption of innocence, *inter alia*, requires that any doubt should benefit the accused, may well be interpreted as implying that a criminal standard of proof should apply.

In any case, even if Art. 6(2) would not require a criminal standard, this does not mean that it does not have any influence at all concerning the standard of proof in proceedings where the POI is engaged. It has been argued that, in light of the requirement of equality of arms, the minimum threshold of evidence must lie at least at $p(x) > 0.5$, *i.e.*, on the balance of probabilities.[121]

It follows that the consequences in regard to CAF proceedings vary, depending on the interpretation adopted. Under the first interpretation, the requirement of Art. 6(2) is satisfied as long as the standard of proof applied in CAF proceedings corresponds to a balance of probabilities.[122] If, however, Art. 6(2) were to be interpreted as requiring a criminal standard of proof, this would create problems in regard to a CAF scheme that corresponds to a criminal charge. In this case, the standard of proof could no longer be a balance of probabilities but should correspond to the criminal standard.

C. Burden of proof

The burden of proof can be viewed as a balance between the rights of the accused person and the fact that the respondent nevertheless, in some situations,

---

[120] See, e.g., *Grayson & Barnham v. The United Kingdom*, appl. 19955/05 and 15085/06, 23.9.2008, para. 42. It is, of course, not impossible to imagine a system in which a criminal conviction with evidence being shown, say, on a balance of probabilities would suffice. But, so far, no such case seems to have come up for the ECtHR, and it is therefore possible that the Court, if presented with such a case, would establish a breach of Art. 6(2), *i.e.*, that Art. 6(2) in fact embodies the standard "beyond reasonable doubt."

[121] See *Strandbakken*, Uskyldspresumsjonen, p. 343. In *Kress v. France*, appl. 39594/98, 7.6.2001, para. 72, the Court defined equality of arms as requiring "each party to be given a reasonable opportunity to present his case under conditions that do not place him at a substantial disadvantage *vis-à-vis* his opponent."

[122] It would also probably mean that, if the evidence was equally divided, the respondent would prevail (see *Cassella*, Asset Forfeiture Law, p. 380). This is not, however, to say that it could not well be argued that Art. 6(2), in light of its nature and purpose, reasonably *should*, and actually does, embody a more stringent minimum requirement in regard to the standard of proof. However, this does not exclude that a higher standard of proof could be required by the right to property under Art. 1 of Prot. 1, although this question will not be discussed here. It can also be noted that a committee on the Judiciary in the U.S. House of Representatives concluded that "a standard of clear and convincing evidence that the property is subject to forfeiture" should be required in CAF proceedings in order to recognise that "that in reality the government is alleging that a crime has taken place. Since civil forfeiture doesn't threaten imprisonment, proof beyond a reasonable doubt is not necessary."(House of Representatives, report 106–192, 18.6.1999, 12). In New York, the statutory standard of proof for non-conviction-based forfeiture is clear and convincing (see New York Forfeiture Statute, sect. 1311(1 b)).

might, to a certain extent, be better placed to show certain facts (provided that his rights are not eroded).[123] A basic requirement of Art. 6(2), as pointed out by the ECtHR in *Barberá*, is that the burden of proof is on the prosecution. In CAF proceedings it is normally for the state to show forfeitability of the property in question. The requirement in Art. 6(2) is therefore usually satisfied. However, for example in cases where third parties claim rights to the property subjected to forfeiture, it might be possible that the onus of proof is shifted, so that the third party must prove innocent ownership on a balance of probabilities (*i.e.*, the claimant would not have to present any evidence negating the defence).[124] If a CAF scheme were to include such a provision, the question arises as to whether this would be in conformity with Art. 6(2).

Although the main rule under the Convention is clear enough, there are exceptions to the requirement that the burden of proof must always be on the state. The question of a reversed burden of proof in relation to criminal confiscation was addressed in *Phillips v. The UK*.[125] The court concluded that Member States may be allowed to reverse the onus as long as it takes into account the importance of what is at stake, maintains the rights of the defence, and respects the requirements of a fair trial in Art. 6(1).[126] In the admissibility decision *Butler v. the UK* (concerning the applicability of Art. 1 Prot. 1), this reasoning was applied to forfeiture proceedings. The court held, with reference to *Phillips*, that the same "considerations must a fortiori apply to the forfeiture proceedings in the instant case, proceedings which did not involve the determination of a 'criminal charge' against the applicant."

Thus, it seems likely that, to the extent that there would be a reversed burden of proof in relation to a respondent/third party, this would be permitted by Art. 6(2) as long as the requirements of a fair hearing are fulfilled.

---

[123] *Jayawickrama et al.*, Forum on Crime and Society 29 (2002). See also, e.g., *United States v. One Parcel of Property Located at 194 Quaker Farms Road*, 85 F.3d 985 (2d Circuit) 4.6.1996, that held that "[b]urden-shifting where one party has superior access to evidence on a particular issue is a common feature of our law" and was therefore not unconstitutional.

[124] This is the case, for example, in US federal forfeiture statute 18 U.S.C. § 983(d)(1): "An innocent owner's interest in property shall not be forfeited under any civil forfeiture statute. The claimant shall have the burden of proving that the claimant is an innocent owner by a preponderance of the evidence." See also *Cassella*, Asset Forfeiture Law, pp. 410–411.

[125] *Phillips v. The United Kingdom*, appl. 41087/98, 5.7.2001. See also *Grayson & Barnham v. The United Kingdom*, appl. 19955/05 and 15085/06, 23.9.2008.

[126] *Salabiaku v. France*, appl. 10519/83, 7.10.1988, para. 28, where the Court explicitly approved of the presumption of fact and law: "[p]resumptions of fact or of law operate in every legal system. Clearly, the Convention does not prohibit such presumptions in principle", but "Article 6 para. 2 (Art. 6-2) does not … regard presumptions of fact or of law provided for in the criminal law with indifference. It requires States to confine them within reasonable limits which take into account the importance of what is at stake and maintain the rights of the defence."

D. The use of legal presumptions

As noted above, some legal systems provide for rebuttable legal presumptions when assessing the forfeitable property. The purpose of the use of presumptions is to assist the party who holds the burden of proof by requiring less evidence than would otherwise be necessary.[127] This can be problematic, as they weaken the position of the respondent (for example, a presumption that concerns property obtained over a long time can be difficult, if not impossible, to rebut).

Presumptions of law and fact have been repeatedly approved of by the ECtHR. The leading case is *Salabiaku v. France*, where the court concluded that "presumptions of fact or of law operate in every legal system" and that "clearly, the Convention does not prohibit such presumptions in principle," as long as they are confined "within reasonable limits which take into account the importance of what is at stake and maintain the rights of the defence."[128] In *Janosevic v. Sweden,* this view was supplemented by the observation that when legal presumptions are being used, a balance must be struck between "the importance of what is at stake and the rights of the defence," such that the means employed are "reasonably proportionate to the legitimate aim sought to be achieved."[129] Considerations of efficiency and execution may be of relevance in this regard. A relevant circumstance in assessing the conformity of the presumption with Art. 6(2) is whether the respondent has a practical possibility of rebutting the legal presumption.[130]

Legal presumptions in CAF proceedings are therefore not in conflict with the ECHR *per se*. It is, however, essential that the respondent has a practical, real, and effective possibility to rebut them. What the reference to "what is at stake" means in practice is not entirely clear, but it does not appear unreasonable that the magnitude of a forfeiture order should potentially be ascribed relevance here.

---

[127] As *Jayawickrama et al.*, Forum on Crime and Society 28 (2002) note, there are three different ways in which a presumption of fact can be constructed and rebutted by the defendant: 1) by raising a reasonable doubt, 2) by a requirement to adduce sufficient evidence to bring into question the truth of the presumed fact, and 3) by a burden to prove on a balance of probabilities the non-existence of the relevant fact.

[128] *Salabiaku v. France*, appl. 10519/83, 7.10.1988, para. 28. The Court also noted (para. 29) that "Even though the 'person in possession' is 'deemed liable for the offence' this does not mean that he is left entirely without a means of defence. The competent court may accord him the benefit of extenuating circumstances (Article 369 para. 1), and it must acquit him if he succeeds in establishing a case of force majeure." On the use of legal presumptions in regard to criminal confiscation, see *Phillips v. The United Kingdom*, appl. 41087/98, 5.7.2001, para. 41–47. The Court concluded that that application to the applicant of the relevant provisions of the Drug Trafficking Act 1994 was confined within reasonable limits, given the importance of what was at stake and that the rights of the defence were fully respected. The operation of the statutory assumption did not deprive the applicant of a fair hearing in the confiscation procedure.

[129] *Janosevic v. Sweden*, appl. 34619/97, 21.5.2003, para. 101(2); *Västberga Taxi Aktiebolag and Vulic v. Sweden*, appl. 36985/97, 21.5.2003, para. 113(2).

[130] *Janosevic v. Sweden*, appl. 34619/97, 21.5.2003, para. 102.

E. *In rem* contra *mens rea*

If a particular CAF scheme is deemed to fall within the scope of Art. 6(2), would this have any bearing on the requirement of *mens rea*?[131] *Mens rea* in essence means that criminal liability must not be imposed unless the individual is sufficiently aware of what he is doing and of the consequences it may have. It also means that it can fairly be said that the individual chose the behaviour and its consequences.[132] One consequence is that people cannot be held criminally liable solely on the grounds that liability and punishment would have a general deterrent effect in hindering further harm. In relation to CAF, this could be held to imply a certain awareness requirement on behalf of the respondent that the property originated in unlawful activity.

Art. 6(2) does not, however, seem to set up a requirement of *mens rea*. The *Salabiaku* case (above) indicates that (even) strict, or objective, criminal liability can be consistent with the Convention as long as the rights protected by the Convention are otherwise respected.[133] Even though CAF would fall within the scope of Art. 6(2), a requirement of fault would not necessarily and automatically follow.

Although CAF, as a civil action *in rem*, is neutral on the conduct of the property holder, the allure of the requirement for a certain level of awareness of the origin of property nevertheless remains. *Worrall* convincingly argues that it is not possible to "separate criminals from the proceeds of their criminal activity" and that this means "that persons whose property is targeted for forfeiture are presumed guilty."[134] *Hadaway* continues this line of argument:

> "Of course, the proponents of civil forfeiture will reply to this argument that, because civil forfeiture is a proceeding in rem, the guilt or innocence of the owner is irrelevant. But such circular reasoning stoops to an unseemly level of intellectual dishonesty because it ignores the punitive nature of in rem forfeiture."[135]

Irrespective of how desirable the postulation is that the respondent should be aware that he, with some degree of probability, is in possession of illicit property, it seems that such a requirement cannot be grounded on Art. 6(2).[136]

---

[131] This differs from criminal confiscation, where *mens rea* is normally required of the triggering crime and is thus indirectly required for confiscation.

[132] See *Ashworth/Horder*, Principles of Criminal Law, pp. 158–159.

[133] See *Harris et al.*, Law of the European Convention, p. 302. *Trechsel*, Human Rights, p. 157, also notes that case law of the ECtHR suggests that the POI does not extend as far as including a requirement of *mens rea*.

[134] *Worrall*, Policing: An International Journal of Police Strategies & Management (2004), 235. See also, similarly, *Naylor*, Crime, Law and Social Change (1999), 41.

[135] *Hadaway*, University of Miami Law Review 115 (2000). See also *Worrall*, Policing: An International Journal of Police Strategies & Management (2004), 235.

[136] If the respondent is *bona fide,* it should either not be possible to recover the property or the magnitude of the recovery should be mitigated. This is the case, for instance, in the UK where the court, pursuant to POCA s. 266(4)(a), may not make a recovery order if the

VII. Concluding Comments

What general conclusions can then be drawn from this analysis of the relation-ship between CAF and Art. 6(2)? Although there is no single type of CAF regime, which means that each scheme needs to be analysed on its own merits, it seems overall unlikely that CAF would be considered a "criminal charge" under the Engel criteria (unless, perhaps, the respondent's procedural position is "totally intolera-ble"). Nor does it seem very likely that a sufficiently strong procedural link could be constructed between a CAF scheme and any prior but discontinued criminal proceedings. The most plausible situation in which the scope of the POI could be extended to CAF is probably, provided that there have been discontinued preceding criminal proceedings, one in which the wording of a particular decision is incrimi-nating (although this would not relate to the CAF scheme as such). A (more) im-portant issue might therefore be, as *Smith, Owen and Bodnar* observe, "what due protections will be available under the scheme, regardless of whether the procedure embodies a 'criminal charge' or not."[137]

The second set of conclusions relate to the question of what the consequences would be if Art. 6(2) were applicable to CAF proceedings. As long as the rights of the ECHR and the requirements of Art. 6(1) are respected, it seems that the POI in itself would not present any real obstacles to CAF schemes. First, case law does not necessarily seem to prevent the nexus between the property to be forfeited and the criminal offence to be decided on a balance of probabilities. If, however, the court would find that Art. 6(2) does indeed imply a criminal standard of proof, the situa-tion would be different. Second, a potential reversed burden of proof is not neces-sarily problematic in light of the ECHR as long as the requirements of Art. 6(1) are respected. And thirdly, the same would apply to the application of statutory pre-sumptions in the assessment of the forfeited property. Nor can any requirement of *mens rea* on behalf of the respondent be grounded on Art. 6(2).

This is not to say that CAF schemes cannot be potentially problematic. Although justified by the important criminal policy's aim of removing criminal proceeds from circulation and from individuals who have no legal right to retain them, CAF schemes can be, while procedurally perhaps impeccable from a civil point of view, at worst substantially unreasonable and unfair.[138] However, it seems reasonable to

---

respondent obtained the recoverable property in good faith and it would be neither just nor equitable to do so.

[137] See *Smith/Owen/Bodnar*, Asset recovery, p. I-1024.

[138] This is shown, e.g., in the American discussion; see, e.g., *Worrall*, Policing: An In-ternational Journal of Police Strategies & Management (2004) and *Hadaway*, University of Miami Law Review (2000). *Alldridge*, Criminal Law Review (2013), 186–187, notes, in regard to the rules on civil recovery in POCA 2002 (Part V), that evidence that would not be admissible in a criminal trial is admitted in civil recovery proceedings, e.g., inferences from silence, evidence of previous behavior, evidence that is illegally obtained as well as hearsay. However, he continues (188), "to the surprise of those who are very concerned

infer that the ECHR will probably not, at least not in light of its current interpretation, provide sufficient ammunition to challenge potential substantive unreasonableness of CAF schemes. The reason for this is, as noted above, that the ECtHR is not mainly concerned with the substantive content of the law but rather with the question of whether the procedure has been fair and transparent, *inter alia*: Has there been a public hearing at which the respondent has been able to produce his own evidence?; Has the respondent had the right of appeal?; Has the evidence been carefully assessed with the final decision being based on that evidence?; Have presumptions been applied in a manner compatible with a fair hearing?

Therefore, it seems that the potential substantive unreasonableness of civil recovery measures will instead have to be challenged by means other than the POI. One alternative approach seems to be, for example, the requirement under Art. 1 Prot. 1 ECHR (right to property) that there must be a reasonable relationship of proportionality between the means employed by the state in the deprivation of property and the legitimate aim which is sought to be realised.[139] Thus, by invoking basic principles of human rights, criminal law, and criminal justice, the responsible policy- and decision-maker will hopefully be made aware of and see the consequences that a too broadly framed CAF scheme could have for both the legal principles in question and for the persons subject to its powers.

Bibliography

Aall, Jørgen, Waiver of Human Rights: Waiver of Procedural Rights According to ECHR Article 6 (Part III/III). Nordic Journal of Human Rights (2011), 206–278.

Alldridge, Peter, Proceeds of Crime Law since 2003 – Two Key Areas. Criminal Law Review (2013), 171–188.

---

about the civil recovery procedure proceedings, it has operated fairly successfully. Significant sums are being seized without generating results that offend popular conceptions of justice, and the presumption of innocence has been protected."

[139] In *R v. Waya* [2012] 1 AC 294, para. 10-18, the UK Supreme Court concluded that the confiscation scheme under s. 6(5) POCA 2002 should be read down so as to include a proportionality requirement, *i.e.*, that "[t]he judge should, if confronted by an application for an order which would be disproportionate, refuse to make it but accede only to an application for such sum as would be proportionate." Waya was later applied in the civil recovery case *Ahmed v. HMCRC* [2013] EWHC 2241 (Admin), para. 49, where Carr J found that there was even greater argument for proportionality when applying Part V (civil recovery) of POCA. See also *Paulet v. the UK*, appl. 6219/08, 13.5.2014, a pre-Waya criminal confiscation case, in which the ECtHR concluded, in establishing a breach of A1P1, that "at the time the applicant brought the domestic proceedings, the scope of the review carried out by the domestic courts was too narrow to satisfy the requirement of seeking the 'fair balance' inherent in the second paragraph of Article 1 of Protocol No. 1."

Andenæs, Johannes, Alminnelig strafferett, 5. utg ved Magnus Matningsdal og Georg Fredrik Rieber-Mohn. 5th ed. Oslo 2004.

Ashworth, Andrew, Four Threats to the Presumption of Innocence. International Journal of Evidence & Proof (2006), 241–279.

Ashworth, Andrew/Horder, Jeremy, Principles of Criminal Law. 7th ed. Oxford 2013.

Ashworth, Andrew/Zedner, Lucia, Preventive Justice. Oxford 2014.

Boucht, Johan, Extended Confiscation and the Proposed Directive on Freezing and Confiscation of Criminal Proceeds in the EU: On Striking a Balance between Efficiency, Fairness and Legal Certainty. European Journal of Crime, Criminal Law and Criminal Procedure (2013), 127–162.

– Utvidgat förverkande enligt norska straffeloven § 34 a – ökad funktionalitet eller obefogat avsteg från hävdvunna rättssäkerhetskrav? Tidsskrift for Strafferett (2012), 382–423.

Cameron, Iain, An Introduction to the European Convention on Human Rights. 6th ed. Uppsala 2011.

Cassella, Stefan D., The case for civil forfeiture. Why *in Rem* proceedings are an essential tool for recovering the proceeds of crime. Journal of Money Laundering Control 11 (2008), 8–14.

– Asset Forfeiture Law in the United States. Huntington (NY) 2007.

De la Cuesta Arzamendi, José Luis (ed.), Resolutions of the Congresses of the International Association of Penal Law (1926–2004), N: 21. Toulouse 2009.

Dworkin, Ronald, Principle, Policy and Procedure. In: Colin Tapper (ed.), Crime, Proof and Punishment: Essays in Memory of Sir Rupert Cross. London 1981.

Emmerson, Ben/Ashworth, Andrew/Macdonald, Allison, Human Rights and Criminal Justice. 3rd ed. London 2012.

Grabenwarter, Christoph/Pabel, Katharina, Europäische Menschenrechtskonvention. Ein Studienbuch. München 2012.

Hadaway, Brant C., Executive Privateers: A Discussion on Why the Civil Asset Forfeiture Reform Act Will Not Significantly Reform the Practice of Forfeiture. University of Miami Law Review (2000), 81–121.

Harris, David/O'Boyle, Michael/Warbrick, Colin, Law of the European Convention on Human Rights. 2nd ed. Oxford 2009.

Jareborg, Nils/Zila, Josef, Straffrättens påföljdslära. 2nd ed. Stockholm 2007.

Jayawickrama, Nihal/Pope, Jeremy/Stolpe, Oliver, Legal provisions to facilitate the gathering of evidence in corruption cases: easing the burden of proof. Forum on Crime and Society (2002), 23–31.

Kennedy, Anthony, Designing a civil forfeiture system: an issues list for policymakers and legislators. Journal of Financial Crime (2006), 132–163.

– Justifying the Civil Recovery of Criminal Proceeds. Journal of Financial Crime (2004), 8–23.

King, Colin, Civil forfeiture and Article 6 of the ECHR: due process implications for England & Wales and Ireland. Legal Studies (2013), 1–24.

Mahmutaj, Klentiana, Cash forfeiture following acquittal: an "affront to public perception" or a breach of fundamental human rights. Criminal Law Review (2009), 783–793.

Mock, William B.T./Demuro, Gianmario (eds.): Human Rights in Europe. Commentary on the Charter of Fundamental Rights of the European Union. Durham 2010.

Naylor, Robert T., Wash-out: a critique of follow-the-money methods in crime control policy. Crime, Law and Social Change (1999), 1–57.

Pellonpää, Matti, Europeiska människorättskonventionen. Helsingfors 2007.

Rui, Jon Petter, Uskyldspresumsjonens vern mot omtale av straffesaker før straffedom og etter frifinnelse. Tidsskrift for strafferett (2014), 119–143.

– The Civil Asset Forfeiture Approach to Organised Crime. Exploring the Possibilities for an EU model. eucrim (2011), 159–167.

– Non Conviction Based Confiscation in the EU – an assessment of Art. 5 of the Proposal for a directive of the European Parliament and of the Council on the freezing and confiscation of proceeds of crime in the European Union. ERA Forum (2012), 349–360.

Smith, Ian/Owen, Tim/Bodnar, Andrew, On asset recovery. Criminal confiscation and civil recovery, Binder I. Oxford 2012.

– On asset recovery. Criminal confiscation and civil recovery, Binder II. Oxford 2012.

Stessens, Guy, Money laundering: a new international law enforcement model. Cambridge 2000.

Strandbakken, Asbjørn, Uskyldspresumsjonen. "In dubio pro reo". Bergen 2003.

Tomlin, Patrick, Extending the Golden Thread? Criminalisation and the Presumption of Innocence. The Journal of Political Philosophy (2012), 1–23.

Trechsel, Stefan, Human Rights in Criminal Proceedings. Oxford 2006.

Träskman, Per Ole, Presumtionen om den för brott misstänktes oskyldighet. In: Olle Höglund/Bertil Bengtsson/Lars Heuman/Hans Ragnemalm (eds.), Festskrift till Lars Welamson. Stockholm 1987.

Worrall, John L., The Civil Asset Forfeiture Reform Act of 2000. A sheep in wolf's clothing? Policing: An International Journal of Police Strategies & Management (2004), 220–240.

List of Abbreviations

CAF	Civil asset forfeiture
ECHR	European Convention on Human Rights
ECtHR	European Court of Human Rights
POCA	Proceeds of Crime Act 2002
POI	Presumption of innocence

Chapter 7

Confiscation and Data Protection

The Bare Necessities

Els De Busser

At first glance, confiscation or asset recovery and the protection of personal data do not seem to have anything in common. Nevertheless, in order to confiscate property – especially in cases in which a person is not able to stand trial – information is necessary on what property is or was owned by this person and where this property is located. Property such as real estate or money sitting in a bank account can be situated in a foreign jurisdiction; thus, international mutual assistance requests could be required to obtain this information. More often than not, this information will include personal data. That means that the legal instruments governing data protection should be respected by the competent authorities of the EU Member States. Additionally, the existing EU legal framework on the protection of personal data is undergoing revision due to challenges introduced by new technologies, on the one hand, and in order to iron out the differences in implementation of the data protection legal instruments in national law, on the other.

Thus, for any type of confiscation, three sets of rules should be considered: the rules on the gathering and processing of information that is not qualified as personal data, the rules on the gathering and processing of personal data, and the rules on confiscation of property. Confiscating property that was used to commit a criminal act or that constitutes proceeds of crime is traditionally done *after* the owner has been convicted. This is the case in most Member States of the EU and was also harmonized in Directive 2014/42/EC of 3 April 2014 on the freezing and confiscation of instrumentalities and proceeds of crime in the EU (hereafter: the Directive).[1] Inspired by national estimates of criminal profit as well as UN estimates that the total amount of criminal proceeds globally was approximately USD 2.1 trillion in 2009, the Commission aimed at strengthening the EU legal framework for confiscation.

In certain Member States and non-Member States, confiscating goods without the conviction of the owner is a possibility.[2] This can be effected either by means

---

[1] O.J. L 127, 29.04.2014, pp. 39–50.

[2] The European Parliament rapporteur *Monica Luisa Macovei* listed the following Member States and non-Member States that have introduced the system of non-conviction-based confiscation after it was first used in the US: Italy, Ireland, United Kingdom, Albania, Bulgaria, Slovakia, Australia, South Africa, the Canadian provinces of Alberta and

of a criminal confiscation procedure or a civil procedure. Gathering and processing information, including personal data, needs to be carried out in both cases, but the set of rules governing the gathering and processing of personal data is different, regardless of whether it concerns a civil or a criminal context. In a 2012 proposal, the Commission aimed at introducing non-conviction-based confiscation in all Member States, but this was removed from the text at a later stage. This paper will show that several legal issues were avoided by taking out this provision. What was kept in the text of the Directive is extended confiscation. In this case, information is gathered that shows a lack of proportionality between the lawful income of the convicted person and the value of his property. The above-mentioned types of confiscation require a considerable amount of information, including personal data. Thus, several questions are at the heart of this contribution: How can the basic data protection standards such as necessity and purpose limitation be reconciled with confiscation? How should personal data that originate from commercial transactions, bank databases, or even employer's files be used for confiscation purposes in accordance with data protection laws? And lastly, how relevant is the current reform of the EU data protection legal framework for the Directive?

In the first part of this paper, the issues sketched above are analysed together with the recent developments that make for a relevant discussion, one which, unfortunately, is often overlooked. Before being able to freeze or confiscate assets, one has to find them first. This operation is usually the result of information exchange that, in many cases, involves crossing one or more national borders. Obviously, this information exchange will include personal data. That, in turn, will trigger the data protection standards that should be complied with. Since they are undergoing revision at the moment, the so-called data protection reform package will also be discussed where necessary. Due to the specificities of confiscation without a criminal conviction and the data protection issues they entail, a short section will be dedicated to this debate. In a second part, the data protection principles will be the focus in an attempt to define the requirement of necessity and the purpose limitation principle in a manner that is both useful and relevant for confiscation under the Directive. Also, part of this second analysis is the information exchange with third states, as this triggers additional data protection concerns.

Ontario. See Report on the proposal for a directive of the European Parliament and of the Council on the freezing and confiscation of proceeds of crime in the European Union (COM(2012)0085 – C7-0075/2012 – 2012/0036(COD)), 20.05.2013.

I. Relevance of Data Protection in Confiscation Matters

A. Finding the Assets

The International Centre for Asset Recovery (ICAR) of the Basel Institute of Governance in Switzerland described asset recovery as a "complex and multi-faceted process which involves several steps that require high levels of technical knowledge and capacity. The actual repatriation of assets stands at the very end of a series of actions."[3] This series of actions starts with a trigger, a piece of information that makes law enforcement agencies suspect money was illegally obtained and/or laundered. The information can originate from a source within an organization, institution, or firm (for example, a whistle-blower); a financial institution (for example, a suspicious transaction report); or intelligence gathering, and can take many forms. Information revealing proceeds of crime can be found in the property register of a typical holiday island or even the admission register of an expensive university or private school at which the children of an offender are or were enrolled. It can include both personal and non-personal data, and it can include both public and private data.

Information that is accessible for the public is not only searched by inquisitive Internet users. It can be and is actually searched and used by public authorities looking for information on a particular person, e.g., a person who is suspected of committing a criminal act. When the Greek Financial and Economic Crime Unit was founded to combat tax evasion, they turned to Google Earth in order to find out that the number of swimming pools built in the suburbs of Athens was more than 52 times greater than the number of legally registered pools.[4] As a reaction, many pool owners turned to camouflage nets to hide their unregistered property. Most published information found on the Internet qualifies as open-source information and is available for everyone without court orders or mutual legal assistance requests. Data that is not accessible through open sources can be obtained either in an informal or in a formal way. Informally searching for information on a person or his activities can be done through networks of personal contacts or even informal networks set up for that particular purpose. Informal networks include the Camden Asset Recovery Inter-Agency Network (CARIN), the Asset Recovery Inter-Agency Network for South Africa (ARINSA), and Red iberoamericana de cooperación jurídica internacional (IberRed). The above-mentioned ICAR is an international network that, since 2006, has not only been assisting national authorities in seizing,

---

[3] Basel Institute of Governance, International Centre for Asset Recovery, Capacity Building in Asset Recovery, 4, url: www.baselgovernance.org/fileadmin/docs/publications/books/Capacity_Building_in_Asset_Recovery.pdf [last visited 10.09.2014].

[4] *Steinvorth*, Greek Government Hauls in Billions in Back Taxes, Spiegel Online, 08.02.2010.

confiscating, and recovering the proceeds of corruption and money laundering but has also been providing training, research, and consultancy on these topics.[5] These initiatives group the experts[6] and knowledge that are necessary to effectively and efficiently handle a complex matter such as asset recovery.

Besides the informal exchange of information, in many instances, the exchange of information has been formalized by means of bilateral or multilateral mutual legal assistance treaties or by information channels provided by organizations and agencies such as Interpol, Europol, Eurojust, and the European Judicial Network (EJN).

In the case of formal searches for information – those searches which are legally regulated and restricted – coercive measures could be necessary or at least a request for mutual legal assistance is required for cross-border cases. Since the definition of personal data focuses on the identified or identifiable individual, both formal and informal searches for information can concern personal data, and both coercive and non-coercive measures can result in personal data. Personal data can be part of a person's private life and therefore require coercive measures, e.g., medical data, but personal data can also exist outside the scope of what is considered a person's private life, e.g., data on the ownership of a house in a property register, and thus be accessed without the use of a court order.

Formal as well as informal exchanges of information can be hindered by differences in national legal systems. In its 2008 Communication on proceeds of organized crime, the Commission highlighted the need for better information exchange in no less than three of the 10 strategic priorities.[7] These priorities included the exchange of information between the Asset Recovery Offices (AROs), which also use the techniques and forms provided for by the 2006 Framework Decision on simplifying the exchange of information and intelligence between law enforcement authorities.[8] In cooperating and exchanging personal data on assets that should be confiscated, the AROs are also obliged to comply with the applicable data protection rules. The same goes for the national judicial and law enforcement authorities, Eurojust and Europol. The applicable data protection rules regulate and restrict the collecting and processing of this information.

---

[5] Url: www.assetrecovery.org [last visited 22.08.2014].

[6] ICAR also hosts a genuine Asset Recovery Experts Network (AREN).

[7] COM(2008)766 final, 20.11.2008, pp. 11–12.

[8] Framework Decision 2006/960/JHA, O.J. L 386, 29.12.2006, pp. 89–100. See also Decision 2007/845/JHA concerning cooperation between Asset Recovery Offices of the Member States in the field of tracing and identification of proceeds from, or other property related to, crime, O.J. L 332, 18.12.2007, pp. 103–105.

B. Umbrella Rules

Before the Lisbon Treaty,[9] which amended the treaties on which the EU was founded, entered into force, the EU's data protection legal framework consisted of three legal instruments in the field of data processing for commercial purposes[10] (the former first pillar) and one Framework Decision covering the field of data protection in criminal matters (the former third pillar).[11] As long as no new legal instruments have been adopted in the post-Lisbon era, these are still valid. At the moment of preparing this contribution, the Commission proposals for a new Directive on the protection of individuals with regard to the processing of personal data by competent authorities for the purposes of prevention, investigation, detection or prosecution of criminal offences, or the execution of criminal penalties, and the free movement of such data[12] as well as a General Data Protection Regulation[13] had both not yet been adopted.

The aforementioned Framework Decision (hereafter: 2008 Framework Decision) relies on the basic standards stemming from the Council of Europe's umbrella convention, the 1981 Convention for the Protection of Individuals with regard to Automatic Processing of Personal Data (hereafter: Data Protection Convention).[14] Europol and Eurojust have adopted their own data protection rules;[15] however, they are also in compliance with the 1981 Data Protection Convention.

The Council of Europe's umbrella convention is often explicitly referred to in other legal instruments governing cooperation in criminal matters, including EU legal instruments, as all Member States have ratified it.[16] Article 5 of this Convention[17] distinguishes quality standards for personal data, on the one hand, and quality standards for the processing of personal data, on the other. As a third group of standards, the 2001 additional protocol[18] to the Data Protection Convention defines

---

[9] Treaty of Lisbon, O.J. C 306, 17.12.2007, pp. 1–271.

[10] Directive 95/46/EC, O.J. L 281, 23.11.1995, pp. 31–50. Regulation (EC) no. 45/2001, O.J. L 8, 12.01.2001, pp. 1–22. Directive 2002/58/EC, O.J. L 201, 31.07.2002, pp. 37–47 amended by Directive 2006/24/EC, O.J. L 105, 13.04.2006, pp. 54–63.

[11] Framework Decision 2008/977/JHA, O.J. L 350, 30.12.2008, pp. 60–71.

[12] COM(2012)10 final, 25.01.2012.

[13] COM(2012)11 final, 25.01.2012.

[14] ETS, No. 108.

[15] Council Decision establishing the European Police Office, O.J. L 121, 15.05.2009, pp. 37–66 and Council, Rules of procedure on the processing and protection of personal data at Eurojust, O.J. C 68, 19.03.2005, pp. 1–10.

[16] For example, Europol Decision O.J. L 121, 15.05.2009, pp. 37–66 and Schengen Implementation Agreement, O.J. L 238, 22.09.2000, pp. 19–62.

[17] This article is modelled on Council of Europe Resolutions with regard to the privacy of individuals vis-à-vis electronic databanks in the public and private sectors: Resolution (73)22, 26.09.1973 and Resolution (74)29, 20.09.1974.

[18] ETS, No. 181.

the rules on transfers of personal data to states that are not bound by the Convention. Derogations to the principles in the Convention and the additional protocol are only allowed in accordance with Article 9 of the Convention that, in turn, is modelled on Article 8 of the ECHR covering the right to a private life.

The Council of Europe's Data Protection Convention includes the requirement that data need to be adequate, relevant, and not excessive in relation to the purposes for which they are stored. Moreover, data should be accurate and, where necessary, kept up to date. The adequacy and relevance requirements aim at demonstrating the qualitative connection between the data and the purpose. If a direct link is non-existent – for example, if the same result can be achieved by other less intrusive means – data cannot be adequate or relevant. On the quantitative level, respecting the proportionality rule means that the data controller should, in each case, determine and distinguish the minimum amount of personal data needed in order to successfully accomplish their purpose and to limit the processing to these data.

Personal data should be obtained and processed fairly and lawfully. This rule was included so as to avoid the use of improper or illegitimate methods for data gathering, which is weighed up by considering the interests of the data subject, the purpose, and the nature of the processing.

Personal data should be stored for specified and legitimate purposes and should not be used in a way that is incompatible with those purposes. This rule is known as the *purpose limitation principle*. What exactly constitutes an incompatible purpose is to be decided on a case-by-case basis. The EU's Data Protection Working Party has developed criteria to assess whether a purpose is compatible or not (cf. *infra*).[19] In accordance with Article 8 §2 ECHR, infringements upon the right to a private life should be legal and necessary in the interests of a legitimate aim. This includes the gathering of personal data as well as the use that is made of these data.[20] Therefore, any use for a purpose other than the original purpose or a compatible purpose should be equally subject to these requirements.

Even when personal data are adequate and relevant at the moment of their collection, it is possible that they no longer are after a certain amount of time. For these reasons, the Data Protection Convention has specified the *data retention principle* or the rule that personal data can be saved in databases for as long as is required for the purpose for which they are retained. After this period of time has passed, the data can still be stored but need to be separated from the name – the identifying factor – of the individual they relate to.

No investigation would be possible if it was not allowed to derogate from both the purpose limitation and the data retention principles. Therefore, inspired by the

---

[19] Article 29 Data Protection Working Party, Opinion 03/2013 on purpose limitation, 02.04.2013, pp. 23–27.

[20] ECtHR, *Leander v. Sweden*, 1987, § 48 and *Rotaru v. Romania*, 2000, § 46.

lawful derogations to human rights in the ECHR, personal data can be collected and processed in breach with the data protection standards if this is legal and necessary in the interests of *inter alia* suppression of criminal offences.

When the gathering of the personal data and the use thereof takes place in two different states, an additional issue arises. In the case where both are EU Member States or when both states have ratified the Data Protection Convention, both are bound by the same ground rules and will therefore not find personal data to be processed in accordance with different – possibly contradictory – principles. In the case where personal data are transmitted from an EU Member State to a third state, however, personal data could possibly enter into a legal framework of data protection that offers lower safeguards than the state of origin. It is not the Data Protection Convention itself, but the 2001 additional protocol that stipulates a special condition to protect personal data in this particular situation. The Member State that plans to transfer personal data to a third state is bound, first, to check the level of data protection in the receiving state. Thus, from an EU point of view, the third state should offer an adequate level of data protection. This requirement is also included in the 2008 Framework Decision on data protection in criminal matters and in Directive 95/46/EC.

Despite its significance, the additional protocol has not been ratified by all Member States. Additionally, so far no adopted legal instrument has presented a binding check-list on aspects to include when assessing the adequacy of other states' data protection legislation. This diverse application of the adequacy requirement creates inconsistencies in the EU data protection scheme.[21]

C. Reform of Data Protection Legal Framework

In 2012, the Commission presented proposals for reforming the EU data protection legal framework. Directive 95/46/EC[22] and the 2008 Framework Decision[23] are both being revised. In accordance with the Lisbon Treaty and the change in legal instruments, the Directive will be replaced by a regulation and the Framework Decision will be replaced by a directive. At the time of writing this contribution, a partial agreement had been reached with regard to the proposed directive for data protection in criminal matters. The relevant changes are dealt with below.

---

[21] See also *De Busser*, eucrim 1 (2010), pp. 30–36.

[22] Proposal for a Regulation on the protection of individuals with regard to the processing of personal data and on the free movement of such data, COM(2012)11 final.

[23] Proposal for a Directive on the protection of individuals with regard to the processing of personal data by competent authorities for the purposes of prevention, investigation, detection or prosecution of criminal offences or the execution of criminal penalties, and the free movement of such data, COM(2012)10 final.

1. Scope

The newly proposed data protection rules incorporate a significant change regarding the scope that these new rules will have once the directive is adopted. Even though the 2008 Framework Decision was originally meant to cover the processing of personal data for the purpose of preventing, investigating and prosecuting criminal offences, and executing criminal sentences, it was adopted with a limited scope after lengthy discussions. The Framework Decision is only applicable to the collecting and processing of personal data received by one Member State's authorities from another Member State's authorities. Domestically collected and processed personal data fell outside of the scope of the Framework Decision and, apart from the implementation of the Data Protection Convention, they were not the subject of harmonised legislation. In the proposed directive, domestically collected and processed personal data will also be subject to the same data protection rules as personal data received from other Member States. Even though all EU Member States are obliged to implement the provisions of the Data Protection Convention, research has proven that many differences still exist in the Member States' legislations.[24]

The proposed directive and its wider scope could therefore bring about specific changes to the handling of personal data, also by authorities responsible for tracing assets for the purpose of confiscation. For example, all personal data stored in commercial databases, such as sales records or personal data stored by financial institutions that have been collected nationally and could be used to prove the purchase of assets, also have to respect the provisions of the proposed directive when they are transferred to another Member State's authorities for the purpose of confiscation.

2. Standards

Looking at the proposed directive, the data protection standards have not undergone substantial changes. Principles such as data minimization and transparency were explicitly present in a leaked draft of the proposed directive but disappeared in the official proposal. Both principles are still included in the current draft, however, be it not so obvious. Data minimization is implicitly included in the data protection principles set forth in Article 4 of the proposed directive, as it includes not only gathering as little personal data as possible but also limiting the processing of personal data to those situations in which the purpose cannot be fulfilled by processing non-personal data.[25] Transparency of data processing is incorporated in the

---

[24] See, for detail, *Korff*, pp. 38–91.

[25] European Parliament legislative resolution of 12 March 2014 on the proposal for a directive of the European Parliament and of the Council on the protection of individuals with regard to the processing of personal data by competent authorities for the purposes of pre-

provisions on the rights of the data subject. Two innovations in the data protection reform are particularly relevant for asset confiscation, especially for the tracing and processing of information on assets.

First, the distinction made regarding different categories of data subjects had never before been laid down in a general data protection legal instrument such as the Data Protection Convention or the 2008 Framework Decision. Eurojust, as one of the main actors in EU judicial and police cooperation in criminal matters, did incorporate this distinction in its own data protection rules.[26] In criminal investigations, it is essential to distinguish personal data relating to a suspect or accused from personal data relating to a relative, witness, victim, or contact person. Again, the rights of fair trial come into play here, as they only apply to the person who has been charged with a criminal offence. Thus, personal data of other persons should be handled with caution. With regard to the tracing of assets and the personal data collected for this purpose, chances are high that personal data from third persons are equally processed, e.g., personal data relating to relatives of the suspect or accused or persons he or she did business with. The fact that the current reform of the data protection legal framework[27] obliges the Member States to integrate this distinction in their national legislation on the processing of personal data is an element to be considered when tracing assets for the purpose of confiscating them.

Second, with regard to the use of unconfirmed data or intelligence, the Council of Europe recommended making a clear distinction between data based on their degree of accuracy and reliability in 1987 already. Recommendation No. R(87)15 on the use of personal data in the police sector has been implemented by, for example, Europol[28] but the accuracy and reliability standard did not make it into the 2008 Framework Decision on data protection in criminal matters despite the Commission having proposed this.[29] Even though Recommendation R(87)15 is recognised as a set of specific data protection rules in other legal instruments, it is still only a non-binding recommendation and its implementation cannot be enforced. Europol is the only actor in judicial and police cooperation in criminal matters that has laid down rules for utilising this distinction in practice. A brochure detailing Europol's information management shows the 4x4 matrix used to evaluate whether a source and the information this source delivers is reliable.[30] This is an example of intelligence assessment that could function as a model for other actors involved in

---

vention, investigation, detection or prosecution of criminal offences or the execution of criminal penalties, and the free movement of such data (COM(2012)0010 – C7-0024/2012 – 2012/0010(COD)).

[26] See Article 17 of Rules of Procedure on the Processing and Protection of Personal Data at Eurojust, O.J. C 68, 19.03.2005, p. 4.

[27] Article 5 of the proposed directive.

[28] See Article 27 Europol Decision.

[29] COM(2005)475 final, 04.10.2005.

[30] Europol Information Management, Products and Services, no. 2510-271, pp. 7–8.

criminal investigations who are handling confirmed and unconfirmed bits of information and intelligence, e.g., in the tracing of assets for the purpose of confiscating them. With the proposed directive, the European Commission requires Member States to ensure that, as far as possible, different categories of personal data undergoing processing are distinguished in accordance with their degree of accuracy and reliability.[31]

D. The Special Case of Non-Conviction-Based Confiscation

On 12 March 2012, the European Commission presented its proposal for the Directive on the freezing and confiscation of instrumentalities and proceeds of crime in the EU.[32] Confiscation of criminal assets was considered not to have been used enough on a national level, thus more possibilities were introduced with this proposal. One of these possibilities was the freezing and confiscation of property irrespective of a prior conviction of its owner by a criminal court, also known as non-conviction-based confiscation.[33] Non-conviction-based confiscation or civil asset forfeiture is unknown in many Member States. Additionally, some Member States do not allow for procedures *in rem* or for procedures against an object rather than a person. Proposing to introduce the system of non-conviction-based confiscation in all Member States was thus quite controversial and the Member States could not agree on keeping it in the text of the Directive. It was considered a bridge too far. Not only because it would be a novelty for the civil law traditions of the EU and cause substantial changes in their national laws, but also because other issues remained. It was, for example, not clear whether the proposed provision aimed at introducing a criminal or a civil procedure and this raised questions regarding data protection.

Moreover, the proposed Article 5 on non-conviction-based confiscation has not been deleted completely. What remains in the Directive is confiscation in cases in which criminal proceedings have been initiated but confiscation based on a final conviction is not possible due to illness or absconding of the suspect or accused. Provided that the proceedings could have led to a criminal conviction if the suspect or accused had been able to stand trial, the confiscation of instrumentalities and proceeds should be established in national law. This means that *de facto* non-conviction-based confiscation is still there, be it only in exceptional circumstances and still in the context of criminal proceedings. The fact that conviction is not reached does not take away the criminal character of the proceedings. The latter is

---

[31] Article 6 of the proposed directive.
[32] COM(2012)85 final, 12.03.2012.
[33] Article 5 of the proposed directive.

essential from a data protection point of view, more specifically with regard to the purpose limitation principle.

The purpose limitation principle requires that personal data are collected for a specific purpose and processed for a purpose that is either identical or compatible therewith. Personal data that are processed to identify and locate proceeds of crime could have been gathered for any purpose, e.g., for commercial, educational, or medical purposes.

Being charged with a criminal offence triggers the protection offered by Article 6, §§2–3 ECHR or the minimum rights to a fair trial. This can create difficulties with regard to the personal data that have been collected for a different incompatible purpose, such as commercial or financial purposes, and used in criminal proceedings unless the legality and necessity requirements that allow derogating from the purpose limitation principle can be met. If non-conviction-based confiscation is considered a criminal procedure, this will not cause problems, since the necessity requirement is fulfilled when the data in question are processed for the purpose of suppression of criminal offences. According to the ECtHR, the fair trial rights of Article 6 even compensate the infringements of the right to a private life of Article 8. The Court concluded an independent relationship between Articles 6 and 8. The latter is generated by the continuing case law pronouncing the right to a fair trial being based on *all* circumstances of the case, rather than merely an interference with an individual's private life by collecting evidence. Personal data can be collected in a way that infringes upon a person's private life and still be successfully used in a criminal procedure.[34]

If the Commission meant to introduce a criminal procedure by proposing the non-conviction-based confiscation in Article 5 in the original proposal, then the questions of complying with the purpose limitation principle and the necessity requirement are not an issue. The personal data that were collected for the purpose of the prior criminal investigation are then not used for a different incompatible purpose, and the use of personal data that were collected for a different purpose before being introduced in a criminal procedure can be justified, as they are necessary for the suppression of criminal offences.

If the proposed Article 5 was meant to introduce a civil procedure, then the fair trial rights embedded in Article 6, §§2–3 ECHR are not activated, and the personal data that were collected in the prior criminal proceedings, or that were collected for other purposes, cannot be used for the purpose of this civil forfeiture. The necessity requirement does not offer any possibility to lawfully derogate from the purpose limitation principle, since the Data Protection Convention limits such

---

[34] See, *inter alia*, *De Smet et al.*, in: Vande Lanotte/Haeck (eds.), Handboek EVRM, Artikelsgewijze commentaar, pp. 468–470; *Vervaele*, Gegevensuitwisseling en terrorismebestrijding, pp. 49–50.

exceptions to measures that are necessary in the interests of protecting state security, public safety, and the monetary interests of the state or the suppression of criminal offences, or in the interests of protecting the data subject or the rights and freedoms of others.

Because none of the pressing social needs that can justify derogating from the purpose limitation principle covers non-conviction-based confiscation as a civil procedure, it is not possible to lawfully use personal data for a non-conviction-based confiscation that were originally collected for another purpose. The only way to enable this use is to expand the pressing social needs listed for derogating from the data protection principles or to consider non-conviction-based confiscation as a compatible purpose, which could work for personal data collected for a prior criminal procedure but not for personal data collected for commercial, financial, or other purposes.

Moreover, considering the jurisprudence of the ECtHR, it should be foreseeable for any given data subject that his or her personal data can be used in a civil procedure following the criminal prosecution. This should be precisely formulated in any national law in order to meet the ECtHR's conditions and in order to rule out any chance of arbitrariness. Fulfilling these requirements should not be too problematic in the case of a prior criminal investigation, since the national legal provisions regarding criminal proceedings could provide this information. Fulfilling the foreseeability requirement with regard to personal data that are collected or with regard to other purposes is more complicated. This would imply that, for every type of data collection, the data subject should be able to anticipate that these data could be used for a civil non-conviction-based confiscation procedure.

Removing the provision on introducing non-conviction-based confiscation in every Member State has also solved the problem explained here, at least for those Member States that do not already have an established civil asset forfeiture system in place. Even though the illustrated data protection question was not the reason why non-conviction-based confiscation was taken out of the Directive, it avoided difficulties with using personal data for confiscating the proceeds of crime in practice.

II. Defining Purpose Limitation

What exactly constitutes a compatible purpose is not defined by the Data Protection Convention or its explanatory report. It was not until 2013 that the EU Data Protection Working Party published an opinion on what is to be understood by the term compatible purpose, not by means of a genuine definition but by means of key criteria to be used on a case-by-case basis in the compatibility assessment.[35]

In order to make the processing of personal data for the purpose of criminal investigations and prosecutions feasible but consistent with the data protection principles, a compatible purpose should have a link with the original purpose for which the data were collected, and the reasonable expectation of the data subject regarding the further processing should be taken into consideration. According to the Data Protection Working Party, the key criteria to be considered when assessing compatibility are, first of all, the relationship between the purposes for which the data have been collected and the purposes of further processing. For this criterion, it is important to emphasise that the substance of the relationship is what matters, not the textual context or language used. The greater the distance between the purposes of collection and the purposes of further processing, the more problematic this would be for the compatibility assessment. As a second key criterion, the Data Protection Working Party lists the context in which the data have been collected and the reasonable expectations of the data subjects as to their further use. This refers to what a reasonable person in the data subject's situation would expect his or her data to be used for regarding the context of the data collection. Thirdly, the nature of the data – sensitive data or those requiring specific protection – and the impact of further processing on the data subjects should be a factor in the compatibility assessment. This criterion refers to those situations in which the processing of data can have a negative effect on data subjects such as discrimination or an emotional impact. Lastly, the Data Protection Working Party considers the safeguards applied by the controller to ensure fair processing and to prevent any undue impact on the data subjects to be a key factor in assessing the compatibility of a purpose. This implies that additional safeguards could compensate for theoretically undue processing.

The Data Protection Working Party mentions explicitly that this list is not fully exhaustive and instead aims at highlighting aspects that should be considered when deciding on the compatibility of the purpose of data processing. Since this is an opinion, it is not legally binding; nevertheless, it offers guidance to data controllers, data protection authorities, or judges deciding on the matter.

III. Defining Necessity

Before authorities can rely on any type of confiscation, information is needed in order to trace the assets. In most cases, personal data will be collected and processed, actions during which infringements to the right to a private life are likely.

---

[35] Article 29 Data Protection Working Party, Opinion 03/2013 on purpose limitation, 02.04.2013, pp. 23–27.

The right to data protection is not laid down in the ECHR as such but the right to a private life in Article 8 ECHR is. It is the jurisprudence of the ECtHR on infringements upon Article 8 that is used here to gain insight into violations of the data protection standards, due to the strong correlation between the two and due to the lawful derogations from the data protection principles in the Data Protection Convention, which are based on the lawful derogations from the right to a private life in the ECHR. The conditions for a lawful derogation from the right to a private life are legality and necessity.

A. Legality

The legality prerequisite relies on two conditions.[36] Firstly, the law should be adequately accessible and, secondly, the law should be foreseeable in order for citizens to assess their own behaviour and the consequences thereof. In order to provide citizens with legal certainty regarding their right to protection against violations of their right to privacy, the law should be sufficiently clear[37] in its terms in order to give individuals a decent indication as to the circumstances and the conditions under which public authorities are entitled to resort to privacy-interfering measures.[38] The law should be understandable by itself and not require any further legal analysis.

In this perspective, the phrase "in accordance with the law" relates not only to the verbatim meaning of the law but also to the quality of the law[39] and its ability to provide sufficient legal safeguards against arbitrary intrusions into individual's private lives.[40]

Thus, an exception to, for example, the purpose limitation principle can be considered foreseeable if it has been formulated with sufficient precision to enable any individual – if need be with appropriate advice – to regulate his or her conduct. The individual must be able to predict the consequences of an action to a reasonable degree. It is not necessary that these consequences are foreseeable with absolute

---

[36] ECtHR, *The Sunday Times v. United Kingdom*, 1979, § 49; ECtHR, *Leander v. Sweden*, 1987, §§ 50–51.

[37] A sufficiently clear legislation does not mean that citizens are expected to infer certain rules from general enactments or principles or to perform an analogical interpretation of legislative provisions or court decisions. ECtHR, *Hüvig v. France*, 1990, § 33.

[38] ECtHR, *Khan v. United Kingdom*, 2000, § 26; ECtHR, *Malone v. United Kingdom*, 1984, § 67.

[39] ECtHR, *Halford v. United Kingdom*, 1997, § 49; ECtHR, *Malone v. United Kingdom*, 1984, § 67.

[40] ECtHR, *Segerstedt-Wiberg and others v. Sweden*, 2006, § 76.

certainty.[41] The requirement implies a responsibility on behalf of a state's legislator to design clear-cut and transparent legal provisions that allow the data subject to know under which circumstances and under which conditions authorities could interfere with his or her right to a private life.[42]

B. Necessity and Proportionality

The principle of necessity and proportionality is embedded in the data protection legal framework in two ways. Firstly, personal data should be collected in a proportionate way in relation to the purpose they are intended for. The proportionality here refers to the relationship between the type and amount of data collected and the purpose of the collection. Secondly, in accordance with the Data Protection Convention, derogations from the data protection principles are allowed in as far as they are legal and the processing of the data is a necessary measure in a democratic society in the interests of protecting state security, public safety, and the monetary interests of the state or the suppression of criminal offences, or in the interests of protecting the data subject or the rights and freedoms of others.[43] In this case, the proportionality refers to the relationship between the infringements of the right to a private life, on the one hand, and the interests for which the collected personal data should be used, on the other. The phrase "necessary in a democratic society" implies that an individual's personal data can be processed in a way that does not correspond to the data protection principles in the case of a pressing social need.[44] The interference with the individual's private life needs to be proportionate to the legitimate aim that is pursued by disregarding a person's private data.[45]

Regardless of which type of confiscation procedure one uses in accordance with the Directive, chances are high that personal data that were originally collected for other purposes will be processed for tracing assets. If this is the case, then the purpose limitation principle must be lawfully derogated from; in other words, the necessity or proportionality requirement must be met.

For example, a businessman is suspected of laundering the proceeds of fraud and a simple chat with his neighbours reveals that he just bought himself a brand-new

---

[41] ECtHR, *Amman v. Switzerland*, 2000, §56 and ECtHR, *The Sunday Times v. United Kingdom*, 1979, § 49.

[42] ECtHR, *Malone v. United Kingdom*, 1984, § 67.

[43] See Article 9 Data Protection Convention.

[44] Mentioned for the first time in a case concerning an alleged violation of Article 10 ECHR: ECtHR, *Handyside v. United Kingdom*, 1976, § 48.

[45] ECtHR, *Leander v. Sweden*, 1987, § 58; ECtHR, *Gillow v. United Kingdom*, 1986, § 55.

Rolls Royce that he would not be able to afford based on his official income. The sales records of the local Rolls Royce dealership – personal data collected for commercial purposes – could then be used to prove that the businessman laundered the proceeds of crime. Possibly, employment or tax records would also be used to prove his lawful income. If the prosecution authorities wish to confiscate the Rolls Royce, then personal data collected for an incompatible purpose are used for a confiscation procedure and the necessity of using these data needs to be proven.

Since non-conviction-based confiscation was removed from the text of the Directive, confiscation in accordance with Article 5 of the Directive implies that a criminal investigation was at least started before turning to the confiscation procedure. The information gathered in this criminal investigation can be used to trace the assets. In those Member States in which civil asset forfeiture or non-conviction-based confiscation does not already exist, confiscation will further be dealt with in a criminal context. This means that the use of personal data for other purposes can be justified as necessary for the suppression of criminal offences. Even though the explanatory report to the Council of Europe's Data Protection Convention states that "suppression of criminal offences" includes the investigation as well as the prosecution of criminal offences, confiscation should logically be a part of it. For a genuine non-conviction-based confiscation that is organised by means of a civil procedure, complying with the necessity requirement is not possible. Member States that have an established civil asset forfeiture system may therefore have problems abiding by the data protection standards when using personal data that was collected for other purposes.

C. Adequate Level of Data Protection

As mentioned before, the transfer of personal data from an EU Member State authority to a third state should follow an assessment of the adequacy of the receiving state's level of data protection. Because this requirement is laid down in an additional protocol to the Data Protection Convention that has not been ratified yet by all Member States, it is not a general condition for transfers of personal data to a third state for the purpose of a criminal investigation or prosecution. It has been laid down in Directive 95/46/EC and is therefore a general requirement for personal data in the context of commercial activities. The adequacy requirement was also included in the 2008 Framework Decision on data protection in criminal matters but, as explained earlier, this legal instrument has a limited scope. Besides the fact that the adequacy requirement is not a general rule in judicial and police cooperation in criminal matters, it is also fraught with confusion regarding its content. To date, no legal instrument has developed a check-list of items that should minimally be included in such an assessment of the adequate level of data protection of a third state. Additionally, Europol and Eurojust have adopted their own assessment procedures for the adequacy requirement, but in their agreements on cooperation in criminal matters with the United States they have not been used.[46]

The difficulties with the adequacy requirement also caught the attention of the European Commission and have been addressed in the proposed data protection reform. An improved procedure, including a check-list of minimum elements to evaluate, has been presented in the proposed directive.

Even though the Directive on confiscation is a legal instrument that is restricted to the cooperation between the EU Member States, asset recovery as a tool will not remain within the EU. Mutual legal assistance requests will frequently have to be made in order to detect whether an offender has acquired or placed assets in one or more third states. This will inevitably also involve the exchange of personal data. Similar to the exchange between the Member States, the rules on data protection cannot be ignored, and, in addition, the level of data protection of the third state will need to be evaluated before transferring personal data to its authorities. For this purpose, it is a welcome development that the Commission has proposed an improved adequacy requirement in the current data protection reform package.

IV. Necessities and Asset Clustering

With its proposal of March 2012, the Commission wanted to offer Member States new tools in the fight against crime. One of these tools is non-conviction-based confiscation. This form of confiscation only survived the decision-making process in a mitigated form. Its advantage is that, even in case of flight or illness of the suspect or accused, seizure of the proceeds of the crime can still take place. As effective as this may be as a tool to hurt offenders where it hurts most, it cannot function effectively if it is not implemented in an appropriate way. In the 2012 proposal, non-conviction-based confiscation was not only imposed upon Member States that would have to make substantial changes to their criminal justice system but it was also not clear whether it was meant to be a criminal or civil procedure. Even though it would make sense to leave the choice of the forum (criminal or civil/administrative courts) up to the Member States from a harmonisation point of view, the provisions were not clear. The consequences of this confusion for the exchange of personal data would have been significant. For this reason, it was a good approach to take non-conviction-based confiscation out of the text of the Directive in its original form, even if that was not the only reason for its removal.

---

[46] See, for greater detail, *De Busser*, Data Protection in EU and US Criminal Cooperation, pp. 416–420.

Relying on "suppression of criminal offences" as a justification for using personal data for any purpose does not work if a procedure is civil in nature. Member States that already have civil asset forfeiture in their national legislation may therefore have difficulty using personal data to trace the proceeds of crime, since most of these data will have been collected for a different purpose. As explained above, the key indicators developed by the Data Protection Working Party will assist authorities in deciding whether or not a purpose is compatible. Nevertheless, in the context of non-conviction-based confiscation, this will be a true challenge.

The processing of information, including personal data for finding assets before freezing or confiscating them, does not always receive the attention it deserves. It is a complex system involving data protection rules and often also mutual legal assistance requests. When cooperation with a state outside the EU is required, additional difficulties caused by different data protection rules can exacerbate the confiscation. The national and the EU legislators should be careful that such differences do not lead to *asset clustering* by offenders, used here in the sense of searching for that particular state which has a more lenient or favourable system for acquiring or positioning one's assets. The knowledge that non-conviction-based confiscation in certain Member States is organised as a civil procedure, and that use of personal data collected in a prior criminal investigation or for other – mostly commercial or financial – purposes will be met with significant data protection-related difficulties, could lead to offenders clustering their assets in these particular Member States.

Bibliography

Basel Institute of Governance, International Centre for Asset Recovery, Capacity Building in Asset Recovery. Basel 2011.

De Busser, Els, Transatlantic Adequacy and a Certain Degree of Perplexity. eucrim 1, 30–36 (2010).

– Data Protection in EU and US Criminal Cooperation. Antwerp 2009.

De Smet, Bart/Lathouwers, Jan/Rimanque, Karel, Artikel 6, §1 [Article 6, §1]. In: Johan Vande Lanotte/Yves Haeck (eds.), Handboek EVRM Artikelsgewijze commentaar [Handbook ECHR Commentary on the Articles] Vol. II. Antwerp 2004–2005.

Greenberg, Theodore S./Samuel, Linda M./Grant, Wingate/Gray, Larissa, Stolen Asset Recovery: A Good Practices Guide for Non-Conviction Based Asset Forfeiture. Washington 2009.

Korff, Douwe, Comparative study on different approaches to new privacy challenges, in particular in the light of technological developments, Working Paper 2: Data protection laws in the EU: The difficulties in meeting the challenges posed by global social and technical developments, European Commission DG Justice, Freedom and Security Report. London 2010.

Rees, Edward/Fischer, Richard/Thomas, Richard, Blackstone's Guide to the Proceeds of Crime Act 2002. 4th ed. Oxford 2011.

Smith, Ian/Owen, Tim (eds.), Asset Recovery: Criminal Confiscation and Civil Recovery. London 2003.

Steinvorth, Daniel, Greek Government Hauls in Billions in Back Taxes. Spiegel Online, 08.02.2010, url: http://www.spiegel.de/international/europe/finding-swimming-pools-with-google-earth-greek-government-hauls-in-billions-in-back-taxes-a-709703.html [last visited: 10.09.2014].

Vervaele, John A.E., Gegevensuitwisseling en terrorismebestrijding in de VS en Neder-land: emergency criminal law? Panopticon, 27–52 (2005).

List of Abbreviations

AREN	Asset Recovery Experts Network
ARINSA	Asset Recovery Inter-Agency Network for South Africa
ARO	Asset Recovery Offices
CARIN	Camden Asset Recovery Inter-Agency Network
ECHR	European Convention of Human Rights
ECtHR	European Court of Human Rights
EJN	European Judicial Network
IberRed	Red iberoamericana de cooperación jurídica internacional
ICAR	International Centre for Asset Recovery

Chapter 8

Civil Asset Forfeiture in Practice

Alan Bacarese and *Gavin Sellar*

I. Introduction

Through the 1990s and into the turn of the new century, the United Kingdom, one of the most important transnational commercial centers in the world and much like the other G20 countries, was proclaiming its willingness to commit to an agenda of recovering the proceeds of crime and corruption. This ignored the steady increase in academic and publically commissioned reports on the subject matter, such as the 1995 Policy Research Group report of the Home Office,[1] which put into sharp perspective the problems that the UK had in terms of its capacity to recover assets in either a criminal or a civil context. The 1995 report, for example, highlighted how ineffective the asset recovery measures had become and how they were hampering efforts to investigate, seize, and confiscate the proceeds of crime.

In 1998, a new government in the UK commissioned a further report. The Cabinet Office Report, prepared by the Performance and Innovation Unit (PIU) and published in 2000, made a number of critical observations and, amongst a broad range of proposals, suggested that there should be a consolidation of existing laws on confiscation and money laundering.[2] At a practical level, the report was damning, claiming that there were deep-rooted concerns such as inadequate levels of response from the law enforcement community and judiciary, a lack of available resources and skills, poor procedures, and insufficient inter-agency cooperation.

There was no escaping the withering reports and therefore, finally, the link between tracing and recovering the proceeds of criminal activity and the fight against crime in the UK, which is essential to both "crime reduction and to public confidence in the rule of law," was made.[3]

---

[1] Police Research Group, Investigating, Seizing and Confiscating the Proceeds of Crime, Crime Detection and Prevention Series Paper no. 61, London: Home Office Police Department – Michael Levi and Lisa Osofsky.

[2] Performance & Innovation Unit (PIU), Recovering the Proceeds of Crime, June 2000.

[3] The report also noted how, in the previous five years, confiscation orders had only been sought in an average of 20% of drugs cases, where such an order was appropriate, and in a mere 0.3% of other crime cases. The enforcement rate fared no better, with approximately 40% or less of the amounts ordered by the courts being seized – paras 4.18–4.26.

This chapter analyses some of the legal and practical issues involved in civil asset forfeiture (also termed "civil recovery" and "non-conviction-based forfeiture"), principally from a UK domestic perspective, with an overview of the challenges that the prosecution agencies and the courts in the UK have faced in the implementation of Part 5 of the Proceeds of Crime Act 2002, the relevant legislation. The chapter also focuses on providing an international and comparative perspective, with a brief overview of the Stolen Asset Recovery (or StAR) Initiative of the World Bank and the United Nations Office on Drugs and Crime, and the lessons that can be learned from its work on the recovery of the proceeds of corruption for the practice of asset recovery in general.

II. Asset Recovery in the UK: A Short History

A. The Need for Change

The UK's position as one of the leading international financial centers as well as its constitutional connections with a number of prominent offshore financial centers in the Crown Dependencies and the Overseas Territories, its position as the lead nation in the Commonwealth of Nations, and its close connections with developing countries have made the UK a safe haven for "dirty money" in the past.[4]

As a result of the PIU Report, the UK government embarked upon a fairly ambitious plan to pass an all-embracing law that would address much of the criticism that had emerged from its analysis of the problems with the recovery of stolen assets. The answer was the Proceeds of Crime Act 2002 (POCA). POCA received Royal Assent on 31 July 2002 and contained twelve parts, which were brought into effect in stages. It also consolidated eleven other separate statutes brought in since 1986, which attempted to do the same.

In one swoop, POCA broadened the scope of legislation relating to the seizure of cash, introduced an "all crimes approach" to money laundering, increased the powers of investigative agencies in relation to restraint, and simplified the confiscation procedure.[5] Was change finally about to be delivered?

---

[4] Transparency International (UK) Combating Money Laundering and Recovering Looted Gains – Raising the UK's Game (2009) – see at http://www.transparency.org.uk/publications/15-publications/154-combating-money-laundering-and-recovering-looted-gains-raising-the-uks-game (last visited: 12.01.2015).

[5] *Bacarese*, Asset recovery in a common law system: the United Kingdom, in: Pieth (ed.), Recovering Stolen Assets.

B. Initial Challenges to the Proceeds of Crime Act 2002

One of the key challenges almost immediately for the new POCA was the question of institutional responsibility for asset recovery, which, in the UK, has been something of a political football over the past decade, as successive administrations (seeking tough-sounding headlines) have created ever-expanding criminal prosecution and investigation agencies. Section 1 of the Proceeds of Crime Act 2002, as enacted, created the Asset Recovery Agency (ARA). The purpose of this entity was to bring civil proceedings in the High Court, using the new civil recovery powers in the High Court to recover the profits of unlawful conduct.[6] Following criticism of the ARA by the National Audit Office in 2007, the ARA was abolished in early 2008 and its operations merged into the Serious and Organised Crime Agency (SOCA). In April 2013, as a sign of further political change, SOCA itself was subsumed into a new umbrella crime-fighting organisation, the National Crime Agency.[7]

It is worth highlighting some of the legal and practical challenges initially faced by the ARA, as an indicator for any others who seek to implement a similar model, be it the EU or another sovereign state. What is striking from the early jurisprudence is how long it seemed to take English practitioners to become accustomed to the new legal landscape represented by the civil recovery provisions in POCA; how often the same arguments were brought against attempts at asset recovery; and how often those arguments were dismissed by the courts, who seemed to adapt to the new requirements of the legislation far more quickly. In case after case, the courts emphasized the civil nature of proceedings over arguments that criminal standards should apply.

In *R (Director of the Assets Recovery Agency) v. He* (unreported decision of 7 December 2004), it was ruled that Article 7 of the European Convention of Human Rights (barring retrospective criminal punishment) did not apply to civil recovery proceedings under POCA, since no penalty was involved.[8]

The appeals continued. In the case of *R (Director of the Assets Recovery Agency) v. Ashton*[9] the High Court again ruled that ECHR Article 7 did not apply, holding that recovery orders were not penal but effectively restitutionary in nature, since

---

[6] For a detailed evaluation of ARA's statistical performance before its merger with SOCA, see *Leong*, The Assets Recovery Agency: future or no future? Comp. Law. 2007, 28(12), 379–380.

[7] http://www.nationalcrimeagency.gov.uk/ (last visited: 12.01.2015).

[8] Furthermore, in *R v. He (no. 2)* [2004] EWHC 3021 (Admin), the High Court confirmed that the standard of proof applicable to the assessment of unlawful conduct was the balance of probabilities – hence the civil standard of evidence. The court also ruled that any interference with the respondent's property rights under Article 1 of Protocol 1 to the ECHR was proportionate to the legitimate aim of crime prevention.

[9] [2006] EWHC 1064 (Admin).

persons in possession of the proceeds of crime have no right to hold such property in the first place. Many of these issues were raised once again in the important case of *Walsh v. Director of the Assets Recovery Agency*,[10] when the Court of Appeal in Northern Ireland rejected submissions from the appellant – who had been acquitted of charges of obtaining property by deception – that ECHR Article 6(2) guaranteeing the presumption of innocence was relevant to the asset recovery proceedings against him and that, because the legislation required a finding of unlawful conduct, such conduct should have to be proven beyond reasonable doubt. The court stated that the proceedings were civil in nature, and their purpose was to recover property rather than impose a penalty. What was interesting to note was that the non-conviction powers were used following an unsuccessful attempt to prosecute the accused for criminal offenses.

The series of cases involving challenges of this kind to the civil recovery regime in POCA came to a head with *Gale v. Serious Organised Crime Agency*,[11] when the Supreme Court, very much echoing the reasoning of the decision in *Walsh*, reconfirmed that it did not breach ECHR Article 6(2) for courts in civil recovery proceedings to apply the civil standard of *proof of a balance of probabilities* to the question of unlawful conduct.

What perhaps seems strange is that a cursory glance at POCA should have made these rules of law perfectly plain for practitioners to begin with, since the asset recovery proceedings in question here were explicitly described as civil in s. 240:

'(1) This Part has effect for the purposes of—

(a) enabling the enforcement authority to recover, in civil proceedings before the High Court or Court of Session, property which is, or represents, property obtained through unlawful conduct.'

Moreover, the standard of proof in these proceedings is specifically stated in POCA s. 241 to be the balance of probabilities:

'(3) The court or sheriff must decide on a balance of probabilities whether it is proved—

(a) that any matters alleged to constitute unlawful conduct have occurred.'

Ultimately, this specter, of the same challenges being brought time after time, seems to have arisen from Part 5's novel non-conviction regime, which seeks to separate an action for recovery of property tainted by association with past criminal conduct from proceedings identifying where liability for that conduct should lie.

The courts have consistently emphasized this separation. In *R (Director of Assets Recovery Agency) v. Taher*[12] the failure of a previous prosecution – after a jury had been unable to reach a verdict and the retrial was discontinued – was found not to prohibit recovery proceedings in respect of the same unlawful conduct, due to the

---

[10] [2005] NICA 6.

[11] [2011] UKSC 49.

[12] [2006] EWHC 3406 (Admin).

differing standard of proof in civil proceedings. Similar reasoning was adopted in *Serious Organised Crime Agency v. Hymans*,[13] in which the High Court reiterated that an acquittal in criminal proceedings did not conclusively establish that a defendant had not committed the unlawful act alleged but showed only that the evidence was insufficient to discharge the enhanced burden of proof. Therefore, an acquittal does not preclude the court in civil recovery proceedings from considering the evidence that formed the basis of the criminal charges.

This arguably represents a seismic shift in the recovery of the proceeds of crime. The case of *R (Director of Assets Recovery Agency) v. E*[14] succinctly summarized the range of powers that Part 5 POCA had bestowed upon law enforcement in the UK. In this case, the applicant was a brothel keeper who had been prosecuted for a number of offenses. The proceedings against him had been stayed as an abuse of process, since the police had allowed his brothels to continue to operate for a number of years, thereby creating a reasonable expectation in the applicant's mind that he would not be prosecuted. However, the High Court ruled that unfairness in continuing criminal proceedings did not necessarily correspond to unfairness in separate civil recovery proceedings: the fact that the police had tolerated the brothel-keeping did not make that conduct lawful, and since it was unlawful, it therefore did not represent an abuse of power preventing the Assets Recovery Agency from seeking to deprive the applicant of his proceeds.

So it follows that the failure of a prosecution by reason of lack of evidence, discontinuance, or abuse of process is not a bar to civil recovery proceedings under POCA Part 5 in respect of the same conduct; nor, indeed, is the termination of criminal proceedings due to a defendant's death.[15] Again, this case law may appear somewhat dissonant to UK criminal practitioners in light of the principles that they traditionally work with.[16]

C. The Irish Experience

In this context, the history of the equivalent Irish legislation seems instructive, since the development of the law of civil recovery there predated the UK experience. Ireland's own Proceeds of Crime Act, which came into force in 1996, similarly applied civil law concepts to criminal profits, giving power to the newly intro-

---

[13] [2011] EWHC 3332 (QB).

[14] [2007] EWHC 3245 (Admin).

[15] *Serious Organised Crime Agency v Lundon (deceased)* [2010] EWHC 353 (QB).

[16] See *Kennedy*, Civil recovery proceedings under the Proceeds of Crime Act 2002: the experience so far, J.M.L.C. 2006, 9(3), 245–264, for an overview of case law *inter alia* involving acquitted and deceased defendants, by the Head of Legal Casework at that time, ARA Northern Ireland office.

duced Criminal Assets Bureau to bring forfeiture proceedings, independent of criminal proceedings and acting *in rem* against property rather than *in personam* against a convicted person and also using the civil standard of proof, namely on a balance of probabilities.

As with the UK legislation, a number of respondents challenged the 1996 Act, alleging constitutional infringement, and their submissions very much foreshadowed those appeals that later followed in the English courts. In the combined cases of *Gilligan v. Ireland, Attorney General, Criminal Assets Bureau and Others* and *Murphy v. GM, PB, PC Ltd, and GH,* the Supreme Court of Ireland's ruling dealt comprehensively with these arguments:[17]

- The 1996 Act did not breach the constitutional prohibition against retrospective punishment (cf. ECHR Article 7), since the acquisition of assets obtained through crime was illegal before the passage of the act and did not become illegal because of the act;

- There was no unfair reversal of the usual burden of proof, since respondents had the opportunity to rebut the suggestion of the unlawful origin of assets;

- The act did not infringe the right to self-incrimination, since disclosures resulting from civil forfeiture proceedings could not be used in the course of a later criminal trial;

- The act also did not breach the right to private property, since the state has a legitimate interest in the forfeiture of the proceeds of crime;

- Above all, forfeiture proceedings under the 1996 Act were civil and not criminal in nature:

    "There is no provision for the arrest or detention of any person, the admission of persons to bail, for the imprisonment of a person for the non-payment of a penalty, for a form of criminal trial initiated by summons or indictment, for the recording of a conviction of any form or the entering of a nolle prosequi at any stage, all elements which would indicate that the Act creates a criminal offence."[18]

The rationale of the Irish courts is evident in the jurisprudence of the UK and was ultimately endorsed by the UK's own Supreme Court in *SOCA v. Gale.*

D. Proving the Unlawful Origin of Assets

Proceedings under Part 5 of POCA attach to property that has been tainted by association with, or derived from, prior criminal conduct. As can be seen from the case law discussed above, Part 5 establishes a scheme whereby such property can

---

[17] [2001] IESC 92.

[18] *Ibid.* at paragraph 12.

be recovered even when establishing the fact of said criminal conduct to the criminal standard of proof has proven impossible. However, there has been some doubt over the extent to which UK law enforcement is required to plead and prove the subsisting criminality from which the alleged recoverable property was said to derive.

This was the issue in *Director of the Assets Recovery Agency v. Green*.[19] In *Green*, the ARA sought recovery of property, inviting the court to infer that it was the proceeds of crime, on the grounds that the defendant could point to no readily identifiable income. Mr. Justice Sullivan disagreed. He held, at paragraph 25, that:

> "the Act deliberately steered a careful middle course between, at the one extreme, requiring the Director to prove (on the balance of probabilities) the commission of a specific criminal offence or offences by a particular individual or individuals and, at the other, being able to make a wholly unparticularised allegation of "unlawful conduct" and in effect require a respondent to justify his lifestyle".

Green confirmed that, although the Part 5 claimant need not specifically plead and justify allegations of specific criminal conduct, no inference could be drawn solely from the defendant being unable to demonstrate the provenance of property held or used to fund his lifestyle.[20] This rule was later tempered in *Director of the Assets Recovery Agency v. Olupitan*[21] in which it was held that, if a defendant gives an explanation of the source of his assets that is inherently incredible or does not stand up to questioning, this will, in practice, be enough to justify the case against him. Moreover, the courts in civil recovery proceedings have consistently taken a very robust view towards unreliable defendants, so that commonsensical (or "irresistible") inferences concerning the true origin of assets may be drawn from the lack of adequate or credible explanation.

How have these principles operated in practice? In *Director of the Assets Recovery Agency v. Prince*[22] the Assets Recovery Agency succeeded in obtaining recovery orders in respect of houses belonging to the siblings of a drug dealer. Although the latter had not, in fact, been convicted of a drug trafficking offense (merely possession), the court nevertheless held that the fact that he had, on his premises, business cards depicting a cannabis leaf, with contact details, and inscribed with the words *"The General or Grandpa at your service day or night"* – taken together with the lack of a credible explanation of how his siblings had been able to finance

---

[19] [2005] EWHC 3168 (Admin).

[20] This contrasts with the approach of the courts to the money laundering offenses contained in Part 7 of POCA, in which an inference can be drawn from circumstantial evidence that the defendant has been engaged in money laundering: *R v Anwoir* [2008] EWCA Crim 1354. The safeguard for the defendant in such circumstances is of course the far higher standard of proof that the prosecution must surmount in order to obtain a conviction.

[21] [2008] EWCA Civ 104.

[22] [2006] EWHC 1080 (Admin).

the purchase of their properties other than by receiving money from him – suggested to the court that the houses could only have been bought using substantial proceeds from his drug dealing.

In *Director of the Assets Recovery Agency v. Jackson*[23] in granting a recovery order against the respondent, the court rejected his contention that large quantities of cash and jewelry seized from his premises had been acquired through legitimate trading in six different businesses, finding this explanation to be implausible given his failure to keep any actual business records and his inability to trace a single customer or produce evidence in support of any sale he had made. A finding of "unexplained wealth" was insufficient to sustain the claim for recovery, but that claim was bolstered by the respondent's explanations being obviously untruthful.

In *Serious Organised Crime Agency v. Qureshi*;[24] a recovery order was granted by the court after there had been a lack of evidence (indeed a lack of response entirely) from the respondent, who had absconded to Pakistan, to undermine the suggestion that his assets had been obtained as a result of fraudulent activity. The credibility of this respondent was perhaps further damaged in the eyes of the court by the fact that emails sent in reply to the court who were trying to serve papers regarding the proceedings, purporting to be from his brother, claimed he had been killed in a bomb blast that occurred during the assassination of Benazir Bhutto. The Metropolitan police could find no evidence that Mr. Qureshi's name had appeared on the list of victims of the attack.

Furthermore, in *Serious Organised Crime Agency v. Kelly*[25] the respondent stated in evidence that a series of large payments into his bank account, on the face of it from a company he claimed never to have heard of, were in fact from successful bets on horse racing and football. The judge gave short shrift to these claims:

"... I regret that I cannot accept Mr Kelly's evidence in this regard. In my view, he would in the real world have noticed who had paid such a sum into his bank account. If his account were right, he would now twice in a fairly short period of time have coincidentally received a payment from a company he had never heard of equal to the amount of a winning bet, and yet no payment from the bookmakers concerned."[26]

The money was found to be the proceeds of drug-related criminal activity and was therefore ruled recoverable.

Finally, in *Serious Organised Crime Agency v. Coghlan*,[27] the court granted a recovery order against a residential property, ruling that it had been acquired through the proceeds of drug dealing. The respondent had never been convicted of a drug

[23] [2007] EWHC 2553 (QB).
[24] [2009] EWHC 3019.
[25] [2010] EWHC 3565 (QB).
[26] [2010] EWHC 3565 (QB) at paragraph 40.
[27] [2012] EWHC 429 (QB).

offense but, against that, the court took account of the lack of evidence of any legitimate source of income, the defendant's association with known drug dealers, and, lastly, the large amounts of cash – and a file containing information on money-laundering legislation – which had been found following his arrest.

In practice, then, defendants may sometimes appear to be their own worst enemy, strengthening the case for civil recovery in which unexplained wealth is insufficient *per se* to found the claim.

E. The UK Experience: Do the Ends Justify the Means?

In sum, at least in terms of law and procedure, and in the attitude of the English courts in civil recovery cases over the past decade – which quickly adapted to the new concepts involved – the cards do seem to be stacked in favor of the enforcement agencies. Many commentators believe this process has gone too far and that the civil recovery regime in POCA has essentially come at the expense of civil liberties and due process protections, which have developed over centuries of jurisprudence and which are now frequently disregarded in favor of administrative expediency.[28]

But, as is well known, the nature of modern organized crime is extremely sophisticated and nebulous: organized crime in the UK alone is estimated to cause social and economic harm worth around £20 billion each year. Furthermore, through access to the financial system, around £3 billion in criminal profits are moved out of the UK annually.[29] Indeed, one of the principal reasons why the Assets Recovery Agency was abolished and subsumed within SOCA (and then the NCA) was the negative reaction to the news that, by 2006, three years after being established, the agency had cost UK taxpayers around £60 million but had only recovered just over £8 million.[30] Looking at the gulf between these figures, it is clear that non-conviction-based forfeiture is a largely uphill task: strong powers of investigation and recovery as well as a robust attitude from the judiciary are all necessary just to make a small dent in the proceeds of crime. This disparity, above all, is why the question of political will and funding of law enforcement agencies responsible for asset recovery continues to be a highly significant underlying consideration in the UK.

---

[28] See, e.g., *Johnson*, Civil recovery: is the erosion of individual rights justified? C.J.Q. 2011, 30(2), 136–142, whose criticism of POCA's legal expenses regime is particularly forceful; see also *Dent*, Filthy lucre and ill-gotten gains, J. Crim. L. 2011, 75(2), 115–121, expressing similar concern that POCA Part 5 respondents are afforded only the bare minimum of procedural fairness.

[29] Both statistics are taken from The Financial Challenge to Crime and Terrorism (HM Treasury, 2007), p. 3.

[30] See http://news.bbc.co.uk/1/hi/uk_politics/5077846.stm (last visited: 04.01.2015).

Some commentators, such as *Peter Sproat*,[31] have questioned the extent to which the POCA regime has truly been successful against organised crime in practice and have gone on to question the professionalism of the law enforcement agencies involved, given the numerical gap between the estimated amount of money controlled by organised crime and the amount that state agencies have recovered. But critics of the apparatus created by POCA Part 5 might heed the rejoinder that bare statistics cannot provide the whole picture here: in short, the ability of enforcement agencies to *disrupt* criminal enterprises, as well as *deprive* criminal proceeds, is an extremely important (and unfortunately for them, harder to measure) part of their work against organised crime.[32]

Imagine how the statistics would read without the use of Part 5 POCA powers!

III. The World Bank's StAR Initiative

Although the UK has seemingly embraced the use of its non-conviction-based powers, it is not alone. There is a move towards non-conviction-based forfeiture at an international level as well, as Kennedy notes:

> "Although pioneered in the US, there now appears to be a global trend to use stand-alone civil proceedings as a means of recovering the proceeds of crime in the hope that they will be more effective than proceedings which are ancillary to a criminal prosecution. Recent examples of jurisdictions which have introduced civil forfeiture legislation include Italy, Ireland, South Africa, Australia, the Australian states of Western Australia, Victoria and New South Wales, and the Canadian provinces of Alberta and Ontario."[33]

The Stolen Asset Recovery (StAR) Initiative, a partnership between the World Bank Group and the UN Office on Drugs and Crime, has been an important champion of the use of non-conviction-based forfeiture. StAR has drawn on comparative material and lessons from several jurisdictions – providing a kind of information-sharing resource; it does not function as an investigative or prosecuting body – whose ultimate goal is to end safe havens for corrupt funds.[34]

Although StAR's remit is specifically to help developing countries combat the laundering of the proceeds of corruption, its published material is of wider use for asset recovery practitioners in general. Of particular note is StAR's 2009 report *"Stolen Asset Recovery: Good Practices for Non-Conviction Based Asset Forfei-*

---

[31] *Sproat*, To what extent is the UK's anti-money laundering and asset recovery regime used against organised crime?, J.M.L.C. 2009, 12(2), 134–150.

[32] *Rider*, More jobs for the boys, J.M.L.C. 2007, 10(3), 213–214.

[33] *Kennedy*, Justifying the civil recovery of criminal proceeds, Comp. Law. 2005, 26(5), 137–145, at 138.

[34] StAR's website is at http://www1.worldbank.org/finance/star_site/ (last visited: 05.01.2015).

ture", which is intended to be a practical tool to help countries recover stolen assets.[35]

Alongside a series of short studies from civil forfeiture professionals from 10 different jurisdictions, this report contains a list of "Key Concepts in Non-Conviction Based Asset Forfeiture", somewhat analogous to the Financial Action Task Force's *Forty Recommendations* on anti-money laundering measures, a prescriptive and quite detailed framework of suggestions for asset recovery legislation. It is worth pointing to as a valuable comparative resource – and not necessarily one that practitioners of whatever nationality will be aware of – based on the essential characteristics of civil forfeiture in all global jurisdictions with such measures in place. These "key concepts" include the following:

- Non-conviction-based (NCB) asset forfeiture should never be a substitute for criminal prosecution. That is, it should be complementary, not alternative, to criminal prosecution.[36]

- The relationship between an NCB asset forfeiture case and any criminal proceedings should be defined. For instance, in Thailand, there is discretion to proceed with asset forfeiture simultaneously with criminal prosecution.

- NCB asset forfeiture should be available when criminal prosecution is unavailable or unsuccessful. This is a question again of the clear separation and delineation of the two proceedings, something made explicit in the Proceeds of Crime Act 2002 s. 240 and in UK jurisprudence, as we have seen.

- Applicable evidentiary and procedural rules should be as specific as possible.

- Assets derived from the widest range of criminal offenses should be subject to NCB asset forfeiture. By way of example, the UK moved from a statutory regime for confiscating the proceeds of only certain crimes, e.g., drug trafficking, to the far more comprehensive and effective approach of targeting the profits of all unlawful conduct.

- The broadest categories of assets should be subject to forfeiture. This would include all kinds of tangible and intangible property, substitute assets, mixed assets, and the proceeds from foreign offenses: a matter of good drafting.

- Tainted assets acquired prior to the enactment of an NCB asset forfeiture law should be subject to forfeiture. That is, asset forfeiture laws must operate retroactively if they are to be effective (on this point, see the case law mentioned above on ECHR Article 7).

---

[35] Available at http://www1.worldbank.org/finance/star_site/publications/non_conviction. html (last visited: 05.01.2015).

[36] Thus, offenders should not be able to effectively buy their way out of criminal liability. Section 2(6) of the Proceeds of Crime Act 2002 indicates the importance of this principle but see *Dent* (note 29 *supra*) for a doubtful view of how this has worked out in practice.

- The specific measures the government may employ to investigate and preserve assets pending forfeiture should be designated.

- Fundamental concepts, such as the standard of proof and use of rebuttable presumptions, should be delineated by statute (see, e.g., POCA 2002 s. 241).

- Defenses to forfeiture should be specified, along with the elements of those defenses and the burden of proof. For example, the defense of *bona fide* purchaser for value is recognized in many jurisdictions.

- Those with a potential legal interest in the property subject to forfeiture are entitled to notice of the proceedings. This is a logical function of natural justice, allowing third parties and victims to make interventions.

- Remedies available to the claimant in the event the government fails to secure a judgment of forfeiture should be specified.

- There should be a system for pre-seizure planning, maintaining, and disposing of assets in a prompt and efficient manner. Receivers or officials may have to be appointed to manage property or ongoing concerns until the end of forfeiture proceedings, if they can render value: some of the more intriguing examples mentioned in the StAR report are a crocodile farm that was taken over by the Anti-Money Laundering Office in Thailand and a fighting school of over 50 pit bulls that was seized by US authorities.

- Extraterritorial jurisdiction should be granted to the courts. Organized crime is a transnational problem that requires transnational legal approaches, as the UK case law shows. Hence also the recommendation that courts should have the authority to enforce foreign provisional and forfeiture orders.

- Correct terminology should be used, particularly when international cooperation is involved. This seems a minor or pedantic point, but there is potential for confusion not just because of language barriers but also because of differences in terminology between civil law and common law systems. Thus, some civil law jurisdictions classify asset forfeiture as a criminal proceeding and may therefore only offer legal assistance to other countries on the condition that the foreign proceeding maintains certain procedural standards. It is therefore recommended that rather than "civil forfeiture" the term used for such proceedings should in fact be "non-conviction-based forfeiture."

In summary, this important list represents a kind of "how to do asset forfeiture" guide for lawmakers, a useful précis of the most effective and fairest legislation internationally. Legal certainty and exactitude are the common threads here. One might add the caveat that, inevitably, not even the most carefully drafted legislation can cover all the practical challenges that targeting organized crime entails, so the law must always remain adaptable, too.

IV. Conclusion

This Chapter has briefly examined the experience with civil asset forfeiture in the UK and also highlighted the transnational resource for asset recovery practitioners represented by the World Bank's StAR initiative. The Irish experience was also considered relevant because it underlines the importance of the political background to civil forfeiture. The driving motive behind the enactment of a non-conviction-based forfeiture regime in Ireland, and the establishment of a well-structured and resourced Criminal Assets Bureau, was the political pressure that had resulted from a high-profile increase in organized crime, exemplified by the murder of the investigative journalist Veronica Guerin by drug lords in 1996. It was recognized that some organized criminals had simply grown beyond the reach of the ordinary criminal law and therefore new solutions were necessary.[37]

What remains to be seen now, from a purely UK perspective, is whether the relatively new National Crime Agency will be able to take advantage of the robust law enforcement principles running through much of the case law (above) and attain greater success in recovering the proceeds of organized crime – and, one might add, in the spirit of a fairer political wind – than its predecessors. At an international level, we shall see where the increased impetus, driven by the work of the StAR initiative and other important international actors, takes us and whether, given the practical experience of the UK and Ireland, the use of non-conviction-based asset recovery powers is adopted as a new and powerful weapon in the armoury of the law enforcement agencies of the world. The criminal fraternity has everything to lose.

Bibliography

Bacarese, Alan, Asset recovery in a common law system: the United Kingdom. In: Mark Pieth (ed.), Recovering Stolen Assets. Bern 2008.

Cheh, Mary M., Constitutional Limits on Using Civil Remedies To Achieve Criminal Law Objectives: Understanding and Transcending the Criminal-Civil Law Distinction. 42 Hastings L.J. (1991), 1325.

Dent, Nick, Filthy lucre and ill-gotten gains. 2011 J. Crim. L. 75(2), 115–121.

Johnson, Yael, Civil recovery: is the erosion of individual rights justified? 2011 C.J.Q. 30(2), 136–142.

---

[37] To take one colourful example, the border farmer and alleged former IRA chief *Thomas 'Slab' Murphy*, whose methodology apparently included a large barn with a door in the Republic of Ireland at one end and a door in Northern Ireland at the other in order to carry out smuggling operations. See news reports at http://www.thesundaytimes.co.uk/sto/news/uk_news/article151398.ece#next (last visited: 05.01.2015) and at http://www.thetimes.co.uk/tto/news/uk/crime/article1873489.ece (last visited: 05.01.2015)

Kennedy, Anthony, Justifying the Civil Recovery of Criminal Proceeds. 2004 Journal of Financial Crime 12(1), 8–23.

– Civil recovery proceedings under the Proceeds of Crime Act 2002: the experience so far. 2006 J.M.L.C. 9(3), 245–264.

Leong, Angela, The Assets Recovery Agency: future or no future? 2007 Comp. Law. 28(12), 379–380.

Performance and Innovation Unit (PIU), Recovering the Proceeds of Crime. June 2000.

Police Research Group, Investigating, Seizing and Confiscating the Proceeds of Crime, Crime Detection and Prevention Series Paper no. 61. London, Home Office Police Department – Michael Levi/Lisa Osofsky (1995).

Rider, Barry, More jobs for the boys. 2007 J.M.L.C. 10(3), 213–214.

Sproat, Peter A., To what extent is the UK's anti-money laundering and asset recovery regime used against organised crime? 2009 J.M.L.C. 12(2), 134–150.

StAR Initiative Stolen Asset Recovery, Good Practices for Non-Conviction Based Asset Forfeiture. World Bank 2009.

Transparency International (UK), Combating Money Laundering and Recovering Looted Gains: Raising the UK's Game (2009).

Abbreviations

ARA	Asset Recovery Agency
ECHR	European Convention on Human Rights
C.J.Q.	Civil Justice Quarterly
Comp. Law.	The Company Lawyer
J. Crim. L.	Journal of Criminal Law
J.M.L.C.	Journal of Maritime Law and Commerce
NCA	National Crime Agency
NCB	Non-conviction-based
PIU	The UK Cabinet Office's Performance and Innovation Unit
POCA	Proceeds of Crime Act 2002
SOCA	Serious Organised Crime Agency
StAR	The Stolen Asset Recovery Initiative

Chapter 9

The Legal Construction that Property Can Do Harm

Reflections on the Rationality and Legitimacy of "Civil" Forfeiture

Joachim Vogel †[*]

In our seminar on civil asset forfeiture, I have been asked to reflect on "the legal construction that property can do harm." In his invitation letter dated 16 February 2012, *Jon Petter Rui* wrote:

> "A fifth important task – perhaps especially in relation to civil law countries – is to analyse the legal construction upon which the civil asset recovery is based; namely that property can do harm."

So I understand my task in the following way: Under U.S. law, civil asset forfeiture has been traditionally construed as an action *in rem* – not *in personam* – and has been traditionally based on the notion that forfeitable property is itself guilty of the respective offence. Such a legal construction and the underlying notion that property can be "guilty" of an offence are difficult or impossible to accept for many jurisdictions, particularly civil law jurisdictions in which criminal guilt is an essentially personal concept and where actions *in rem (United States v. $22,474.00 in United States Currency)* do not exist. However, it might be possible and acceptable for such jurisdictions to base civil or non-conviction-based forfeiture[1] on the notion that forfeitable property can do (or can be used to do) (criminal) harm, so that the harm principle – and not the principle of culpability – might legitimize such forfeitures.

---

[*] *Joachim Vogel* passed away in August 2013 before having had a chance to revise this manuscript for publication. Therefore, his manuscript is printed here as is. Footnote 1 has, however, been brought up to date by his assistant, *Dominik Brodowski*.

[1] The EU Commission proposal for a Directive of the European Parliament and of the Council on the freezing and confiscation of proceeds of crime in the European Union, COM(2012) 85 final of 12 March 2012 contained a requirement for member states to provide a non-conviction based confiscation regime (Art. 5) and proposed a preponderance of evidence-based standard of proof for confiscation proceedings (Art. 4). The adopted legislation however – Directive 2014/42/EU of the European Parliament and of the Council of 3 April 2014 on the freezing and confiscation of instrumentalities and proceeds of crime in the European Union, OJ L 127 of 29 April 2014, p. 39 – only calls for a confiscation procedure where criminal proceedings have at least been initiated and "such proceedings could have led to a criminal conviction if the suspected or accused person had been able to stand trial" (Art. 4 para. 2 Directive 2014/42/EU).

Indeed, it is clear that the harm principle does play a major role in criminal law in most jurisdictions, including civil law jurisdictions. It is also clear that property which can do criminal harm is a kind of "natural" object of forfeiture – even if it is obvious that, as a rule, it is not the property itself but its abuse for criminal purposes that causes the respective harm so that we should more appropriately refer to it as "property which can be (ab-) used to do criminal harm:" A firearm as such will not be subject to forfeiture; rather, it will be an illegal firearm or a firearm used by or found in the possession of a criminal offender. Even so, it is questionable whether the full scope of asset forfeiture can be explained and legitimized through – and only through – the notion that forfeitable property can do harm or be (ab-) used to do harm.

In my presentation, I would like to make the following three points:

– "Civil" and "criminal" forfeiture differ primarily in procedure and only secondarily in nature. Therefore, the question of how to legitimize forfeiture as such can (and must) be answered independently of the civil or criminal procedure background (*infra* I.).

– The harm principle does play a major role in criminal sanctioning, and criminal conduct may result in legal consequences or measures with a view to preventing harm even if the conduct was not "culpable." However, asset forfeiture is a complex matter which cannot be based fully and comprehensively on the notion of preventing harm (*infra* II.).

– Instead, the public policy considerations explaining and legitimizing asset forfeiture vary and depend on the nature of the property involved: contraband; proceeds; instrumentalities (*infra* III.).

I. "Civil" and "criminal" forfeiture

It is well known that the concept of civil forfeiture is historically rooted in U.S. law, although today it has spread into many foreign jurisdictions including some belonging to the civil law family, e.g., Italian or Liechtenstein law.[2] Therefore, any discussion of the legal construction upon which civil forfeiture is based should start with the U.S. discourse on this matter. If I understand U.S. forfeiture law correctly,[3] the distinction between "criminal" and "civil" forfeiture is primarily based on

---

[2] In Italy, cf. Act no. 1423 of 27 December 1956 and Act no. 575 of 31 May 1965 *(Disposizioni contro la Mafia)*, as amended by Act no. 646 of 13 September 1982; in Liechtenstein, cf. §§ 353 et seq. Liechtenstein Code of Criminal Procedure; §§ 20 et seq. Liechtenstein Criminal Code.

[3] See, *inter alia*, *Blair*, Federal Forfeiture Practice Manual; *Cassella*, Asset Forfeiture Law in the United States; *Edgeworth* (ed.), Asset Forfeiture; *McGowan/Grovsten* (eds.), Forfeiture, Conspiracy, Venue.

the *procedural* environment whereas the *nature* – objects, preconditions, impacts and purposes – of "criminal" and "civil" forfeiture is more or less the same.

Criminal forfeiture under U.S. law is an *in personam* action and follows a criminal conviction of the property owner: After a finding of guilt, the jury is asked to consider, by special verdict, which property identified in the indictment is subject to forfeiture; upon a jury's finding that the property is forfeitable, the court may enter a preliminary order of forfeiture, allow discovery to locate the property, and hold hearings to litigate any third-party claims to the property. The procedural standards are those for criminal convictions, including burden of proof and Fourth (seizure), Fifth (due process), and Sixth (right to counsel) Amendment protections. The forfeiture order applies only to the property of the convicted defendant (including substitutes); third parties' property may not be forfeited, even if the third party is him- or herself guilty of participation in the crime. There is no criminal forfeiture without a conviction (be it following a trial or based on a guilty plea). If the State cannot or does not prosecute an offence, e.g., because the defendant is unknown or deceased or evidence is inadmissible, a criminal forfeiture is impossible even if it is clear that the property concerned is, e.g., proceeds from or instrumentality of a crime.[4]

In contrast, civil forfeiture is an *in rem* action – the property itself is the defendant which results in case titles such as *U.S. v. $22,474.00 in U.S. Currency*.[5] The jurisdiction lies with civil courts (traditionally in the district where the *res* has been found or seized). The rules of civil procedure apply, including the civil procedure standard of proof: preponderance of probabilities. This only requires that it is more probable that the *res* has been used for or stems from criminal activities than that it is not the case. Neither the offence nor the connection of the property with the offence must be proven beyond reasonable doubt. Not finding the wrongdoer or him being deceased does not interfere with a civil forfeiture, as long as the property can be identified and seized. Constitutional guarantees that are specific to criminal procedure such as the Fourth and Sixth Amendment do not apply, at least not in principle. Since property, rather than a person, is considered to be the offending or guilty thing, it is, in principle, irrelevant whether the owner is guilty – which, in principle, enables the state to forfeit property belonging to innocent third parties and even belonging to victims of the offence.[6]

---

[4] This is neither a law of nature nor of logic or legal principle. Instead, many jurisdictions recognize "objective" forfeiture proceedings in a criminal procedure context and provide for "non-conviction-based forfeitures." See, in German law, § 76a German Criminal Code, §§ 440–442 German Code of Criminal Procedure.

[5] 236 F.3d 1212 (9th Cir. 2001).

[6] Refer to the infamous case *Bennis v. Michigan*, 516 U.S. 442 (U.S. SCt. 1996). See *infra* at note 39 for details.

Interestingly enough, U.S. legal doctrine has recently focused on a third way to forfeit property, the "administrative" forfeiture.[7] Again, the defining aspect is primarily of a procedural nature: In principle, administrative forfeiture is uncontested civil forfeiture. Under U.S. federal law, the Government must give owners and third parties with an interest in the property notice of the forfeiture and an opportunity to contest it. The matter becomes a civil case in federal court only if at least one claimant responds within the narrow deadlines and files a claim. Otherwise, the forfeiture is finalized without any judicial proceedings and thus retains a purely administrative character. Indeed, as many as 80 % of federal forfeitures go uncontested, either because owners are not aware of the notice or because they do not challenge the forfeiture on account of self-incrimination concerns. In such cases, the seizure of the property on probable cause may, in effect, result in forfeiture.

It is true that the substantive law of criminal forfeiture on the one hand and of civil forfeiture on the other, is not identical: Criminal forfeiture requires criminal culpability whereas civil forfeiture is, in principle, even possible if the owner of the forfeitable property is innocent. Third parties' property may only be forfeited under civil forfeiture law. And the rules on the forfeiture of substitutes differ.

It seems, however, that criminal and civil forfeiture do not, in principle, differ in nature, that is to say with regard to objects and purposes. Both criminal and civil forfeiture encompass contraband, proceeds and instrumentalities. The repressive and preventive purposes of criminal and civil forfeiture are identical. Indeed, *Stefan Cassella* writes:[8]

"The nature of the relationship between the property and the crime, and the social and political objectives of the forfeiture, cannot depend on the procedure by which the forfeiture is accomplished."

"In a civil forfeiture case, the objectives are the same [scil. as in a criminal forfeiture case]: to recover the proceeds of crime and the property used to facilitate it; but the procedure is different."

And – discussing the "legal fiction" that the property itself has done something wrong in civil forfeiture cases – *Stefan Cassella* adds:

"That is no longer the theory underlying civil forfeiture; rather, it is viewed simply as a procedural device for resolving all objections to the forfeiture of property at one time in a single proceeding."

In another recent U.S. contribution on forfeiture procedure, we read:[9]

"The [...] civil/criminal distinction is not a meaningful one, at least not tied to compelling and well-defined public policy. Both are occasioned by illegal conduct, and both serve essentially the same 'punitive and deterrent' purposes. [...] Neither logic nor good public policy supports the distinction [...]. CAFRA makes criminal forfeiture available

---

[7] See *Pimentel*, 13 Nevada Law Journal 9 (2012).

[8] *Cassella*, Asset Forfeiture Law in the United States, p. 837.

[9] *Pimentel*, 13 Nevada Law Journal 40 (2012).

everywhere civil forfeiture is already available [... scil. and] attempts to treat the two procedures as virtually interchangeable..."

Indeed, the U.S. model of civil forfeiture seems to simply fill in gaps where criminal proceedings are not available under U.S. law but where forfeiture is nevertheless justifiable, e.g., when the wrongdoer is unknown; when he is a fugitive, is prosecuted or has been convicted abroad, or has died; or when the interests of justice do not require a criminal conviction.

But even the sharp procedural distinction between criminal and civil forfeiture must not be overestimated.

On the one hand, the U.S. model of civil forfeiture has a decidedly criminal justice background since it is the police and public prosecution that initiate and pursue civil forfeitures. And it should be noted that there is neither a law of nature nor of logic nor a legal principle that make it impossible to integrate civil claims and civil procedures into a criminal procedure. For instance, many jurisdictions permit the victim to claim civil damages in a criminal procedure against the defendant – in such a case, the victim becomes *partie civile* of the criminal procedure. Insofar, some arguments in favour of civil forfeiture lose their *prima facie* persuasiveness: It is true that third parties who own forfeitable property cannot or need not be defendants in a criminal procedure against the (main) perpetrator. However, there is no law of nature nor of logic or a legal principle that makes it impossible to include such third parties as participants in the criminal procedure insofar as the forfeiture is concerned – a solution which is well known in many jurisdictions. Of course, due process must not be violated, and the third party must be heard and given the opportunity to raise objections against the forfeiture. Concerning the problems posed by deceased or fugitive defendants, it is neither logically nor legally impossible to establish "objective" criminal procedures in which forfeitures may be ordered – which is the solution in German law.

On the other hand, it has often been criticized in U.S. legal doctrine that civil forfeiture is, actually, an attempt to circumvent strict standards and guarantees of criminal procedure, in particular with a view to lowering the evidentiary standard of proof beyond reasonable doubt.[10] Indeed, insofar as forfeiture has a genuine criminal nature and is a criminal sanction, it is hardly acceptable to abandon standards and guarantees of criminal procedure by simply shifting the procedure to the civil realm – or, it might be said, to simply re-label a genuinely criminal procedure as civil in nature. The Serious Organized Crime Agency's (SOCA) order to forfeit £2.000.000 in proceeds from drug trafficking offences allegedly committed by Mr. Gale after he has been finally acquitted for lack of evidence is acceptable only if and insofar as forfeiture is not, by its very nature, a criminal punishment so that the

---

[10] See, *inter alia*, *Williams et al.*, Policing for Profit.

prohibition of double jeopardy *(ne bis in idem)* and the standards of proof for criminal convictions do not apply.[11]

Therefore, any theory of civil forfeiture must be based on a theory of forfeiture in general. Once such a theory has been established, a "fitting" procedural scheme may be developed and fine-tuned to meet practical conditions and contingencies – but not vice versa. So, the problem I would like to tackle now is whether forfeiture may be theoretically based on the harm principle.

II. The harm principle: Criminal law in general and forfeiture in particular

The harm principle is a traditional principle of liberal ethics, political liberalism, and also a legal principle of particular significance in criminal law. The famous sentences in *John Stuart Mill*'s "On Liberty"[12] read:

> "[…] the only purpose for which power can be rightfully exercised over any member of a civilized community, against his will, is to prevent harm to others.
>
> […] for such actions as are prejudicial to the interests of others, the individual is accountable, and may be subjected either to social or to legal punishments, if society is of opinion that the one or the other is requisite for its protection."

Conduct not meeting the harm principle test must not be criminalized, in particular neither offensive conduct not yet detrimental to the rights or interests of others nor conduct concerning only the actor's rights or interests. Similarly, 19th century German criminal law doctrine developed a "principle of protection of legal interests" *(Rechtsgüterschutzprinzip)* which requires that criminal conduct must negatively affect others' individual or collective legal interests.[13] To be sure, neither the harm principle nor the *Rechtsgüterschutzprinzip* are uncontested, and they certainly do not reflect important parts of positive criminal law,[14] which can be more easily explained by an "offence principle" as proposed by *Joel Feinberg*[15] or by legal paternalism.[16]

However, the traditional discussion of the role of the harm principle in criminal law is focused on the criminalization as such: the question as to whether specific conduct may be prohibited and punished. The problem whether forfeiture may be

---

[11] To this effect: *Gale v. SOCA*, 2011 UKSC 49 (U.K. Supreme Court).

[12] *Mill*, On Liberty, pp. 40, 182.

[13] *Binding*, Die Normen und ihre Übertretung, p. 189.

[14] For instance, consummation of drugs (including "hard" drugs) does not, in itself, affect third parties' legal interests.

[15] *Feinberg*, Offense to Others.

[16] *Feinberg*, 1 Canadian Journal of Philosophy 105 (1971).

based on the legal notion that property can do harm has a different source: it concerns the legal consequences of criminal conduct. And it has a different object: it concerns property as such but only indirectly human conduct.

It is remarkable that we find a quite interesting discussion of the problem in "On Liberty" in which *John Stuart Mill* asks whether the sale of poisons may legitimately be prohibited or at least regulated under the harm principle. The example, says *John Stuart Mill*,[17]

> "opens a new question; the proper limits of what may be called the functions of police; how far liberty may legitimately be invaded for the prevention of crime [...]. It is one of the undisputed functions of government to take precautions against crime before it has been committed, as well as to detect and punish it afterwards. The preventive function of government, however, is far more liable to be abused, to the prejudice of liberty, than the punitory function; for there is hardly any part of the legitimate freedom of action of a human being which would not admit of being represented, and fairly too, as increasing the facilities for some form or other of delinquency. Nevertheless, if a public authority, or even a private person, sees any one evidently preparing to commit a crime, they are not bound to look on inactive until the crime is committed, but may interfere to prevent it. If poisons were never bought or used for any purpose except the commission of murder, it would be right to prohibit their manufacture and sale. They may, however, be wanted not only for innocent but for useful purposes, and restrictions cannot be imposed in the one case without operating in the other."

Looking at today's discussion, we see that the harm principle or, more precisely, the harm prevention principle plays a major if not overwhelming role in criminal sentencing – both in the field of traditional punishment and in the field of modern legal consequences or measures:

Since *Cesare Beccaria*'s battle cry: *punitur ne peccetur*,[18] prevention of re-offending, that is to say prevention of harm done by re-offending, has been a major rationale of criminal punishment, in particular of prison sentences. In European terminology, criminal justice being done effects "general prevention" and "special prevention,"[19] in American terminology general and special deterrence, incapacitation and rehabilitation.[20] And since *Immanuel Kant*'s dissent: *punitur quia peccatum*,[21] the fundamental question is whether the consequentialist approach behind the harm prevention theories is fair and just or whether the starting point of any theory of punishment should be the deontological position, that is to say retribution or just desert.

---

[17] *Mill*, On Liberty, pp. 185–186.

[18] *Beccaria*, Über Verbrechen und Strafe, p. 74.

[19] See, *inter alia*, *Weber*, in: Baumann/Weber/Mitsch (eds.), Strafrecht Allgemeiner Teil, § 3 at 25 et seq.

[20] See, *inter alia*, *Robinson*, Criminal Law, § 1.2.

[21] See *Kant*, Metaphysik der Sitten, pp. 196–197 (where the Latin formula which dates back to *Lucius Annaeus Seneca*, De Ira 1, XIX 7 is not mentioned).

In any case, traditional punishment has long ago been supplemented by a "second track" of legal consequences for criminal conduct, which are based exclusively on a harm prevention principle, that is to say on the dangerousness of the defendant regardless of his or her personal culpability. In Germany, such measures are called "measures of correction and prevention" *(Maßregeln der Besserung und Sicherung)*. Most jurisdictions allow for preventive detention of dangerous insane defendants or for drug treatment of addicts. Some jurisdictions (notably Germany[22]) provide for preventive detention of fully responsible defendants even after they have fully served the prison sentence if there is still a major risk of major reoffending.

Forfeiture belongs to a "third track" of legal consequences for criminal conduct which dates back to 19th century admiralty and maritime law but has developed substantially during the U.S. wars on drugs, organized crime, and terrorism: asset recovery *(Vermögensabschöpfung)*. The rationale behind the "third track" is quite complex. In 1997, *Stefan Cassella* said in his testimony before the House Committee on the Judiciary that forfeiture exists to (1) seize contraband; (2) take the property that facilitates crime out of circulation; (3) seize the proceeds of crime; (4) return the proceeds of crime to victims; (5) deter crime; and (6) punish criminals.[23] An example given by him in a later publication[24] is the forfeiture of an airplane used by a drug dealer to smuggle drugs:

> "[We] want to take title to the plane for all the usual reasons: punishment, deterrence, keeping the plane from being used again, disrupting the operation of a criminal organisation, etc."

Similarly, the U.S. Supreme Court characterized the policy behind forfeiture in terms of "punitive and deterrent purposes."[25]

The complexity of the legal notions behind forfeiture is also mirrored in German law. The German Federal Supreme Court says that the forfeiture of proceeds (*Verfall*, § 73 German Criminal Code) is a "measure *sui generis*" of a non-punitive character to prevent unjust enrichment through crime.[26] In contrast, the forfeiture of instrumentalities (*Einziehung*, § 74 German Criminal Code) has a punitive character with a general and special preventive background insofar as instrumentalities owned by perpetrators or accomplices are forfeited. However, the forfeiture of

---

[22] See §§ 66–66b German Criminal Code. The criminal policy trend in Germany was to ever tighten the rules on "Sicherungsverwahrung." It has been stopped by landmark decisions of the European Court of Human Rights (Judgment of 17 December 2009 – 19359/04 *M vs. Germany*, EuGRZ 2010, 25) and by the German Federal Constitutional Court (Judgement of 4 May 2011 – 2 BvR 2365/09, Official Series vol. 128 p. 326).

[23] *Cassella*, 105th Cong. 112 (1997).

[24] *Cassella*, The Case for Civil Forfeiture, p. 3.

[25] *Calero-Toledo v. Pearson Yacht Leasing Co.*, 416 U.S. 663, 686 (1974).

[26] German Constitutional Court, Decision of 14th January 2004, 2 BvR 564/95; German Constitutional Court, Decision of 14th June 2004, 2 BvR 1136/03.

dangerous objects or typical instruments of crime is a non-punitive preventive measure, regardless of culpability and ownership.[27]

Although the legal notion that property can do or can be used to do harm does play a role in forfeiture law, I do not feel that it is the general or overarching principle behind forfeiture. Rather, the unifying idea is a manifestation of some sort of economic analysis of criminal law: The starting point is that crime is often committed for profit, and that the commission of a crime often goes hand in hand with costs. Forfeiture, it is said, takes the profit out of crime and raises its costs. Therefore, it is seen as a powerful counter-incentive against crime. In this sense, the U.S. President's Commission on Organized Crime recommended "a strategy aimed at the [...] economic basis of organized crime" in its 1986 final report and identified forfeiture as an important element of such a strategy.[28] It is a double-faced strategy: Retrospectively, forfeiture guarantees that "crime must not pay" – which has a decidedly punitive overtone, and forfeiture practitioners often say that forfeiture serves as an instrument "to take the criminals' toys away," e.g., expensive cars or luxury homes. Prospectively, forfeiture has a preventive character – forfeited proceeds cannot be reinvested in crime, forfeited instrumentalities cannot be used to commit or facilitate crime, and as a matter of general deterrence, successful forfeitures spread the news that crime does not pay and remove a powerful incentive to engage in criminal activities.

Of course, such a construction is quite general, and it might very well be asked whether it is a legal or rather an economic construction. Therefore, *David Pimentel* has recently argued that we should distinguish between the different objects of forfeiture in order to identify specific public policies, rationales or legal constructions that explain and legitimize forfeiture and, as the case may be, civil forfeiture.[29] I believe this is the way forward.

III. Forfeiture of contraband, proceeds and instrumentalities

In his dissenting opinion in *Bennis v. Michigan*,[30] U.S. Justice *John Paul Stevens* classified forfeitable property into three categories: (1) "pure contraband," (2) "proceeds of criminal activity," and (3) "tools of the criminal's trade." Indeed, many jurisdictions differentiate between these three categories. In German law, for

---

[27] See § 74 (2) No. 2, (3) German Criminal Code.

[28] President's Commission on Organized Crime, The edge: organized crime, business, and labor unions, p. 308.

[29] *Pimentel*, 13 Nevada Law Journal 40 et seq. (2012).

[30] 516 U.S. 442, 459 (1996).

instance, we find rules on the forfeiture of proceeds on the one hand (§§ 73–73e German Criminal Code) and on the forfeiture of instrumentalities on the other (§§ 74–74f German Criminal Code). In addition, we find an often neglected referral to "special provisions" in § 74 (4) German Criminal Code which, in substance, concerns contraband, e.g., drugs (see § 33 German Narcotics Act, § 74d German Criminal Code).

Pimentel has recently argued that it is important to keep these three different types of forfeitures – forfeiture of contraband, proceeds, and instrumentalities – separate when discussing criminal policy, as they all come from different sources and are implemented for different reasons.[31] I agree and would like to underline that guarantees and procedures differ.

A. Forfeiture of contraband

Traditionally, the law of contraband forms part of the law of war and implies a belligerent party's right to confiscate cargo intended for the enemy's warfare, even if delivered by a neutral party.[32] In a modern and civil sense, contraband is property whose mere possession is illegal.[33] Far from being exhaustive, examples for contraband include:

– illegal drugs,
– illegal firearms,
– adulterated food and beverages,
– counterfeit money, counterfeit products,
– piracy copies,
– illegal obscene material.

Forfeiture of contraband does not raise major policy or legal problems: If the law prohibits possession, forfeiture is a logical response to possession because it restores legality, i.e., non-possession. Of course, the legitimacy of contraband forfeiture depends on the legitimacy of the respective prohibition of possession. Often, contraband will imply a threat to public safety and health. Then seizure and forfeiture serve the function of removing the contraband items from public circulation where they may do harm. In the case of obscene material, public morals might deserve protection.

---

[31] *Pimentel*, 13 Nevada Law Journal 41 et seq. (2012).

[32] Cf. *Pimentel*, 13 Nevada Law Journal 11–12 (2012).

[33] See 18 U.S.C. § 983 (d) (4): "contraband or other property that it is illegal to possess."

We also do not encounter major problems of guarantees and criminal procedure. Forfeiture of contraband is triggered by illegal possession as such but does not require that the owner or possessor has also committed an offence: If illegal drugs are found in my rental car, the drugs may be forfeited even if they were placed in the car by a corrupt employee of the rental car company without my knowledge. Therefore, there is no issue over the source of the property or how strong the nexus is between the property and the crime, and the burden of proof is of no particular significance – the contraband is what it is, and the question is at most whether it is illegal contraband or not. There is no innocent owner problem because possession and, *a fortiori*, ownership is illegal. Insofar, notice and hearing requirements are not particularly important. However, it is quite clear that contraband forfeiture does not extend to substitutes of the contraband: If the public policy is to remove the contraband from circulation to protect public health and safety, forfeiture of substitute assets, e.g., the money received when the contraband was sold, does nothing to serve that purpose.

Indeed, forfeiture of contraband is a natural candidate for a "police" or "administrative forfeiture:" A classical task of police and (e.g., customs) administration is to counter threats to public safety and health. Of course, judicial review must be guaranteed – but not necessarily in criminal courts and in criminal procedures.

B. Forfeiture of proceeds

Forfeiture of proceeds differs markedly from forfeiture of contraband. Usually, proceeds of crime are not harmful in themselves; rather, it is money or other valuable property proceeding from, say, trafficking in illegal drugs or commercial fraud. Money "*non olet*" and is not, per se, a harmful object. Even if it is true that profits from crime may be an incentive to further engage in crime, and that they may be reinvested to commit further crime (for instance, if a drug dealer spends his profits to finance new drug deliveries), it is at least possible and by no means uncommon that profits from crime are laundered and invested in per se legal property or companies.

It follows that forfeiture of proceeds cannot be primarily based on the harm prevention principle – which implies a marked difference from forfeiture of contraband. Rather, forfeiture of proceeds rests on the morally and legally evident consideration that "crime must not pay," that criminals should be deprived of the fruits of their criminal acts, that the wrongdoer should be denied the benefit of his or her ill-gotten gains. It is the principle of avoiding unjust enrichment which legitimizes forfeiture of proceeds, because it is at least a matter of equity that the property-holder is not entitled to retain ill-gotten gains. Practically all jurisdictions in the world recognize that unjust enrichment triggers restitution duties in civil law. This principle can and should be transferred into the field of criminal law.

For this reason, forfeiture of proceeds is, in itself, not a genuine criminal sanction. Certainly, it is connected with deterrence because asset forfeiture tries to attack criminal incentives by taking the profit out of crime and stripping criminal organizations of the financial means to organize future crime. It has even been said that many criminals fear the loss of their vacation homes, fancy cars, businesses, and bloated bank accounts far more than the prospect of a jail sentence.[34] However, it must be noted that the forfeiture of proceeds does not deter by punishment but instead by denying the criminal the benefits of his or her crime. Indeed, the deterrent effects might be called into question. It is often argued that if you limit forfeiture of proceeds to the net profits (see *infra*), the worst that can happen to a criminal is that he or she will be deprived of the profits – which will result in the same economic situation as if the crime would not have been committed – hence it is rational to commit the crime if there is a chance to escape criminal justice.

It is not only the principle of avoidance of unjust enrichment that links the forfeiture of proceeds to civil law but also the necessity to coordinate it with civil claims of crime victims. It would be manifestly unjust if property which stems, say, from commercial fraud through a Ponzi scheme would be forfeited in favour of the state but fraud victims would be left out in the cold if they tried to enforce their respective tort claims against a debtor deprived of property. In some jurisdictions (such as Germany), the problem is solved by a priority of private claim enforcement over forfeiture, which is legally excluded if and insofar as private claims exist or are being enforced; these jurisdictions trust in private initiative to make civil claims, which guarantees that the criminal will be deprived of unjust enrichment. There are situations, however, where such trust is not well justified, e.g., if many individual victims suffer only small damages, which add up to a huge unjust enrichment. Therefore, many jurisdictions do not recognize such a priority but stipulate that the proceeds are forfeitable regardless of victims' civil claims, but that forfeited property must be paid out to victims who are entitled to civil claims.

Forfeiture of proceeds under the unjust enrichment concept does not require that the owner is guilty of the offence: any enrichment remains "unjust" and requires restitution, even if culpable conduct cannot be proven. Therefore, the rule of German law that forfeiture of proceeds requires the commission of an unlawful offence but that the wrongdoer need not necessarily have acted in a culpable way is in line with the unjust enrichment principle. Even innocent third parties may be subject to forfeiture of proceeds: Enrichment can remain "unjust," i.e., can lack a legal basis, even if the person is enriched through another person's wrongdoing or mistake. Therefore, donees of forfeitable property can be subject to forfeiture themselves,

---

[34] H.R. Rep. No. 105-358, pt. 1, at 22–23.

even if they acted in good faith; however, forfeiture is limited to the donees' enrichment, so that the value they spent to acquire the forfeitable property must be deducted. The gratuitous transfer of proceeds of crime to, say, family members, does not stand in the way of forfeiture even if they did not have any clue that the property constituted proceeds of crime. Otherwise, it is – again – necessary to harmonize forfeiture law on proceeds with civil law on unjust enrichment and bona fide acquisitions.

The unjust enrichment principle creates a compelling case for allowing the forfeiture of substitute assets: It would squarely run against the idea of avoiding unjust enrichment on the part of the property owner if he could avoid forfeiture by exchanging proceeds for other property of value.

Concerning guarantees and procedure, proceeds forfeiture is a natural candidate for "civil forfeiture" – which does not necessarily mean that it should be formally separated from criminal justice and criminal proceedings. However, the constitutional regime governing proceeds forfeiture is shaped by the constitutional protection of property as such but not, at least not in principle, by the constitutional guarantees applying to punishment *sensu strictu*. Furthermore, the procedural regime need not necessarily follow criminal procedure but may take up elements of civil procedure. It depends on the jurisdiction in question if and to what extent differences arise. The major aspects are:

– Burden and standard of proof concerning the offence and the nexus offence-property. Reversals of the burden of proof – e.g., that the property holder is required to provide evidence of the legal origin of the property – are much more problematic in criminal law than in civil law. Whereas the standard of proof in criminal and civil procedures does not differ in many civil law jurisdictions, in which the claimant must prove the facts underlying his or her claim beyond reasonable doubt, common law jurisdictions only require a preponderance of probabilities in civil procedures.

– Double jeopardy. If criminal justice principles apply, proceeds forfeiture would not be possible following an acquittal (e.g., if the offence could not be proven beyond reasonable doubt); in a civil law context, forfeiture would still be possible.

– Retroactivity. If criminal justice principles apply, it would be prohibited to introduce or facilitate proceeds forfeiture *ex post facto*; in a civil law context, retroactivity might be considered (subject to considerations of proportionality and reasonable reliance on existing laws).

– Proportionality. Unjust enrichment is unjust, and therefore, in principle, the question of proportionality between offence on the one hand and forfeiture, on the other, does not arise.[35]

---

[35] Still, U.S. courts have occasionally applied the Eighth Amendment "excessive fines" prohibition to forfeiture of proceeds. See *United States v. Jalaram, Inc.*, 599 F.3d 347,

In any case, property owners need an opportunity to contest and litigate the question of whether the property is indeed the product of criminal activity. Therefore, due process, meaningful notice and hearing requirements are important regardless of the civil or criminal procedural environment.

It has often, and rightly, been held that the unjust enrichment rationale is compelling only when limited to the net profit of the crime.[36] Not only in the U.S. but also in many jurisdictions throughout the world, criminal policy strives towards forfeiting gross revenues generated by criminal activity.[37] In cases of co-perpetrators and accessories, courts throughout the world tend to forfeit total proceeds from each single party to the crime – also in the case of lowly accessories from whom sums far in excess of their individual profit are forfeited.[38] In these cases, proceeds forfeiture can be harshly punitive, and proceeds forfeiture operates as a punitive fine – with all the problems that arise in punitive instrumentalities forfeiture, and with the consequence that the standards and guarantees of criminal procedure need apply.

C. Forfeiture of instrumentalities

At first glance, the forfeiture of "tools of crime" seems both a traditionally recognized and, in terms of criminal policy and legal principles, hardly questionable form of forfeiture: The burglar should be deprived of the crowbar used in the crime, or the hacker deprived of the notebook used to hack highly personal data. Indeed, forfeiture of instrumentalities overlaps with contraband forfeiture insofar as the respective "tools of crime" are per se illegal, that is to say property whose mere possession is illegal, e.g., illegal weapons. Insofar, forfeiture of instrumentalities shares the rationales and principles of contraband forfeiture (see *supra* III.A.).

However, forfeiture of instrumentalities needs a separate analysis concerning property which is per se legal but has been used as a tool of crime, to make possible, or to facilitate a crime. Examples are

– maritime vessels in traditional contraband cases (see *supra* III.A.);

354–357 (4th Cir. 2010) (applying the Eighth Amendment excessive fine prohibition analysis to forfeiture of proceeds); *United States v. Corrado*, 227 F.3d 543, 552 (6th Cir. 2000) (stating that courts can reduce forfeiture of illegal proceeds to make the forfeiture proportional to the seriousness of the offense, so as not to violate the Eighth Amendment's prohibition against excessive fines); *United States v. Browne*, 505 F.3d 1229, 1281–1282 (11th Cir. 2007) (applying Eighth Amendment analysis to proceeds forfeiture in a RICO case).

[36] See, *inter alia*, *Rönnau*, Vermögensabschöpfung, 191.

[37] For Germany, see, *inter alia*, German Constitutional Court, Decision of 14 June 2004 – 2 BvR 1136/03.

[38] See, e.g., *United States v. Levesque*, 546 F.3d 78, 80–82 (1st Cir. 2008): A single, unemployed mother acting as a drug runner for a marihuana conspiracy, earning a net profit of $37,284, was subjected to a $3 million forfeiture for the full amount of the gross proceeds obtained by all the conspirators.

– automobiles used for or in the commission of criminal activities;

– real estate used in such a way.

Such property may either belong to the criminal(s) or to third parties who may or may not be innocent.

Further, forfeiture of smuggled goods or values which are not illegal, per se, merits a special analysis because such forfeiture may be placed in between forfeiture of contraband and that of instrumentalities. Hence, cigarette smuggling will result in the forfeiture of the smuggled cigarettes or failure to declare currency to the customs authorities will result in the forfeiture of the currency in many jurisdictions.

Traditionally, U.S. law permits the "civil" forfeiture of instrumentalities even if they belong to innocent third parties – which has led to harsh consequences: Mr. *Bennis* engaged in sex with a prostitute in the family car belonging to him and his wife in joint ownership; the car was forfeited as an instrument of illegal prostitution, and the forfeiture encompassed Mrs. *Bennis'* joint ownership.[39] Mentally unstable *Thomas* grew marihuana plants in the garden of his parents' house; the house was forfeited as an instrument of illegal drug production.[40] Cases like these have prompted reform in the U.S. and in federal forfeiture law, an innocent owner defence has been installed.

Nevertheless, instrumentalities forfeiture still gives rise to grave problems of criminal policy and legal principles which can be illustrated by the case *U.S. v. Bajakajian*:[41] Mr. *Bajakajian*, a Syrian national and member of the Armenian minority with a profound distrust of government, failed to declare $350,000 in U.S. currency on the customs form when leaving the U.S. Although there was no indication that the cash had an illegal background, the entire sum was forfeited under U.S. customs law – which was deemed excessive under the Eighth Amendment by the U.S. Supreme Court.

Looking for the rationale of forfeiture of instrumentalities, we find complex considerations that boil down to four reasons: It is (1) additional punishment for actual criminals and meant to (2) deter potential criminals, (3) an incentive for noncriminal owners to take care that their property will not be abused for facilitating crime, and (4) an instrument to remove "tools of crime" from circulation. Do these reasons bear scrutiny?

1. Forfeiture of instrumentalities belonging to criminals themselves may easily be understood as punishment and is actually understood so in many jurisdictions.[42]

---

[39] *Bennis v. Michigan*, 516 U.S. 442 (U.S. SCt. 1996).

[40] The Pittsburgh Press, 11 August 1991.

[41] 524 U.S. 321 (1998).

[42] *Austin v. United States*, 509 U.S. 602, 618 (1992).

The consequence is that there is no "civil" forfeiture of such instrumentalities but that the constitutional regime of crime and punishment applies. Indeed, U.S. courts tend to apply the Eighth Amendment prohibition of excessive fines to forfeiture of instrumentalities.[43] However, the problem remains that punishment through the forfeiture of instrumentalities is difficult to integrate into just and proportional sentencing. Firstly, it is an "extra" punishment in addition to "normal" punishment (prison or fines), which results in complicated sentencing considerations: It is clearly unfair that drug dealer A, who completed a drug deal in a rental car, is sentenced to two years in prison, whereas drug dealer B, who completed the same drug deal in his own car, is sentenced to two years in prison plus forfeiture of his car valued at $20,000. Rather, the "extra" $20,000 must be "translated" into some sort of "prison discount," say three months so that the sentence would be one year nine months for drug dealer B.[44] Secondly, instrumentalities forfeiture does not necessarily reflect the gravity of the offence which is a lead factor in just and proportional sentencing. The $350,000 forfeiture in *U.S. v. Bajakajian* might be acceptable if the offence had been money laundering but not if – as was the case – the money was perfectly legal and the offence amounted to nothing more than a failure to declare the money in the customs form.

2. Certainly, forfeiture of instrumentalities may have strong deterrent effects: If I stand to lose my house by growing marihuana in the basement (or by letting my tenant grow marihuana there), I have a strong incentive to refrain from the criminal act (or to intervene against it, see *infra* 3.). The problem is that deterrence associated with the threat of forfeiture of instrumentalities has an arbitrary quality that is difficult to reconcile with the rule of law. Setting proportionality (and, in the U.S., Eighth Amendment) considerations aside, the perpetrator's car will be forfeited regardless of the nature and gravity of the offence committed in the car, be it a brutal rape or the sale of 1 gram of marihuana. What remains is general deterrence embodied in the threat of a genuinely arbitrary penalty, unrelated to the wrongfulness of the conduct or the extent of the harm, and the specific deterrence that once the instrument of the crime has been forfeited, it cannot be used to commit further crimes. That flies in the face of the principle that the severity of the penalty – and consequently the quantum of deterrence – is tied to the reprehensibility of the criminal act and that arbitrary penalties can violate due process.[45]

---

[43] See the leading Supreme Court cases *Austin v. United States*, 509 U.S. 602 (1993), *United States v. James Daniel Good Real Property* – 510 U.S. 43 (1993), and *United States v. Bajakajian*, 524 U.S. 321 (1998).

[44] In U.S. sentencing law, we encounter the additional difficulty that sentencing guidelines might stand in the way of adapting the "normal" sentence to the "extra" punishment by means of forfeiture. Insofar, forfeiture of instrumentalities runs against the policy of uniform and determinate sentencing in the U.S., see *Pimentel*, 13 Nevada Law Journal 52 (2012).

[45] It is true that, in U.S. law, a constitutional requirement for proportional sentences is highly disputed, especially when it comes to non-death penalty sentences.

3. Most jurisdictions do not permit forfeiture of instrumentalities if the respective instrumentality belonged to a person who was not criminally liable for the respective offence. A notable exception to the rule is U.S. law which traditionally permits "civil" forfeiture of instrumentalities, even if the owner is completely innocent. In many jurisdictions, such a rule would be flatly unconstitutional. Even the U.S. Congress had doubts and introduced the "innocent owner defence," an affirmative defence that the owner did not know of the conduct giving rise to forfeiture, or upon learning of such conduct did all that reasonably could be expected under the circumstances to terminate such use of the property. This rule does not go far enough. It does not exclude that non-criminal conduct – simple knowledge or even simple negligence – results in severe and disproportional loss of property – e.g., of a tenement block if the owner cannot prove sufficient cooperation with police and/or private security to terminate drug trafficking on the premises. Since (and insofar as) the owners are not criminally liable, forfeiture of instrumentalities cannot be justified as punishment but has to be defended as being remedial: as a way to provide incentives to property owners in order to ensure that their property is not misused for criminal purposes. This shifts some of the responsibility for policing wrongdoing from law enforcement to property owners:[46] In order to avoid forfeiture, owners of immovable property, for example, may need to hire private security services to police their land and buildings to ensure that criminal activity is not carried out there. However, it must be noted that common property owners already have incentives to ensure that their property is not misused for criminal purposes: A common car owner will not lend his or her automobile to a drunk person out of concern for the lives and safety of potential accident victims and because he or she fears destruction of the car; a conventional firearms owner will keep the weapons secured for similar reasons. It seems unlikely that the risk of government forfeiture of such property plays a more serious role in prompting owners to take precautions, or to augment the precautions the owner is already taking.

4. What remains is the public interest in removing the instruments of crime from circulation, out of the reach of criminals who might otherwise use them for future criminal activity. This is a harm prevention argument, and there are certainly cases in which it bears everyday logic. Consider, for instance, a 1925 bootlegging case in the U.S.: If police stopped an automobile full of illegal liquor, and arrested the driver, returning the vehicle to the owner merely would have facilitated future bootlegging activity. In such a situation, the forfeiture is neither a punishment, nor an example to deter others from attempting such crimes, but a remedial effort to suppress the wrongdoing by removing the means of such criminal activity from the wrongdoer's control, and perhaps even from the public sphere altogether. This rationale works well for property whose primary uses are directly related to criminal

---

[46] *See Goldsmith Jr.-Grant v. U.S.*, 254 U.S. 505 at 510–511 (1921).

activity, such as automatic weapons[47] or equipment to outfit a drug laboratory – cases that are already close to contraband cases, see *supra* III.A. But usually forfeited instrumentalities are "nothing even remotely criminal,"[48] e.g., real estate, motor vehicles, airplanes or monetary instruments (cash, cards, etc.). In fact, such property often is not removed from circulation in the economy – it is merely reallocated within the economy when the State, as it usually does, sells forfeited real estate or vehicles or spends forfeited money. In such cases, the harm prevention principle justifies the forfeiture of instrumentalities only if the State can prove a substantial likelihood that, without forfeiture, the property would be used for criminal activities in the future.[49]

In any case, the procedure of forfeiture of instrumentalities should satisfy the standards of criminal procedure. This is clear if forfeiture of instrumentalities is an "extra" punishment for wrongdoers. But it would also be highly questionable if innocent or guilty third parties, whose property has been abused for criminal purposes, would be afforded less legal protection.

Bibliography

Beccaria, Cesare, Über Verbrechen und Strafe [On Crimes and Punishment]. Livorno 1764.

Binding, Karl, Die Normen und ihre Übertretung [Norms and Their Transgression], vol. 1. 1st ed. Leipzig 1872.

Blair, Montgomery, Federal Forfeiture Practice Manual. eBook Version 3.0, 2009.

Cassella, Stefan, Asset Forfeiture Law in the United States. 2nd ed. Huntington 2012.

– The Case for Civil Forfeiture: Why In Rem Proceedings are an Essential Tool for Recovering the Proceeds of Crime. 25th Cambridge International Symposium on Economic Crime, 7 September 2007. Available at http://works.bepress.com/cgi/viewcontent.cgi?article=1019&context=stefan_cassella [5.8.2014].

– Statement in the Hearing on H.R. 1835 – Civil Asset Forfeiture Reform Act –, 105th Cong. 112, 1997.

---

[47] See *U.S. v. One Assortment of 89 Firearms*, 465 U.S. 354 (1984).

[48] *One 1958 Plymouth Sedan v. Pennsylvania*, 380 U.S. 693 at 699 (1965).

[49] *Pimentel*, 13 Nevada Law Journal 63 at note 287 (2012) discusses the following example: "Officers make a valid traffic stop on a vehicle and obtain consent to search the vehicle. They find a concealed compartment that has been specifically built into the vehicle which contains a large quantity of drugs. The registered owner is a 'mule' who admits driving drugs from Mexico to the US and takes currency back to Mexico inside the concealed compartment. The vehicle makes regular runs between Mexico and the US. CBP documents numerous entries by this vehicle into the US over the past six months. The vehicle is not contraband. There is no evidence that the vehicle was purchased with drug proceeds."

Edgeworth, Dee R. (ed.), Asset Forfeiture: Practice and Procedure in State and Federal Courts. 2nd ed. Chicago 2009.

Feinberg, Joel, The Moral Limits of the Criminal Law, vol. 2: Offense to Others. New York 1985.

– Legal Paternalism. 1 Canadian Journal of Philosophy 105–124 (1971).

Kant, Immanuel, Metaphysik der Sitten [Metaphysic of Morals]. Königsberg 1798.

McGowan, Ryan E./Grovsten, Colin H. (eds.), Forfeiture, Conspiracy, Venue. Hauppauge 2011.

Mill, John Stuart, On Liberty. 2nd ed. London 1863.

Pimentel, David, Forfeitures Revisited: Bringing Principle to Practice in Federal Court. 13 Nevada Law Journal 1–73 (2012); available at: http://works.bepress.com/david_pimentel/12 [5.8.2014].

President's Commission on Organized Crime, The edge: organized crime, business, and labor unions. Washington D.C. 1986.

Robinson, Paul H., Criminal Law. New York 1997.

Rönnau, Thomas, Die Vermögensabschöpfung in der Praxis [Asset Forfeiture in Practice]. München 2003.

Weber, Ulrich. In: Jürgen Baumann/Ulrich Weber/Wolfgang Mitsch (eds.), Strafrecht Allgemeiner Teil [Criminal Law – General Part]. 11th ed. Bielefeld 2003.

Williams, Marian R./Holcomb, Jefferson E./Kovandzic, Tomislav V./Bullock, Scott, Policing for Profit. 2010, available at http://www.ij.org/images/pdf_folder/other_pubs/asset forfeituretoemail.pdf [5.8.2014].

List of Abbreviations

Cir.	Circuit
COM	European Union Commission documents
F.3d	Federal Reporter, Third Series
H.R. Rep.	House of Representatives Report
pt.	part
RICO	Racketeer Influenced and Corrupt Organizations Act
scil.	scilicet
SCt.	Supreme Court
SOCA	Serious Organized Crime Agency (UK)
U.K.	United Kingdom
UKSC	United Kingdom Supreme Court
U.S.	United States of America
U.S.C.	Code of Laws of the United States of America

Chapter 10

Non-Conviction-Based Confiscation in Europe

Bringing the Picture Together

Jon Petter Rui and *Ulrich Sieber*

I. Introduction

1. On the basis of the foregoing contributions, this chapter identifies and elaborates upon some main findings that might further develop the concept of NCBC. The focus of this last chapter is on non-conviction-based confiscation as defined in the introduction to this book. Thus, it does not deal primarily with traditional confiscation or with extended confiscation, which also raises issues such as whether to limit the requirement of proof for the nexus between a crime and the confiscated gain. Instead, it concentrates on confiscation systems that do not require *any* criminal conviction.

With respect to these specific cases of NCBC, the *first* important observation originating from the foregoing contributions is that there is not one single concept of NCBC. At least four approaches to NCBC have been identified: the common law, the Italian, the German-Scandinavian, and the EU approach.

A *second* interesting observation is that the NCBC rules of the four approaches, different as they may be, were developed in response to the same problem: namely, it is often impossible to obtain a criminal conviction, which is a requirement for traditional confiscation. One explanation for this is that the defendant or owner of property is not available for a criminal trial, i.a. because of flight from prosecution, illness, or death. Another obstacle originates from the evidence problem: persons involved in organized crime use their resources to distance themselves from the crimes they mastermind. Thus, it is impossible to prove a link between the persons, the crimes they have committed, and the property derived from these crimes. In the latter cases, however, it may be possible to prove that there is a link between property and criminality, in the sense that the property represents or is financed by crime. In these circumstances, the inability to remove the tainted property from circulation in the legal economy would seem to be a problematic result.

Thirdly, even though the rationales for developing NCBC rules are the same, they have developed differently. In the UK and Ireland, NCBC was introduced through legislation that created a complete scheme for NCBC. In contrast, the development of NCBC legislation in Italy was piecemeal: At the very beginning, the legislation was anchored in rules enabling *preventive* confiscation directed towards persons. Then, gradually, the requirements concerning the link between a likely offender and the crime were reduced. According to *Panzavolta* and *Flor,* however, "Italian law has taken steps to move in the direction of creating an *actio in rem*, but it has not quite got there yet."[1] The piecemeal approach has, according to *Cassella*, been taken in the United States as well.[2] The German-Scandinavian approach to NCBC differs from both the common law and the Italian approaches in that there are only a few single constellations enabling confiscation without a criminal conviction of the offender. Thus, one cannot refer to a comprehensive NCBC system or regime. The rules, which seem to have grown out of pragmatic considerations, are partly based on the fact that, while property is sometimes linked to crime, there is often no known or available person to charge and convict for that crime. Thus, there is a practical need for a confiscation provision so as to enable confiscation without a conviction. An experience shared by Germany and Norway is that the NCBC procedure is rarely used in practice.

Fourthly, the approaches to NCBC in different jurisdictions are based on different policy considerations. In Italian law, NCBC legislation is considered to be a preventive measure, that is, a measure imposed to prevent a criminal offense from taking place. The measure may be imposed, regardless of whether or not criminal proceedings are ultimately initiated.[3] Preventive confiscation, just like all other preventive measures, is wholly independent of a criminal conviction.[4] The first stage of the legislation (1965) was to regard anyone suspected of mafia crime as a danger to society and hence liable to be subjected to a preventive measure.[5] At the second stage (1982), when a system of financial preventive measures was established, the main underlying logic was that mafia *properties* were to be considered just as dangerous as the single individuals.[6] By the third stage (2011), the legislature attempted to extinguish entirely the need for a link between the dangerous person and the property. It did not fully succeed, however. In contrast, the common law approach is based on a different policy consideration, namely, the need to remove from society property that could be linked with crime.[7] Such property must be taken out of circulation because it gives an unfair advantage to those with access to it. In German law, confiscation as such is not regarded as a criminal measure. The rationale follows two lines of argumentation: Firstly, confiscation is aimed at removing property that could lead to the commission of future crimes, were it not removed; hence, confiscation has a preventive goal.[8] Secondly, while the (criminal)

---

[1] See *supra Panzavolta/Flor*, p. 147.

[2] See *supra Cassella*, p. 20.

[3] See *supra Panzavolta/Flor*, p. 119.

[4] See *supra Panzavolta/Flor*, p. 123.

[5] See *supra Panzavolta/Flor*, p. 119.

[6] See *supra Panzavolta/Flor*, p. 121.

[7] See *supra Smith*, p. 31; *supra Bacarese/Sellar*, pp. 213–215.

[8] See *supra Esser*, p. 79.

absorption of profits is designed to correct an unlawful allocation of property, confiscation has taken over functions of civil compensation.[9]

A *fifth* finding is that NCBC systems are either placed within the criminal (procedural) law of the jurisdiction or outside of it.

2. Considering the variety of these approaches, at first glance, there does not seem to be an easy answer as to whether NCBC is a criminal measure or not: it depends on the classification in national law enacted by the national legislature. The foregoing contributions show that there are different views on the purpose of NCBC legislation in various jurisdictions. A clear trend is that NCBC – in its different facets in different jurisdictions – is not considered a criminal measure. This is the case for both the Irish and the UK NCBC systems.[10] In Germany, it is clear that the NCBC provision in Section 76a 1 Criminal Code is not a criminal sanction.[11] Furthermore, the highest German courts (Supreme Court and Federal Constitutional Court) have consistently held that confiscation of assets in general is not a criminal measure: it is neither a punishment as such nor does it resemble a punishment.[12] Similarly, confiscation is not regarded as a penal measure in Denmark,[13] Finland,[14] Norway,[15] or Sweden. However, as shown, classification in national law is only one of three criteria applicable when the European Court of Human Rights analyzes whether a measure should be regarded as "criminal" in the context of the ECHR.

If NCBC were to be regarded as a criminal measure for Convention purposes, several questions would arise: is the evidence threshold in NCBC proceedings compatible with the presumption of innocence in ECHR Art. 6 No. 2? Is there a reversed burden of proof for third parties claiming rights to the property (the common law model), and is such a reversed burden compatible with the same Article? How should the conditions enabling the third party to speak and produce evidence (common law model) be configured in light of his right to remain silent and not incriminate himself (Art. 6 No. 1)? A further area of potential conflict is the option of launching an NCBC procedure after a final acquittal in a criminal case. ECHR Protocol 7 Art. 4 contains a prohibition on double jeopardy *(ne bis in idem)*. The notion of what constitutes a "criminal" case in the Article is to be understood mainly under the same terms as the content of Art. 6 *(Engel* criteria).[16] Last but not

---

[9] *Op. cit.*

[10] See *supra Smith*, pp. 33–34; *Bacarese/Sellar*, pp. 213–215.

[11] See *supra Esser*, p. 79.

[12] See *supra Esser*, p. 78.

[13] *Toftegaard Nielsen*, Strafferet, p. 305.

[14] *Frände*, Allmän straffrätt, pp. 362–363.

[15] *Andenæs*, Alminnelig strafferett, p. 513.

[16] *Sergey Zolotukhin v. Russia*, application no. 14939/03, Grand Chamber Judgment of 10 February 2009 paras. 52–57; *Glantz v. Finland*, application no. 37394/11, Judgment of

least: if NCBC is regarded as a criminal measure in terms of Art. 7 ECHR, the prohibition on retroactivity will apply. Hence, the notion of "criminal" in Art. 7 is
identical with that in Art. 6. *Smith, Esser, Panzavolta/Flor, Boucht, De Busser,* and
Bacarese have all discussed most of these aspects.

Thus, there is a need for an analysis independent of national classifications
(Querschnittsanalyse),[17] i.a. for jurisdictions that are considering implementing
NCBC legislation. For these reasons, it is obvious that we need to decide on a "me-
ta level" – a level detached from formal national classification – regarding whether
NCBC is a criminal sanction or not. Since NCBC has to be considered in close
connection with other confiscation rules, the analysis should also touch upon
whether confiscation in general is a penal measure or not.

But what approach should be taken in order to decide this question? One solution
is to adhere to the method of the ECtHR and to use the well-established *Engel* criteria. On the one hand, it is obvious that this approach should be taken into consideration when analyzing whether NCBC is a criminal measure or not. On the other
hand, the *Engel* criteria are well suited to a concrete, case-by-case oriented approach. However, they provide only rather limited guidance from the perspective of
the legislature. When legislating NCBC, a certain logical and coherent system is
necessary. Expressed in other terms: the *Engel* criteria are well suited to an *ex post*
evaluation of a measure based on a given case. They do not, however, provide a
very secure and helpful approach when legislating NCBC (and other legal
measures) from an *ex ante* perspective. This kind of policy-oriented approach
would require the differentiation of the various construction models available to
legislatures. The following text will refer to this proactive or *ex ante* approach as
the "policy-oriented approach"; it must be distinguished from the retrospective, *ex
post* control-oriented approach of the ECtHR.

3. On the basis of a general theoretical framework, the following text will create
such a policy-oriented approach with models for legislatures. For this reason, section II will develop the theoretical and practical concepts for this approach. Section
III will analyze whether this policy-oriented "*ex-ante*" concept comports with the
"*ex post* control" concept developed by the ECtHR. Since NCBC systems aim to
develop non-criminal confiscation systems, section IV will analyze which human
rights guarantees are applicable outside the criminal sphere. Section V will describe
the development of NCBC at the EU level. Lastly, section VI will provide some
recommendations for the drafting of NCBC legislation at the national level.

---

20 May 2014 paras. 48–51; *Häkkä v. Finland,* application no. 758/11, Judgment of 20 May
2014 paras. 37–40; *Nykänen v. Finland,* application no. 11828/11, Judgment of 20 May
2014 paras. 38–41, and *Pirttimäki v. Finland,* application no. 35232/11, Judgment of 20
May 2014 paras. 45–48.

[17] *Sieber,* Strafrechtsvergleichung im Wandel, pp. 115–116.

II. Developing a Policy-Oriented NCBC Approach

A. Methodology

The starting point of the policy-oriented approach is not the development of general evaluation criteria (such as the *Engel* criteria) but the differentiation of distinct models allowing for the confiscation of supposedly tainted property. This process of model-building requires analysis of the various legal disciplines that could be used for confiscation purposes. These disciplines are repressive criminal law, preventive police law (separate from criminal law in many states), and civil law.

A first look at these disciplines indicates that they provide three fundamentally different approaches and legal constructions under which property could be confiscated:

– Criminal law could confiscate property by means of sanctions;
– Police law could confiscate property in order to prevent future damage caused by or with this property;
– Civil law could take away property on the basis of the principle of unjustified enrichment, thus attempting to re-establish the situation before the offense took place (at least with respect to the enriched person).

An additional tax law approach would also be possible if the perpetrator did not pay taxes on his gains. However, this approach is not discussed in detail here since it could only apply to a certain percentage of the perpetrator's gains and would not lead to full confiscation of profits. In addition, such an approach would cause considerable difficulties at the international level as some countries tax criminal gains, whereas such an approach is controversial in others. Nevertheless, the tax law approach is interesting in the present context because it shows the broad powers of tax authorities to estimate the proceeds of tax fraud without being hampered by strict rules of proof.

This legal regime-oriented policy approach has four distinct advantages over the general approach of the ECtHR: Firstly, this concept identifies three clearly defined models that the legislature could use and evaluate. Secondly, the differentiation between these models, their limits, and their evaluations can lead to much more precise results than the *Engel* criteria, which develop general limits and evaluations for *all* different types of NCBC. Thirdly and above all: If the respective NCBC models were in line with the concepts of police or civil law, this would already be a strong argument for the legality of this model. Fourthly and finally, the following public and civil law concepts offer the legislature several options regarding where to codify the resulting models: either in the legal regimes of public and civil law or in the criminal code (public law models, e.g., for the incarceration of mentally ill or dangerous people; or civil law models, e.g., with respect to the concepts of *partie civil* in French criminal law or *Adhäsionsverfahren* in German criminal law).

For this reason, the following text will start by differentiating and analyzing the general characteristics of criminal sanctions and (public) police law as well as civil law concepts of confiscation based on unjust enrichment. In order to guarantee the legal conformity of this approach, the next section will then analyze whether this differentiating regime-oriented and phenomenological approach comports with the *Engel* criteria developed by the ECtHR.

B. The Criminal Law Model: What Characterizes a Penalty?

Described in the simplest and most basic way, a penalty is a retrospective phenomenon. It is a reaction of the state to an unlawful act or omission that has taken place in the past. The reaction takes the form of imposing something negative on the person who has acted or refrained from acting (omission). In addition, the state-inflicted reaction is designed to have a negative effect on the person. These characteristics are uncontroversial, widely recognized, and commonly used to explain the concept of a penalty. As *Esser* points out, the German Constitutional Court has defined a penalty along these lines for constitutional purposes.[18] The same characteristics are used to describe what punishment is, e.g., in Norwegian,[19] Swedish,[20] Danish,[21] and Finnish[22] law. Literature on legal theory defines the concept of punishment and penalty in broadly the same terms.[23] According to objective characteristics (retrospective reaction by the state, directed towards an individual, having a negative effect on the individual), it is inevitable that a penalty is, in fact, a retributive sanction.

Applying the term "retribution" when discussing criminal law has a certain effect among legal scholars. The person using it runs a great risk of being labeled a "retributivist" or "deontologist" who adheres to *Kant's* deontological morality philosophy. *Fletcher* points out that retributive theories are generally thought to be closely aligned with the imperative to seek justice in the criminal process, and the label "deontologist" is often used to describe this family of arguments about punishment as a requirement of justice. Retributivists defend this commitment to do justice on the ground that it incidentally serves to affirm the dignity of the offender. Retribution recognizes the criminal as a responsible human actor, someone who deserves punishment for his crime. Blaming and punishing offenders as a matter of justice

---

[18] See *supra Esser*, pp. 78–79.

[19] Rt. 1977 s. 1207 (Norwegian Supreme Court); *Andenæs*, Alminnelig strafferett, p. 10.

[20] *Asp et al.*, Kriminalrättens grunder, pp. 48–49.

[21] *Toftegaard Nielsen*, Strafferet, p. 20.

[22] *Frände*, Allmän straffrätt, pp. 1–2.

[23] *Hart*, Punishment and Responsibility, pp. 4–5; *Fletcher*, The Grammar of Criminal Law, pp. 227–233.

avoids using the suspects as a means to the end of social protection. Retribution stands for punishment of only the guilty and only because they are guilty.[24]

The opposite camp might be called social protectionists. The genesis of social protection as a rationale for punishment lies in the utilitarian theory developed by *Beccaria* and *Bentham*: the suffering of the prisoner is justified as necessary in order to achieve the greater good of improving the welfare or happiness of society. Social protectionists respond to the strict Kantian retributivists with a mixture of disdain and disbelief. The idea of making criminals suffer for the sake of a transcendental ideal of justice makes many moderns cringe. How can anyone seriously propose a program of punishment that disregards human welfare? Also, what is the origin of the modern State's authority to seek ultimate justice? The problem of eternal justice should be reserved for God. The state should act in the here and now, with a view to improving the lives of its citizens.[25]

This shows that the traditional camps of retributivists and social protectionists discuss the notion of penalty from an aim and purpose angle. As mentioned above, we argue that it is possible to answer to a certain extent the question of what a penal measure is and what it is not, without taking a final stand on why we punish. The distinction between what a penalty is, on the one hand, and its aim and purpose, on the other, has been correctly and precisely articulated by the German Constitutional Court, which has held that "a penalty is the imposition of a legal disadvantage because of an unlawful and illicit act. It is – notwithstanding its function to discourage the commission of future crimes and to resocialize the offender – an appropriate reaction to an action prohibited by criminal law. The evil comprised in every punishment is designed to compensate the culpable violation of a legal norm; it is an expression of retributive justice."[26] According to this line of thinking, there is no conflict between holding that a penal measure is in fact a retrospective retributive sanction and arguing that a penal measure can pursue several aims and purposes, i.a. general (positive or negative) prevention and special prevention (rehabilitation of the offender). Relatively new research on why we punish has revealed important nuances in the traditional approaches[27] and developed new approaches as well.[28] While the topic of the aims and purposes of punishment has been, is, and will remain complex and controversial, there is quite a widespread and common perception of what a penal measure in fact *is*.

---

[24] *Fletcher*, The Grammar of Criminal Law, p. 249.

[25] *Op. cit.*, pp. 249–250.

[26] See *supra Esser*, pp. 78.

[27] E.g., *Frände*, Allmän straffrätt, pp. 20–30; *Asp et al.*, Kriminalrättens grunder, pp. 30–32, both with further references.

[28] E.g., *Tadros*, Criminalization and Regulation, pp. 163–190; *Berman*, Two kinds of retributivism, pp. 433–457.

C. The Civil Law Model: Distinguishing Measures that Re-Establish the Status Quo Ante from Penal Measures

A penalty and a measure that re-establishes the *status quo* before an unlawful act was committed are both retrospective measures. However, a penalty is characterized as a measure imposing something negative on the person who has committed an act. Furthermore, a penalty is inflicted on the person by the state, with the purpose of having a negative effect. This is something more than the function of a measure designed to re-establish the *status quo ante*: *such a measure does not go beyond re-establishment.* Expressed in other terms, a retributive measure has to imply something more than the mere re-establishment of the situation before the criminal act took place. In addition, the state does not want a re-establishing measure to have a negative effect on the person affected by the measure. The desire of the state in this context is only to restore the situation back to the state before the unlawful act took place. Another feature distinguishing re-establishment from retributive measures is as follows: Re-establishment amounts only to the re-allocation of property, e.g., money, real estate, or moveable property, to establish the situation before the unlawful act. Re-establishment does not depend on the gravity of the unlawful act that has been carried out. In addition, the culpability of the person who has committed the unlawful act is irrelevant to the question of how much property needs to be re-allocated. These two factors are essential, however, to the establishment of a penal sanction. Furthermore, while illicit enrichment is only one of several relevant factors taken into consideration in the meting out of a penalty, enrichment is the only factor to consider when meting out a measure of re-establishment.

When applied to confiscation, a confiscation order or judgment that requires a person to turn over to the state the economic gains of an unlawful act (thus re-establishing the situation before the unlawful act) cannot be characterized as a penalty. This is the reason why confiscation is not considered a penalty in several national legal systems. As we have seen, in German law, the (criminal) absorption of profits is designed to correct an unlawful allocation of property. In other words, the function of confiscation legislation is to re-establish the situation that existed before the crime that created the economic gain was committed. In UK law, NCBC rules are designed to enable the state to remove from circulation the proceeds of crime: it is a proprietary remedy. At first glance, this reasoning is somewhat different from the reasoning in German law. It rests on the assumption that criminal property gives those with access to it an unfair advantage in business compared with those who have to earn their money and property the legal way. However, the legislation aims to correct the unfair situation and re-establish the economic situation before the tainted property came into circulation. Thus, the rationale behind the UK legislation is also to re-establish the status before the criminal act.

It is interesting to note that US confiscation law is built on diverse rationales: the non-punitive purpose of taking the profit out of crime, prevention, and restitution/restoration. In addition, confiscation is considered a form of punishment.[29] This is a different situation compared with German law. How can it be that confiscation legislation in German and US law pursues such different aims and purposes? *Cassella* states that

"if the procedures governing forfeiture were different depending on the Government's theory or motive there would be endless litigation over exactly what theory or motive applied in a given case, with the prosecutor arguing that he was proceeding under the theory that invoked the less burdensome procedures and the claimant arguing the reverse. Given the overlapping and mutually reinforcing motives and theories that apply in asset forfeiture cases, determining which procedures apply in a given case based on the Government's motive or theory would be a prescription for chaos in the courtroom."[30]

In other words, the US legislature has developed its confiscation legislation by means of a piecemeal approach. Some legislation is obviously considered non-criminal, e.g., with regard to the (non-)applicability of the presumption of innocence embodied in the Bill of Rights[31] and the double jeopardy clause of the Fifth Amendment. However, other legislative provisions undoubtedly serve penal purposes. *Cassella* writes:

"In money laundering cases, for example, the Government may forfeit all property involved in a money laundering offense, *including untainted property* that is commingled with the criminal proceeds at the time the money laundering offense takes place. In racketeering cases brought under the RICO statute, the Government may forfeit all property affording the defendant a 'source of influence' over the racketeering enterprise, *whether the property is tainted by the offense or not.* And in terrorism cases, the Government is entitled to the forfeiture of *every item of property that the terrorist has* (emphasis added)."[32]

In these examples, confiscation legislation is not limited to re-establishing the situation before the criminal act was committed. Thus, confiscation cannot be considered a solely restitutionary measure. In fact, confiscation that goes beyond establishing the status before the crime took place must be seen as a retributive measure. There is no other reason for such confiscation other than the state inflicting something negative on an offender with the purpose of having the measure negatively impact him and deterring others. For that reason, confiscation according to the "civil law model" should be limited to the net profit of crime.[33] In our opinion, this reveals that the distinction between re-establishment of the situation before the crime, on the one hand, and a retributive measure, on the other, is a precise and practical criterion for drawing the line between a retrospective measure that is criminal and a non-criminal retrospective measure.

---

[29] See *supra Cassella*, pp. 14–15.
[30] See *supra Cassella*, p. 19.
[31] See *supra Cassella*, p. 26.
[32] See *supra Cassella*, p. 18.
[33] See *supra Vogel*, p. 238.

254 Jon Petter Rui / Ulrich Sieber

D. The Police Law Model: Distinguishing Preventive Measures from Penal Measures

Both retributive measures and measures re-establishing the *status quo ante* are retrospective phenomena. Attention is drawn to an unlawful act that has taken place in the past, and the measures are directed towards remedying the wrong already committed. Preventive measures have an opposite focus. No unlawful act has yet been committed, but a measure is required in order to prevent it from taking place in the future. A common requirement for a preventive measure is that either a person or a property poses a danger that an unlawful act will be committed. To prevent this from happening, a measure is imposed. Thus, preventive measures do not amount to a penalty.

Defining and separating penal repressive measures from preventive measures is not a new invention. *Panzavolta* and *Flor* point out that crime prevention has always been the legitimate aim of every civilized country, often considered nobler than mere repression. *Blackstone*, for instance, recognized as commendable that English laws provided for means of crime prevention,

"since *preventive justice* is upon every principle, of reason, of humanity, and found policy, preferable in all respects to *punishing justice*; the execution of which, though necessary, and in its consequences a species of mercy to the commonwealth, is always attended with many harsh and disagreeable circumstances."[34]

Vogel reveals that the distinction between the preventive function and punitive function of sanctions is found in *Mill*'s "On Liberty," in which Mill asks whether the sale of poisons may legitimately be prohibited or at least regulated under the harm principle. The example, says Mill:

"(O)pens a new question; the proper limits of what may be called the functions of police; how far liberty may legitimately be invaded for the prevention of crime ... It is one of the undisputed functions of government to take precautions against crime before it has been committed, as well as to detect and punish it afterwards. The preventive function of government, however, is far more liable to be abused, to the prejudice of liberty, than the punitory function; for there is hardly any part of the legitimate freedom of action of a human being which would not admit of being represented, and fairly too, as increasing the facilities for some form or other of delinquency. Nevertheless, if a public authority, or even a private person, sees any one evidently preparing to commit a crime, they are not bound to look on inactive until the crime is committed, but may infer to prevent it ..."[35]

Considering the deeply rooted distinction between preventive and retributive measures, it is no surprise that we find it operative in several national jurisdictions, including, for example, Austria,[36] Denmark,[37] Finland,[38] Germany,[39] Italy,[40] the

---

[34] See *supra Panzavolta/Flor*, p. 111.

[35] See *supra Vogel*, pp. 230–231.

[36] *Kühne*, Strafprozessrecht, p. 750.

[37] *Smith et al.*, Straffeprocessen, pp. 100–105.

Netherlands,[41] Norway,[42] and the United Kingdom.[43] A common denominator for legal systems adhering to the distinction between preventive and retributive measures is that the former are not considered penal. In addition, preventive measures are not a part of the criminal law system but a part of administrative law (police law/*Polizeirecht*).

The clearest distinction between retrospective-retributive and preventive measures applied to confiscation is found in Italian law. In fact, as *Panzavolta* and *Flor* reveal, the entire system of NCBC in Italian law, which is defined as non-criminal, rests on this distinction: Italian law distinguishes between criminal confiscation and preventive confiscation, where the latter is considered a non-criminal measure by both the legislature[44] and the Supreme Court.[45] *Vogel* shows that such preventive confiscation can also be found in other legislation, esp. with respect to contraband and instrumentalities.[46]

E. Conclusion

Applying the policy-oriented approach, the following observations can be made:
- A penal measure is a reaction of the state to an unlawful act or omission that has taken place in the past. The state-inflicted reaction is designed to have a negative effect; it should inflict hardship on the offender.
- A retrospective measure, which only re-establishes the status before the unlawful act was committed and does not bear the aforementioned characteristics, is not a penal measure. If it goes beyond re-establishment, however, and in fact imposes something in addition to re-establishment, the "surplus" amounts to a penalty. Such a surplus may lead to a spillover effect, the consequence being that the measure as such has to be characterized as a penal measure.
- A measure that is a reaction to a supposed unlawful act in the future is a preventive measure; it is neither retrospective nor retributive. It is applied because either a person or a property poses a danger that an unlawful act will be committed in the future. Preventive measures applied in an appropriate manner do not amount to a penalty.

---

[38] *Frände*, Finsk straffprocessrätt, pp. 35–36, pp. 129–130.

[39] *Kühne*, Strafprozessrecht, pp. 106–110.

[40] See *supra Panzavolta/Flor*, pp. 111–112, 114.

[41] *Kühne*, Strafprozessrecht, p. 777.

[42] *Hov*, Rettergang, pp. 798–799.

[43] *Asworth/Zedner*, Preventive Orders, pp. 61–65.

[44] See *supra Panzavolta/Flor*, pp. 123–124.

[45] See *supra Panzavolta/Flor*, pp. 134, 141.

[46] See *supra Vogel*, pp. 234–235, 238–242.

III. Compliance of the Policy-Oriented Approach with the *Engel* Criteria

A. Introduction

Several of the contributions have highlighted the *Engel* criteria that were created by the ECtHR in the plenary case of *Engel and Others v. the Netherlands* in 1976. Since then, the criteria have been clarified and developed further in a vast number of judgments of the Court. Several of the authors have pointed out that the criteria are applied in order to determine whether a measure should be regarded as a criminal measure, making the guarantees of ECHR Art. 6 (fair trial, principle of self-incrimination, presumption of innocence), Art. 7 (no punishment without law, prohibition on retrospective penalties), and Protocol 7 Art 4 (*ne bis in idem*/double jeopardy) applicable.

The raison d'être of the *Engel* criteria is straightforward: if national authorities were able, at their discretion, to classify a measure as non-criminal, the operation of the fundamental clauses of the Convention applicable to criminal cases would be subordinated to their sovereign will. This much latitude might lead to results incompatible with the purpose and object of the Convention. Thus, the *Engel* criteria may be appropriately described as an anti-subversion doctrine.[47] Its function in our context is to prevent manipulation of the framework described above, which underpins the policy-oriented approach.[48]

The *Engel* criteria are (1) the classification of the measure in national law, (2) the nature of the offense, and (3) the degree of severity of the penalty risked.

– The *first criterion* (classification in national law) works only one way. If the measure is classified as criminal in national law, it will, as a rule, be regarded as the same for Convention purposes.

– The *second criterion* (nature of the offense) draws attention to the norm (not the underlying act). If the norm has some of the characteristics of a criminal law offense, the ECtHR is likely to conclude that it is a criminal offense for Convention purposes. The Court also attaches weight to the aim and purpose of the offense when analyzing its nature. If the provision aims at punishment and retribution, it will be regarded as criminal. If, however, the offense pursues reestablishment of the *status quo ante* or is compensatory in nature, it will not be regarded as "criminal." The nature of the offense is extremely important: Firstly, a measure will be regarded as criminal irrespective of the degree of severity of the penalty. In *Öztürk v. Germany*,[49] the Court concluded that a traffic fine of

---

[47] *Ashworth/Zedner*, Preventive Orders, p. 76.
[48] See *supra Boucht*, pp. 156 et seq.
[49] Application no. 8544/79, Judgment of 21 February 1984.

DM 60 constituted a criminal measure for Convention purposes, i.a. holding: "There is in fact nothing to suggest that the criminal offense referred to in the Convention necessarily implies a certain degree of seriousness."[50] In *Öztürk*, the Court concluded that the nature of the offense was criminal because the norm had the characteristics of a criminal law provision: it had been moved from the sphere of criminal law to that of administrative law *(Ordnungswidrigkeitsrecht)* in order to decriminalize petty offenses. In addition, the ECtHR attached importance to the fact that the aim and purpose of the provision was to punish and deter. *Secondly*, the jurisprudence of the Court shows that the degree of severity of the penalty has a very limited weight.

– With the exception of measures imposing a prison sentence, the *third Engel* criterion (degree of severity) does not lead to a measure being classified as criminal if the nature of the offense is not regarded as criminal. In *Porter v. the United Kingdom*,[51] the applicant was subjected to a fine of GBP 26 million. After having stated that Ms. Porter did not risk a prison sentence in default of paying the fine, the Court held: "While the risk of a prison sentence is not decisive for the classification of an offense as criminal ... the Court does not consider that the size of a monetary liability, which is rather compensatory rather than punitive in nature, can operate to bring the matter within the criminal sphere. It is equally conceivable, for example, that a person be found liable to pay very substantial sums in civil proceedings, and run the risk of bankruptcy in the event of non-payment."[52]

The following three sections will focus on the relationship between the policy-oriented approach to confiscation as outlined above and the *Engel* criteria. The question is whether and to what extent the policy-oriented approach complies with the *Engel* criteria. As regards the latter, the analysis seeks to explore the boundary between the discretion given to national legislatures when drafting confiscation legislation and the anti-subversion Strasbourg doctrine.

---

[50] Para. 53.

[51] Application no. 15814/02, Decision of 8 April 2003.

[52] The law, para. 1.1. (Applicability of Article 6 § 1). See also *Welch v. the United Kingdom*, application no. 17440, Judgment of 9 February 1995 para. 32, in which the Court held, when analyzing whether a substantial confiscation order amounted to a penal measure connection to a substantial confiscation order: "The Court agrees with the Government and the Commission that the severity of the order is not in itself decisive, since many non-penal measures of a preventive nature may have a substantial impact on the person concerned."

B. The *Engel* Criteria and the Distinction Between Penal Measures and Measures that Re-establish the Status Quo Ante

Welch v. the United Kingdom[53] sheds light on the distinction between penal and re-establishing measures and the use of the anti-subversion doctrine operationalized through the second *Engel* criterion: the nature of the offense. Mr. Welch was found guilty of several drug offenses and given an overall sentence of twenty-two year's imprisonment. In addition, the trial judge imposed a confiscation order pursuant to the Drug Trafficking Act 1986 in the amount of GBP 66,914. In default of payment of this sum, Mr. Welch would have been required to serve a consecutive two year prison sentence. The operative provisions of the 1986 Act came into force on 12 January 1987. The offenses for which Mr. Welch was convicted and on which the confiscation order was based had been committed before the entry into force of the 1986 act. After having exhausted national remedies, he brought the case to Strasbourg. He complained that the confiscation order amounted to the imposition of a retrospective penalty contrary to ECHR Art. 7.

Assessing the nature and purpose of the confiscation order (second *Engel* criterion), the Court, after having stated that the severity of the order in itself was not decisive, held:

> "However, there are several aspects of the making of an order under the 1986 Act which are in keeping with the idea of a penalty as it is commonly understood even though they may also be considered as essential to the preventive scheme inherent in the 1986 Act. The sweeping statutory assumptions in section 2 (3) of the 1986 Act that all property passing through the offender's hands over a six-year period is the fruit of drug trafficking unless he can prove otherwise … the fact that the confiscation order is directed to the proceeds involved in drug dealing and is not limited to actual enrichment or profit… the discretion of the trial judge, in fixing the amount of the order, to take into consideration the degree of culpability of the accused… and the possibility of imprisonment in default of payment by the offender … – are all elements which, when considered together, provide a strong indication of, inter alia, a regime of punishment."[54]

It was no surprise that the government's arguments were quashed. The government had contended that the true purpose of the confiscation order was twofold: firstly, to deprive a person of the profits he had received from drug trafficking, and secondly, to remove the value of the proceeds from possible future use in the drug trade. The Court's reasoning is in line with the policy-oriented approach. It is of great significance that the confiscation order was not limited to the actual enrichment or profit. This factor is, in fact, sufficient to conclude that a measure is not re-establishing but penal according to the policy-oriented approach.

---

[53] Application no. 17440/90, Judgment of 9 February 1995.

[54] Para. 33.

In *Walsh v. the United Kingdom*[55] the Court again faced the question of whether confiscation proceedings were criminal in nature. Mr. Walsh had an extensive criminal record, commencing in February 1980. It included some 132 road traffic offenses, one offense of conspiracy to rob, four of burglary, eight of theft, and 14 of being equipped for theft, together with other miscellaneous convictions. On 13 June 2003, Mr. Walsh, together with other co-defendants, was acquitted of offenses of obtaining services and property by means of deception. The restraint order issued regarding Walsh's property pending any eventual confiscation order on conviction was discharged. On 2 July 2003, the Assets Recovery Agency served a summons on Mr. Walsh for the purpose of recovery proceedings (NCBC). The Agency sought recovery of the sum of GBP 70,250 allegedly paid to his solicitor in 2001 for buying a house and the sum of GBP 5,969 held in a bank account, alleging that these were the proceeds of unlawful conduct within the meaning of the Proceeds of Crime Act 2002 ("POCA"). Thus, one might say that it was the NCBC system of the United Kingdom that stood trial in Strasbourg. At an interlocutory hearing, it was contended on behalf of Mr. Walsh that the proceedings for recovery of his assets were not "civil" but criminal in nature and that the guarantees of Art. 6 §§ 1 and 2 ECHR applied, in particular as regards the standard of proof.

After having tried his case in all available national courts, Mr. Walsh turned to the ECtHR. He complained that he had been denied the presumption of innocence in the recovery proceedings, as the civil standard of proof had been applied, and that the proceedings were conducted entirely by affidavit without hearing any witnesses. After finding that the measure was classified as civil in national law, the Court went on to analyze the confiscation measure in light of the second and third *Engel* criterion:

> "As to the second, the domestic courts considered that the purpose of the proceedings was not punitive or deterrent but to recover assets which did not lawfully belong to the applicant... The Court also notes that there was no finding of guilt of specific offences and that the High Court judge in making the order was careful not to take into account conduct in respect of which the applicant had been acquitted of any criminal offence. Lastly, the recovery order was not punitive in nature; while it no doubt involved a hefty sum, the amount of money involved is not itself determinative of the criminal nature of the proceedings (see *Porter v. the United Kingdom*, (dec.), no. 15814/02, 8 July 2003, where the applicant was liable to pay some GBP 33 million in respect of financial losses to the local authority during her mandate as leader)."[56]

In contrast to *Welch*, the Court accepted the government's argument that the purpose of the measure was not punitive. The NCBC legislation was drafted in accordance with its purpose, namely, to recover assets that did not lawfully belong to Mr. Walsh. It did not provide for the confiscation of proceeds that could not be linked to unlawful conduct.

---

[55] Application no. 43384/05, Decision of 21 November 2006.

[56] The law, para. 1.

A last case of interest for our analysis is *Dassa Foundation and Others v. Liech-tenstein*.[57] The case concerned the Dassa Foundation, the Lefleur Foundation, and Mr. Attilio Pacifico (the applicants). The latter was suspected of having bribed several judges in Rome in the 1990s and of having transferred the proceeds of those offenses to the two foundations in order to conceal that the money had originated from criminal acts. A court ordered the seizure of all assets that the foundations had deposited in Neue Bank, Liechtenstein. The seizure was prolonged several times. In one of the court decisions prolonging the seizure order, seizure was based on section 20b § 2 of the Liechtenstein Criminal Code. This provision had entered into force on 19 December 2000. The applicants argued that the criminal provision of section 20b § 2 had thus been applied retrospectively, in breach of the prohibition on retroactive punishment. The applicants' argument was not successful in national courts. They brought the case to Strasbourg, arguing i.a. that seizure and forfeiture on the basis of section 20b § 2 had to be regarded as a criminal measure, making the prohibition on retroactive penalty in ECHR Art. 7 applicable. Analyzing the second *Engel* criterion, the Court held:

> "There are in fact several elements which make seizure and forfeiture, in the manner in which these measures are regulated under Liechtenstein law, more comparable to a restitution of unjustified enrichment under civil law than to a fine under criminal law. In particular, seizure and forfeiture under Liechtenstein law are limited to assets which originate from a punishable act (see section 20b § 2 of the Criminal Code). If the suspicion that the seized assets stem from a punishable act proves to be true, forfeiture is thus restricted to the actual enrichment of the beneficiary of an offence – a factor which distinguishes the present case from the case of *Welch*... in which such a limitation did not exist. Moreover, other than in the *Welch* case... there are no statutory assumptions under Liechtenstein law to the effect that property passing through the offender's hand prior to the offence was the fruit of crime unless he could prove otherwise. Likewise, other than in the *Welch* case... and other than in the case of criminal-law fines, the degree of culpability of the offender is irrelevant for fixing the amount of assets declared forfeited. Furthermore, unlike the confiscation orders at issue in the case of *Welch*... the forfeiture orders under Liechtenstein law cannot be enforced by imprisonment in default of payment."[58]

The Court concluded that "given in particular the nature of forfeiture under Liechtenstein law which makes it comparable to a civil law restitution of unjustified enrichment, the orders of seizure made against the applicant foundations in view of a subsequent forfeiture of their assets did not amount to a 'penalty' within the meaning of Art. 7 § 1, second sentence of the Convention."[59] It is of special significance that the Court emphasized that seizure and forfeiture under Liechtenstein law "are limited to assets which originate from a punishable act" and that "forfeiture is restricted to the actual enrichment of the beneficiary of an offense."

---

[57] Application no. 696/05, Decision of 10 July 2007.
[58] The law. C. Complaint under Article 7 of the Convention.
[59] The law. C. Complaint under Article 7 of the Convention.

As the Court emphasizes, these factors distinguish the Liechtenstein confiscation system from the system tested by the Court in the *Welch* case.

The cases presented above reveal that the core of the Court's anti-subversion doctrine is an objectivized scrutiny of the reasons adduced by the national government for supporting a civil (non-criminal) classification of a confiscation measure. A crucial factor in the Court's evaluation is whether the measure goes beyond re-establishment of the situation before the unlawful act or is limited to the actual enrichment. The Court takes other factors into consideration as well, such as whether the degree of culpability of the offender is relevant in fixing the amount of assets declared forfeited, whether statutory assumptions operate, and whether the possibility of imprisonment in default of payment by the offender exists. According to the policy-oriented approach, it suffices to bring a measure from the re-establishment realm to the penal realm if the confiscation order amounts to something more than re-establishment.

When a legislature establishes such NCBC models, it should, however, be aware that the overall sanctioning effect of the criminal law system lies not only in the legal consequences of a judgment (e.g., imprisonment or a fine) but also in the ethical blame connected with a criminal conviction. This ethical aspect can be observed in the current German discussion on the establishment of criminal liability for companies. One of the main reasons for the industries' objection to replacing the old system of *Ordnungswidrigkeiten* with a system based on criminal responsibility is that this new system would label them as "criminals." For this reason, any NCBC system developed in accordance with the civil law model must avoid such ethical blame. This will be easier, however, in NCBC systems (not requiring a crime and taking away only the actual "unexplained" profit) than in conviction-based systems.

Thus, the policy-oriented approach is in compliance with the ECtHR's anti-subversion doctrine.

C. The *Engel* Criteria and the Distinction between Penal and Preventive Measures

As pointed out by *Panzavolta* and *Flor*, the ECtHR has on several occasions scrutinized the Italian labeling of NCBC confiscation as a preventive, non-criminal measure. The Court has repeatedly held that the Italian preventive seizure/confiscation system cannot be considered a criminal penalty.[60] According to *Panzavolta* and *Flor*, it seems that the Court has done so mostly because it

---

[60] See *supra Panzavolta/Flor*, pp. 143–145.

acknowledges the peculiarity of the Italian situation with regard to the pressing need to fight organized crime.[61]

It is interesting to note that, in cases against other states, the Court has also accepted the national classification of NCBC rules as preventive, non-criminal measures. In *Butler v. the United Kingdom*,[62] for example, the key question was whether the preventive NCBC cash confiscation rules in the Drug Trafficking Act of 1994 could be appropriately classified as preventive and not penal. A friend of Mr. Butler was stopped in Portsmouth by a customs officer. When asked how much cash he was carrying, he replied GBP 500. A subsequent search of the boot of the car he was driving revealed GBP 240,000 in a green hold-all. The friend then stated that the money belonged to Mr. Butler, that he was taking it out of the country for Mr. Butler, that Mr. Butler wanted to use it to buy an apartment in Spain, and that he was travelling to Barcelona, Spain. The money was seized in accordance with section 42 of the Act. Some time later, the customs authorities made an application under sections 43 of the Act for the forfeiture of the seized amount, on the grounds that they believed the money was directly or indirectly the proceeds of drug trafficking. The Court issued an order for the confiscation of the money and ordered Mr. Butler to pay the costs of the hearing.

Section 42 (1) provides as follows:

"A customs officer or constable may seize and, in accordance with this section, detain any cash which is being imported into or exported from the United Kingdom if... he has reasonable grounds for suspecting that it directly or indirectly represents any person's proceeds of drug trafficking, or is intended by any person for use in drug trafficking."[63]

Section 43 of the Act states:

"A Magistrates' court ... may order the forfeiture of any cash which has been seized under section 42 of this Act if satisfied, on an application made while the cash is detained under that section, that the cash directly or indirectly represents any person's proceeds of drug trafficking, or is intended by any person for use in drug trafficking... The standard of proof in proceedings on an application under this section shall be that applicable to civil proceedings; and an order may be made under this section whether or not proceedings are brought against any person for an offence with which the cash in question is connected."[64]

Mr. Butler appealed the Court's decision without success. The court of appeal noted that the money was contaminated to a limited extent by cannabinoids and that Mr. Butler's friend had with him in the hire car a plan showing a route through Spain to Malaga. The court further observed that the cash seized included a large proportion of Scottish notes, which were typically used by drug traffickers to finance drug deals conducted abroad, and that the southern coast of Spain was

---

[61] See *supra Panzavolta/Flor*, p. 147.
[62] Application no. 41661/98, Decision of 27 June 2002.
[63] See under "B. Relevant domestic law".
[64] See under "B. Relevant domestic law".

known to customs officials as the source of a large number of consignments of drugs destined for the United Kingdom. With regard to the strong circumstantial evidence, the court found the explanations given by Mr. Butler and his friend as to why cash was being carried to Spain wholly unbelievable. Thus, the court concluded: "We do find it more probable than not that this money was to be used for trafficking."

Mr. Butler brought his complaint to the ECtHR, holding that the confiscation proceedings were criminal in nature and, as such, should invoke the safeguards of a criminal process, in particular his right to be presumed innocent. The government opposed: It stressed that no "offense" is charged against a person from whom cash is seized and forfeited and that there is no "offense" in domestic law of intending to use money for drug trafficking or if a third party was to use it for that purpose on his behalf. The forfeiture order against the applicant was a preventive measure. There was no finding by the domestic courts that the applicant had committed a criminal offense, and a perceived association between the cash forfeited and criminal activity is not sufficient to make forfeiture proceedings determinative of a criminal charge. The forfeiture order could therefore not be considered a penalty or punishment. The Court held that:

> "the forfeiture order was a preventive measure and cannot be compared to a criminal sanction, since it was designed to take out of circulation money which was presumed to be bound up with the international trade in illicit drugs. It follows that the proceedings which led to the making of the order did not involve 'the determination ... of a criminal charge' (see the Raimondi v. Italy judgment of 22 February 1994, Series A no. 281-A, p. 20, § 43; and, more recently, *Arcuri and Others v. Italy* (no. 54024/99, inadmissibility decision of 5. July 2001 [unreported]); *Riela v. Italy* (no.52439/99, inadmissibility decision of 4 September 2001 [unreported])."[65]

Thus, the Court accepted the government's classification, concluding that the confiscation measure in question was not penal but preventive in nature in accordance with the Convention's autonomous concept of a penalty.[66] This conclusion is not self-evident. The Court could have held that sections 42 and 43 represent a circumvention of the presumption of innocence in ECHR Art. 6 No. 2: firstly, section 42 implies the finding of criminal guilt, as the money confiscated represents "any person's proceeds of drug trafficking;" secondly, section 43 lowers the burden of proof to that applicable in civil proceedings. Reading this case together with the Italian cases mentioned by *Panzavolta* and *Flor*, it appears to be a trend for the Court to give national authorities broad discretion in drawing the line between punitive and preventive measures. In fact, in the Arcuri v. Italy case,67 the Court held that the confiscation legislation in question "forms part of a crime-prevention policy;

---

[65] The law, B. Applicability of Article 6 of the Convention under its criminal heading.

[66] See also *Webb v. the United Kingdom*, application no. 56054/00, Decision of 10 February 2004.

[67] Application no. 52024/99, Decision of 5 July 2001.

it considers that in implementing such a policy, the legislature must have a wide margin of appreciation both with regard to the existence of a problem affecting the public interest which requires measures of control and the appropriate way to apply such measures."[68]

D. Results

1. The policy-oriented approach applied in an appropriate manner when drafting confiscation legislation will not lead to breaches of *ECHR rights*, which apply in cases considered "criminal" according to the *Engel* criteria.

– As to the distinction between penal measures and those with the goal of re-establishing the *status quo ante*, it is crucial to observe that in the latter case legislation does not allow the confiscation of more than the actual enrichment of the unlawful act. Thus, the amount has to be calculated in accordance with the net principle. Adhering to a gross principle will lead to a confiscation order going further than re-establishing the situation before the unlawful act. The surplus cannot be regarded as a penalty. This will most likely taint the entire confiscation proceedings, making them a penal measure in Convention terms. Allowing confiscation of property that is untainted will clearly lead to the confiscation being classified as a penalty. The same could be true if a so-called re-establishing measure were to convey the ethical blame of having committed a crime.

– As to the distinction between penal and preventive measures, the Court allows the national authorities more discretion. At a certain point, however, the Court will draw a line. Thus, policy makers can provide for confiscation of property under the umbrella of preventive measures only if the respective legal provision requires a certain risk for other legal goods or if the provision limits its scope to precisely described situations that imply a certain probability that the confiscated property is dangerous or might be abused by its owner in a dangerous way.

2. The above conclusions for the ECHR of the Council of Europe are similar to the results for the *Charter of Fundamental Rights of the European Union* (Art. 6 § 2 TEU). This is based on the fact that the standards of protection under the Charter are generally interpreted in light of the jurisprudence of the ECtHR in a way that these standards are at least as high as the standards of the corresponding rights in the ECHR (Art. 52 § 3 1st phrase EUC). Up until now, there are also no indications that the ECJ will interpret the presumption of innocence (Art. 48 § 1 EUC) and especially the scope of application of the Charter for non-criminal measures in

---

[68] The law, para. 1.

a different way as the ECtHR, particularly as far as the *Engel* criteria are concerned.[69]

3. Similar results can be found on the *national level*. In Germany, for example, the presumption of innocence prohibits the imposition of any measure on the accused without a lawful proof of guilt. The presumption of innocence also applies only to punishments or treatment similar to punishment and not to legal consequences without a punitive character. This is why the Federal Constitutional Court does not consider the absorption of illegally obtained profits to be a retributive sanction, as long as the measure only aims at a correction of illegally developed assets. Thus, the re-establishment of the financial situation before a crime is not, in itself, a repressive act. For that reason, in the example of Germany, the results for the specific human rights safeguards (esp. the presumption of innocence) are similar to those on the European level.[70] This harmonious result is different from the situation in the field of human rights outside the sphere of criminal sanctions, which will be considered in the following.

IV. Human Rights Outside the Criminal Sphere Applicable to NCBC Proceedings

Since NCBC is not covered by the special human rights guaranties for criminal penalties, emphasis must be put on the question of whether NCBC measures are limited by non-criminal human rights, particularly by guarantees for the protection of property and the right to a fair trial in civil or public proceedings. Unlike the situation created by the presumption of innocence and the related *Engel* criteria for criminal law guarantees,[71] the corresponding non-criminal human rights are not covered by a similarly well-developed jurisprudence of the ECtHR in accordance with EU fundamental rights and national constitutional law. In the area of general human rights, the situation is more diverse. Thus, the analysis of the non-criminal-law-specific guarantees in the European multilevel human rights system must differentiate from the very beginning between three legal regimes: the ECHR system, the fundamental rights system of the EU, and the safeguards of national constitutional law.

---

[69] See *supra Esser*, pp. 91–95

[70] See *supra Esser*, pp. 77–82

[71] Especially for the presumption of evidence see *supra Boucht*, pp. 157–160.

A. The Legal System of the ECHR

1. Applicability of Art. 1 of Protocol No. 1 of the ECHR
(Protection of Property)

Art. 1 of Protocol No. 1 to the ECHR entails the protection of property ("biens" in the French version) and reads as follows:

> "Every natural or legal person is entitled to the peaceful enjoyment of his possessions. No one shall be deprived of his possessions except in the public interest and subject to the conditions provided for by law and by the general principles of international law.
>
> The preceding provisions shall not, however, in any way impair the right of a State to enforce such laws as it deems necessary to control the use of property in accordance with the general interest or to secure the payment of taxes or other contributions or penalties."

As the Court has held on many occasions, the wording of this provision entails four requirements: an *interference with property rights ("possessions")* must be *prescribed by law* and *pursue one or more legitimate aims;* in addition, there must be a reasonable relationship of *proportionality* between the means employed and the aims sought to be realized. In other words, the Court must determine whether a balance has been struck between the demands of the general interest and the interests of the individuals concerned. In doing so, the Court leaves the State a wide margin of appreciation with regard both to choosing the means of enforcement and to ascertaining whether the consequences of enforcement are justified in the general interest for the purpose of achieving the object of the law in question.[72]

As to the requirement of an interference with property rights, it is no surprise that the Court has found that confiscation proceedings directed towards *third parties* claiming *bona fide* interests amounts to an interference in those persons' property rights.[73] Somewhat less obvious, however, is the fact that Art. 1 of Protocol No. 1 in principle affords protection when a person has committed an unlawful act, and proceeds or instrumentalities in his possession are confiscated.

> In the recent Paulet case,[74] Mr. Paulet successfully applied for three jobs in the United Kingdom using a false French passport. He had used the false passport to support his assertion that he was entitled to work in the United Kingdom. All of his employers subsequently stated that they would not have employed him had they known of his true immigration status. The falsity of the passport was revealed when Paulet applied for a provisional driving license. By that time, he had earned a total gross salary of GBP 73,293 from his employments. He had total savings of GBP 21,649.

---

[72] E.g., *Silickiene v. Lithuania*, application no. 20496/02, Judgment of 10 April 2012 para. 63 with further references.

[73] *AGOSI v. the United Kingdom*, application no. 9118/80, Judgment of 24 October 1986; *Air Canada v. the United Kingdom*, application no. 18465/91, Judgment of 5 May 1995; *Denisova and Moiseyeva v. Russia*, application no. 16903/03, Judgment of 1 April 2010, and *Silickiene v. Lithuania*, application no. 20496/02, Judgment of 10 April 2012.

[74] Application no. 6219/08, Judgment of 13 May 2014.

Paulet was charged and pleaded guilty i.a. to three counts of dishonestly obtaining a pecuniary advantage by deception. In addition to a custodial sentence and a recommendation for deportation, the prosecution sought a confiscation order in respect of Paulet's earnings. After deducting tax and national insurance payments, it was calculated that the benefit Paulet received from his earnings was GBP 50,000. It was agreed that – of the GBP 50,000 – Paulet still had assets of GBP 21,949. On this basis, the trial judge imposed a confiscation order in the sum of GBP 21,949 upon Paulet, with a consecutive sentence of twelve month's imprisonment to be served in default of payment. Thus, the confiscation order had the effect of depriving Paulet of all the savings he had accumulated during the four years of employment.

After having exhausted national remedies, Paulet brought his case to Strasbourg, claiming that the confiscation order amounted to a breach of his right to peaceful enjoyment of his property secured in Art. 1 of Protocol No. 1. The government did not dispute that the confiscation order amounted to interference. The Court commented briefly that "it is clear from Phillips v. the United Kingdom... that confiscation orders fall within the scope of the second paragraph of Art. 1 of Protocol No. 1, which, inter alia, allows the Contracting States to control the use of property to secure payment of penalties."[75]

It is, *de lege ferenda*, questionable whether the property a person has acquired through criminal offenses should be given legal protection as a human right, especially under the right to property in Art. 1 of Protocol No. 1. In most jurisdictions, the civil law of the country basically denies any legal protection to criminally acquired property.[76] As pointed out in a dissenting opinion in the *Paulet* case, "there is a fundamental difference between possessions acquired in a lawful way and possessions acquired through crime."[77] The dissenting judge further held:

"The confiscation of the proceeds of crime is a criminal-law measure that may be based on natural justice. One of its aims is to ensure that a crime does not profit the perpetrator. Illegal gains should not be protected under the Convention and should not be considered to fall within the scope of application of Article 1 of Protocol No. 1. This last provision comes into play, however, when the parties dispute the source of some possessions. The paradox of the approach adopted by the majority is that possessions obtained as a result of crime enjoy protection under Article 1 of Protocol No. 1 against excessive interference. According to the approach proposed by the majority, they may be retained by a criminal if their confiscation would not strike a fair balance between the individual and public interests at stake."[78]

In *Denisova and Moiseyeva v. Russia*,[79] the Court indeed touched upon the matter of whether proceeds of crime should in principle be protected by Art. 1 of Protocol No. 1. Here, the Court discussed whether the applicants, who were third parties in the confiscation proceedings, had a legitimate claim to the property in

---

[75] Para. 64.

[76] *Denisova and Moiseyeva v. Russia*, application no. 16903/03, Judgment of 1 April 2010, Dissenting Opinion of Judge Vajic.

[77] Dissenting Opinion of Judge Wojtyczek para. 5.

[78] Dissenting Opinion of Judge Wojtyczek para. 5. See also *Denisova and Moiseyeva v. Russia*, application no. 16903/03, Judgment of 1 April 2010, Dissenting Opinion of Judge Vajic: "As in most countries, Russian civil law basically denies any legal protection to criminally acquired property."

[79] Application no. 16903/03, Judgment of 1 April 2010 paras. 47–54.

question, i.e., whether they argue that they had "at least a reasonable and 'legitimate expectation' of obtaining effective enjoyment of a property right or a proprietary interest." Thus, there is some tension between the Court's approach in the *Paulet* case and in *Denisova and Moiseyeva.*

The *legitimate aim requirement* in Art. 1 has never led the Court to assume a violation of human rights. In only one case has it found a violation because the national procedure for confiscation was not prescribed by law.[80] Thus, the proportionality requirement is the most interesting for our purposes.

In the vast majority of cases concerning the confiscation of a person's property acquired through criminal offenses committed by him, the Court concludes that confiscation is also *proportionate.*[81] The cases in which the Court finds a violation in our opinion reveal *exceptional circumstances* that lead the Court to find the confiscation order in question disproportionate.[82]

> In the above-mentioned Paulet case, the national courts concluded that they did not have any discretion to interfere with the Crown's decision to confiscate all of Mr. Paulet's assets. The only reason the Court concluded that Art. 1 of Protocol No. 1 had been violated was because "the scope of review carried out by the domestic courts was too narrow to satisfy the requirement of seeking the 'fair balance' inherent in the second paragraph of Article 1 of Protocol No. 1."[83] Even though it is not a part of the operative reasoning of the judgment, it seems to have had a certain effect on the Court that the money confiscated was not directly linked to a criminal offense, such as the proceeds of selling narcotics. The confiscated money instead had a more remote connection with Mr. Paulet's criminal activity (using a false passport to acquire jobs). Another fact mentioned in the judgment, which might have had an impact on the Court's conclusion, is that, after Mr. Paulet's case, it had changed its view on the competences of the UK courts as to the scope of review in confiscation proceedings: it had held that a judge should, "if confronted with an application for an order which would be disproportionate, refuse to make it but accede only to an application for such sum as would be proportionate."[84]

In *Ismayilov v. Russia,*[85] the Court also found that the confiscation in question was disproportionate.

---

[80] *Baklanov v. Russia*, application no. 68443/01, Judgment of 9 June 2005 para. 47.

[81] *Raimondo v. Italy*, application no. 12594/87, Judgment of 22 February 1994; *Arcuri and Others v. Italy*, application no. 52024/99, Decision of 5 July 2001; *Phillips v. the United Kingdom*, application no. 41087/98, Judgment of 5 July 2001; *Butler v. the United Kingdom*, application no. 41661/98, Decision of 27 June 2002; *Webb v. the United Kingdom*, application no. 56054/00, Decision of 10 February 2004 and *Saccoccia v. Austria*, application no. 69917/01, Judgment of 18 December 2008.

[82] The cases are *Ismayilov v. Russia*, application no. 30352/03, Judgment of 6 November 2008; *Waldemar Nowakowski v. Poland*, application no. 55167/11, Judgment of 24 July 2012 and *Paulet v. the United Kingdom*, application no. 6219/08, Judgment of 13 May 2014.

[83] Para. 68.

[84] Para. 38.

[85] Application no. 30352/03, Judgment of 6 November 2008.

Mr. Ismayilov arrived in Moscow from Baku carrying with him USD 12,348, which represented the proceeds from the sale of his ancestral dwelling in Baku. However, he only reported USD 48 on the customs declaration, whereas Russian law required that any amount exceeding USD 10,000 be declared to customs. A customs inspection uncovered the remaining amount in his luggage. He was charged with smuggling (which was a criminal offense), and the money was appended to the criminal case as physical evidence. Some time later, a court found Ismayilov guilty as charged and imposed a sentence of six months' imprisonment conditional on six months of probation. As regards the money, the Court held: "Physical evidence – 21,348 US dollars stored in the Central cash desk of the Sheremetyevo Customs Office – shall revert to the State."[86] After having unsuccessfully appealed, Ismayilov brought the case to the ECtHR, claiming a breach of Art. 1 of Protocol No. 1. The Court found the confiscation order to be disproportionate.

At the outset, the Court held that the criminal offense of which Ismayilov was convicted consisted of a failure to declare to the customs authorities the USD 21,300 he had been carrying. It is important to note that the act of bringing foreign currency into Russia in cash was not illegal under Russian law. Not only was it lawful to import foreign currency as such, but also the sum that could be legally transferred or, as in the present case, physically carried across the Russian customs border was not in principle restricted."[87] The Court then pointed out that the lawful origin of the confiscated cash was not contested: Ismayilov possessed documentary evidence, including the will and the sale contract, showing that he had acquired the money through the sale of a Baku flat that he had inherited from his mother. On this ground, the Court "distinguishes the present case from the cases in which the confiscation measure extended to the assets which were the proceeds of a criminal offense... which were deemed to have been unlawfully acquired... or were intended for use in illegal activities."[88] The Court found that the confiscation amounted to a penal measure. Viewed together with the prison sentence imposed, the confiscation order was disproportional.

In *Paulet,* the confiscated money had a rather remote connection with Mr. Paulet's criminal activity. In the present case, the property confiscated had an even more remote connection with the criminal offense. The direct proceeds of the crime in this case were the amount of customs tax evaded. The money smuggled into Russia was instead the instrument used to commit the offense. In addition, the difference between the direct proceeds of the crime and the amount confiscated was substantial.

On the basis of these observations, some conclusions can be drawn. Art. 1 of Protocol No. 1 is in principle applicable to NCBC legislation. However, legislation limited to the confiscation of the direct economic advantage of criminal offenses, i.e., what has been earned by criminal activity, will, as a rule, not be regarded as disproportionate.[89] Issues in relation to proportionality may arise, however, if the legislation allows for confiscation of proceeds that have a remote link with the unlawful act(s) that has triggered confiscation proceedings or the confiscation of instrumentalities. In addition, Art. 1 of Protocol No. 1 requires persons claiming

---

[86] Para. 7.

[87] Para. 35.

[88] Para. 36.

[89] See *supra Vogel*, p. 237.

rights to the property to put forward the argument of innocent ownership *(bona fide)*. Furthermore, the court deciding on confiscation must have the ability to carry out an evaluation of the proportionality of the confiscation and must in fact carry out such an evaluation.

These limitations under the principle of proportionality are supported by the basic justifications of the concepts of unjust enrichment and re-establishment. In many of the cases dealt with by the ECtHR under the proportionality principle, it was highly problematic to treat the respective property as criminal gain. In *Ismayilov v. Russia,* it is quite clear that the confiscated money could not be considered unjust enrichment or proceeds of crime, since its owner had earned it in a substantially and – formally – completely legal way. In the *Paulet* case, one could also argue that *Paulet,* in essence, had earned his salary through his work and that his crime was only a formal infringement of labor rules.

Thus, the civil law model of re-establishment supports the above decisions of the ECtHR as well as the differentiation pointed out in the dissenting opinion in the *Paulet* case that "there is a fundamental difference between possessions acquired in a lawful way and possessions acquired through crime." However, the "policy model" discussed above can often provide more precise rules and arguments for cases in which the link between a crime and its gain is indirect or highly remote. Thus, the present "regime-oriented" approach and the principle of proportionality could serve to limit the abuses that can be found in many countries that make excessive use of the NCBC approach, thus corrupting its positive aspects.

2. Applicability of Art. 6 No. 1 ECHR
(The Right to a Fair Trial in Civil Matters)

As confiscation proceedings determine a dispute relating to property rights, the ECtHR has in many cases held that such proceedings amount to "civil rights and obligations."[90] Thus, a person either subject to or part of an NCBC proceeding enjoys the rights enshrined in Art. 6 No. 1. The article gives the person the right to:

> "a fair and public hearing within a reasonable time by an independent and impartial tribunal established by law. Judgment shall be pronounced publicly but the press and public may be excluded from all or part of the trial in the interests of morals, public order or national security in a democratic society, where the interests of juveniles or the protection of the private life of the parties so require, or to the extent strictly necessary in the opinion of the court in special circumstances where publicity would prejudice the interests of justice."

---

[90] E.g. *Air Canada v. the United Kingdom*, application no. 18465/91, Judgment of 5 May 1995 para. 56; *Saccoccia v. Austria*, application no. 69917/01, Judgment of 18 December 2009 para. 58–65, and *Dimitar Krastev v. Bulgaria*, application no. 26524704, Judgment of 12 February 2013 para. 57. For a critical evaluation of this classification as "civil rights,", see *infra* p. 301.

These rights for NCBC proceedings have to be observed both when legislating NCBC and when applying the legislation in concrete cases.[91]

A condition for an effective NCBC system is legislation that affords the possibility at an early stage of the process to freeze the property that is subject to confiscation. As to the applicability of Art. 6 No. 1 to freezing proceedings, the Court's decision in *Nedyalkov and Others v. Bulgaria*[92] is enlightening. Here, the Court discussed the applicability of Art. 6 No. 1 to freezing proceedings in the course of an NCBC procedure. Analyzing previous case law, the Court held that it had been a "long-standing position that interim measures in civil proceedings do not engage that provision. However, in the subsequent Grand Chamber case of *Micallef v. Malta* the Court reversed its earlier position and held that Art. 6 § 1 applies to such measures if the right at stake in both the main and the interim proceedings is civil, and if the interim measure can be considered effectively to determine that right."[93] As the rights of the applicants affected by the freezing orders were considered to be civil and the restrictions resulting from those orders substantial, the Court found that Art. 6 No. 1 was applicable to the freezing proceedings. On the basis of the Court's reasoning, it has to be taken as a general rule that Art. 6 No. 1 is applicable to freezing proceedings in an NCBC procedure.

However, an important distinction was made: the applicants claimed that there had been a violation of Art. 6 No. 1 because the court deciding on freezing had not held a "public hearing." The Court stated that:

> "the first-instance proceedings leading to the making of the freezing orders were conducted on the papers and *ex parte*. However, no issue arises in relation to that. To be able to serve their purpose of preventing the dissipation of forfeitable assets, applicants for freezing orders need to be heard without notice, and that is not in itself incompatible with the requirements of Article 6 § 1 of the Convention... The position in relation to the appeal proceedings is different. They were *inter partes*, but were likewise conducted on the papers. However, a public hearing was arguably required, in view of what was at stake for the applicants – the potentially long-term freezing of a considerable number of assets, including their bank accounts."[94]

Thus, Art. 6 No. 1 does not apply to initial proceedings leading to the freezing orders but only to a later procedure at which the freezing order is contested. As the applicants had not made any request for a public hearing in the later proceedings concerning the validity of the freezing order (appeal proceedings), the Court found no Convention violation.

---

[91] For guidance, see, e.g., *Harris et al.*, Law of the European Convention, pp. 235–299; *White/Ovey*, The European Convention , pp. 242–277.

[92] Application no. 663/11, Decision of 10 September 2013.

[93] Para. 18.

[94] Para. 117–118.

3. Consequences of Art. 1 of Protocol No. 1 and Art. 6 No. 1 ECHR
for Evidentiary Requirements

With respect to confiscation, and mainly NCBC, the most interesting question now is whether, in non-criminal-law-based proceedings, the human rights guarantees discussed above of Art. 1 of Protocol No. 1 of the ECHR (protection of property) and Art. 6 No. 1 ECHR (right to a fair trial) have consequences for the standards of proof, not only with respect to the nexus between a crime and its proceeds but also to the existence of a crime at all.[95]

a) The ECtHR dealt with this question extensively in its May, 2015, decision *Gogitidze and others v. Georgia*.[96] The decision concerns the new Georgian "administrative confiscation," which has co-existed since 2004 with the "criminal confiscation" provision. The case deals with unexplained wealth of a high-ranking public official and his family. It is strongly oriented towards the containment of corruption in the public service, as illustrated by its detailed analysis of the various international instruments for confiscation, such as the UN Convention against Corruption, which invites States parties to consider that an offender has to "demonstrate the lawful origin of such alleged proceeds of crime or other property." Thus, the question as to extent to which the findings can be generalized is justified. However, the merits of the decision are quite general and clear, both with respect to the protection of property (Art. 1 of Protocol No. 1 of the ECHR) and the right to a fair trial (Art. 6 No. 1 ECHR). The court judges the administrative conviction provision as a "civil action in rem aimed at the recovery of assets wrongfully or inexplicably accumulated by the public officials concerned and their close entourage" (paras. 91–94). With respect to Art. 1 of Protocol No. 1 of the ECHR, the court rejects the claim that the person concerned had "to bear an individual and excessive burden":

> "the Court observes that common European and even universal legal standards can be said to exist which encourage, firstly, the confiscation of property linked to serious criminal offences such as corruption, money laundering, drug offences and so on, without the prior existence of a criminal conviction. *Secondly, the onus of proving the lawful origin of the property presumed to have been wrongfully acquired may legitimately be shifted onto the respondents in such non-criminal proceedings for confiscation, including civil proceedings in rem (emphasis added)*. Thirdly, confiscation measures may be applied not only to the direct proceeds of crime but also to property, including any incomes and other indirect benefits, obtained by converting or transforming the direct proceeds of crime or intermingling them with other, possibly lawful, assets. Finally, confiscation measures may be applied not only to persons directly suspected of criminal offences but also to any third parties which hold ownership rights without the requisite *bona fide* with a view to disguising their wrongful role in amassing the wealth in question."[97]

---

[95] For the consequences of Art. 6 Section 2 concerning evidentiary requirements see *supra Boucht*, pp. 180–184, and *Vogel*, p. 229.

[96] ECtHR, *Gogitidze and others v. Georgia*, 12 May 2015, no. 36862/05.

[97] Para. 105.

The court provided a detailed definition of the requirements of proof:

"As regards property presumed to have been acquired either in full or in part with the proceeds of drug-trafficking offences or other illicit activities of mafia-type or criminal organisations, the Court did not see any problem in finding the confiscation measures to be proportionate even in the absence of a conviction establishing the guilt of the accused persons. The Court also found it legitimate for the relevant domestic authorities to issue confiscation orders on the basis of a preponderance of evidence which suggested that the respondents' lawful incomes could not have sufficed for them to acquire the property in question. Indeed, whenever a confiscation order was the result of civil proceedings *in rem* which related to the proceeds of crime derived from serious offences, the Court did not require proof "beyond reasonable doubt" of the illicit origins of the property in such proceedings. Instead, proof on a balance of probabilities or a high probability of illicit origins, combined with the inability of the owner to prove the contrary, was found to suffice for the purposes of the proportionality test under Article 1 of Protocol No. 1."[98]

b) In the same decision, the Court deduced a similar result from Art. 6 § 1ECHR (right to a fair trial for civil rights):

"Be that as it may, the Court reiterates its well-established case-law to the effect that proceedings for confiscation such as the civil proceedings *in rem* in the present case, which do not stem from a criminal conviction or sentencing proceedings and thus do not qualify as a penalty but rather represent a measure of control of the use of property within the meaning of Article 1 of Protocol N. 1, cannot amount to "the determination of a criminal charge" within the meaning of Article 6 § 1 of the Convention and should be examined under the "civil" head of that provision."[99]

And continued:

"As to the applicants' argument that they should not have been made to bear the burden of proving the lawfulness of the origins of their property, the Court reiterates there can be nothing arbitrary, for the purposes of the "civil" limb of Article 6 § 1 of the Convention, in the reversal of the burden of proof onto the respondents in the forfeiture proceedings in rem after the public prosecutor had submitted a substantiated claim."[100]

c) In sum, it can be said that in this decision, the ECtHR has very clearly extended its quite generous jurisprudence with respect to the nexus between a proven crime and its proceeds (developed in − esp. extended− confiscation proceedings):[101] in its new jurisprudence, it has lowered the evidential requirements with regard to the proof of the very existence of a crime. As will be shown below, this is a key element for NCBC.

---

[98] Para. 107.

[99] Para. 121.

[100] Para. 122.

[101] See, for former generous standards in confiscation proceedings e.g. *Grayson & Barnham v. The United Kingdom*, 23 September 2008, para 39–50; *Yakiya Minhas against the United Kingdom*, 10 November 2009, no. 7618/07, The law, B; *Noel Young v. the United Kingdom*, 6 May 2014, no. 38759/12, para 36–40, 44–48. However, see also *Geerings v. The Netherlands*, 1 March 2007, no. 30810/03, para 41, 44–49

B. The Legal System of the EU

The European Union has recognized the Charter of Fundamental Rights of the European Union (Art. 6 § 2 TEU). The standard of protection under the Charter must be interpreted in light of the jurisprudence of the ECtHR in a way that it is at least as high as the standards of the corresponding rights in the ECHR (Art. 52 § 3 1st phrase EUC). The EU also recognizes the rights enumerated in the ECHR as common principles of European Union Law (see. Art. 6 § 3 TEU). The Charter, however, is applicable only when Member States are "implementing Union law." Yet, this requirement has been interpreted quite generously since the *Fransson* and the *Melloni* decisions of the ECJ.[102]

The right to property is protected by Art. 17 EUC in a narrower sense than in Art. 1 of Protocol No. 1 to the ECHR since Art. 17 is limited to "lawfully" acquired possessions. There are no indications, however, that the ECJ and the ECtHR interprete the provision in substantially different ways. The same holds true with respect to the principle of proportionality, which is a general safeguard for all fundamental rights of the charter (Art. 52 § 1 phrase 2). It seems, however, that the ECJ applies this principle in a more cursory way than, for example, the German Federal Constitutional Court does. Yet, there are no decisions that provide an indication of whether the ECJ would judge an asset forfeiture provision in a more generous way (similar to the ECtHR) or in a more strict way (similar to the German Federal Constitutional Court).[103] This uncertainty also exists with respect to the discussed evidentiary requirements, esp. if one considers the differing jurisprudence of the German Federal Constitutional Court, described in the following.

C. National Constitutional Law

On the level of national constitutional law, the situation can be quite different. In Germany, for example, the protection of property by Article 14 of the German Constitution ("Basic Law") is accorded a high value, and the principle of proportionality is handled quite strictly on the basis of a long tradition of constitutional law. There is also detailed jurisprudence that deals specifically with laws on the evidentiary requirements for confiscation.

The German legislature has enacted legislation based on various approaches that could have permitted broad confiscation and removal of property, such as when a perpetrator's income, estate, and previous acts indicated that the unlawfulness of the existing property was so likely that an objective observer would consider any-

---

[102] See *supra Esser*, pp. 101–102
[103] See *supra Esser*, pp. 103–106.

thing else to be inconceivable. However, the Constitutional Court and the Federal Supreme Court have limited or rejected these approaches.

Section 73d of the Criminal Code on "extended confiscation" requires the owner to have committed at least one specific "unlawful act." Only if this act is proven can other assets – assets that were obtained in a supposedly illegal way – be confiscated on a proportional basis. Yet, despite this requirement of a proven "unlawful act", the Federal Supreme Court held that this provision requires the court, after exhausting all available evidence, *"to be convinced* that the assets concerned were obtained illegally" (emphasis added). The Federal *Supreme Court* stated that only on the basis of this limiting interpretation is the provision compatible with the basic rights of the German Constitution, including Art. 14 on the protection of property. The Federal *Constitutional Court* upheld this decision by confirming that *"based on this interpretation"* the provision is in accordance with Art. 14. At the same time, it did not explicitly define an "outer limit" of constitutionality. [104] Nevertheless, there is good reason to assume that a confiscation decision based on the preponderance of evidence would infringe Art. 14 of the German Constitution.

The German Federal Constitutional Court has also developed strict principles for the removal of property in its decision on the so-called confiscatory expropriation penalty (the former *"Vermögensstrafe,"* originally enacted as Section 43a German Criminal Code). This provision allowed the imposition of a monetary sanction on a convicted person based not on the perpetrator's income but on his assets. The Court considered this to be unconstitutional, esp. with respect to the lacking definiteness of the provision.[105]

D. Conclusions

The protection of human rights in Europe is based on a multilevel system of legal regimes consisting of the European Convention on Human Rights of the Council of Europe, the Fundamental Rights of the European Union, and the various national constitutional laws. An NCBC system based on lowered requirements of proof for the nexus between crime and confiscated property would comply with the ECHR and the existing case law of the ECtHR. It would also seem not to contravene the fundamental rights system of the EU, yet there is insufficient case law for a reliable evaluation. However, this kind of NCBC system would contradict the national constitutional law at least in Germany. Thus, a harmonized European solution for NCBC with a "preponderance of evidence" standard could hardly be introduced; instead, the harmonized solution would require much stricter standards of proof.

---

[104] Decision of the Federal Supreme Court 40, 371–374; Decision of the Federal Constitutional Court 110, 1 (23–27).

[105] Federal Constitutional Court 105, 135 (152–172).

V. NCBC at the EU Level

A. Introduction

On 3 April 2014, the EU Directive on the freezing and confiscation of instrumentalities and proceeds of crime in the European Union was enacted. Art. 4 No. 1 of the Directive obliges the Member States to enable confiscation of instrumentalities and proceeds of crime "subject to a final conviction for a criminal offence." Art. 5 of the Directive states that the Member States must adopt the necessary measures to enable extended confiscation of property belonging to a person "convicted of a criminal offence." Thus, Art. 4 No. 1 and Art. 5 address *conviction-based confiscation*.

The relevant provision for our purposes is, however, Art. 4 No. 2, which demands that legislation in Member States afford the option of confiscation in certain cases in which there is no criminal conviction (NCBC). In the following, section B will deal with the legislative history of Art. 4 No. 2 of the Directive, and section C will analyze the content of Art. 4 No. 2. Lastly, section D will provide an analysis of the road ahead at the EU level.

B. Legislative Process

On 12 March 2012, the Commission presented a Proposal for a Directive of the European Parliament and of the Council on the freezing and confiscation of proceeds of crime in the European Union. Art. 5 had the heading "Non-conviction based confiscation" and read as follows:

> "Each Member State shall take the necessary measures to enable it to confiscate proceeds and instrumentalities without a criminal conviction, following proceedings which could, if the suspected or accused person had been able to stand trial, have led to a criminal conviction, where:
>
> (a) the death or permanent illness of the suspected or accused person prevents any further prosecution; or
>
> (b) the illness or flight from prosecution or sentencing of the suspected or accused person prevents effective prosecution within a reasonable time, and poses the serious risk that it could be barred by statutory limitations."

The interpretation of the proposal provision raised several questions and was open to criticism on a number of points.[106] A comparison of this provision with the enacted version in the Directive, Art. 4 No. 2 reveals that some changes were made. Detailed information on the legislative process from the Commission's proposal to the text of the enacted Directive is not accessible. It is obvious, however, that the NCBC provision was a controversial one. The Committee on Civil Liberties, Jus-

---

[106] *Rui*, Non-conviction based confiscation in the European Union, Journal of the Academy of European Law 3/2012, pp. 349–361.

tice and Home Affairs of the European Parliament was of the opinion that the provision proposed by the Commission had to be reinforced and made more efficient so that it would "actually serve the purpose of preventing the use of proceeds of crime for committing further crimes or their reinvestment into licit activities."[107] To this end, several insertions were proposed.[108]

However, these proposals are not part of the enacted NCBC provision of the Directive. An inter-institutional file reveals that, during the legislating process, "a number of informal contacts have taken place between the Council, the European Parliament and the Commission with a view to reaching an agreement on this dossier at first reading, thereby avoiding the need for second reading and conciliation."[109] Another inter-institutional file shows that, in the course of the process, six so-called trilogues were held. Further, "various technical and other informal meetings took place."[110] Thus, the present NCBC provision of the Directive is the result of an intransparent debate that took place over a relatively short period of time and led to a compromise.

C. Content of Art. 4 No. 2 of the Directive

Art. 4 of the Directive of the European Parliament and of the Council on the freezing and confiscation of instrumentalities and proceeds of crime in the European Union[111] has the heading "Confiscation." It reads as follows:

"1. Member States shall take the necessary measures to enable the confiscation, either in whole or in part, of instrumentalities and proceeds or property the value of which corresponds to such instrumentalities or proceeds, subject to a final conviction for a criminal offence, which may also result from proceedings in absentia.

2. Where confiscation on the basis of paragraph 1 is not possible, at least where such impossibility is the result of illness or absconding of the suspected or accused person, Member States shall take the necessary measures to enable the confiscation of instrumentalities and proceeds in cases where criminal proceedings have been initiated regarding a criminal offence which is liable to give rise, directly or indirectly,

---

[107] European Parliament, Committee on Civil Liberties, Justice and Home Affairs: Report on the proposal for a directive of the European Parliament and of the Council on the freezing and confiscation of proceeds of crime in the European Union, Com(2012)0085 – C7-0075/2012 – 2012/0036(COD), 20.5.2013, p. 34.

[108] See *supra Rui*, pp. 6, 8–10; *supra Cassella*, pp. 17, 19, 21–22.

[109] Council of the European Union: Interinstitutional File, 2012/0036 (COD), 6744/14, Brussels, 4 March 2014, p. 1.

[110] Council of the European Union: Interinstitutional File, 2012/0036 (COD), 16861/13, Brussels 28 November 2013, p. 2.

[111] Directive 2014/42/EU of the European Parliament and of the Council of 3 April 2014 on the freezing and confiscation of instrumentalities and proceeds of crime in the European Union, published in the Official Journal of the European Union L 127, Volume 57, 29 April 2014.

to economic benefit, and such proceedings could have led to a criminal conviction if the suspected or accused person had been able to stand trial."

The text of Art. 4 No. 2 of the Directive is quite complex. Thus, careful analysis is required of (1) its substantive requirements for confiscation, (2) its procedural elements for the embedded *in absentia* procedure, (3) its form of decision, and (4) the codification of the proposed measure in the criminal justice system. The separation and analysis of these various elements enables (5) a better understanding of the provision and allows it to be characterized as traditional and conviction-based and, as a result, lagging behind standards that have been adopted by many European and especially common law countries.

1. Substantive requirements for confiscation

a) The substantive requirements of Art. 4 No. 2 of the Directive for confiscation are described by the definition of *"cases where criminal proceedings have been initiated regarding a criminal offence* which is liable to give rise, directly or indirectly, to economic benefit, *and such proceedings could have led to a criminal conviction if the suspected or accused person had been able to stand trial."* The essential hypothetical element of this definition describing the *nexus between a person and a crime* demands a *criminal conviction* of the suspected or accused person, thus requiring full proof of a crime committed by said person. According to the principles discussed above, this proof must be based on the presumption of innocence without any change in the burden of proof. This necessary nexus between an offender and a crime makes it clear that, in substance, Art. 4 No. 2 has nothing to do with a typical NCBC decision.

In addition, the provision is limited to criminal offenses that are "liable to give rise, directly, to economic benefit." Furthermore, these offenses are restricted by Art. 3 to a list of specific serious crimes.

b) Unlike the nexus between the offender and the crime, the *relationship between the crime and the confiscated property* is not described in detail: Art. 4 No. 2 only requires Member States to "take the necessary measures to enable the confiscation of instrumentalities and proceeds."

The text does not become much clearer even if read in combination with Art. 2, which defines *"instrumentalities"* ("any property used or intended to be used, in any manner, wholly or part, to commit a criminal offence or criminal offences," No. 3), *"proceeds"* ("any economic advantage derived directly or indirectly from a criminal offence; it may consist of any form of property and includes any subsequent reinvestment or transformation of direct proceeds and any valuable benefits," No. 1), and "property" ("property of any description, whether corporeal or incorporeal, moveable or immovable, and legal documents or instruments evidencing title or interest in such property," No. 2). The same holds true for Art. 4 No. 1, which defines the object of confiscation as "in whole or in part, of instrumentalities and proceeds of property, the value of which corresponds to such instrumentalities or proceeds".

Thus, No. 2 does not provide any details concerning which proceeds can be confiscated under which conditions. This is especially important with regard to the evidentiary requirements for the relationship between the crime and the confiscated property. It also does not answer the question of whether the national rules should take the form of a re-establishing measure based on a net principle or of a penal measure that adheres to the gross principle. As mentioned above, confiscation according to the latter would be regarded as a "criminal charge" in terms of the ECHR, thus making the guarantees of the Convention Arts. 6, 7 and Protocol 7 Art. 4 applicable. As a result, it is not possible to classify the confiscation proceedings called for in Art. 4 No. 2 either as criminal or as non-criminal in terms of the *Engel* criteria.

2. Procedural requirements for in absentia procedures

Art. 4 No. 2 is further limited to cases "where confiscation on the basis of paragraph 1 is not possible, at least where such impossibility is the result of illness or absconding of the suspected or accused person." These requirements are typical of *in absentia* procedures. At first glance, it appears that No. 2 requires Member States to apply a low threshold for convictions *in absentia* ("illness or absconding of the suspected or accused person"). However, legislation on criminal convictions *in absentia* in Member States must also adhere to the minimum standards of a fair trial in Art. 6 No. 1 ECHR, more precisely the accused's right to be present at the trial. Although not mentioned expressly in Art. 6, the ECtHR has repeatedly held that a person charged with a criminal offense is entitled to take part in the hearing.[112] Furthermore, the Court has stated that "a denial of justice ... undoubtedly occurs when a person convicted *in absentia* is unable subsequently to obtain from a court which has heard him a fresh determination of the merits of the charge, in respect of both law and fact, where it has not been established that he has waived his right to appear and defend himself ... or that he intended to escape trial."[113] The government has to prove that the person is "seeking to evade justice" "of his own free will."[114]

Hence, "illness" of the offender is not per se sufficient to render a judgment *in absentia*. As long as the suspected or accused person has not deliberately injured

---

[112] *Sejdovic v. Italy*, Application no. 56581/00, Grand Chamber Judgment of 1 March 2006 para. 81.

[113] Para. 82.

[114] *Sejdovic v. Italy*, Application no. 56581/00, Grand Chamber Judgment of 1 March 2006 paras. 86–88.

himself or otherwise deliberately made himself too sick to stand trial, he has not of his own free will sought to evade justice. As a consequence, he has the right to a retrial when he has recovered. In practice, it means that the confiscation process must be halted and the proceedings must be "rewound" to the starting point. In other words, if a confiscation process builds on a judgment *in absentia*, and the reason why the accused did not stand trial was illness, the judgment loses its res judicata force when the accused recovers. One can imagine the problems and costs involved for national governments in reversing confiscation proceedings – for example, where property has been confiscated and then resold.

If the suspected or accused person lies about being too sick to stand trial and simulates illness, ECHR Art. 6 No.1 will of course not be an obstacle to rendering a judgment against him *in absentia*. However, the reason for seeking to evade justice is in that case not "illness" but a lie. Thus, the Directive's use of illness as a reason for a judgment *in absentia* is misleading, as it states that, in the case of "illness ... of the suspected or accused person ... Member States shall take the necessary measures to enable the confiscation of instrumentalities and proceeds" through an *in absentia* conviction of the sick person. The Directive cannot on this point be interpreted and implemented into national law according to its wording. As the term "absconding" also covers the situation in which a person simulates illness to avoid criminal proceedings, the term "illness" should have been removed.

As to the absconding criterion in Art. 4 No. 2, the minimum requirements of Art. 6 for conviction *in absentia* have to be met. If a person flees from prosecution of his own free will, seeking to evade justice, the conditions for rendering a judgment *in absentia* according to the ECHR Art. 6 are met. However, the extent to which convictions *in absentia* are possible under national law varies considerably.

3. Form of Decision

The legal consequence described by No. 2 requires Member States to "take the necessary *measures* to enable the *confiscation of instrumentalities and proceeds.*" A decisive difference between this provision and traditional *in absentia* provisions is that, under No. 2, absence of the perpetrator does not lead to a *criminal conviction* of the accused person in which a sentence to a traditional *penalty* is combined with a confiscation, but only to a decision on the *confiscation of property*. For this reason, Art. 4 No. 2 demands less than the traditional *in absentia* procedures and also less than Art. 4 No. 1 of the Directive, which leads to a *conviction-based* confiscation (either in the presence or in the absence of the accused).

This distinction between an *in absentia conviction* decision (No. 1) and an *in absentia confiscation* decision (No. 2) explains the need for the two separate provisions of the Directive: Art. 4 No. 2 simply requires the creation of an absentia procedure that does not lead to a conviction but (only) to a confiscation decision.

This distinction has two consequences: (a) Member States whose legal systems provide for generally applicable *in absentia* procedures (so that the resulting conviction can include confiscation) already fulfill the requirement of No. 2, since their courts can easily render a criminal *conviction* that also contains – in addition to or instead of a criminal penalty –a confiscation decision; (b) in contrast, Member States that do not have and that do not want to create generally applicable absentia procedures that may lead to a conviction are not obliged to introduce such procedures but instead have the option (and the duty) to create "reduced" or "castrated" *in absentia* procedures that can only lead to a confiscation decision. This interpretation is confirmed by para 15 of the preamble to the Directive:

> "Subject to a final conviction of a criminal offense, it should be possible to confiscate instrumentalities and proceeds of crime, or property the value of which corresponds to such instrumentalities or proceeds. Such final conviction can also result from proceedings in absentia. When confiscation on the basis of a final conviction is not possible, it should nevertheless under certain circumstances still be possible to confiscate instrumentalities and proceeds, at least in the cases of illness or absconding of the suspected or accused person. *However, in such cases of illness or absconding, the existence of proceedings in absentia in Member States would be sufficient to comply with this obligation.* When the suspected or accused person has absconded, Member States should take all reasonable steps and may require that the person concerned be summoned to or made aware of the confiscation proceedings" (emphasis added).

A document from the British Parliament, House of Commons, European Scrutiny Committee confirms this interpretation. Firstly, it states that the provision "has been the most contentious Article throughout negotiations." Secondly, it is revealed from the negotiations that

> "(m)ost Member States do not have civil non-conviction based confiscation regimes and do not face the same problem with this Article as we do. In general, Member States have sought to change Art. 5 so that they can comply with it without having to create new non-conviction-based confiscation powers. Negotiations have reshaped the Article so that Member States can implement it by using *in absentia* prosecutions to achieve a conviction."[115]

Thus, Art. 4 No. 2 only requires Member States to have the possibility to confiscate the property of an accused in criminal proceedings *in absentia*, and not more. And if a Member State does not want to enact generally applicable *in absentia* procedures, it is sufficient for it to create a kind of "limited" *in absentia* procedure (allowing only for confiscation but not conviction *in absentia*).

---

[115] European Scrutiny Committee – Sixth Report. Document considered by the Committee on 27 June 2012. No. (33758), 7641/12, Draft Directive of the European Parliament and of the Council on the freezing and confiscation of proceeds of crime in the European Union (http://www.publications.parliament.uk/pa/cm201213/cmselect/cmeuleg/86-vi/86vi 07.htm, last retrieved 01.07.2014), p. 2.

4. Codification in the Criminal Justice system

It is difficult to read No. 2 to mean anything other than a requirement for a procedure placed within the criminal (procedural) law of the Member State, since it demands that "criminal proceedings have been initiated regarding a criminal offence."[116] The preamble to the Directive (para. 16) also supports reading Art. 4 as requiring proceedings within the criminal (procedural) law of the Member State: it specifies that the term "illness" "should be understood to mean the inability of the *suspected or accused person* to attend the *criminal proceedings*, as a result of which proceedings cannot continue under normal conditions" (emphasis added).

5. Character of the required decision

The foregoing discussion shows that, in a formal way, one could indeed say that Art. 4 No. 2 deals with a confiscation decision without a prior conviction decision. However, since the confiscation decision of No 2 requires all elements of a conviction decision to be fulfilled, it has nothing to do with a real common law "non-conviction-based confiscation," which does not require a culpable perpetrator. Instead and in substance, No. 2 deals only with a confiscation without an *express* conviction. Furthermore, this kind of a formal or pseudo "non-conviction based confiscation" is – strictly speaking – not even demanded by Art. 4, as the requirement of this provision can be satisfied by an *in absentia* procedure for conviction decisions.

Thus, the Directive deprives NCBC of its main added value of enabling confiscation, namely in cases in which the evidence suffices to assume the illicit origin of the goods in question without proving the guilt of the accused. Additional support for the claim that Art. 4 does not deal with or require a true NCBC can be drawn from the fact that it calls for proceedings directed at a person and not against property. For this reason, it would be substantively wrong to consider Art. 4 No. 2 a demand for a common law approach to NCBC. That might also be the reason why the heading of the provision was changed from the Directive proposal Art. 5 ("Non-conviction-based confiscation") to the current heading of Art. 4 ("Confiscation").

Art. 4 No. 2 also has nothing to do with the Italian model for preventive confiscation. Instead, it deals with a type of a retrospective measure similar to the German-Scandinavian approach, which can be applied when a suspected or accused person has absconded. However, there are major differences between the EU approach and the German-Scandinavian concept: while the German-Scandinavian

---

[116] The wording of the provision does not absolutely exclude civil or administrative proceedings following unsuccessful criminal proceedings. However, it gives a strong indication that the legislature foresees a confiscation decision within the criminal justice decision.

approach allows for confiscation even if there is no known suspect or accused, Art. 4 prescribes confiscation only for the circumstance that the person is ill or has absconded. In addition, Art. 4 does not even contain any requirements concerning the calculation of the confiscation.

As a consequence, Art. 4 No. 2 is not a step towards a more efficient confiscation approach. In addition: According to the preamble para. 5, the purpose of the provision is to "approximate the Member States' confiscation regimes, thus facilitating mutual trust and effective cross-border cooperation." Yet, with all due respect, Art. 4 No. 2 is quite far from fulfilling this purpose.

D. The Road Ahead

1. Current Position at the EU Level

In conjunction with a provisional agreement between the Council and the Parliament of 28 November 2013 on the text of the Directive on the freezing and confiscation of instrumentalities and proceeds of crime in the European Union,[117] two declarations were agreed upon. With respect to the introduction of *common rules* on the confiscation of property, the first states:

"The European Parliament and the Council *call on* the Commission to analyze, at the *earliest possible opportunity* and taking into account the differences between the legal traditions and the systems of the Member States, the feasibility and possible benefits of introducing further *common rules* on the confiscation of property deriving from activities of a criminal nature, *also in the absence of a conviction of a specific person or persons for these activities* (emphasis added)."[118]

The second addresses *mutual recognition* and reads as follows:

"An effective system of freezing and confiscation in the EU is inherently linked to well functioning mutual recognition of freezing and confiscation orders. Considering the need of putting in place a comprehensive system for freezing and confiscation of proceeds and instrumentalities of crime in the EU, the European Parliament and the Council call on the Commission to present *a legislative proposal on mutual recognition of freezing and confiscation orders* at the earliest possible opportunity, in relation to which the concept of freezing should be further examined (emphasis added)."[119]

The first declaration is a clear message to the Commission to analyze the possibility of EU legislation giving the opportunity to confiscate property deriving from activities of a criminal nature "also in the absence of a conviction of a specific person or persons for these activities." It points towards a desire for more far-reaching confiscation including NCBC legislation at the EU level. In this connection, the

---

[117] Council of the European Commission: Interinstitutional File, 2012/0036 (COD), 16861/13, ADD 1, Brussels 28 November 2013.

[118] See *supra Rui*, p. 1.

[119] See *supra Rui*, p. 2.

Special Committee on Organized Crime, Corruption and Money Laundering of the European Parliament notes in its comprehensive Report of 10 June 2013 that it:[120]

> "Calls on the Member States, on the basis of the *most advanced national legislations*, to *introduce models of civil law asset forfeiture*, in those cases where, *on the balance of probabilities* and subject to the permission of a court, it can be established that the assets in question result from criminal activities or are used to carry out criminal activities" (emphasis added).[121]

Furthermore, the Committee:

> "Considers that, in compliance with constitutional national guarantees and without prejudice of the right of property and the right of defense, provision could be made for *preventive models* of confiscation, which should be applicable only following a court decision" (emphasis added).[122]

The former citation seems to refer to the common law approach to NCBC, while the latter refers to the Italian preventive approach. As described above, the two approaches differ substantially from one another and both are more far-reaching than Directive Art. 4.

The current position at the EU level appears to be that the Parliament advocates the extended use of NCBC in the Member States. In order to achieve this goal, three approaches can be identified: harmonization of common substantive rules for NCBC (*infra* 2), procedural legislation for mutual recognition of freezing and confiscation orders (*infra* 3), and encouragement and recommendations for Member States to establish comprehensive legislation ("models") for NCBC (*infra* 4). These approaches will be further explored below.

2. Harmonization of Common Substantive Rules for NCBC (Art. 83 TFEU)

a) The EU is built on the principle of conferred powers. The question of whether and to what extent it has competence to harmonize substantive rules on NCBC through a directive depends on the existence of a specific basis in the Treaty of the European Union (TEU) or in the Treaty of the Functioning of the European Union (TFEU).[123] The provisions on confiscation fall within the ambit of Art. 3 No. 2 TEU, according to which the Union should "offer its citizens an area of freedom, security and justice without internal frontiers." Within this realm, legislative competence is shared between the Member States and the EU, the latter having subsidiary competence (Art. 4 No. 1 and 2 TFEU). The legislating powers of the Union

---

[120] European Parliament, Special Committee on Organised Crime, Corruption and Money Laundering: Draft report on organized crime, corruption and money laundering: recommendations on action initiatives to be taken 2009–2014, 2013/2107 (INI), 10 June 2013.

[121] Para. 12.

[122] Para. 13.

[123] *Klip*, European Criminal Law, p. 35.

can therefore be exercised only according to a specific legal competence as well as the principles of subsidiarity and proportionality.[124]

The legal basis for a possible competence of the EU to create substantive rules on NCBC could be found in Art. 83 Sec. 1 TFEU. It deals with the harmonization of substantive criminal law and confers power on the Union to "establish minimum rules concerning the definition of criminal offenses *and sanctions* in the areas of particularly serious crime with a cross-border dimension resulting from the nature or impact of such offenses or from a special need to combat them on a common basis" (emphasis added). However, it is not clear what constitutes a "sanction" in the sense of this provision.

One approach to finding a definition of the term "sanction" would be to apply the above described *Engel* criteria. On this basis, the Legal Service of the Council of the European Union has expressed the following view on the possibility of legislating NCBC in the current directive on confiscation: "Notwithstanding its denomination in national law as civil confiscation, Article 83 (1) TFEU does not exclude this type of confiscation, as long as it can be qualified as 'criminal sanction' according to the criteria developed in the *Engel* judgement (sic) of the ECTHR (be of a criminal nature, the severity of penalty). The 'criminal nature' of such a confiscation is a condition for any harmonization under Article 83 (1) TFEU…"[125]

According to these criteria, legislation on confiscation that follows the (preventive) Italian and the (enrichment-based) common law approach could not be considered criminal measures. Similarly, the German-Scandinavian approach could not generally be seen as criminal if the amount of confiscation is stipulated on a net principle with the goal of re-establishing the situation before the unlawful act occurred. Thus, based on the *Engel* criteria, these "non criminal" confiscation models could not simply be harmonized with reference to Art. 83 (1) TFEU. To bring these types of legislation into the criminal sphere and to make them comply with the *Engel* criteria, especially with respect to the "nature of the offense" (second *Engel* criterion), the legislation would have to imply something more than re-establishment of the situation prior to an unlawful act. With respect to the German-Scandinavian approach based on the net principle, this "something more" could be justified by the above-mentioned ethical blame that is connected with a confiscation by means of an – express or embedded – conviction for a punishable criminal act. In this case, the sanction would not only consist of the duty to restore gains but also of the ethical blame connected with the respective decision of conviction. Another argument in favor of classification as a conviction-based "sanction" in these

---

[124] *Op. cit.* pp. 164–165; *Hecker*, Europäisches Strafrecht, pp. 280–283.

[125] European Parliament, Committee on Civil Liberties, Justice and Home Affairs: Report on the proposal for a directive of the European Parliament and of the Council on the freezing and confiscation of proceeds of crime in the European Union, Com(2012)0085 – C7-0075/2012 – 2012/0036(COD), 20.5.2013, p. 22. See also p. 19.

cases can be found in the first *Engel* criteria, according to which a measure is regarded as criminal if it is classified as such by the national legislation.

There is also another approach that would also support such a broad concept of "sanctions": One could argue that the interpretation of the term "sanction" in a competence norm (Art. 83) need not necessarily be identical with the interpretation of the same term in a norm guaranteeing human rights: established rules of legal methodology permit the interpretation of one and the same term differently, depending on the context.[126] Based on this approach, one could consider interpreting the competence norm of Art. 83 on "minimum rules concerning the definition of criminal offences and *sanctions*," not in the sense of the *Engel* criteria but in the sense of "minimum rules concerning the definition of criminal offences and their negative *legal consequences.*" This would also be supported by an *argumentum a maiore ad minus*: if the EU has the competence to harmonize serious sanctions (e.g., confiscation according to the gross principle), it should – especially with respect to the principle of proportionality – also have the competence to demand similar but less strict consequences for crimes (e.g., confiscation according to the net principle). In addition, there is the practical argument that the harmonization and mutual recognition of confiscation measures should not differentiate too much between various types of confiscation for practical reasons.

Thus, there are good reasons to justify a general competence of the EU for the above-mentioned Directive on the freezing and confiscation of instrumentalities and proceeds of crime in the European Union without differentiating and speculating too much about the legal character of the respective confiscation measures. General commentaries on Art. 83 TFEU, which state without further differentiation that forfeiture and confiscation are criminal sanctions in the sense of this provision, seem to follow this line of thinking.[127]

It is, however, an open question whether this also applies to a real (i.e., common-law-based) NCBC. The essential difference between a common law-based NCBC and traditional confiscation measures is that NCBC is not designed as an individual measure that targets a (criminal) person but rather as a measure that targets property. In addition, a goal of the common law-based NCBC model is to avoid any ethical blame so as to avoid triggering the application of guarantees for penal sanctions. It could be considered to be equally distant from a criminal confiscation regime as a system for taxing illegal gains. For these reasons, the distance between the common-law-based NCBC model and a criminal sanction is much greater than the distance between the German-Scandinavian confiscation model and a criminal

---

[126] This is based on the fact that the interpretation of a term in a certain provision must consider not only its wording but also the aim and the context of the provision, which may be different in the context of defining competences and of defining legal safeguards.

[127] See *Böse*, in: *Böse* (ed.), Europäisches Strafrecht, p. 158 f.; *Velev*, Modelle der Vermögensabschöpfung, p. 297; *Vogel*, in: *Grabitz/Hilf/Nettessheim*, Art. 82 AEUV No. 37.

sanction, even if the confiscation model is based on the net principle. Confiscation in accordance with the NCBC model is so different from an individual personal "sanction" in the sense of Art. 83 that one cannot assume that it was the will of its creators to include it within the provision on Art. 83 dealing with sanctions. Thus, Art. 83 must be limited to traditional sanctions (such as imprisonment or fine) and the traditional system of alternative personal measures (such as forfeiture or confiscation *in personam*) and should exclude new legal measures that are not based on individual responsibility. As a result, common law-based NCBC models can hardly be considered to be minimum rules for "sanctions" against persons according to Art. 83.[128]

Leaving the criminal sanction requirement aside, an NCBC policy based on Art. 83 (1) TFEU could create additional difficulties. Firstly, NCBC legislation made in accordance with Art. 83 (1) TFEU must be limited to specific crimes, namely "terrorism, trafficking in human beings and sexual exploitation of women and children, illicit drug trafficking, illicit arms trafficking, money laundering, corruption, counterfeiting of means of payment, computer crime and organised crime." The Commission was aware of this limitation, as it stated:

> "As the main legal basis for this proposal is Article 83(1) TFEU, its scope is limited to the offences in the areas listed in that Article, namely terrorism, trafficking in human beings and sexual exploitation of women and children, illicit drug trafficking, money laundering, corruption, counterfeiting of means of payment, computer crime and organised crime. Illicit arms trafficking is covered where that crime is committed in the context of organised crime.
>
> One of the listed areas of crime is "organised crime". The proposal will therefore cover other criminal activities not specifically listed in Article 83(1) where those activities are committed by participating in a criminal organisation as defined in Framework Decision 2008/841/JHA on the fight against organised crime."[129]

Therefore, as Art. 83 (1) TFEU limits the legislative competence of the EU to specific types of crime, it could not serve as a basis for harmonizing a typical common law model of NCBC legislation that does not link confiscation to certain crimes or types of crime. None of the NCBC models explored in this book has a limitation that could render NCBC confiscation legislation ineffective, as a link between specified crimes or crime types and the property confiscated would have to be proved. As *Asp* correctly points out, since rules on confiscation are often applied horizontally in relation to many types of crime, they do not fit very well into the framework of Art. 83 TFEU.[130] However, one might overcome these arguments

---

[128] See also *Simonato*, New Journal of European Criminal Law 2015, 221.

[129] Proposal for a Directive of the European Parliament and of the Council on the freezing and confiscation of proceeds of crime in the European Union, COM(2012) 85 final, 2012/0036 (COD), Brussels 12.3.2012 p. 8.

[130] *Asp*, The Substantive Criminal Law Competence, p. 100. Another obstacle to Art. 83 (1) TFEU giving effective legislative competence as regards NCBC is that only "minimum rules" could be established. Thus, it is doubtful whether the Article could serve as a legal

for limiting NCBC by seeing the resulting limitations as a welcome consequence of the principle of proportionality.

b) To sum up, Art. 83 (1) TFEU cannot serve as a basis for the EU to enact a common law model of NCBC legislation. The same must be said about Art. 83 (2) TFEU, which contains the same requirements as No. 1 on "criminal … sanctions." In addition, confiscation rules under Art. 83 (2) TFEU can only be adopted once an EU policy has first been harmonized.[131] As yet, however, no such policy can be identified in the context of confiscation.

3. Procedural Legislation on Mutual Recognition of Freezing and Confiscation Orders (Art. 82 TFEU)

a) Mutual recognition can also be supported without or with little harmonization of substantive law. As a result, the question arises as to whether the Union has at least the competence to enact procedural legislation that requires mutual recognition of non-conviction-based freezing and confiscation orders. This might be justified by the fact that non-conviction-based freezing and confiscation orders cause difficulties when it comes to their enforcement in countries that do not have operative NCBC legislation.[132] Thus, legislation providing for mutual recognition of NCBC orders would then represent significant progress, even in the absence of harmonization of substantive law.

The question of a possible competence of the EU for mutual recognition is regulated in Art. 82. Whereas Art. 83 covers substantive criminal law, Art. 82 deals with procedural law, especially judicial cooperation in criminal matters: Art. 82 sec. 1 lays down and provides for the principle of "mutual recognition of judgments and judicial decisions;" in addition, sec. 2 permits to a limited degree the adoption of procedural minimum rules to "facilitate mutual recognition of judgments and judicial decisions and police and judicial cooperation *in criminal matters* having a cross-border dimension."

b) The scope of this procedural concept in Art. 82 for *mutual recognition* of "judgments and judicial *decisions*" in *criminal matters* is different from and broader than the substantive concept of "(criminal) *sanctions*" in Art. 83 (discussed above). This is due, firstly, to the fact that "judgments and decisions" according to Art. 82 are not limited to "judgments and decisions *on sanctions.*" Secondly, it is

---

basis for the EU to make detailed and comprehensive NCBC legislation (NCBC model) through a directive.

[131] *Vogel*, Die Strafgesetzgebungskompetenzen, p. 46; *Forsaith et al.*, Study for an impact assessment, p. 190.

[132] *Hofmeyr*, Navigating, pp. 141, 142; *Greenberg et al.*, Stolen Asset Recovery. pp. 95, 96; Eurojust: Annual Report 2011 p. 28.

based on the fact that, in addition, the concept of "criminal matters" is understood in a broader sense as "criminal sanctions."

Literature defines criminal matters as procedures for investigating, prosecuting, or adjudicating crimes. It expressly includes procedures for forfeiture and confiscation as well as criminal proceedings in which civil restitution claims (such as the German *Adhäsionsverfahren*) are addressed.[133] This broad interpretation of the concept of *"criminal matters"* is justified by the fact that a decisive difference between civil matters, on the one hand, and public (including criminal) matters, on the other, is that the former deal with the relationship between citizens while the latter deal with the relationship between citizens and the state. The coercive power of the state when it confiscates property for itself (and uses the confiscated property for public interest or social purposes according to Art. 10 Sec. 3 of the Directive) cannot be considered a civil measure solely because the respective impoverishment of the citizen is limited to the amount of his unjust enrichment. In other words: Whereas the question of whether a norm represents a sanction or the deprivation of an unjust enrichment depends on the value of the confiscated property, the classification of a norm to public law (including criminal law) or to civil law depends primarily on the status of the respective (state or private) actors involved. For this reason, it is not relevant for the term "criminal matters" whether the substance of a confiscation order of the state (especially if codified within the criminal justice system) is based on the civil concept of unjust enrichment or on the concept of a sanction.

c) Due to this classification, European cooperation and mutual recognition with respect to conviction- and non-conviction-based confiscation can indeed be based on Art. 82 (judicial cooperation in criminal matters) and not on Art. 81 (dealing with cooperation in civil matters). Thus, according to Art. 82 (2), the European Parliament and the Council can "(a) lay down rules and procedures for ensuring recognition throughout the Union of all forms of judgments and judicial decisions; (b) prevent and settle conflicts of jurisdiction between Member States; (c) support the training of the judiciary and judicial staff; (d) facilitate cooperation between judicial or equivalent authorities of the Member States in relation to proceedings in criminal matters and the enforcement of decisions."

d) In addition, with respect to harmonization, Art. 82 (2) states that "To the extent necessary to facilitate mutual recognition of judgments and judicial decisions and police and judicial cooperation in criminal matters having a cross-border dimension, the European Parliament and the Council may... *establish minimum rules*" (emphasis added). However, these (procedural) minimum rules may only concern "(a) mutual admissibility of evidence between Member States; (b) the rights of individuals in criminal procedure; (c) the rights of victims of crime." Also,

---

[133] See *Vogel*, in: *Grabitz/Hilf/Nettessheim*, Art. 82 AEUV No. 12 and 13. See also *Hess*, in: *Grabitz/Hilf/Nettessheim*, Art. 81 AEUV No. 16.

"(d) any other specific aspects of criminal procedure which the Council has identified in advance by a decision can only be adopted by a unanimous decision of the Council and the consent of the European Parliament." Furthermore, Art. 82 (2) is not an end in itself but provides only a limited supportive function for better mutual recognition. In addition, it is limited by the requirement of "minimum rules" and the principles of subsidiarity and proportionality. As a result, Art. 82 does not provide broad powers for harmonizing procedural rules for conviction- or non-conviction-based confiscation decisions.

e) As a consequence, Art. 82 enables the development of rules on mutual recognition of confiscation decisions (including NCBC decisions). For this purpose, it contains a very limited competence for the harmonization of confiscation rules, e.g., for minimum rules on the above-mentioned issues, especially the harmonization of the rights of the individuals or victims of crime concerned. Thus, there is indeed some room for furthergoing obligations on the part of the EU.

f) Due to the various standards of proof analyzed above, it would be difficult for the EU Member States to agree upon a mutual recognition system for confiscation proceedings. For example, an English confiscation order based on a "preponderance of evidence" would probably contradict German constitutional requirements and even raise problems of *"ordre public."* The problem could be solved by demanding minimum rules with high standards of evidence for all countries. This solution, however, might not be compatible with the English position upholding its preponderance of evidence concept. For this reason, a second solution is: the rules on mutual recognition could limit recognition of confiscation decisions to cases in which confiscation would also be possible under the law of the requested state. However, this would not be efficient. Thus, the third and best option is to make obligatory mutual recognition conditional on the fulfillment of certain minimum requirements defined in the respective directive (including minimum rules of evidence). This would not preclude more extensive, purely national solutions.[134]

4. Establishment of NCBC Legislation
at National Levels

As outlined above, the Special Committee on Organised Crime, Corruption and Money Laundering of the European Parliament has called on Member States to introduce substantive legislation on NCBC models, i.e., legislation along the lines of the common law model and the Italian preventive model. Resorting to encouragement and recommendations is perhaps somewhat surprising in the *post*-Lisbon era, in which the EU has reformed both its legislative competence and the use of this competence. As the Union lacks the competence to legislate NCBC broadly, however, this is the only viable option.

---

[134] For this legal technique see *Sieber*, ZStW 2009, pp. 35–39.

At first glance, harmonizing by encouragement and recommendations could be deemed an ineffective and old-fashioned approach at the EU level. However, taking into account the very different NCBC approaches in Europe, enacting legislation – if it had been possible within the competences of the Union – would also have been a difficult task and one with an uncertain outcome. The drafting history of Art. 4 No. 2 reveals how controversial and difficult it is to legislate NCBC at the EU level.

An additional argument against further legislating action for NCBC at the Union level is that such legislation might have a negative effect on legal systems that already have NCBC legislation in place. The United Kingdom eventually decided not to take part in the adoption of the Directive (preamble para. 43). An important reason for this decision was highlighted by the UK Parliament's European Scrutiny Committee:

> "Were the UK to opt in to the Directive and implement Article 5 using our civil recovery regime there is a real risk that, in a future challenge, the fact that we would be relying on civil measures to implement a criminal law instrument could be relied on to assert that civil recovery powers are in fact criminal in nature and so criminal procedural protections should apply. This would risk greatly weakening our civil recovery powers and hinder our attempts to tackle organized crime."[135]

Taking these aspects into consideration, a recommendation and guideline approach is clearly an alternative option for the Union to contribute to the enactment and approximation of NCBC legislation in Europe. There are no obstacles for the Union to resort to such "soft law" guidelines in the case of NCBC. Even though soft law is not used frequently in the field of criminal policy, there are some examples.[136] Thus, some general guidelines for drafting NCBC legislation at national levels in Europe should be of value, irrespective of whether the Union decides to issue such guidelines. In the following section, some general recommendations are proposed that could prove relevant when legislating NCBC at the national level.

VI. Recommendations for the National Level

The starting point for any reform on confiscation law must be the decision as to which type of confiscation regime should be developed for which purpose (*infra* A). Based on this decision, the main elements of the envisaged confiscation system can be determined, e.g., whether it should amend or replace the existing confiscation rules, be based on a conviction or a non-criminal decision, be built as an *in*

---

[135] European Scrutiny Committee – Twenty-Second Report. 9 Freezing and confiscation of proceeds of crime, 13 December 2012. No. (33758), 7641/12, Draft Directive of the European Parliament and of the Council on the freezing and confiscation of proceeds of crime in the European Union (http://www.publications.parliament.uk/pa/cm201213/cmselect/cmeuleg/86-xxii/86xxii13.htm, last retrieved 01.07.2014) p. 2.

[136] *Klip*, European Criminal Law, pp. 30, 31.

personam or an *in rem* procedure, and whether it should be codified within the criminal, civil, or public justice system (*infra* B). Last but not least, the question of whether and to what degree the achieved aims can be reached under the applicable human rights law must be analyzed (*infra* C). The following text will analyze these aspects with respect to the main question of this book, namely whether European continental law countries should adopt the common law-based NCBC approach towards creating a re-establishing confiscation procedure.

A. The Starting Point for Criminal Policy: Classification of NCBC as Civil, Preventive, or Criminal?

1. The Need for Classification

The first and most important issue when drafting confiscation legislation is to thoroughly consider what type of measure is needed for which purpose, i.e., the classification of the measure. The answer to this question should be based on the policy approach developed above. Is the legislation required because of a need to punish offenders of criminal acts? Or should the legislation re-establish the status before an unlawful act was committed? Or is legislation required because there is a need to prevent criminal offenses in the future? If these distinctions are not taken as a point of departure, negative effects will follow. One such effect is a lack of clarity as to whether and to what extent the legislation is in compliance with human rights requirements. Another is a lack of foreseeability. A third is inefficient legislation: a lack of clarity with respect to the aim and the classification of the legislation could lead to confiscation being regarded as a penalty. That is of course not a problem if punishment is the purpose. But if the purpose is re-establishment of the *status quo ante* or future prevention, these purposes might not be fulfilled to a maximum extent because of the limitations that follow when a measure is regarded as a penalty. Thus, the policy-oriented approach should be the point of departure for considerations of NCBC legislation.

2. The Criminal Law Model

When the classification of NCBC legislation is settled, another important point it is to draft the legislation strictly in accordance with the approach chosen. If the goal of the NCBC legislation is to punish a person for having committed criminal offenses, the Convention guarantees of the ECHR in cases concerning a "criminal charge" apply. As shown, none of the NCBC models in Europe are considered penal measures.

Apart from *in absentia* procedures, it is difficult to imagine a *criminal* confiscation measure in the absence of the criminal conviction of an offender. In other words, apart from *in absentia* procedures, it would be somewhat of a contradiction in terms to talk about non-conviction-based confiscation and at the same time to accept that the confiscation measure is a penal measure. As pointed out above, Art. 4 No. 2 of the Directive requires that confiscation proceedings be an option even when the offender is not present during the criminal proceedings. However, as illustrated above, confiscation following a conviction *in absentia* cannot be regarded as a true non-conviction-based confiscation (especially under a regime that requires a hypothetical conviction if the accused could have stood trial). Thus, the NCBC approach to confiscation is not recommended if the legislation is needed to punish an offender for crimes he has committed.

3. The Preventive Model

The other two options are either to classify the NCBC legislation as a measure that re-establishes the *status quo ante* or as a preventive measure that aims at preventing criminal acts in the future. The latter approach has been chosen in Italian legislation: the entire NCBC system rests upon its classification as preventive. In the UK, the cash forfeiture procedure provides for both, a preventive option and a civil option. Choosing to classify NCBC legislation as preventive, i.e., as a security measure to prevent future crime, has the advantage of being potentially very effective. As shown above, the ECtHR has afforded Member States of the Council of Europe a generous margin of discretion in drawing the line between punitive and preventive measures. However, the lack of such a boundary in positive law combined with the inherently vague and unclear distinction between punitive and preventive measures calls for some restraint.

Confiscating with the purpose of preventing future crime from taking place has to be kept within certain limits in a state that adheres to the rule of law *(Rechtsstaat)*. It is commonly agreed that deprivation of liberty of persons based on prevention (i.e., preventing them from committing crimes in the future) must be subject to strict limits. Even though confiscation is a far smaller intrusion on a person's integrity, the same principle applies. *Mill's* warning that the preventive function of government is liable to abuse, remains.[137] It is also worthwhile to recall that the Italian experience shows how difficult it is to extinguish entirely the link between a person and criminality when the preventive approach to NCBC is chosen. Thus, when adhering to the preventive approach, NCBC legislation should entail some limitations.

The cash forfeiture procedure in UK law, which was tested by Strasbourg in the *Butler* and *Webb* cases, serves as a good example of the use of limitations within the framework of a preventive approach to NCBC: if only cash is subject to forfeiture, it additionally has to be proven that the cash represents a person's proceeds

---

[137] See *supra Vogel*, pp. 230–231.

from drug trafficking or that it is intended to be used in drug trafficking. A *carte blanche* provision allowing the forfeiture of any property found by the authorities to represent a danger of being used to commit crime in the future is something completely different. In addition, in a preventive model, the principle of proportionality should determine whether the confiscation should be permanent or only temporary, i.e., whether it would have to be lifted as soon as the risk is over (e.g., death of the owner and inheritance by his children).

Thus, the main field of application for the preventive confiscation model could be the confiscation of instruments used and specifically tailored for crime. With respect to money, the preventive model should be used only if there are clear and concrete indications that it will be used to commit a crime, e.g., for a perpetrator who was convicted of terrorist financing and who has not changed his mind since the conviction.

4. The Model of Re-establishment

The third possibility is to classify NCBC as a measure that re-establishes the status before an unlawful act was committed. In other words, the state has to ensure that the perpetrator does not profit from crime ("crime should not pay"). Such a re-establishment regime is legitimate based on natural justice.[138] However, there are also several pragmatic policy considerations that support this approach. One is that property that is or represents proceeds of crime has to be taken out of circulation in the economy because it gives an unfair competitive advantage to those with access to it. The tainted proceeds have a negative impact on the market. If substantial amounts of proceeds of crime come into circulation, they have the potential to destabilize the legal economy. At its most extreme, tainted property circulating in the legal economy gives the persons having control over it the power to influence politics and government institutions. Another consideration is that confiscation measures that re-establish the *status quo ante* compensate for what civil law is not able to accomplish, as civil law can at most deny the validity of an illegal transaction. In addition, in cases in which there are no persons affected by a crime who can take legal steps to restore the *status quo ante*, the state must become involved.

An advantage of the re-establishment approach over the preventive approach is that it does not have the same potential to be pushed too far or even abused. As seen above, a condition for a re-establishing confiscation measure is the limitation of the amount confiscated to the exact proceeds of crime. If the amount exceeds the proceeds of crime, i.e., if untainted property is confiscated as well, confiscation of the surplus cannot be regarded as anything other than as punishment, leading to the measure being classified as penal.

---

[138] *Paulet v. the United Kingdom*, application no. 6219/08, Judgment of 13 May 2014, Dissenting Opinion of Judge *Wojtyczek* para. 5.

Another advantage is that the property confiscated under a re-establishing regime must have a relatively close connection to crime. Issues in relation to proportionality (Art. 1 of Protocol No. 1 ECHR) and problems with the concept of restitution arise if the legislation allows for confiscation of proceeds that have only a remote link to the unlawful act that has triggered confiscation proceedings. The proportionality limitation applies, in principle, to preventive confiscation as well. However, as the dangerousness of the property is what must be proven in preventive confiscation proceedings, the proportionality test is less suitable for limiting the amount that can be confiscated. In addition, the requirement of enrichment from criminal sources provides an additional limitation on the confiscation of property that does not originate from crime but rather from other activities and that is only incidentally related to criminal conduct.

A third advantage of the re-establishment approach is that the link to a specific person's criminal conduct is far less problematic than in preventive confiscation proceedings. In the latter, the dangerousness of the person must be proven in the proceedings: most property is not dangerous in and of itself (e.g., money, immovable/movable property); rather, it is "dangerous" due to the fact that it is owned or under the control of a person who is capable of using it in a manner dangerous to society. In contrast, the fact that must be proven in re-establishment confiscation proceedings is far more objective, namely, whether the property (on the balance of probabilities, preponderance of evidence) can be linked to crime.

Despite all these points, for the introduction of a re-establishment approach, however, it is essential to precisely develop its safeguards. This is not only true for the aforementioned gains from formal infractions and for cases with an indirect link between the crime and the gain. It also applies to the probability that confiscated property originates from illegal activities. Furthermore, the procedural question arises as to whether testimony in civil NCBC can be used in subsequent criminal proceedings. A possible solution to this problem is not to allow the subsequent use of testimony given by a person who is later charged in criminal proceedings in order to avoid an infringement of the principle "nemo tenetur se ipsum accusare."[139]

Thus, the respective safeguards must be carefully developed under the human rights regimes described above, including the national constitutions. In addition, at the level of practical implementation, care must be taken to prevent authorities responsible for confiscation from financially profiting from the confiscated goods, as this is the cause of abuse of confiscation in some countries.

The conclusion is that the re-establishment approach is the better one when legislating NCBC. The preventive approach is also acceptable, provided that it is kept

---

[139] See, e.g., ECtHR *Saunders v. the United Kingdom*, no. 19187/91, 17 October 1996, para. 67 et seq.; ECtHR *I.J.L. and others v. the United Kingdom*, no. 29522/95; 30056/96, 30574/96, 19 September 2000, para. 79 et seq. However, further going, ECtHR *Shannon v. the United Kingdom*, no 6563/03, 4 October 2005.

within reasonable limits. Thus, the following remarks will focus on the re-establishment approach.

B. The Main Elements for the Re-establishment Model: Identifying and Evaluating the Constructive Differences of Common Law and Continental Law Models

Evaluation of the various models for confiscation is difficult not only because of the differences among the various elements of these models; it is also difficult because it is unclear which elements are essential and formative, which characteristics derive from these key elements, and which elements are merely incidental. The following discussion of these elements is based on the policy-oriented approach developed above: it focuses on the creation of an independent, non-criminal confiscation regime for re-establishing the financial status before the crime.

1. Creation of an Independent, Non-Criminal Confiscation Track for Re-establishment

The policy-oriented approach developed above illustrates the main difference between the common law and the continental law confiscation models: from the perspective of an international meta-structure, the *common law* provides an independent confiscation model that is not sanction-based but rather is based on the principles of unjust enrichment and re-establishing the situation before the commission of a crime.[140] The decisive argument in these countries for this construction is simple: due to the assumed non-punitive character of this confiscation measure and its proximity to civil restitution measures, the strict guarantees of criminal law (especially the principle of innocence) do not apply; instead, the nexus between crime and confiscated property may be proven on the basis of the more lenient evidence standards of "civil" law (such as the preponderance of evidence). An additional causal link between a criminally responsible *person* and the crime or the property is not necessary.

Continental law countries also make a distinction between criminal sanctions (with special guarantees) and non-criminal (restitutive or preventive) measures. When dealing with constitutional and criminal law, lawyers and courts in continental law countries analyze the differences between these two types of confiscation measures in even more detail than do their common law colleagues. In an approach methodologically similar to that of the common law, for example, Georgian law in 2004 created two separate procedures for the forfeiture of property: one on "criminal confiscation" (following a final criminal conviction establishing the accused's

---

[140] See supra pp, 250–251; 258–261; see *supra Vogel*, p. 232.

guilt), and the other on "administrative confiscation" (aimed at recovering wrong-fully acquires property and unexplained wealth from a public official).[141] Italy has also developed a separate track for confiscation; confiscation in Italy is not, how-ever, designed as re-establishment but rather for preventive purposes. Yet, many continental law countries have not developed in a consequent way the distinction between punitive and restitutive confiscation into a second mode of confiscation that is more efficient, thanks to less arduous guarantees.

This lack of a second confiscation track for re-establishing the gains of crime can – at least at a first glance – be regarded as a disadvantage. This is especially the case since, in today's risk society, criminal law is being increasingly amended and enhanced by non-criminal measures, such as preventive police laws, intelligence-led investigations, measures of international humanitarian law, and self-regulatory systems. As long as these alternative measures are in fact substantively non-criminal (and not merely labeled as such) and respect their own human rights sys-tem, they can be valuable amendments to criminal law.[142] This means that – at least from the starting point of the "second track approach" – the common law model could be a valuable contribution to a more effective confiscation policy.

However, before a final evaluation of this new approach can be undertaken, its consistence with the human rights guarantees of criminal *and* non-criminal law must be considered. This aspect will be addressed in more detail following the analysis of the various elements of the NCBC system.

2. Creation of "Non-Conviction-Based" Confiscation

The most significant difference between the German-Scandinavian confiscation model and the common law NCBC model is often seen in the fact that the first ap-proach requires a conviction for a criminal offense, whereas the second approach does not go along with a criminal conviction.

However, the EU directive discussed above with its *in absentia* proceedings shows that, in specific cases, there can also be *non*-conviction based decisions that require criminal law standards similar to those that apply to traditional criminal proceedings convictions at which the accused is present. This is based on the fact that the EU deals with a *formally* "non-conviction-based confiscation" for in-absentia confiscations in cases where – *in concreto!* – "such proceedings could have led to a criminal conviction if the suspected or accused person had been able to stand trial." Thus, by judging the EU directive according to its substance as a

---

[141] See ECtHR, *Gogitidze and others v. Georgia*, 12 May 2015, No. 36862/05, pp. 49–54.

[142] See *Sieber*, in: Manacorda/Nieto (eds.), Criminal Law between War and Peace, 2009, pp. 35–69 (66 et seq.).

"conviction-based" model, one could uphold the above differentiation that criminal law-based decisions are conviction-based and re-establishing confiscations are not.

Based on the underlying concept for re-establishment and the *Engel* criteria, this "non-conviction-based" construction of the common law approach is consistent, since the re-establishment model is not based on the conviction of an individual person but only on a causal relationship between crime and property. Since the *Engel* criteria demand that confiscations designed to re-establish the *status quo ante* avoid the blame for a criminal act, they should also avoid criminal convictions against individual perpetrators. Ascertaining the criminal origin of the confiscated property is sufficient for this concept. Thus, non-conviction-based procedures are the logical consequence of these re-establishing confiscation measures.

3. Proceedings Directed Towards a Person or Property

Another significant difference between the German-Scandinavian confiscation model and the common law NCBC model can be identified if German-Scandinavian confiscation is regarded as directed against a *person* and common law NCBC is regarded as directed against *property*. At first glance, this would seem to be a fundamental difference. A second look, however, indicates that the difference may well be merely formal, since it does not seem to matter much whether the confiscation of a bank account is filed, indexed, and executed under the name of its owner or under the number of the bank account. It is clear that an action against an asset can have implications for the human rights of its owner. This puzzlement leads to the question concerning the essential elements behind the labels referring to *in rem* and *in personam* procedures.

These essential differences between *proceedings against a person* and *proceedings in rem* cannot automatically be equated with the different legal guarantees in the criminal confiscation model and the re-establishing confiscation model, which have been identified as the underlying key elements of this differentiation. A procedure *in rem* need not be free of criminal law guarantees for its owner, since it might be based on a formal (and even false) label, as illustrated by the bank account example given above. And similarly, a procedure against a person is not necessarily associated with the standards for a criminal law conviction (especially in the cases of preventive confiscation or confiscations designed to re-establish the *status quo ante* discussed above). Thus, these labels cannot automatically be equated with the decisive differences between the common law and the continental confiscation models. Instead, they have to be evaluated independently.

In this evaluation, there are good reasons to name, index, and conduct non-criminal confiscations as proceedings *in rem*, since this would clearly illustrate to the public the non-criminal character of these proceedings. This labeling also has the advantage of avoiding or reducing the ethical blame of the owner of confiscated goods. Furthermore, it provides a simple construction for property owned by un-known persons, without additional justifications or provisions for procedures against unknown persons (as regulated, for example, in Section 76a German Crim-inal Code on an "independent order" for an autonomous confiscation). As a conse-quence, there are no objections but instead there are good logical reasons for label-ing and constructing re-establishing confiscations as *in rem* proceedings.

4. Codification in the Criminal Justice System or in Other Regimes

A fourth difference between the various models of confiscation and also an im-portant construction element for non-criminal confiscation concerns the question of whether the confiscation regime should be codified in a country's criminal justice system or in its civil or public law codifications. The German-Scandinavian ap-proach opts for the first option while the common law and Italian approaches have chosen the second one.

The placement of NCBC legislation outside the codification of criminal law could provide a clear message, namely that the confiscation measure is not a crimi-nal instrument associated with personal blame. However, the placement of NCBC legislation in the national criminal laws does not necessarily lead to it being re-garded as a criminal measure. Also, according to the *Engel* criteria, not all measures codified in *criminal legislation* are in fact criminal. Examples include provisions that permit the resolution of civil claims for compensation in the course of a criminal trial; measures applicable to persons who, due to their mental incapac-ity, cannot be punished; and various types of preventive measures. Thus, NCBC with proceedings directed towards property (and not persons) might well be placed within the national criminal laws.

Practical aspects provide strong arguments for such a solution. A first reason for choosing the criminal justice system is the fact that existing criminal justice institu-tions (i.e., investigating, prosecuting, and adjudicating authorities) are experienced in handling criminal cases (e.g., an experienced prosecutor is familiar with the tran-sition between a criminal and a non-criminal acquisition of property). A second reason is that, in practice, a shift from an *in rem* confiscation to an *in personam* conviction (and vice versa) is possible if the so-called NCBC is codified in the criminal justice system (the need for such a shift may arise due to the procedural situation or the available evidence in a concrete case). Thus, the better solution with respect to codification is to place NCBC within the criminal justice system.[143]

---

[143] See also *Meyer*, ZStW 2015, 260, 263–265.

5. Consequences and the Decisive Follow-Up Question

Comparison of the various confiscation models together with an analysis of their essential construction elements leads to a clear result: in the interest of an effective confiscation regime, it makes sense to create a non-criminal model for confiscations designed to re-establish the *status quo ante*. This model should be introduced as a second track alongside the traditional criminal law-based confiscation model. It should follow the common law model in that it should be unrelated to a criminal conviction and be possible on the basis of a decision that has proven the existence of an unjust criminal enrichment. Furthermore, it should take the form of an *in rem* procedure against property, similar to the common law model. Due to the close nexus with criminal law and for practical reasons, however, this re-establishment model should be codified in the criminal justice system.

Based on the concept of unjust enrichment and re-establishment of the status before the crime, the essential substantive element for this type of confiscation would be the requirement that the property in question originate from crime. Based on the principle of proportionality, one might also limit the applicability of this kind of confiscation to a list of specific serious crimes; this, however, would hinder the efficiency of the measure, since the owner could claim that the property originated from a non-listed crime.

Up until now, however, a decisive question, namely that of the evidentiary requirements for the nexus between the crime and the confiscated property, has been left unanswered: If the confiscation model against unjust enrichment were to evaluate the nexus between a crime and the resulting property using the evidentiary requirements of civil common law procedures (e.g., simple preponderance of probabilities), the model would lead to much more efficient confiscation. However, if this nexus were to be evaluated in accordance with traditional criminal procedures (e.g., beyond reasonable doubt), the whole construction would be in vain. This leads to the final and most important point of this analysis, i.e., appropriate evidence rules.

C. The Standard of Proof

The question of whether the standard of proof for non-criminal confiscation can be lower than that for criminal sanction-based confiscation is not only the most important theoretical question for NCBC models; it is also the most important practical question. Up until now, however, despite the large number of scholarly articles on NCBC, these standards of proof have not been analyzed sufficiently from a comparative perspective. There are deficits in research and open questions on human rights requirements with regard to two standards.

First, in the field of criminal law, it is quite clear that the presumption of innocence is a generally accepted human rights guarantee. This presumption applies to the law of criminal procedure in the various national and international legal orders. However, the degree to which the legislature can create deviating rules of evidence for specific questions or reach a similar result by changing the definitions of substantive criminal law – e.g., in the areas of defense or the origin of property in confiscation clauses – is not clear on the international and comparative levels. In this context, there also seem to be considerable differences between common law and continental law countries.[144]

Second, the evidence laws of *legal regimes other than criminal law* also need more attention. The discussion of NCBC usually refers to the standards of "civil" procedure. However, as illustrated, there is no detailed discussion of the fact that instruments that enable the state to take unjust enrichment away from citizens and redistribute it for social purposes do not regulate the relationship between citizens but rather the relationship between the state and citizens; thus, they are a part of public not civil law.[145] For this reason, one could say that the "civil" part of the term "civil forfeiture" is a misnomer, and it is an open question as to whether the analogy of the NCBC model to the standards of evidence in civil procedures is correct or whether an analogy to the standards of evidence in specific areas of public law (e.g., even tax law) would not be more appropriate. This is the case at least, if confiscation is conducted primarily for the state and not for individual victims.

This lack of analysis also exists with respect to the questions of whether and to what extent such standards derive from *national human rights guarantees*, such as the protection of property. The preceding analysis shows that the German Federal Constitutional Court derives results from the constitutional guarantees protecting property that are quite similar to the presumption of innocence. This does not mean that the German constitutional jurisprudence is generally ideal for all confiscation cases, even for other jurisdictions, without exception. However, this jurisprudence points out the lack of comparative (esp. constitutional and human rights-based) research, particularly with respect to the guarantees for property. Fundamental differences, such as those as between German constitutional law on the protection of property and the current common law confiscation systems, are not only important with respect to the harmonization of confiscation law; they may also be relevant for the more moderate aim of mutual recognition of confiscation decisions – which could be rejected due to the national *ordre public*. [146]

If these problems with constitutional law were to be analyzed in more detail, however, the comparative analysis might lead to a solution similar to that devel-

---

[144] See *supra* pp. 272–275; see *supra Vogel*, p. 227; Meyer, ZStW 2015, 265–272.

[145] See *supra* pp. 287–288; see also *supra Vogel*, p. 228 et seq.

[146] See *supra* p. 290.

oped by the Norwegian Supreme Court: In NCBC cases, the Court demands a higher evidence threshold than in civil cases (preponderance of evidence/balance of probabilities) but lower than in criminal trials (beyond reasonable doubt).[147] Thus, it is likely that "civil" NCBC decisions could lead to considerable progress in the confiscation of the proceeds of crime but that such proceedings could not be executed as extensively (especially with such a low threshold of proof) as some of the confiscation laws currently in force in common law countries allow.

D. Conclusion

The conclusion of the analysis undertaken here is that the so-called NCBC legislation should be seen as a promising venture for future national legislation in Europe. Such legislation ought to be based primarily on the policy-oriented (so-called civil) approach of measures designed to re-establish the *status quo ante*. Proceedings for this type of legislation should be independent of the criminal conviction of a possible perpetrator and should also be independent of *in absentia* proceedings. At least in continental law countries, this kind of confiscation system can best be established in the form of independent *in rem* proceedings.

The most decisive and problematic element of this legislation is the level of proof required for the nexus between crime and property. In the future, this level must be based on a more extensive analysis of national human rights guarantees, especially those bearing on the protection of property. Depending on the various national constitutional requirements, this might be a standard somewhere between the so-called civil law-based preponderance of evidence, on the one hand, and the criminal law-based proof beyond reasonable doubt (which goes hand in hand with the principle of innocence), on the other. However, it is an open question whether this standard would be acceptable in all countries.

We hope that the discussion and the findings in this book – combined with other NCBC guidelines and comparative studies of existing NCBC legislation[148] – will contribute to the discussion of these new types of legislation in various jurisdictions. Despite its controversial nature, properly designed NCBC legislation can be a valuable tool for the prevention of harm to society caused by the proceeds of crime. At the same time, however, such legislation must have proper limits and safeguards that derive from human rights law and constitutions as well as from the inherent limits of the underlying concepts of re-establishment of the *status quo ante*.

---

[147] See e.g. the judgments of the Norwegian Supreme Court Rt. 1999 s. 14, Rt. 2007 s. 1217, Rt. 2008 s. 1409.

[148] See, e.g., *Greenberg et al.*, Stolen Asset Recovery, published by the Stolen Asset Recovery (StAR) Initiative. (http://star.worldbank.org/star/publications?keys=&sort_by=score&sort_order=DESC&items_per_page=10, last visited 14.07.14).

Bibliography

Andenæs, Johs., Alminnelig strafferett. 5th ed. with Magnus Matningsdal and Georg Fredrik Rieber-Mohn. Oslo 2004.

Asp, Petter, The Substantive Criminal Law Competence of the EU. Stockholm 2012.

Asp, Petter/Ulväng, Magnus/Jareborg, Nils, Kriminalrättens grunder. Uppsala 2010.

Ashworth, Andrew/Zedner, Lucia, Preventive Orders: A Problem of Undercriminalization? In: R.A. Duff/Lindsay Farmer/S.E. Marshall/Massimo Renzo/Victor Tadros, The Boundaries of the Criminal Law. Oxford 2010, pp. 59–87.

Berman, Mitchell N., Two kinds of retributivism. In: R.A. Duff/Stuart P. Green, Philosophical Foundations of Criminal Law. Oxford 2011.

Böse, Martin (ed.), Europäisches Strafrecht. Baden-Baden 2013.

Fletcher, George P., The Grammar of Criminal Law. American, Comparative and International. Volume One: Foundations. Oxford 2007.

Forsaith, James/Irving, Barrie/Nanopoulos, Eva/Fazekas, Mihaly, Study for an impact assessment on a proposal for a new legal framework on the confiscation and recovery of criminal sets, Technical Report, RAND Europe. European Union 2012.

Frände, Dan, Allmän straffrätt. Helsingfors 2004.

– Finsk straffprocessrätt. Helsingfors 2009.

Grabitz, Eberhard/Hilf, Meinhard/Nettesheim, Martin, Das Recht der Europäischen Union, Looseleaf, Supplement 55, Munich 2015.

Greenberg, Theodore S./Samuel, Linda M./Grant, Wingate/Grey, Larissa, Stolen Asset Recovery. A Good Practices Guide for Non-Conviction Based Asset Forfeiture. Washington 2009.

Harris, D.J./O'Boyle, M/Bates, E.P/Buckley, C.M., Law of the European Convention on Human Rights. 2nd ed. Oxford 2009.

Hart, H.L.A., Punishment and Responsibility: Essays in the Philosophy of Law. Oxford 1968.

Hecker, Bernd, Europäisches Strafrecht. 4th ed. Berlin/Heidelberg 2012.

Hofmeyr, Willie, Navigating between mutual legal assistance and confiscation systems. In: Mark Pieth, Recovering Stolen Assets. Bern 2008, pp. 135–146.

Hov, Jo, Rettergang II. Oslo 2010.

Klip, André, European Criminal Law. An Integrative Approach. 2nd ed. Cambridge 2012.

Kühne, Hans-Heiner, Strafprozessrecht. Eine systematische Darstellung des deutschen und europäischen Strafverfahrensrechts. Heidelberg 2010.

Meyer, Frank, „Reformiert die Rückgewinnungshilfe!" – Denkanstöße für eine Generalüberholung der Vermögensabschöpfung. ZStW 2015, 241–283.

Rui, Jon Petter, Non-conviction based confiscation in the European Union – an assessment of Art. 5 of the proposal for a directive of the European Parliament and of the Council on the freezing and confiscation of proceeds of crime in the European Union, ERA Forum. Journal of the Academy of European Law, No. 3/2012, pp. 349–361.

Sieber, Ulrich, Strafrechtsvergleichung im Wandel. In: Ulrich Sieber/Hans Jörg Albrecht, Strafrecht und Kriminologie unter einem Dach, Kolloquium zum 90. Geburtstag von Professor Dr. Dr. h.c. mult. Hans Heinrich Jescheck. Freiburg 2006, pp. 78–151.

– Blurring the Categories of Criminal Law and the Law of War. In: Stefano Manacorda/Adán Nieto (eds.), Criminal Law between War and Peace. Cuenca 2009, pp. 35–69.

– Die Zukunft des Europäischen Strafrechts. ZStW 2009, 1–67.

Simonato, Michele, Directive 2014/42/EU and Non-Conviction Based Confiscation. New Journal of European Criminal Law 2015, pp. 213–228.

Smith, Eva/Jochimsen, Jørgen/Kistrup, Michael/Lund Poulsen, Jakob, Straffeprocessen, 2nd ed. Copenhagen 2008.

Tadros, Victor, Criminalization and Regulation. In: R.A. Duff/Lindsay Farmer/S.E. Marshall/Massimo Renzo/Victor Tadros, The Boundaries of Criminal Law, Oxford 2010.

Toftegaard Nielsen, Gorm, Strafferet I. Ansvaret. Copenhagen 2001.

van Dijk, Pieter/van Hoof, G.J.H./Yukata, Arai, Theory and Practice of the European Convention on Human Rights. 4th ed. Antwerpen 2006.

Velev, Boris, Modelle der Vermögensabschöpfung. Hamburg 2014.

Vogel, Joachim, Die Strafgesetzgebungskompetenzen der Europäischen Union nach Art. 83, 86 und 325 AEVU. In: Kai Ambos (ed.), Europäisches Strafrecht post-Lissabon. Göttingen 2011, pp. 41–56.

White, Robin C.A./Ovey, Clare, The European Convention on Human Rights. 5th ed. Oxford 2010.

List of Abbreviations

ECHR	European Convention on Human Rights
ECtHR	European Court of Human Rights
i.a.	inter alia
i.e.	id est
NCBC	Non-conviction-based confiscation
StAR	Stolen Asset Recovery

List of Authors and Editors

Alan Bacarese
Director Anticorruption & Asset Recovery, Stream House AG
London/UK

Professor Dr. *Johan Boucht*
University of Oslo, Faculty of Law
Oslo/Norway

Dr. *Els De Busser*
Head of section of European Criminal Law, Max Planck Institute for Foreign and
International Criminal Law
Freiburg/Germany

Stefan D. Cassella
Assistant U.S. Attorney Chief, Asset Forfeiture and Money Laundering Section
Baltimore/USA

Professor Dr. *Robert Esser*
Chair for German, European and International Criminal Law, Criminal Proce-
dure Law and Economic Crime, University of Passau
Passau/Germany

Adjunct Professor Dr. *Roberto Flor*
Adjunct Professor for ICT Criminal Law and International Criminal Law, Uni-
versity of Verona
Verona/Italy

Associate Professor Dr. *Michele Panzavolta*
Associate Professor, Catholic University Leuven; Assistant Professor, Maastricht
University
Leuven/Belgium, Maastricht/The Netherlands

Professor Dr. *Jon Petter Rui*
University of Bergen
Bergen/Norway

Gavin Sellar
Barrister, Parliamentary Councel at The Scottish Government
Edinburgh/UK

Professor Dr. Dr. h.c. mult. *Ulrich Sieber*
  Director at the Max Planck Institute for Foreign and International Criminal Law
  Freiburg/Germany

Ian Smith
  Barrister (England and Wales)
  London/UK

Professor Dr. *Joachim Vogel* †
  Chair for Criminal Law, Criminal Procedure Law and Economic Crime, Ludwig
  Maximilian University
  Munich/Germany

Schriftenreihe des Max-Planck-Instituts für ausländisches und internationales Strafrecht

Die zentralen Veröffentlichungen des Max-Planck-Instituts für ausländisches und internationales Strafrecht werden in Zusammenarbeit mit dem Verlag Duncker & Humblot in den folgenden vier Unterreihen der „Schriftenreihe des Max-Planck-Instituts für ausländisches und internationales Strafrecht" vertrieben:

- „Strafrechtliche Forschungsberichte",
- „Kriminologische Forschungsberichte",
- „Interdisziplinäre Forschungen aus Strafrecht und Kriminologie"
- „Publications of the Max Planck Partner Group for Balkan Criminology" sowie
- „Sammlung ausländischer Strafgesetzbücher in deutscher Übersetzung".

Diese Publikationen können direkt über das Max-Planck-Institut unter <www.mpicc.de> oder über den Verlag Duncker & Humblot unter <www.duncker-humblot.de> erworben werden.

Darüber hinaus erscheinen im Hausverlag des Max-Planck-Instituts in der Unterreihe „research in brief" zusammenfassende Kurzbeschreibungen von Forschungsergebnissen und in der Unterreihe „Arbeitsberichte" Veröffentlichungen vorläufiger Forschungsergebnisse. Diese Veröffentlichungen können über das Max-Planck-Institut bezogen werden.

Detaillierte Informationen zu den einzelnen Publikationen des Max-Planck-Instituts für ausländisches und internationales Strafrecht sind unter <www.mpicc.de> abrufbar.

The main research activities of the Max Planck Institute for Foreign and International Criminal Law are published in the following four subseries of the "Schriftenreihe des Max-Planck-Instituts für ausländisches und internationales Strafrecht" (Research Series of the Max Planck Institute for Foreign and International Criminal Law), which are distributed in cooperation with the publisher Duncker & Humblot:

- "Strafrechtliche Forschungsberichte" (Reports on Research in Criminal Law),
- "Kriminologische Forschungsberichte" (Reports on Research in Criminology),
- "Interdisziplinäre Forschungen aus Strafrecht und Kriminologie" (Reports on Interdisciplinary Research in Criminal Law and Criminology),
- "Publications of the Max Planck Partner Group for Balkan Criminology," and
- "Sammlung ausländischer Strafgesetzbücher in deutscher Übersetzung" (Collection of Foreign Criminal Laws in German Translation).

These publications can be ordered from the Max Planck Institute at <www.mpicc.de> or from Duncker & Humblot at <www.duncker-humblot.de>.

Two additional subseries are published directly by the Max Planck Institute for Foreign and International Criminal Law: "research in brief" contains short reports on results of research activities, and "Arbeitsberichte" (working materials) present preliminary results of research projects. These publications are available at the Max Planck Institute.

Detailed information on all publications of the Max Planck Institute for Foreign and International Criminal Law can be found at <www.mpicc.de>.

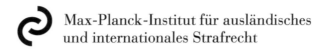 Max-Planck-Institut für ausländisches
und internationales Strafrecht

Auswahl aus dem strafrechtlichen Veröffentlichungsprogramm:

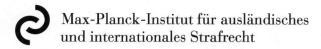 Max-Planck-Institut für ausländisches
und internationales Strafrecht

Auswahl aus dem strafrechtlichen Veröffentlichungsprogramm:

S 128.1.1 *Ulrich Sieber / Konstanze Jarvers / Emily Silverman* (eds.)
National Criminal Law in a Comparative Legal Context
Volume 1.1: Introduction to National Systems
2013 • 314 Seiten • ISBN 978-3-86113-822-8   € 40,00

S 128.1.2 Volume 1.2: Introduction to National Systems
2013 • 363 Seiten • ISBN 978-3-86113-826-6   € 43,00

S 128.1.3 Volume 1.3: Introduction to National Systems
2014 • 297 Seiten • ISBN 978-3-86113-818-1   € 40,00

S 128.1.4 Volume 1.4: Introduction to National Systems
2014 • 391 Seiten • ISBN 978-3-86113-810-5   € 43,00

S 128.2.1 *Ulrich Sieber / Susanne Forster / Konstanze Jarvers* (eds.)
National Criminal Law in a Comparative Legal Context
Volume 2.1: General limitations on the application
of criminal law
2011 • 399 Seiten • ISBN 978-3-86113-834-1   € 43,00

S 128.3.1 *Ulrich Sieber / Susanne Forster / Konstanze Jarvers* (eds.)
National Criminal Law in a Comparative Legal Context
Volume 3.1: Defining criminal conduct
2011 • 519 Seiten • ISBN 978-3-86113-833-4   € 46,00

S 114.1   *Ulrich Sieber/Karin Cornils* (Hrsg.)
Nationales Strafrecht in rechtsvergleichender Darstellung
– Allgemeiner Teil –
Band 1: Grundlagen
2009 • 790 Seiten • ISBN 978-3-86113-849-5   € 55,00

S 114.2   Band 2: Gesetzlichkeitsprinzip – Internationaler Geltungs-
bereich – Begriff und Systematisierung der Straftat
2008 • 470 Seiten • ISBN 978-3-86113-860-0   € 41,00

S 114.3   Band 3: Objektive Tatseite – Subjektive Tatseite –
Strafbares Verhalten vor der Tatvollendung
2008 • 490 Seiten • ISBN 978-3-86113-859-4   € 41,00

S 114.4   Band 4: Tatbeteiligung – Straftaten in Unternehmen,
Verbänden und anderen Kollektiven
2010 • 527 Seiten • ISBN 978-3-86113-842-6   € 45,00

S 114.5   Band 5: Gründe für den Ausschluss der Strafbarkeit –
Aufhebung der Strafbarkeit – Verjährung
2010 • 718 Seiten • ISBN 978-3-86113-841-9   € 55,00

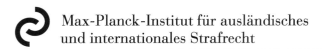

Max-Planck-Institut für ausländisches und internationales Strafrecht

Auswahl aktueller Publikationen aus dem kriminologischen Veröffentlichungsprogramm:

BC 1   *Anna-Maria Getoš Kalac, Hans-Jörg Albrecht, Michael Kilchling* (eds.)
Mapping the Criminological Landscape of the Balkans
A Survey on Criminology and Crime
with an Expedition into the Criminal Landscape of the Balkans
Berlin 2014 • 540 Seiten • ISBN 978-3-86113-248-6   € 44,00

K 169   *Andreas Schwedler, Gunda Wössner*
Elektronische Aufsicht bei vollzugsöffnenden Maßnahmen
Implementation, Akzeptanz und psychosoziale Effekte des baden-württembergischen Modellprojekts
Berlin 2015 • 126 Seiten • ISBN 978-3-86113-252-3   € 25,00

K 167   *Christopher Murphy*
**"Come in Spinner" – Money Laundering
in the Australian Casino Industry**
Berlin 2014 • 152 Seiten • ISBN 978-3-86113-250-9   € 29,00

K 166   *Ramin Tehrani*
**Die „Smart Sanctions" im Kampf gegen den Terrorismus
und als Vorbild einer präventiven Vermögensabschöpfung**
Berlin 2014 • 256 Seiten • ISBN 978-3-86113-247-9   € 35,00

K 165   *Daniela Cernko*
Die Umsetzung der CPT-Empfehlungen im deutschen Strafvollzug
Eine Untersuchung über den Einfluss des Europäischen Komitees
zur Verhütung von Folter und unmenschlicher oder erniedrigender
Behandlung oder Strafe auf die deutsche Strafvollzugsverwaltung
Berlin 2014 • 455 Seiten • ISBN 978-3-86113-246-2   € 39,00

K 164   *Franziska Kunz*
Kriminalität älterer Menschen
Beschreibung und Erklärung auf der Basis von Selbstberichtsdaten
Berlin 2014 • 387 Seiten • ISBN 978-3-86113-244-8   € 35,00

K 163   *David Jensen*
Maras
A study of their origin, international impact, and the measures
taken to fight them
Berlin 2013 • 245 Seiten • ISBN 978-3-86113-243-1   € 35,00

K 161   *Gunda Wößner, Roland Hefendehl, Hans-Jörg Albrecht* (Hrsg.)
Sexuelle Gewalt und Sozialtherapie
Bisherige Daten und Analysen zur Längsschnittstudie „Sexual-straftäter in den sozialtherapeutischen Abteilungen des
Freistaates Sachsen"
Berlin 2013 • 274 Seiten • ISBN 978-3-86113-241-7   € 35,00

K 159   *Andreas Armborst*
Jihadi Violence
A study of al-Qaeda's media
Berlin 2013 • 266 Seiten • ISBN 978-3-86113-119-9   € 35,00